The
Greatest
Football
Stories
Ever Told

The
Greatest
Football
Stories
Ever Told

Twenty Tales of Gridiron Glory

EDITED BY
ERIC NOE

THE LYONS PRESS
Guilford, Connecticut
An imprint of The Globe Pequot Press

The Lyons Press is an imprint of The Globe Pequot Press.

10 9 8 7 6 5 4 3 2

Printed in the United States of America

ISBN 1- 59228-087-0

Library of Congress Cataloging-in-Publication Data

The greatest football stories ever told / edited by Eric Noe
    p.   cm.
  ISBN 1-59228-087-0 (hardcover)
    1. Football—United States— Miscellanea. 2. Football stories. I. Noe, Eric.

GV950.5.G75 2003
796.332—dc22

2003021934
CIP

Contents

Introduction

When I was seven years old, my family convened in the den of our suburban Atlanta home on a winter Sunday afternoon to watch our hometown Atlanta Falcons take on the Dallas Cowboys in the NFL playoffs. The traditionally moribund Falcons had taken the NFL by storm that year and surged into the playoffs as a chic pick to reach the Super Bowl. Facing the Cowboys, perennial winners boasting the irritating "America's Team" moniker, was the chance to finally see my team accomplish something and exorcise the inferiority complex that cheering for a crappy team gave an impressionable, sports-crazed kid.

A block and a half away, my best friend and his family were experiencing a similar ritual, but from the opposite perspective. My friend's family had relocated from Dallas several years earlier, and his father had raised a family of diehard Cowboys' fans. During sleepovers, I was always clad in my Falcons' pajamas while my friend donned his Cowboys' gear, and when we tossed the pigskin in the yard I was Steve Bartkowski to his Danny White. I spent a good portion of my childhood hearing his father, a passionate football fan with an encyclopedic knowledge of Cowboys' history, recount heroic tales about their past championships, stars like Ed "Too Tall" Jones, and their saintly coach, Tom Landry. I hated it.

And though I told no one about it and I knew their obsession with their team was no more insidious than my own, I despised the Cowboys. I wanted some glory stories to tell. And more than anything else, I was ready to see my Falcons give the Cowboys their come-uppance. When the ball was kicked off that afternoon, I was convinced it was finally the day I would get some long-awaited and much deserved vindication for my lifetime devotion.

My dad, sadly afflicted with a sports obsession similar to my own, was in rare form for that game. A scientist and college professor by trade, he has always been a reserved, stoic figure to most who know him. But not on this day. We cheered for every first down, every defensive stand, and every Cowboys' miscue. I can actually remember my dad leaping up from his recliner, bouncing on his feet, knocking over his giant Tupperware popcorn bowl, and clapping his hands with glee for one particularly big play. It appeared to me that he actually wanted the win more than I did. But as the game wore on, the Cowboys began manhandling our Falcons and pulling away on the scoreboard. A familiar feeling of despair settled over the room, and it was clear by the fourth quarter that a miracle was needed. I decided to ask for just that. I walked downstairs to the basement, a place where I'd used a Nerf football and a fertile imagination to choreograph great Falcons' victories in my mind, and I dropped to my knees and prayed.

I prayed for the Falcons and for my favorite players Bartkowski, William Andrews, and Alfred Jenkins. Valiant battlers all, and I was sure they deserved a win. I prayed for my dad, taking particular note of how important this game obviously was for him and noting how crushed he would inevitably be by another loss. Would he quit his job? Walk out on the family? Wander the streets aimlessly searching for the meaning in it all? And of course, being basically a selfish kid by nature, I prayed for myself. It was my turn to tell the stories. My turn to visit my friend's house and wear my Falcons pajamas with pride. It was my turn for victory.

But it wasn't to be. The Cowboys won 30-27 and went on to play the San Francisco 49ers the next week in the NFC Championship game.

More than two decades removed from that day, I've been able to put the game into a perspective that was obviously beyond the grasp of a seven-year-old. With a firmer understanding that more important things happen in the adult world than football—supporting a family, paying a home mortgage, forging a career—I will now concede that it's possible I overestimated my dad's need for a win that day. And I realize that I may have even overestimated the effect the loss would have on my own life (turns out, there was very little). But I still have questions.

What could work a mild-mannered, low-key, academic man like my dad into a frenzy on a Sunday afternoon in his living room? What could make a similarly bookish doctor like my friend's father verbally replay a game in lavish detail for anyone within earshot? What can make two kids spend hours dreaming of gridiron heroics when we know our time would be better spent doing homework or dreaming of inventing a cure for cancer? And what to this day can turn me, a relatively well-adjusted adult with many interests, into a mental primate with no interest in the rest of the world for three hours every Saturday or Sunday?

The answer: Football.

If baseball is still America's Pastime, then I firmly believe that football has become America's obsession. Of all the sports addicts I know—and there are many—I can't think of a one who wouldn't choose football as his or her obsession of choice. Football appears to have been formatted to fit on the television. The line of scrimmage fits concisely onto the screen, and when the ball is snapped all eleven players are in full view. It's the perfect sport for the video game age, and the perfect sport for a sport-obsessed culture. From late August to late January, most of America's sports-viewing public is transfixed by actions played out in high school stadiums, in college campus cathedrals, and under the bright lights and media mania surrounding the NFL.

The game itself is an amalgam of physical prowess, combining all range of athletes from small, quick receivers and defensive backs to huge, lumbering lineman. It mixes power, speed, intelligence, and cohesiveness. You can appreciate the relentlessness of linebackers zooming from sideline to sideline, tracking ball-carriers and wrestling them to the turf. Jumbo offensive tackles pancake opponents and then look for someone else to plow through. In no other sport is there a field general akin to the quarterback, who holds the balance of the game in his hand on every snap. And of course, there is the violence. Today's football players are modern day gladiators, thrilling audiences with their ability to afflict vicious punishment on their opponents and take a beating in response. Football combines all the attributes of sport into one diverse, dramatic package.

When I was looking for stories to fill these pages, I tried to find works that represent the diversity of the game. Included are true accounts of games that played out on real fields, with real competitors and real outcomes. I found some stories about the football's all-time great players and their thoughts and feelings about the game. I added a few stories ancillary to the sport, dramatic life events in which football was a linchpin. And I discovered a few literary short stories that represent the themes, emotions, and cultural significance of football.

Are these the *greatest* football stories ever told? That's certainly to be determined by the reader. But they're all great stories, and I hope you have as much fun reading them (in the off-season, no doubt) as I did.

—ERIC NOE, SUMMER 2003

The Harris Fetko Story

MICHAEL CHABON

Father–son dynamics take on an added dimension in football families. Michael Chabon's "The Harris Fetko Story" is a darkly humorous take on one such relationship.

The hard-ass dad is often a staple of the football family, and Harris Fetko's famous father is your garden variety sports parent. Harris's college nickname, "Frankenback," suggests a childhood spent under the watchful eye of an overbearing dad who designed his son's life to create a football player—the literary Todd Marinovich. Marinovich, a one-time star quarterback at USC and first-round draft pick of the Oakland Raiders, has become a cautionary tale for sports parents. The kid who had supposedly never eaten a McDonald's cheeseburger and was known as a robo-quarterback—a reference to his father's obsession with grooming the ultimate physical specimen to play the position—flamed out of professional football and was eventually arrested on drug charges. That Chabon's Harris Fetko never achieved the football success his father envisioned for him and apparently cracked under the stress and turned to drugs is eerily similar to the real-life Marinovich saga.

The phallic Fetko reconciliation underlines young Harris's emasculation from a childhood-turned-science-experiment and humorously offers him a chance at redemption. His efforts to prevent his half-brother's banishment to a similar fate, not to mention an imminent groin injury, are side-splittingly funny. But his eventual willingness to forgive his father and participate in his half-baked "comeback" suggests a complicity in his initial demise, and the fact that the comeback involves a made-up sport called Powerball is ridiculous.

But of course Harris Fetko, Powerball star, is not such an outlandish idea. In a time when pseudo-celebrities are recycled on a whim for made-for-TV events, it is hardly a stretch to imagine Todd Marinovich, American Gladiator.

The hotel in Tacoma was a Luxington Parc. There was one in Spokane, one in Great Falls, and another in downtown Saskatoon. It was half motor lodge, half state-of-the-art correctional institution, antacid-pink with gun-slit windows. There was a stink of chlorine from the waterfall in the atrium where the chimes of the elevators echoed all night with a sound like a dental instrument hitting a cold tile floor. A message from Norm Fetko, Harris's father, was waiting at the desk on Friday night when the team got in. It said that on the previous Friday Fetko's wife had given birth to a son and that the next afternoon, at three o'clock, they were going to remove his little foreskin, of all things, in a Jewish religious ceremony to be held, of all places, at Fetko's car dealership up in Northgate. Whether by design or hotel policy, the message was terse, and Harris's invitation to his half brother's bris was only implied.

When Harris got upstairs to his room, he sat with his hand on the telephone. The passage of four years since his last contact with Fetko had done little to incline him to forgiveness. He tended, as did most commentators on the Harris Fetko story, to blame his father for his own poor character and the bad things that had happened to him. He decided it would be not only best for everyone but also highly satisfying not to acknowledge in any way his father's attempt at renewing contact, an attempt whose motives, with an uncharitableness born of long experience, Harris suspected at once.

He picked up the receiver and dialed Bob Badham. There was no answer. Harris set the receiver down on the floor of his room—it was in his contract that he got a room to himself—lay down alongside it, and squeezed out the one thousand abdominal crunches he had been squeezing out every night since he was eleven years old. When he had finished, he got up, went into the bathroom, and looked at himself in the mirror with approval and dispassion. He was used from long habit to thinking of his body as having a certain monetary value or as capable of being translated, mysteriously, into money, and if it were somehow possible, he would have paid a handsome sum to purchase himself. He turned away from the mirror and sat down on the lid of the toilet to trim the nails of his right hand. When his nails were clipped and filed square, he went back out to pick up the telephone. It was still ringing. He hung up and dialed Bob's work number.

"Screw you, Bob," Harris said cheerfully to Bob Badham's voicemail box. "I mean, hello." He then left a detailed account of his current whereabouts and telephone number, the clean result of his most recent urine test, and the next destination on the team's schedule, which was Boise, a Holiday Inn, on July 5.

Harris possessed the sort of wild, formless gift that attracted the gaze of harsh men and disciplinarians, and the whole of his twenty-six years had been lived under the regimens of hard-asses. Bob Badham was merely the latest of these.

There was a knock at the door. Harris went to answer it in his pin-stripe bikini briefs, hoping, not quite unconsciously, that he would find an attractive female member of the Western Washington Association of Mortgage Brokers (here for their annual convention) come to see if it was really true that the briefly seminotorious Harris Fetko was in the hotel.

"Why aren't you in bed?" said Lou Sammartino.

The coach of the Regina Kings club of the North American Professional Indoor Football League was not, as it happened, a hard-ass. He indulged his players far more than most of them deserved—housing them with his family when things went badly for them; remembering their birthdays; nudging them to save receipts, phone their wives, pay their child support. He was an intelligent man of long experience who, like many coaches Harris had played for, believed, at this point in his career rather desperately, in the myth of the football genius, a myth in which Harris himself, having been raised by a football genius, had learned by the age of seventeen to put no stock whatever. Lou Sammartino believed that the problem of winning at football was surely one susceptible to the systematic application of an inspired and unbiased mind. His lifetime record as a coach, including a stint in the short-lived Mexican Football League of 1982, was 102–563. He pushed past Harris and barked at his quarterback to close the door. He was hunched and rotund, with a jowly, pocked face and immense black-rimmed spectacles. The smell of his cologne was exactly like that of the tiny red cardboard pine trees that dangle from the rearview mirrors of taxicabs.

"What's the matter?" said Harris. He looked out into the hallway, in both directions, then closed the door against the stiff artificial breeze that came howling down the deserted corridor.

"We need to talk." Lou sat down on the bed and studied Harris. His watery brown eyes behind the lenses of his glasses were beautiful in a way that suited his losing record. "You called your PO?"

"I left a message."

"Aren't you supposed to see him in person when you're home?"

"I'm *not* home," said Harris. "Technically. My *home* is Seattle. We're in *Tacoma.*"

"Technically," said Lou. "A word much beloved of screwups."

"Something to drink?" Harris went to the minibar. There was nothing in it except for a rattling ice tray and a ghostly smell of caulk. The minibars were always empty in Luxington Parcs and in most of the other hotels the Regina Kings patronized. Often they were not even plugged in. "I'm supposed to have six bottles of mineral water," Harris said. He tried not to sound petulant, but it was difficult, because he was feeling petulant.

"Aw," said Lou.

"I'm sick of this!" Harris slammed the refrigerator door shut. "Every time I walk into my room and open the minibar door, there's supposed to be six bottles of mineral water in there." The slammed door rebounded and bashed into the wall beside the minibar. Its handle gouged a deep hole in the wallboard. Crumbs of plaster spattered the floor. Harris ran his fingers along the edges of the hole he had made in the wall. A feeling of remorse took wing in his chest but with an old, sure instinct, he caught it and neatly twisted its neck. He turned to Lou, trying to look certain of himself and his position. The truth was that Harris didn't even like mineral water; he thought it tasted like saliva. But it was in his contract. "So, okay, talk. It's past my bedtime."

"Harris, in a minute or two there's someone coming up here with a proposition for you." Just as he said this, there was another knock at the door. Harris jumped. "He wants to offer you a job."

"I already have a job."

Lou turned up the corners of his mouth but somehow failed to produce a viable smile.

"Lou," said Harris, and his heart started to pound. "Please tell me the league isn't folding."

There had been rumors to this effect since before the season even began; attendance at games in all but a few sports-starved cities was declining by a thousand or more every weekend, the owner of the Portland team had been murdered by Las Vegas wiseguys, and the Vancouver bank on whose line of credit the NAPIFL depended for its operating costs was under investigation by the government of Canada.

Lou stroked the bedspread, smoothing it, watching the back of his hand.

"I just want to play out the schedule," he said sadly. "I could be happy with that."

"Harris?" said a man on the other side of the door. "You there?"

Harris put on his jeans and went to the door.

"Oly," he said. He took a step back into the room. The man at the door was enormous, six feet eight inches tall, just shy of three hundred pounds. Like Norm Fetko a member of the 1955 national champions and—unlike Fetko—a successful businessman, purveyor of a popular topical analgesic, Oly

Olafsen had always been the biggest man Harris knew, a chunk of the northern ice cap, a piece of masonry, fifteen tons of stone, oak, and gristle supporting eight cubic inches of grinning blond head. He wore silver aviator eyeglasses and a custom-tailored suit, metallic gray, so large and oddly proportioned that it was nearly unrecognizable as an article of human clothing and appeared rather to have been designed to straiten an obstreperous circus elephant or to keep the dust off some big, delicate piece of medical imaging technology.

"How's my boy?" said Oly.

It had been Oly Olafsen's money, more or less, that Harris had used, more or less without Oly's knowing about it, to purchase the pound of cocaine the police had found under the rear bench of Harris's 300 ZX when they pulled him over that night on Ravenna Avenue. He gave Harris's hand a squeeze that compressed the very bones.

"So," he went on, "the coach has got himself another son after all these years. That's a thought, isn't it? Wonder what he's got cooked up for this one."

This remark angered Harris, whom the sporting world for two hectic and disappointing collegiate seasons had known as Frankenback. Among the failings of his character exposed during that time was a total inability to stand up to teasing about any aspect of his life, his father's experimentation least of all. With a great effort and out of an old habit of deference to his father's cronies, he got himself to smile, then realized that Oly wasn't teasing him at all. On the contrary, there had been in Oly's soft voice a disloyal wrinkle of concern for the fate, at his great idol's hands, of the latest little Fetko to enter the world.

"Yeah, he asked me out to the showroom tomorrow," Harris said. "To the thing where they, what's that, circumcise the kid."

"Are you people Jewish?" said Lou, surprised. "I didn't know."

"We're not. Fetko isn't. I guess his new wife must be."

"I'll be there. Ah!" Gingerly—his knees were an ancient ruin of cartilage and wire—Oly lowered himself into the desk chair, which creaked in apparent horror at the slow approach of his massive behind. "As a matter of fact, I'm paying for the darn thing." Oly smiled, then took off his glasses and pinched the bridge of his nose. When he put the glasses back on, he wasn't smiling anymore. "The coach has got himself into a little bit of a tight spot out there in Northgate," he said, pressing his palms together as if they represented the terrific forces that were putting the squeeze on Fetko. "I know things haven't been, well, the greatest between you two since . . . everything that happened, but the coach—Harris, he's really putting his life back together. He's not—"

"Get to the point," said Harris.

An odd expression came over Oly's generally peaceful and immobile face. His eyebrows reached out to each other over the bridge of his nose, and his tiny, pale lips compressed into a pout. He was unhappy, possibly even actively sad. Harris had never imagined that Oly might ever be feeling anything but hunger and gravitation.

"Harris, I'm not going to lie to you, the old man could really use a little help," said Oly. "That's what I want to talk to you about. I don't know if Lou has mentioned it, but the coach and I—"

"I told him," said Lou. "Harris isn't interested."

"Isn't he?" Oly looked at Lou, his face once again a region of blankness, his eyes polite and twinkling. He had pleasant, vacant little eyes that, along with his bulk and a recipe purchased in 1963 from a long-dead Chinese herbalist in the International District for $250, had enabled him to do what was necessary to make Power Rub the number-three topical analgesic in the western U.S. "Somebody might think he would be very interested in finding another job, seeing as how this outfit of yours is about to go bellyup." He turned his flashbulb eyes toward Harris now. "Seeing as how what they call gainful employment is a condition of his parole."

"If that happens, and I don't personally feel that it will, Harris can find another job. He doesn't need any help from you."

"What is he going to do? He doesn't know how to do anything but be a quarterback! It's in his genes, it's in his blood particles. It's wired into his darn brain. No, I figure he has to be very interested in hearing about an opportunity like this. A chance to actually *redefine the position,* at twice his present salary, in front of a guaranteed national cable audience of *forty-four million homes.*"

Harris was accustomed to having his disposition discussed and his fate decided, in his presence, by other people; it was part of that same mysterious alchemy that could transmute his body into cash and of the somewhat less obscure process that had sent him to Ellensburg for nineteen months. But at the mention of cable television, he could not restrain himself.

"What is it?" he said. "What opportunity?"

Oly reached into the breast pocket of his jacket and withdrew a manila envelope, folded in half. He took a color brochure from the envelope and handed it to Harris. Harris sat down on the bed to read. It was a prospectus designed to attract investors to a league that would feature a sport that the brochure called Powerball, "the first new major American sport in a hundred years," to be played in every major city in the U.S., apparently by men in garish uniforms that were part samurai armor and part *costume de ballet,* one of whom was depicted, on the airbrushed cover of the brochure, swinging across the playing arena from a striped rappelling cable. The description was vague, but, as far as Harris could tell, Powerball appeared to be an amalgam of rugby, professional wrestling, and old pirate movies. It was not football or anything close to football. Once Harris realized this, he skimmed through such phases as "speed, drama, and intense physical action . . . the best elements of today's most popular sports . . . our proposed partnership with the Wrestling Channel . . . all the elements are in place . . . revolutionary, popular, and, above all, profitable . . ." until he turned to the last page and found a photograph of his father beside a caption that identified him as "coaching great Norm Fetko, inventor of Powerball, part owner and coach of the Seattle franchise."

"Fetko invented this crap?" said Harris, tossing the brochure onto the floor.

"It came to him in a dream," said Oly, looking solemn. He raised his hands to his eyes and spread his thick fingers, watching the air between them as it shimmered with another one of Norm Fetko's lunatic visions. "A guy . . . with a football under his arm . . . swinging from a rope." Oly shook his head as if awestruck by the glimpse Harris's father had vouchsafed him into the mystic origins of the future of American sport. "This will be big, Harris. We already have a line on investors in nine cities. Our lawyers are working out the last few kinks in the TV contract. This could be a very, very big thing."

"Big," said Harris. "Yeah, I get it now." For he saw with admiration and to his horror, that at this late stage of his career Fetko had managed to come up with yet another way to ruin the lives and fortunes of hapless elevens of men. None of Fetko's other failures—his golf resort out in the Banana Belt of Washington, his "revolutionary" orange football, his brief (pioneering, in retrospect) foray into politics as a candidate with no political convictions, his attempt to breed and raise the greatest quarterback the world would ever see—had operated in isolation. They had all roped in, ridden on the backs of, and ultimately broken a large number of other people. And around all of Fetko's dealings and misdealings, Oly Olafsen had hovered, loving sidekick, pouring his money down Fetko's throat like liquor. "That's why he called. He wants me to play for him again."

"Imagine the media, Harris, my gosh," said Oly. "Norm and Harris Fetko reunited, that would sell a few tickets."

Lou winced and sat down on the bed next to Harris. He put his hand on Harris's shoulder. "Harris, you don't want to do this."

"No kidding," said Harris. "Oly," he said to Oly. "I hate my father. I don't want to have anything to do with him. Or you. You guys all screwed me over once."

"Hey, now, kid." Another crack of grief opened in the glacial expanse of his face. "Look, you hate me, that's one thing, but I know you don't—"

"I hate him!"

Inside Harris Fetko the frontier between petulance and rage was generally left unguarded, and he crossed it now without slowing down. He stood up and went for Oly, wondering if somewhere in the tiny interval between the big man's jaw and shoulders he might find a larynx to get his thumbs around. Oly started to rise, but his shattered knees slowed him, and before he could regain his feet, Harris had kicked the tiny chair out from under him. A sharp pain went whistling up Harris's shin, and then his foot began to throb like a trumpet. The right foreleg of the wooden chair splintered from the frame, the chair tipped, and Oly Olafsen hit the flecked aquamarine carpet. His impact was at once loud and muffled, like the collision of a baseball bat and a suitcase filled with water.

"I'm sorry," Harris said.

Oly looked up at him. His meaty fingers wrapped around the broken chair leg and clenched it. His breath blew through his nostrils as loud as a horse's. Then he let go of the chair leg and shrugged. When Harris offered a hand, Oly took it.

"I just want to tell you something, Harris," he said, smoothing down his sleeves. He winched up his trousers by the belt, then attended to the tectonic slippage of the shoulder pads in his jacket. "Everything the coach has, okay, is tied up in this thing. Not money. The coach doesn't have any money. So far the money is mostly coming from me." With a groan he stooped to retrieve the fallen brochure, then slipped it back into its envelope. "What the coach has tied up in this thing, it can't be paid back or defaulted on or covered by a bridge loan." He tapped the rolled manila envelope against the center of his chest. "I'll see you tomorrow."

"No, you will not," said Harris as Oly went out. He tried to sound as though he were not in terrible pain. "I'm not going."

Lou lifted Harris's foot and bent the big toe experimentally. Harris groaned. A tear rolled down his cheek.

"You broke it," said Lou. "Aw, Harris."

"I'm sorry, Coach," said Harris, falling backward on the bed. "Damn Fetko, man. It's all his fault."

"Everything else, maybe it was Fetko's fault," said Lou, though he sounded doubtful. He picked up the telephone and asked room service to bring up a bucket of ice. "This was your fault."

When the ice came, he filled a towel with it and held it against Harris's toe for an hour until the swelling had gone down. Then he taped the big toe to its neighbor, patted Harris on the head, and went back to his room to revise the playbook for tomorrow. Before he went out, he turned.

"Harris," he said, "you've never confided in me. And you've never particularly followed any of the copious advice I've been so generous as to offer you over the last few months."

"Coach—"

"But regardless of that, I'm foolishly going to make one last little try." He took off his glasses and wiped them on a rumpled shirttail. "I think you ought to go to that thing tomorrow." He put his glasses back on again and blinked his eyes. "It's your brother that'll be lying there with his little legs spread."

"Screw the little bastard," said Harris, with the easy and good-natured callousness that, like so much about the game of football, had always come so naturally to him. "I hope they slice the damn thing clean off."

Lou went out, shaking his big, sorrowful head. Ten minutes later there was another knock at the door. This time it was not a lady mortgage broker but a reporter for the *Morning News Tribune* come to poke around in the embers of the Harris Fetko conflagration. Harris lay on the bed with his foot in an ice pack and told, once again, the sorry tale of how his father had ruined his life and made him into all the sad things he was today. When the reporter asked him what had happened to his foot and the chair, Harris said that he had tripped while running to answer the phone.

They beat Tacoma 10–9, on a field goal in the last eight seconds of the game. Harris scrambled for the touchdown, kicked the extra point with his off foot, and then, when in the last minute of the game it became clear that none of the aging farm implements and large pieces of antique cabinetry who made up his backfield and receiving corps were going to manage to get the ball into the end zone, he himself, again with his left foot, nailed the last three points needed to keep them happy for one more day back in Regina.

When the team came off the field, they found the Kings' owner, Irwin Selwyn, waiting in the locker room, holding an unlit cigar in one hand and a pale-blue envelope in the other, looking at his two-tone loafers. The men from the front office stood around him, working their Adam's apples up and down over the knots of their neckties. Selwyn had on blue jeans and a big yellow sweater with the word KINGS knit across it in blue. He stuck the cigar between his teeth, opened the blue envelope, and unfolded the letter from the league office, which with terse, unintentional elegance regretfully informed the teams and players of the NAPIFL that the standings at the end of that day's schedule of games would be duly entered into the record books as final. Lou Sammartino, having coached his team to first place in its division and the best record in the league, wandered off into the showers and sat down. Irwin Selwyn shook everyone's hand and had his secretary give each player a set of fancy wrenches (he owned a hardware chain) and a check for what the player would have been owed had Lou Sammartino been granted his only remaining desire. Shortly thereafter, twenty-five broken giants trudged out to the parking lot with their socket wrenches and caught the bus to the rest of their lives.

Harris went back to his room at the Luxington Parc, turned on the television, and watched a half-hour commercial for a handheld vacuum device that sheared the bellies of beds and sofas of their eternal wool of dust. He washed his underpants in the sink. He drank two cans of diet root beer and ate seven Slim Jims. Then he switched off the television, pulled a pillow over his head, and cried. The serene, arctic blankness with which he was rumored, and in fact did struggle, to invest all his conscious processes of thought was only a hollow illusion. He was racked by that particular dread of the future that plagues superseded deities and washed-up backs. He saw himself carrying an evening six-pack up to his rented room, wearing slacks and a name tag at some job, standing with the rest of the failures of the world at the back of a very long line, waiting to claim something that in the end would turn out to be an empty tin bowl with his own grinning skull reflected in its bottom. He went into the bathroom and threw up.

When he reemerged from the bathroom, the queasiness was gone but the dread of his future remained. He picked up the phone and called around town until he found himself a car. His tight end, a Tacoma native, agreed, for a price they finally fixed at seventeen dollars—seventeen having been the number on the tight end's 1979 Washington State Prep Championship jersey—to bring his brother's car around to the hotel in half an hour. Harris showered, changed into a tan poplin suit, seersucker shirt, and madras tie, and checked out of his room. When he walked out of the Luxington Parc, he found a 1979 Chevrolet Impala, eggplant with a white vinyl top, waiting for him under the porte cochere.

"Don't turn the wipers on," said Deloyd White. "It blows the fuse on the radio. Be honest, it blows a lot of fuses. Most of them."

"What if it rains?"

Deloyd looked out at the afternoon, damp and not quite warm, the blue sky wan and smeary. He scratched at the thin, briery tangle of beard on his chin.

"If it rains you just got to drive really fast," he said.

As Harris drove north on I-5, he watched nervously as the cloak of blue sky grew threadbare and began to show, in places, its eternal gray interfacing of clouds. But the rain held off, and Harris was able to make it all the way out to Northgate without breaking the speed laws. The Chevy made a grand total of seven cars parked on the lot of Norm Fetko's New and Used Buick-Isuzu, an establishment that had changed hands and product lines a dozen times since Pierce Arrow days. It sat, a showroom of peeling white stucco, vaguely art deco, next to a low cinder-block garage on one of the saddest miles of Aurora Avenue, between a gun shop and a place that sold grow lights. Fetko had bought the place from a dealer in Pacers and Gremlins, banking on his local celebrity to win him customers at the very instant in history when Americans ceased to care who it was that sold them their cars. Harris pulled in between two Le Sabres with big white digits soaped onto their windshields, straightened his tie, and started for the open door of the dealership.

A tall, fair-haired salesman, one of the constantly shifting roster of former third-stringers and practice dummies Fetko could always call upon to man the oars of his argosies as they coursed ever nearer to the maelstrom, was propped against the doorway, smoking a cigarette, as Harris walked up. He was stuffed imperfectly into his cheap suit, and his face looked puffy. He lounged with a coiled air of impatience, tipping and rocking on the balls of his feet. His hair was like gold floss.

"Hey, Junior," he said. He gestured with a thumb. "They're all in the back room."

"Did they do it already?"

"I don't think so. I think they were waiting for you."

"But I said I *wasn't* going to come," said Harris, irritated to find that his change of heart had come as a surprise only to him.

He walked across the showroom, past three metal desks, three filing cabinets, and three wastebaskets, all enameled in a cheery shade of surgical glove; three beige telephones with rotary dials; a dismantled mimeograph; and an oak hat rack that was missing all of its hooks but one, from which there hung an empty plastic grocery sack. There was no stock on the floor, a bare beige linoleum expanse layered with a composite detritus of old cigarette ash and the lost limbs of insects. The desk chairs were tucked neatly under the desks, and the desktops themselves were bare of everything but dust. Aside from a bookshelf filled with the binders and thick manuals of the automobile trade and a few posters of last season's new models tacked up amid black-and-white photographs of the owner, in his glory days, fading back to pass, there was little to suggest that Norm Fetko's New and Used was not a defunct concern and had not been so for a very long time.

"I knew you'd come," said Fetko's wife, hurrying across the back room to greet him. She was not at all what he had imagined—an ample, youngish bottle blond with an unlikely suntan and the soft, wide-eyed look, implying a certain preparedness to accept necessary pain, that Fetko had favored in all the women he had gotten involved with after Harris's mother. She was small, with thin arms and a skinny neck, her hair like black excelsior. Her eyes were deep set. She was certainly no younger than forty. Her name was Marilyn Levine.

"I almost didn't," he insisted. "I'm, uh, not too wild about . . . these things."

"Have you been to a bris before?"

Harris shook his head.

"I'm not even going to be in the room," Marilyn said. "That's what a lightweight I am." She was wearing a loose burgundy velvet dress and ballet shoes. This was another surprise. Over time, most of the women in Fetko's life allowed themselves to become, as it were, themed, favoring grass-green muumuus patterned with stiff-arming running backs, goalposts, and footballs turning end over end. Marilyn touched a hand to Harris's arm. "Did you know the coach stopped drinking?"

"When did he do that?"

"Almost a year ago," she said. "Not quite."

"That's good news," said Harris.

"He isn't the same man, Harris," she told him. "You'll see that."

"Okay," said Harris doubtfully.

"Come say hi."

She led him past the buffet, three card tables pushed together and spread with food enough for ten times as many guests as there were in attendance. Aside from one or two of Fetko's employees and a dozen or so members of Marilyn's family, among them an authentic-looking Jew, with the little hat and the abolitionist beard, whom Marilyn introduced as her brother, the room was empty. A few women were huddled at the back of the room around a cerulean football that Harris supposed must be the blanketed new Fetko.

In the old days, at a function like this, there would have been a great ring of standing stones around Fetko, dolmens and menhirs in pistachio pants, with nicknames like Big Mack and One-Eye. Some of the members of the '55 national champions, Harris knew, had died or moved to faraway places; the rest had long since been burned, used up, worn out, or, in one case, sent to prison by one or another of Fetko's schemes. Now there remained only Oly Olafsen, Red Johnnie Green, and Hugh Eggert with his big cigar. Red Johnnie had on a black suit with a funereal tie, Oly was wearing another of his sharkskin tarpaulins, and Hugh had solved the troublesome problem of dressing for the dark ritual of an alien people by coming in his very best golf clothes. When they saw Harris, they pounded him on the back and shook his hand. They squeezed his biceps, assessed his grip, massaged his shoulders, jammed their stubbly chins into the crook of his neck, and, in the case of Hugh Eggert, gave his left buttock a farmerly slap. Harris had been in awe of them most of his life. Now he regarded them with envy and dismay. They had grown old without ever maturing: quarrelsome, salacious boys zipped into enormous rubber mansuits. Harris, on the other hand, had bid farewell to his childhood eons ago, without ever having managed to grow up.

"Harris," said Fetko. "How about that." The tip of his tongue poked out from the corner of his mouth, and he hitched up the waist of his pants, as if he were about to attempt something difficult. He was shorter than Harris remembered—fatter, grayer, older, sadder, more tired, more bald, with more broken blood vessels in his cheeks. He was, Harris quickly calculated, sixty-one, having already been most of the way through his thirties, a head coach in Denver with a master's in sports physiology, before he selected Harris's mother from a long list of available candidates and began his grand experiment in breeding. As usual he was dressed today in black high-tops, baggy black ripstop pants, and a black polo shirt. The muscles of his arms stretched the ribbed armbands of his shirtsleeves. With his black clothes, his close-cropped hair, and his eyes that were saved from utter coldness by a faint blue glint of lunacy, he looked like a man who had been trained in his youth to drop out of airplanes in the dead of night and strangle enemy dictators in their sleep.

"Son," he said.

"Hey there, Coach," said Harris.

The moment during which they might have shaken hands, or even—in an alternate-historical universe where the Chinese discovered America and a ten-year-old Adolf Hitler was trampled to death by a passing milk wagon—embraced, passed, as it always did. Fetko nodded.

"I heard you played good today," he said.

Harris lowered his head to hide the fact that he was blushing.

"I was all right," he said. "Congratulations on the kid. What's his name?

"Sid Luckman," said Fetko, and the men around him, except for Harris, laughed. Their laughter was nervous and insincere, as if Fetko had said something dirty. "Being as how he's a Jewish boy." Fetko nodded with tolerant, Einsteinian pity toward his old buddies. "These bastards here think it's a joke."

No, no, they reassured him. Sid Luckman was an excellent choice. Still, you had to admit—

"Luckman's the middle name," said Harris.

"That's right."

"I like it."

Fetko nodded again. He didn't care if Harris liked it or not. Harris was simply—had always been—there to know when Fetko wasn't joking.

"He's very glad to see you," said Marilyn Levine, with a hard edge in her voice, prodding Fetko. "He's been worrying about it all week."

"Don't talk nonsense," said Fetko.

Marilyn gave Harris a furtive nod to let him know that she had been telling the truth. She was standing with her arm still laced through Harris's, smelling pleasantly of talcum. Harris gave her hand a squeeze. He had spent the better part of his childhood waiting for Fetko to bring someone like Marilyn Levine home to raise him. Now he had a brief fantasy of yanking her out of the room by this warm hand, of hustling her and young Sid Luckman into the aubergine Chevy Impala and driving them thousands of miles through the night to a safe location. His own mother had fled Fetko when Harris was six, promising to send for him as soon as she landed on her feet. The summons never came. She had married again, and then again after that, and had moved two dozen times over the last fifteen years. Harris let go of his stepmother's hand. Probably there was no such safe place to hide her and the baby. Everywhere they went, she would find men like Fetko. For all Harris knew, he was a man like Fetko, too.

"Hello?"

Everyone turned. There was a wizened man standing behind Harris, three feet tall, a thousand years old, carrying a black leather pouch under his arm.

"I am Dr. Halbenzoller," he said regretfully. He had a large welt on his forehead and wore a bewildered, fearful expression, as if he had misplaced his eyeglasses and were feeling his way through the world. "Where are the parents?"

"I'm the boy's father," said Fetko, taking the old man's hand. "This is the mother—Marilyn. She's the observant one, here."

Dr. Halbenzoller turned his face toward Marilyn. He looked alarmed.

"The father is not Jewish?"

Marilyn shook her head. "No, but we spoke about it over the phone, Dr. Halbenzoller, don't you remember?"

"I don't remember anything," said Dr. Halbenzoller. He looked around the room, as if trying to remember how he had got to the outlandish place in which he now found himself. His gaze lingered a moment on Harris, wonderingly and with evident disapproval, as if he were looking at a Great Dane someone had dressed up in a madras jacket and taught to smile.

"I'm an existential humanist," Fetko told him. "That's always been my great asset as a coach. Over the long series, an atheistic coach will always beat a coach who believes in God." Fetko, whose own lifetime record was an existential 163–162, had been out of coaching for quite a while now, and Harris could see that he missed being interviewed. "Anyway, I don't feel I could really give the Jewish faith a fair shake—"

Dr. Halbenzoller turned to Marilyn.

"Tell them I'd like to begin," he said, as if she were his interpreter. He took the pouch from under his arm. "Where is the child?"

Marilyn led him over to the back of the room, where, beside the huddle of women, a card table had been set up and draped in a piece of purple velvet. Dr. Halbenzoller undid the buckles on his pouch and opened it, revealing a gleaming set of enigmatic tools.

"And the sandek," he said to Marilyn. "You have one?"

Marilyn looked at Fetko.

"Norm?"

Fetko looked down at his hands.

"Norm."

Fetko shrugged and looked up. He studied Harris's face and took a step toward him. Involuntarily, Harris took a step back. "It's like a godfather," Fetko said. "To the kid. Marilyn and I were wondering."

Harris was honored, and wildly touched, but he didn't want to let on. "If you want," he said. "What do I have to do?"

"Come stand next to me," said Dr. Halbenzoller slowly, as you would speak to a well-dressed and intelligent dog.

Harris went over to the velvet-covered table and stood beside it, close enough to Dr. Halbenzoller to smell the steam in his ironed suit.

"Do you have to be a doctor to do this?" he asked.

"I'm a dentist," said Dr. Halbenzoller. "Fifty years. This is just a hobby of mine." He reached into the pocket of his suit coat and took out a slim volume of cracked black leather. "Bring the child."

Sidney Luckman Fetko was brought forward and placed into Harris's arms. He was wide awake, motionless, his lumpy little pinch-pot face peering out from the blue swaddling cloth. He weighed nothing at all. Fetko's wife left the room. Dr. Halbenzoller opened the little book and began to chant. The language—Hebrew, Harris supposed—sounded harsh and angular and complaining. Sid Luckman's eyes widened, as if he were listening. His head hadn't popped entirely back into place yet after his passage through Marilyn Levine, and his features were twisted up a little on one side, giving him a sardonic expression. This is my brother, thought Harris. This is Fetko's other son.

He was so lost in the meaning of this that he didn't notice when several seconds had gone by in silence. Harris looked up. Dr. Halbenzoller was reaching out to Harris. Harris just looked at his hands, calloused and yellow but unwrinkled, like a pair of old feet.

"It's all right, Harris," said Fetko. "Give him the baby."

"Excuse me," Harris said. He tucked Sid Luckman under his arm and headed for the fire door.

He sprinted across the back lot, past a long, rusting, red-and-white trailer home with striped aluminum awnings in which Harris's mother had once direly predicted that Fetko would end his days, toward a swath of open land that stretched away behind the dealership, a vast tangle of blackberry brambles, dispirited fir trees, and renegade pachysandra escaped from some distant garden. In his late adolescence, Harris had often picked his way to a large clearing at the center of the tangle, a circular sea of dead grass where for decades the mechanics who worked in the service bays had tossed their extinguished car batteries and pans of broken-down motor oil. At the center of this cursed spot, Harris would lie on his back, looking at the pigeon-colored Seattle sky, and expend his brain's marvelous capacity for speculation on topics such as women's breasts, the big money, and Italian two-seaters.

These days there was no need to pick one's way—a regular path had been cleared through the brush—and as they approached the clearing, Harris slowed. The woods were birdless, and the only sounds were the hum of traffic from Aurora Avenue, the snapping of twigs under his feet, and a low, hostile grunting from the baby. It had turned into a cold summer afternoon. The wind blew in from the north, smelling of brine and rust. As Harris approached the clearing, he found himself awash in regret, not for the thing he had just done nor for shanked kicks or lost yardage nor for the trust he had placed, so mistakenly, in others during his short, trusting, mistaken life, but for something more tenuous and faint, tied up in the memory of those endless afternoons spent lying on his back in that magical circle of poison, wasting his thoughts on things that now meant so little to him. Then he and Sid fell into the clearing.

Most of the trees around it, he saw, had been brought down, while those that remained had been stripped of their lower branches and painted, red or blue, with a white letter, wobbly and thin, running ten feet up the trunk. Exactly enough trees had been left, going around, to spell out the word POWER-BALL. Harris had never seen a painted tree before, and the effect was startling. From a very tall pole at the center of the circle, each of nine striped rappelling cables extended, like the ribs of an umbrella, toward a wooden platform at the top of each of the painted trees. The ground had been patiently tilled and turned over, cleared of grass and rubbish, then patted down again, swept smooth and speckless as an infield. At the northern and southern poles of the arena stood a soccer-goal net, spray-painted gold. Someone had also painted a number of imitation billboards advertising Power Rub and the cigarettes, soft drinks, spark plugs, and malt liquors of fantasy sponsors, and nailed them up at key locations around the perimeter. The lettering was crude but the colors were right and if you squinted a little you might almost be persuaded. The care, the hard work, the childish attention to detail, and, above all, the years of misapplied love and erroneous hopefulness that had gone into its planning and construction seemed to Harris to guarantee the arena's inevitable destruction by wind, weather, and the creeping pachysandra of failure that ultimately entangled all his father's endeavors and overwhelmed the very people they were most intended to avail. Fetko was asking for it.

"Look what Coach did," Harris said to Sid, tilting the baby a little so that he might see. "Isn't that neat?"

Sid Luckman's face never lost its dour, sardonic air, but Harris found himself troubled by an unexpected spasm of forgiveness. The disaster of Powerball, when finally it unfolded, as small-scale disappointment or as massive financial collapse, would not really be Fetko's fault. Harris's entire life had been spent, for better or worse, in the struggling company of men, and he had seen enough by now to know that evergreen ruin wound its leaves and long tendrils around the habitations and plans of all fathers, everywhere, binding them by the ankles and wrists to their sons, whether the fathers asked for it or not.

"Get your ass back in there," said Fetko, coming up behind them, out of breath. "Asses."

Harris didn't say anything. He could feel his father's eyes on him, but he didn't turn to look. The baby snuffled and grunted in Harris's arms.

"I, uh, I did all this myself," Fetko said after a moment.

"I figured."

"Maybe later, if you wanted to, we could go over some of the fine points of the game."

"Maybe we could."

Fetko shook himself and slapped his palms together. "Fine, but now come on, goddammit. Before that little Jewish gentleman in there seizes up on us."

Harris nodded. "Okay," he said.

As he carried Sid past their father, Harris felt his guts contract in an ancient reflex, and he awaited the cuff, jab, karate chop, rabbit punch, head slap, or boot to the seat of his pants that in his youth he had interpreted as a strengthening exercise designed to prepare him for his career as an absorber of terrible impacts but that now, as Fetko popped him on the upper arm hard enough to make him wince, touching him for the first time in five years, he saw as the expression of a sentiment at once so complicated and inarticulate, neither love nor hatred but as elemental as either, that it could only be expressed by contusing the skin. Harris shifted Sid Luckman to his left arm and, for the first time ever, raised a fist to pop Fetko a good one in return. Then he changed his mind and lowered his hand and carried the baby through the woods to the dealership with Fetko following behind them, whistling a tuneless and impatient song through his teeth.

When they got back, Harris handed over Sid Luckman. Dr. Halbenzoller set the baby down on the velvet cloth. He reached into his pouch and took out a rectangular stainless-steel device that looked a little like a cigar trimmer. The baby shook his tiny fists. His legs, unswaddled, beat the air like butterfly wings. Dr. Halbenzoller brought the cigar trimmer closer to his tiny panatela. Then he glanced up at Harris.

"Please," he said, nodding to the fitful legs, and Harris understood that somebody was going to have to hold his brother down.

Soul Survivor

GARY SMITH

Devard and Devaughn Darling's odyssey from the Bahamas to Houston, Texas, to Tallahassee, Florida, and the Florida State University football team could have been an inspirational tale about the bond between brothers and their love of football. But when the Darling twins were forever separated one morning during the Seminoles' infamous mat drills, it instead became one of heart-wrenching loss.

In one early-morning workout, Devard Darling was robbed of his soul mate and nearly had his lifelong dream stolen. Reading this story, I tried to imagine what it would be like to lose a family member, a best friend, or a spouse, but as Gary Smith points out, what Devard Darling lost was bigger than any of those things. Smith explores the lives of identical twins who share a bi-ological and cultural bond that is unlike anything else in life. As Smith points out in the story's first sentence, Devard Darling lost a lifelong teammate and a best friend. He also lost part of himself, and before that wound healed he was forced face a challenge that could have robbed him of his dream.

Devard Darling's single-minded determination to continue the path to a career in football that he and his brother began is in the end as uplifting as it is devastating.

Thne golden helmet gleamed upon the pedestal beneath the foyer light. It stopped the boy as he came through his mother's front door. It held his eyes. He'd searched everywhere else. Why not here? Devard Darling lifted the helmet from the pedestal and peered inside. After all, if the soul resided in the mind, and the mind resided in the cranium, and the cranium resided—during his identical twin's moments of greatest hope and aliveness—inside this golden Seminoles helmet . . . then couldn't it be here?

It *might* fit inside a helmet. It wasn't a complete soul, mind you. Just half of one. Devard and his twin had gone halvers on everything their entire lives—a splendid arrangement right up to the day that Devaughn, pursuing their dream, worked himself to death. But now that Devaughn was gone. . . .

Devard pulled the helmet over his head. He walked into the living room, then the kitchen. He looked at the newspaper. Patience. It might take awhile to lure the half-soul back.

His mother and two sisters stole glances. It was an odd sight, a boy walking around the house in street clothes and a football helmet—heartbreaking and humorous and eerie all at once. But they were wise, and they kept silent.

He returned to the foyer—and froze. There, in the flash of the mirror by the bathroom door, in the glimpse of eyes framed by the headgear, he'd almost sensed it, felt it, found it. The mirror pulled him closer . . . closer. . . .

He swallowed what rose in his throat as he stared at his eyes. He removed the helmet and returned it to the pedestal.

No. His half-soul wasn't in the helmet. He'd have to keep searching.

Science can't explain it. Now and then, once in about every 250 human conceptions, the fertilized egg splits, creating two distinct embryos containing identical genetic material. There's magic in this sudden duplication, a powder keg of psychic implications for the pair of children born. This was understood long ago and over there, where the ancestors of Devard and Devaughn Darling lived.

African tribes created rituals and totems to contain this magic—some even built fences around the homes of newborn twins. Some killed one or both twins upon birth; others rejoiced and made offerings. Some tribes buried a dead twin as swiftly as possible, or not at all, leaving the body sitting on a rock and then fleeing without looking back. The Yoruba, of Nigeria, sensed that identical twins possessed just one soul between them, and they understood the spiritual emergency when a child's double died. That's why they carved a wooden figurine for the deceased twin's half-soul to reside in, an object for the survivor to wash and clothe and feed, to reach for whenever he felt half of himself missing and needed something—God, *something*—to hold onto.

Somewhere in the clang of manacle and chains and the stench of a slave ship's lower deck, such understanding began to be lost. And so one day in the second month of 2001, as Devaughn Darling lay dying in front of his twin at the end of an off-season football conditioning workout at Florida State, Devard had to begin his search on his own, without figurines or ceremonies to see him through the trauma. On his own, amid a tribe whose principal ritual occurred in stadiums thronged with thousands of people worshiping strength and speed, youth and vitality. God only knew how he'd find his missing half-soul, how he'd keep his brother's memory alive, but it would have to be with a football.

Of course, he had a loving family trying to console him. Of course, he had sympathetic friends and teammates from Austin–Fort Bend High School, just outside Houston—where the twins had become blue-chip prospects sought by large universities across the land—and new friends at Florida State, where the Darlings had displayed their promise as freshmen: Devard, the 6'3" wide receiver with 4.3 speed; Devaughn, the 225-pound linebacker who devoured quarterbacks. But all who knew the twins knew it was impossible to know the depth of Devard's loss; their attempts at empathy felt futile. This was one mind in two bodies, says their aunt Yvonne Moncur. A chemistry like you've never seen between two human beings, says their high school teammate, Nick Nichols. For God's sake, marvels their cousin Frank Rutherford, they even had to *take leaks* at the same time. They were harmonized, synchronized, two hearts that beat as—

Wait a minute. If one heart had failed under the glare and bark of a football coach, couldn't—*wouldn't*—the identical one fail as well? How could Florida State risk it? Sorry, son. Take off your helmet. No more football, Devard.

Find your half-soul some other way.

This is a ghost story. The ghost isn't Devaughn, the dead twin. It's Devard. Sometimes it's the living who haunt. Have you ever loved someone enough to do that?

The place where they began: Maybe that's where Devard's spirit would find what had been ripped from it. A few months after his brother's death he flew to the Bahamas, where they had lived their first dozen years. He went to their old home in Nassau. He stood in front of the two-story house with the big backyard and the plum tree that their godfather had planted—the wise sapling that forked into two trunks, one for each twin to perch on—and stared, watching their past unfold. It wobbled and blurred through his tears, but he could still make it out.

It's a Sunday, and they're so damn happy to have each other all day, because it's the year of that failed experiment, in which grown-ups tried to pull them apart. The year school administrators placed them in separate second-grade classes to help them become individuals—*miserable* individuals—and their mother, trying to heed the experts' warnings about blurred identity, attempted to dress them differently. *No, Mummy,* they protested, with that lovely Bahamian lilt that turned the phrase into a question. *We want to keep dressing the same, Mummy, so just buy two of everything and put it in the same drawer. Can't we be in the same class again,* please, *Mummy?*

The school would surrender at the end of second grade. Mummy? She lasted only a day or two, melted by those four sad brown eyes, so they're back in matching outfits, right down to their football undies. It's a force larger than her, has been from that moment on the delivery table when Devard came forth and the obstetrician's eyes popped: What's that wrapped around the newborn's ankle? A . . . *hand?* Yes, a hand—here comes another one! One heartbeat, the dumbstruck doc kept saying. That's all he'd ever heard.

Thank goodness cousin Enith Darling spotted that tiny birthmark on the bridge of Devaughn's nose and concocted the ditty that the extended family would repeat to tell the two apart—*Vaughnie's got a mole/And Vardie's got a cold*—because even the twins can't look at photographs and tell themselves apart. Truth is, it doesn't much matter. Each answers to both names, no worries. Same pals, same birthday cake, same sick days, same toy bank to stash their allowance, same adorable hip shimmy when the reggae starts. Same glow on their faces and on those of everyone who meets them—so why pry them apart?

But they're torn today, because it's Sunday. Torn between the joy of jiggling on Daddy's knees in front of the TV and catapulting off when his beloved Miami Dolphins score touchdowns and watching emotions they didn't know he had pour out of him—and the bliss of pretending to be Miami Dolphins scoring touchdowns in the big backyard. Look at 'em bolt, man: Speed and agility are in their blood. Their cousin Frank will soon become the first Bahamian ever to win an Olympic track and field medal, a bronze in the triple jump in Barcelona in 1992, and a three-time NCAA champ at the University of Houston. Their older brother, Dennis, will captain Houston's track team and twice win the 200 and 400 meters in the Conference USA indoor championships. Their aunt Yvonne would've been a cinch to make the '64 Olympics in the sprints if she hadn't gotten pregnant, and their great-uncle George Knowles won the European Commonwealth's middleweight boxing crown. Those two long-armed rascals even run the same, trained by cousin Frank on his visits from Houston, their wrists flicking up on the backswing as if they're shooing gnats riding in their draft.

Let 'em pretend to be Marino and Duper in the yard. They don't know yet that kids like them can't play in the NFL because there's no high school football in the Bahamas. They don't know yet that their upper-middle-class life as the sons of the Bahamas' deputy treasurer—maid, two cars, private schools, big-screen TV, vacations at Disney World—will be shattered in just a few years, that the cops will surge through the front door at 5 a.m. and Daddy will end up in handcuffs on the front page of the *Bahamian Tribune*, wrongly accused after $2 million vanishes from the national treasury. That their parents' marriage will crumble, even after Daddy is found innocent in court, and they'll drift with Mummy from house to house, unable to pay the electric bill even though she works as a government clerk by day and delivers pizzas at night—*the butter floating in the ice cooler* is how brother Dennis will describe their altered state.

Devard stared at their old home, rubbing the wetness from his eyes, then turned and trudged away. His half-soul wasn't there.

Have you ever had someone you could lie down in the dark with and talk to about anything? Maybe you're lucky. Maybe you have.

He was me and I was him, says Devard. Devard was the shy and quiet twin, the one few could imagine pouring out his heart to anyone, at any hour. The one who'd softly talk Devaughn out of sacking their toy bank and blowing their life's savings on candy bars, the one a few minutes older and wiser but assured enough to let Devaughn function as the leader. Their grandfather, a Baptist minister, predicted that Devard would become a preacher too. . . . So what in the Lord's name was the silent, sober one doing now, returning to the house his family had moved into on the outskirts of Houston and screaming a name in the middle of the night: *Devaughn! DEVAUGHN!*

There he *is,* pile-driving Devard's rear end right through the bedroom wall and apologizing in the same grunt—the dispute settled before the dust has. It's here that they show what they're made of, immigrants thrown into the swarm after their world collapsed in Nassau and their divorced mother turned north, to America, with her 12-year-old twins and two daughters. Here where they learn to mimic Mummy, who just keeps taking blows, smiling and stepping into tomorrow. Here where they grab mops at night to help her swab the library and the courthouse in Sugarland for a few bucks an hour, then sardine together at bedtime, all six of them—Mummy, the twins, Monique and Stacey and Stacey's child, Rashayne—into one bedroom, where Mummy will dip her finger into olive oil and anoint their foreheads, and then they'll link hands and pray and fall asleep.

Father, aunts, uncles, grandparents, cousins, friends, school, status, *home:* The twins lost so much when they left behind the Bahamas. What can America possibly offer to compensate?

Football! Daddy's favorite! Shoulder pads, hip pads, helmets, jerseys, cleats: The twins adorn themselves in these sacred new vestments, unsure whether to howl in delight or kneel in reverence. Well, then, Devaughn could howl and Devard could kneel, for distinct personalities have emerged in Sugarland, their *twoness* as well as their *oneness.* Devaughn's their mouthpiece in this new world. The one who makes all the phone calls, the jokes, the peace. He'll croon the corniest songs and dance the silliest dance without blushing: "The Big Man Dance!" he'll bellow, remaining motionless except for thrusting his chest out and in, and soon everyone will be flushed out of the shadows, boogying around the big teddy bear.

Funny thing, though. The girls Devaughn flushes from cover usually go for the silent one, the mystery man: Devard. The brothers harvest each other's fruits that way. Devard can hang back and feel his way, pulled along in Devaughn's bubbly wake. Devaughn can let his impulses howl, knowing Devard will whisper in his ear if they howl too loud.

Football begins to carve two distinct physiques as well. Devaughn starts jacking up monster weights and wolfing down monster bowls of frosted cereal to become the monster linebacker. Devard remains the whippet, uncannily strong but 30 pounds lighter than Devaughn by the time they graduate from high school.

At first their classmates find it strange that the twins talk funny and don't curse. Soon they too find themselves saying *rawp* instead of *rap,* and *ting'um* instead of *thing* and *golleee!* or *shoots!* or, in a very wicked adjectival moment, *freakin'.* In the beginning they find it odd that the twins won't smoke or drink but will, at the mere loss of a football game, start sniffling, then dabbing an eye, then . . . weeping. By the ninth grade all their teammates are weepers too. Initially they find it hokey that the twins, at Mummy's urging, hang posters on their bedroom walls with a list of yearly football and scholastic goals beneath a Bible verse, but then the members of the G.C. Fam—the nickname for the twins' circle of friends that formed at Garcia Middle School—begin to hang them on their bedroom walls as well. Everyone wants to want something as dearly as the Darlings do.

Mummy gets a job taking care of a multiple sclerosis sufferer by day and a stroke victim by night, kissing the twins goodbye each Sunday night and not returning home until Thursday. No ma at home, no pa at home—guess what those two teen anarchists stay up half the night doing? Lying in bed clutching the cushion footballs Mummy bought them, hatching their blood-brothers pact: They'll both major in sports medicine at one of America's elite football colleges, then become the first identical twins from the Bahamas ever to play in the NFL, then buy matching black Lamborghini Diablos and houses a few doors apart, then start a youth football program in their homeland and make sure that Mummy never works another day in her life. They set the alarm clock for 7 a.m. in the dead of summer to make it all come true.

To the weight room. To the track. To the football field. To the VCR, combing their performances for flaws so many times it makes their friends groan. At a voluntary workout on a chilly morning during the Christmas holidays, no-body on the track team shows up—except coach Dennis Brantly, Devard and Devaughn. Unheard-of drive, says the twins' pal Reggie Berry. The highest integrity and character you can imagine—a coach's dream, says their football coach, Tom Stuart. I didn't know people could be like that, says their buddy Godwin Nyan.

Every teenager around them is burning so much psychic energy searching for his *other,* for the mirror in which to find his own identity. The twins were born possessing that, freeing them to funnel all their fuel into the engine of their dreams. Their grades? Up: 3.8 for Devard when he graduates, 3.5 for Devaughn. Their bench presses? Up: 305 for Devaughn, 275 for Devard. Their times in the 100 meters? Down: 10.31 for Devard, 10.50 for Devaughn. When the two co-captains of the football and track teams, the two humblest, fastest, strongest and damn near smartest kids at Austin–Fort Bend High, are out of earshot, the rest of the G.C. Fam says, "Man, their life's too perfect. Something bad gotta happen."

But how could it? Devaughn wouldn't *allow* it. Have you ever had someone grasp both your hands and begin jumping and screaming, telling you how much he believed in you and how quickly he'd be there if ever you got in trouble? Until you started jumping and screaming and believing too?

Devard did. Maybe that was where he'd find his missing half-soul, in the high school locker room where they jumped and hollered face mask-to-face mask before every game, or on the field where they fought three years of autumn wars together. He wandered back and stared. All the spirit they'd spilled here couldn't just evaporate . . . could it?

No, *look,* there goes Devaughn! Hitting that wall of flesh against Elkins High, spinning away somehow for that 65-yard run. Cramping up from playing both ways in the Texas heat, hobbling off and then back on to flatten blockers and quarterbacks in a single burst that ends in Devard's waiting arms as the crowd roars and recruiters from Kansas and Kansas State and Arizona and Purdue and Texas A&M and Auburn and Michigan State and Tennessee and Syracuse and Florida State rise to their feet, each awaiting a pair of nods.

Devard will choose their college. Devaughn insists on it, knowing that he can maul and maim anywhere but that his twin—an All-District jet mostly stranded on the tarmac in a landlubbing offense—needs to find a coach and a quarterback who believe in bombs away.

Devard chooses Florida State. Tears fill the twins' eyes when they sign their letters of intent. All their 1 a.m. plans are coming true. Why, then? Why, in the still of night when Devaughn falls asleep, does Devard keep staring at his twin's face and feeling desperation in his gut, rushing in like the wave that sucked Devaughn out to sea when they were seven and nearly drowned him? Devard lies there, crying and telling himself how ridiculous this feeling is, that his twin won't die until they're old, and then, somehow, they'll do it like they do everything else: together. Have you ever done that? Loved someone so much that you mourned his death as he slept?

The last bedroom they shared. Devard kept sneaking back into it: How could NO TRESPASSING apply to a ghost? He'd slip away from the apartment he'd moved into with his brother Dennis—who had come to see him through the school year and the grief—and drift back to Burt Reynolds Hall, where Florida State's freshman and sophomore players lived. He'd pull out the key he hadn't turned in, enter the silence and sag onto one of their old beds, waiting . . . listening . . . watching.

There they are, the two of them coming back from study hall on a winter Sunday night and ordering a pizza. It's seven weeks after their freshman season ended. It's their last night together.

Their dream's on track. They've learned that they belong in the big time, with Devaughn pegged to start as a sophomore and Devard to be one of four receivers in the Seminoles' rotation. Their coaches call both of them a coach's dream.

They've learned something else after their freshman physicals: They both have the sickle-cell trait. But so what? So do 8% of all blacks in America, including plenty of gifted athletes. It's a generally benign hereditary condition marked by one abnormal gene for hemoglobin that causes the production of some red blood cells with a sickle shape, instead of the smooth-flowing spherical one, and thus potentially reducing the blood's oxygen-carrying capacity. The NCAA medical handbook warns that the trait might be linked to exercise-associated sudden death—in military training, not in sports—but so rarely that no specific restrictions should be placed on an athlete who carries the trait. Only that he, like all athletes, should avoid dehydration during workouts and get into condition gradually over several weeks before engaging in exhaustive exercise regimens, and that team doctors and trainers should familiarize themselves with the medical literature. The only caution flag waved at the twins is this: Be careful making babies. If their partners have the same trait, they run a high risk of conceiving a child with sickle-cell anemia, an often fatal disease in which the sickle-shaped blood cells are rampant.

The twins are not thinking about multiplying as they polish off the pizza—just about surviving. Just a few more mat drills remain to be completed. To a man, ex-Seminoles who've gone on to NFL two-a-days in July or to Marine Corps boot camp agree: Nothing compares to Florida State's off-season mat drills. Former Seminoles tailback John Merna, a Marine, called the drills "a true test of a man's physical and moral courage." Former Seminoles defensive lineman James Roberson said they were like "stepping into a gas chamber." Players who had finished four years of them came back and thanked Coach Bobby Bowden for the rewards they reaped from them and for the lessons they learned about themselves and about life.

The drills are a battery of noncontact running, jumping, crouching, diving and rolling exercises that Bowden borrowed from Bear Bryant nearly five decades ago. "We want to push you to the breaking point," is how Bowden explained them to players. "Not over it, but to it."

Trash cans are placed within staggering distance of the three stations through which the players rotate. Both twins have already vomited into them. Ten Seminoles vomited on the first day of mat drills the previous year, some so intimidated that they puked before the drills even began. Former FSU offensive lineman Eric Luallen, a Tallahassee sports-talk-show host, wrote a column about mat drills on a website just a week and a half before, "It was always chilling to hear [former Seminoles assistant] Chuck Amato address the team the first day of mat drills," Luallen wrote. "While he would point out the trash cans and what they were to be used for, he would always throw in this confidence-building quote: 'Just remember, gentlemen, the body is a wonderful machine. You will pass out before you die. If you pass out, the trainers will take care of you.'"

It's 11:30 p.m. Devaughn's got a head cold that he caught from Devard, and mat drills begin in six hours and 15 minutes. Devaughn pops a couple of nighttime cold and flu pills. The twins reread the New Year's goals on their wall posters. Devaughn has dared to write *All-America first team* on his and keeps urging Devard to take the dare too. They say their prayers, asking God to be there at dawn when they need him, and they fall asleep.

Bang! Bang! Bang! That's the big metal spoon striking door after door, spreading dread through Burt Reynolds Hall at 5 a.m. *Bang! Bang! Bang!* That's the traditional wake-up call for Florida State mat drills. *Bang! Bang! Bang!* Devard could almost hear it four months later as he stood and peered at the door at 3 a.m. on a summer night, because someone else lived there and he could no longer search inside.

There they go, out that door on their final morning together, trudging down those stairs, bludgeoned by fatigue. Into the darkness, onto the dirt road through the construction zone, taking the short walk to Moore Athletic Center.

No time for breakfast or to brush their teeth. No time for more than a few swallows of water. Silence between them, except for Devaughn's one remark: "I can't wait for this to be over and for us to go home for spring break." Devard nods. They enter the trainer's room, where Devaughn gets his sore ankle wrapped. They go upstairs and stretch on the mats in the Rubber Room. The bullhorn shrieks at 5:45. Time for hell.

Devaughn and Devard go separate ways with their position groups. Devaughn completes his first two segments in the gym downstairs. Short sprints, running drills through ropes and agility drills, crouched beneath PVC pipes. The twins pass each other in the hallway between stations. Devard sees the faraway look in Devaughn's eyes. No time to speak or gulp from the water fountain as the coaches hurry the players to their next tasks. Devard touches Devaughn's hand to give him strength.

Devaughn ascends the stairs. Into the fire. Into the Rubber Room, where players form lines of four on the mats, legs pistoning furiously, and at the order or gesture of a coach . . . hit the floor! Roll left! Roll right! Jump up! Sprint! Again and again, and then once more if anyone in your foursome can't keep up. Peer pressure builds, because no one wants to make his buddies repeat, or get a failing grade and an order to report at 5 a.m. for an extra session back-to-back with a scheduled one. No one wants the coaches to win, to snap his will, because that's the dynamic at work: Us against Them.

No one, most of all Devaughn, who's feeling it happen again: the cramps and the dizziness and then the blackness, the world going dark the way it did the week before, when he vomited and passed out. Quit? Be the weak link? The kid who coded his computer to pipe out the FSU fight song every time he turned it on, the kid who never missed a day of classes in four years of high school, the two-way player they called the Beast in high school because he kept coming back from the dead like a monster in the movies?

Pain rips through his chest. He bends and presses his hands against it. Yes, the coaches have told the players to see the trainers if they're in trouble, but what have the upperclassmen poured into the freshmen? You *don't* quit mat drills. You *can't* quit mat drills. They're how we build unity and how we build pros. They're who we are in the fourth quarter on a 90° September Saturday afternoon in Tallahassee. Devaughn begins to stagger, to sway, to gasp to teammates that his chest hurts, that he can't breathe, that he can't see. But he keeps going. The coaches and trainers will say later that they never heard him, that they wish to God they had, that he looked no worse than other players struggling to finish.

A coach commands Devaughn to hit the floor. He falls forward like a board. He needs help to get up. "Come on!" his teammates cry. "You got to go four quarters!" They clap to try to rally him, they grab his arms and hold him upright and do the drills with him—just as they've done in previous mat drills when he has struggled—never dreaming that they're dragging and exhorting him to his death. His foursome is ordered back to redo a set of drills, and when he falls behind again he's sent back once more, the last man, finishing alone.

In the gym downstairs Devard finishes. No vibe, no sixth sense that his twin's in trouble one floor above. Why? Didn't people say that twins do that in a crisis?

Devaughn staggers to the wall at the end of the drill and drops to his knees. Randy Oravetz, the head trainer, goes to his side and begins to ask him questions. Devaughn's breaths are shallow. He doesn't reply.

The team members are regathering in the Rubber Room to hear their grades. Devard sees Devaughn sitting beside the trainer with ice packs on his neck, but it's just fatigue, he thinks, it'll pass "C'mon, Devaughn," he says. Suddenly he sees teammate O.J. Jackson and the trainer carrying his twin out the door as a coach calls out, "There goes our only F."

"I gotta go check on my brother!" cries Devard. He rushes downstairs and into the training room, glimpses his brother on a table with ice bags packed around him, a mask over his mouth, the trainers frantically pumping his chest. No pulse! His eyes are rolling back into his head! Call EMS! Somebody shoves Devard out of the room.

Devard starts screaming, cursing the coaches and their mat drills, running upstairs to tell everyone what they've done to his twin, then turning—his brother needs him!—and running back. Corey Simon, the former Florida State defensive lineman who has just finished his rookie year with the Philadelphia Eagles, comes down the hallway on his way to lift weights and sees Devard's panic and the anger building in the gathering knot of players. He pulls Devard away. He gets him on his knees to pray.

An ambulance arrives. Paramedics rush into the trainers' room. Players hold hands in the hallway. Players howl at coaches, players wail to God.

The trainers' room door opens. Out comes Devaughn on a stretcher, into the ambulance. Devard bolts to the front seat. It's like a movie now, it's not real, it's not real, it's not real. "C'mon, Devaughn!" he keeps shouting back as they race toward Tallahassee Regional Memorial. "C'mon, Devaughn! *Breathe!*"

The paramedics rush Devaughn into the emergency room. Devard is left in the waiting room. A receptionist hands him forms and a pen. He can't fill in a single blank. A nurse sees his desperation. She takes him to his twin. He sees all the tubes and EKG leads attached to him, screams to his brother, touches his leg—God, it feels so *hard*—wheels and staggers out of the room. He stabs at his cellphone, blurts craziness to Mummy.

"Devard, calm down," she says. "He'll be all right."

"No, Mummy. . . . I hate these coaches! I *hate* them!"

Half the team is in the waiting room, crying, praying, trying to console Devard. An E.R. doctor enters.

Devard sees his face.

Devard knows.

His 18-year-old twin is dead.

His hands go to his chest, as if it's happening to him. He starts ripping off his shirt because he can't rip off his skin and rip up his heart. He whirls, glimpses a mirror and jerks his head away. Seeing himself is seeing Devaughn!

He collapses and sobs. Devaughn always told Devard he'd never go anywhere without him. But he had, he had, he had. . . .

At the memorial service, Bowden—who had never lost a player in all those decades of mat drills—apologized to the Darling family and said, "I hope this won't hit anyone the wrong way . . . but he's the first player I've coached in 47 years who actually worked himself to death. . . . He said, 'I will not quit. I will die before I give up.' That's a great virtue. I don't have it. Oh, God, what a role model You have created for us to follow."

Devard walked into their bedroom when the service ended, and at the bottom of his goals poster he wrote: *First-team All-American*. At the funeral he wrapped his arms around Devaughn's helmet and hugged it to the end. *Someone else* hadn't died. Half of him was dead.

And so a boy who had never come to know aloneness the way other human beings do—little by little, as a side effect of breathing—suddenly knew an aloneness with no bottom. He clutched at almost anything as he hurtled down that shaft. The tattoo that Devaughn had had etched on his left biceps just after his 18th birthday (an idea Devard wanted no part of at the time) now blazed on Devard's left biceps: a cross wrapped in barbed wire beneath the nickname Devaughn had given himself, THE BLESSED ONE. He carried Devaughn's key chain, wore Devaughn's helmet in his mother's house and, when that wasn't enough, wore Devaughn's jersey, too. He talked out loud to Devaughn as if Devaughn were still at his elbow. On their birthday he ordered two cakes at the bakery counter, one with his name and one with Devaughn's. Mummy had to walk out. She couldn't bear it. He cried himself to sleep night after night, month after month.

He roamed everywhere he might find his missing half. Back onto the field at Doak Campbell Stadium, which they'd charged onto together as firebreathing freshmen; back to the trainers' room where life leaked out of his brother; back to the hallway at Moore Athletic Center where their hands touched for the last time; back to Burt Reynolds Hall, where Dennis would find him at frightful hours murmuring, "That's where I'm supposed to be," then hug him and lead him away. Everywhere except the Rubber Room. Devard couldn't make his legs go through that door.

And still, no matter how painstaking his search, his half-soul always seemed a whisper, a shadow, a sudden glance away. There was only one way to save himself—and Devaughn too—from the bottom of that shaft. But couldn't football kill Devard, too?

Two days after the funeral he walked into the office of a Houston cardiologist to find out if something inside him, too, lay in ambush. He underwent a series of tests and awaited the results with his stomach in a fist. Relief gusted through him when they came back negative. Then confusion when the cardiologist wouldn't give him clearance to play.

"I'm going to carry out our dream," Devard declared. His family closed ranks around him. We want to see Devaughn live through Devard, said cousin Frank.

Devard called the football office at Florida State, requesting a weightlifting program he could follow while he grieved with his family for a few weeks in Sugarland. No one would send one. Oravetz, the trainer, started philosophizing on the phone about how a college degree was more important than playing football. Uh-oh. . . .

"We can't *wait* for you to get back." Hadn't Bowden told him that at the memorial service? Maybe, Devard began to think, the coaches no longer wanted him around—a ghastly facsimile, a daily reminder of who was gone and why. Already they'd had to snuff the flames of rebellion that flashed through the freshmen players: Many wanted to transfer, blaming the coaches for the horror, and some, like Devard, wanted never to set foot in the Rubber Room again. Already the coaches had begun reevaluating mat drills, a process that would lead them to introduce two mandatory four-minute water breaks, along with an ambulance and a defibrillator on site.

Devaughn's autopsy report was issued. No definitive cause of death was found, but sickle-shaped red blood cells—the ones that could form a sludge in the vessels and threaten the flow of oxygen in the blood, especially during a state of dehydration, when the overall volume of blood is reduced— were found diffused throughout his body, and the sickle-cell trait was noted as a possible underlying cause. Florida State University police filed a 300-page report finding no wrongdoing on the university's part.

Devard returned to Florida State and was promptly sent to a local cardiologist, Dr. John Katopodis. Katopodis voiced doubt that Devard should play football again. Tears rushed to Devard's eyes. Katopodis ordered a battery of tests, many of the same ones Devard had undergone in Houston. Blood tests, exercise stress tests, electrocardiograms, echocardiograms, bubble studies, MRIs of the chest and heart, oxygen saturation tests, volume oxygen tests and, hey, would he mind taking an electrophysiologic test, the one in which a wire is pushed through a tube sent up the groin and through blood vessels to the heart, so it can be microelectrically shocked into going haywire to see if it can regain its natural beat—with just a tiny, tiny risk of death? Oh? He would mind?

The cardiologist, of course, also asked Devard some questions. Yes, Devard admitted, he'd experienced some light-headedness and seen dots during rigorous workouts—but then, he thought, hadn't every athlete who ever pushed himself to his limit in the Texas and Florida heat? Yes, Devard admitted, an uncle of his had died from a heart problem—but what the cardiologist didn't realize, said cousin Frank, was that the uncle's heart had been banging from an overdose of drugs. The new tests on Devard came back negative, but Katopodis, citing Devard's family history and his experiences of light-headedness, decided to do the safest thing. He refused medical clearance and told Devard that his football life was done.

Please, son, stay, continue your studies on scholarship, the Seminoles' coaches and athletic director urged him. They weren't running him off, and couldn't he understand their position: How could the school and the cardiologist live with themselves if this tragedy unfolded *twice?* Devard broke down. The kid's arms had been cut off when his twin died, said Godwin Nyan, and just when he was learning to live with that, they cut off his legs.

No. It wasn't just to soothe the surviving twin that the Yoruba washed and fed and clothed the wooden image of the deceased twin. It was to appease the departed twin's spirit so it wouldn't lure the living one to join it in death.

Could that be what was happening now, as Devard decided to defy the doctor's decision, to leave Florida State, to find a college that would let him run the risk of following his twin to the other side? Where would he go? He pulled out the list of suitors who had come calling the year before, when the twins were being wooed in high school, and imagined how thrilled they'd be to have a second chance to bag a Darling.

He started with Texas A&M, the school that would allow him to remain near home as he tried to start life over as *one,* and the program that had flooded his living room with seven coaches one night just before signing day. At first the Aggies seemed excited to hear from him, but then came silence, and then a reference to the shock their football program had undergone 10 years earlier when kicker James Glenn died of a heart problem before practice . . . and then, no thank you, Devard, we're sorry.

Next he contacted Tennessee. Yes, said the Volunteers, come see us on the double. They sat him down, indicated that they had a scholarship open, set him up with a counselor to arrange classes and told him they'd express-mail the forms he'd need to sign. Tennessee, man! Nearly on a par with Florida State! He arranged an apartment in Knoxville, read a story of his reported transfer in *The Tennessean,* went home and waited for the scholarship papers to arrive.

And waited. And waited. Cousin Frank kept calling the Tennessee football office to learn what was causing the delay. Well . . . uh . . . we're sorry, a coach finally told him, but the scholarship we thought we had to offer, we don't have.

The news found Devard at his mother's house. Halfway up the stairs, he dropped and wept. How could it be? All the advantages he'd reaped in 18 years as Devaughn's twin suddenly were turning against him. Guilt by association, that's how it felt, but who—in a land of lawyers licking their chops— could take on the liability of Devaughn Darling's double?

He tried blasphemy next: Miami, the Seminoles' archenemy. Coach Larry Coker's remorse sounded real: Oh, if only Devard had called two weeks earlier, before that last scholarship was bestowed, perhaps he could've been a Hurricane. The clock was ticking. Summer and scholarships were vanishing, the next school year drawing near. Cousin Frank contacted Arizona. Sorry. No interest. A question began to gnaw at Devard: Have I been blacklisted?

He tried Purdue next. Sure, said the Boilermakers, come visit, and his hopes rose again. He flew there and was asked to take virtually all of those tests a third time. More injections, more tubes, more straps, clips, mouthpieces and monitors. More invasion, more waiting. He hung his head and became a piece of meat again, then went home. He felt no connection there.

Southern Cal grew interested. He had barely gotten off the plane, it seemed, when he was asked to submit to the same tests yet again. Couldn't he forward the results of all the ones he'd already taken and re-taken? No. How many times, he wanted to scream, must his body prove its innocence? But he was Devard, not Devaughn, so he clamped his lips and walked away with his suitcase and his unspeakable loneliness.

My God, this is crazy! Devard stared out the window as the airplane descended over a million miles of wheat. *Where am I?* That's all he could see, an ocean of gold grass swelling and dipping across the hills of eastern Washington.

Washington State was his next hope. Everything was wrong about the place: the distance from Houston and Mummy and friends, the light-years from Nassau and relatives, from reggae and rice. The sheer isolation and smallness of this town—what did they call it? Pullman? The winter freeze waiting to take hold of it, and of a boy from the Caribbean if he were obsessed enough to stay.

Everything was right about the place: From the top—head coach Mike Price—on down, the staff at Washington State felt to Devard like family. The team trainer and doctor seemed ready to fight for his right to play, if they could find a way for him to do it safely. The Cougars' offense filled the sky with foot-balls, a wide receiver's kingdom come, and the trash cans were tucked away in corners and beneath desks, not set up around the gym. John Lott, the strength coach at the University of Houston when cousin Frank ruled the triple jump there, had moved on to the New York Jets and relayed word of Devard's plight to Jet offensive assistant Eric Price . . . who just happened to be Mike Price's son. Presto, Devard was walking through Pullman, trying to conceive of himself starting fresh there, among total strangers on the continent's far corner.

He talked it over with Devaughn. Somehow, in the hush of a Pullman night, he came to a realization. Here there was no one and nothing to take his eyes off his mission. Here was the perfect place for a solitary, single-minded man.

He started classes and moved into an apartment at the end of the sum-mer of 2001. Devaughn's mouth guard, wristband and gloves went up on the wall. No roommate could match the one he'd had all his life, so he wanted no roommate at all.

His family's lawyers readied a wrongful-death lawsuit against Florida State, charging the university with negligence in both the hydration and the supervision of a player in physical distress—"straight murder," cousin Frank called it. But the family was quick to sign a form freeing Washington State of liability should disaster recur. Still, the university needed more before it could let him take the field: a medical authority willing to counter Dr. Katopodis's opinion, willing to risk his reputation, and perhaps Devard's life, by clearing him to play. And so week after week, as the medicine men pored over reams of Devard's data and peppered the sickle-cell-trait experts with queries, he waited, suffocating from homesickness and living on his cellphone, agonizing as the season trickled away, rushing straight from classes to the football offices each day to ask if anyone had heard anything. Sorry, kid, they kept saying. Nothing yet. He came oh so close to quitting and going home, but he couldn't get past the framed picture of Devaughn on his nightstand.

Finally, in late October, Gust Bardy—a renowned Seattle cardiologist and the man on whom Washington State settled to make the call—invited Devard to his office and rendered his verdict: *Yes.* If Washington State was willing to take some precautions, Devard could play football. Somehow Devard made it all the way to the parking lot before the tears rolled down his cheeks.

It was too late to play in 2001, but two days later Devard adorned himself in the sacred vestments and bolted onto the practice field, so much adrenaline surging through him that he barely felt the bone-deep chill as he thumped his heart twice and pointed to something in the sky. The second week of practice, as he crunched through the first snow of his life and shivered uncontrollably under three layers of sweats, Coach Price sidled up to him and muttered, "How dumb are you to come here?" and they both puffed out smoky plumes of laughter.

The Cougars purchased four defibrillators, installed a new digital radio system to call EMS, rationed Devard's conditioning sprints and watered him as if he were an orchid transplanted to the desert. He was rusty at first, but by spring practice he was turning on the jets and plucking balls out of the sky with those octopus arms, power-cleaning more weight than anyone except two behemoth linemen, and by opening day of 2002 there was a determination in his eyes that his mates marveled at, a sense of urgency in him that smoked like burning rubber. He scrawled Devaughn's high school and college numbers on the tape he wrapped around his socks. Inside his shoulder pads, over his heart, was a picture of his twin, and over the pads he wore a new number, the loneliest number: 1.

He caught six passes in his first game, against Nevada. Then he caught five, two for touchdowns, and scored a third time on an end-around against Idaho, double-thumping his chest and pointing to heaven each time. Then came six more catches and a TD against Ohio State. Through 11 games he led the Cougars with 657 receiving yards—no small task on a team featuring three receivers with NFL potential. His 10 touchdown receptions were one shy of the school record, and his 46-yard scoring catch on a tipped ball, which sealed a 32–21 win over Oregon that briefly vaulted his team to No. 3 in the AP and BCS rankings, was replayed on *SportsCenter* so many times that Devaughn couldn't possibly have missed it.

"He gets open so quickly with his speed and strength, it's like watching a man among boys," said Cougars quarterback Jason Gesser. "It's clear this is just a stepping-stone for him. He'll be playing Sundays. His brother's on his shoulders, and he's taking him to the NFL. We haven't even scratched the surface with him yet."

He seemed to his teammates to be much older than they were, and he moved through the locker room wafting a certainty that no circumstance could stop him now, that nothing could hurt or shake him more than he'd already been hurt and shaken.

One thing could: the pressure he put on himself, the feeling that he couldn't let a dead man down. A few dropped passes in practice were all it took for him to cocoon himself inside his apartment and his headphones for a few days, for him to burn his retinas watching and rewatching the mistakes on video. After Mummy and his sisters flew up and watched Washington State's Nov. 2 victory over Arizona State, a game in which Devaughn muffed a pass and managed just two receptions, they waited for nearly an hour in his living room while he holed up in his bedroom, clutching Devaughn's picture and sobbing.

It was far from over, his long trek into twinlessness. At any moment, at kinesiology class or a hamburger joint or the 20-yard line, he would find himself right back in that horrifying moment—a flashback so electric that his body jumped.

Anger, too, still coursed through him—the thought that a breather and a water bottle or two might've saved Devaughn's life sometimes sent his fist into whatever was nearby. "It was inhumane," Devard says. "Pure negligence. Then they [the Seminoles coaches] wanted me to disappear, because every time I appeared on that field, Devaughn's name would be mentioned. They just wanted me out of there. But I wanted to go back and play there, whether a lawsuit was filed or not. My brother died there and was buried in that uniform. That's where my heart is. I'll be a 'Nole for life.

"I'm playing for two people now. Devaughn's living through me. I know I'm going to make the NFL, because there's nothing the world can send at me that's harder than what I've gone through."

Something began to shift in Devard in the second year of his twin's absence. His friends in Houston shook their heads over the way he would call them, expressing his feelings and getting as silly as someone else they used to know. They piled into Reggie Berry's car when Devard came home, talking old times as they drove around, and Devard smiled and blurted, "Let's go find some women!" and then actually approached a few when they took him to a dance club. The G.C. Fam members blinked at each other, and Reggie look Devard in the eye. "Man, *who* are you?" he demanded. "Who the hell *are* you?"

Devard bear-hugged his friends before heading back to college. "It was amazing," said James Lucas. "I felt Devaughn in him. It's like they've become the same person."

Devard flew back to Washington, landed in Spokane and crossed that hour and a half of emptiness to Pullman. He looked out the window, just one heartbeat like the doctor once said, and as usual in those parts, a dust dervish began to stir, then to funnel and fly across the land like a spirit.

He stared at it. Naaaaah. Couldn't be out there, or anywhere else . . . because it had always been inside him.

North Dallas Forty

Sunday

PETER GENT

Peter Gent's renowned novel *North Dallas Forty* offers a front row seat to a side of football that does not register big television ratings points. Gent gives the reader a glimpse into the day-to-day physical and mental punishment that grown men take to play what is often described as a kids' game. But he also shows how grown men playing a kids' game operate in a realm separate from the fans who ultimately fund their livelihood.

The novel's dark tone and Gent's efforts to distance the characters from the purity of the sport underscore the brutal, conflicted, violent reality that professional football players face during their careers. The grocery list recitation of game day activities regurgitated in "Sunday" suggest that the athletes' motives are often far removed from the wins and losses that fans brood over season after season. And the fact that Gent himself is a former professional football player gives the novel a validity that sports writers could never hope for.

Maxwell got the wake-up call after one ring. He groaned into the mouthpiece and then slammed the receiver back to its cradle.

"What time is it?" I asked, not moving my head from the pillow.

"Eight o'clock. Breakfast at eight-thirty, meeting at nine, nondenominational devotional at nine-thirty, Bullwinkle at ten. See, it all works out for those in the hands of the Lord."

Maxwell loved Bullwinkle Moose like he was kinfolks, and he worried whenever we played in a different time zone that team activity might be scheduled during "The Bullwinkle Show."

Seth crawled out of bed coughing and clearing great hunks of sludge from his breathing apparatus. He stumbled into the bathroom while I lay in bed and thought about my dream.

I had dreamt that I was late for the game and the bus had left without me. I couldn't find the stadium, although I could hear the noises of the game quite clearly. Finally I hitched a ride with Mickey Mantle, who told me Yankee Stadium was a nice place to visit, but he wouldn't want to live there. He dropped me at the stadium and disappeared. I started down the tunnel to the dressing rooms. The winding passages got very dark and I began to have difficulty keeping my eyes open. There were rats and spiders everywhere, but I could only glimpse them. Everything was dark and blurry. I kept running into giant spider webs, knocking hairy yellow-and-black spiders onto the back of my neck.

Then suddenly I was naked and standing in the dugout. The stadium was full and the game was in progress. I could see Rufus Brown, our clubhouse attendant, waving me to the other side of the field. He had my equipment and uniform. I started across the field and got caught up in the game. I was still naked. Maxwell threw me a pass but I wouldn't take my hands from covering myself. I was agonizingly embarrassed. The ball bounced off my face, breaking my nose. I could breathe again. I ground my jaw so hard from frustration and fear that all my teeth broke off. Then the tape around my thigh unwound and my leg fell off. I had the ball and I was crawling naked toward the end zone, still trying to hide by hugging my stomach to the ground. Then B.A. took me out of the game and told me to quit fooling around and made me sit alone on the bench. I was still naked and my nose was bleeding. Everyone was looking at me. . . .

"Come on, poot," Maxwell said, toweling off his freshly shaven face.

I jumped quickly out of bed and pulled on my pants.

"B.A. said we could wear turtlenecks, didn't he?"

"Yeah, but no love beads." He held one arm crooked over his head as he rolled on copious amounts of deodorant. It seemed peculiar, in light of the day's schedule.

The bulletin in the elevator listed Empire Rooms I and II as the locations for our meeting, pregame breakfast, and devotional. The rooms would also be used for much of the simple ankle and knee taping.

"MMMM . . . there's a delicious smell," I said, lifting my nose and following it to the entrance of Empire I. "Eggs and analgesic. Just like Momma used to make."

I stopped at the doorway and checked out the tables set for breakfast. Most of the team was seated, waiting for the food.

Maxwell brushed past me into the room, singing. It was his favorite George Jones song.

. . . a man come round today and said he'd haul my things away,
If I didn't get my payment made by ten . . .

I stood in the entrance and surveyed the two rooms, waiting for Maxwell to choose what table he would grace while he took his pregame coffee and cigarettes. It was an important part of his game plan to choose the right table at which to smoke and drink coffee, tell jokes, and generally pump up the frightened men around him. The players he selected each Sunday were picked according to criteria known only to himself. We often split up at pregame meals because of my unpopularity with some of the men Maxwell chose.

The partition between I and II had been pushed back and the six breakfast tables were crowded into the front of Empire I. Near the partition several players in shirt sleeves and undershorts waited their turns to be taped.

My stomach began to churn as the endocrine glands redistributed vital juices for the coming contest. I yawned and stretched, suddenly feeling very tired, the first sign of nervous fear.

In Empire II, chairs, a blackboard, and B.A.'s ever-present portable podium were set up for the last-minute strategy review and the nondenominational team devotional.

Maxwell sat down with Jo Bob Williams, Tony Douglas, O. W. Meadows, and a couple of others. I walked to the nearest table and joined several blacks, including Delma Huddle and the wayward running back Thomas Richardson.

"Hey, Bubba," Huddle said, holding out his palm to be slapped. I obliged and the cold wetness of our palms made a soggy pop.

He was wearing a white silk shirt monogrammed on the cuff, a wide green tie, a light green cashmere coat, and boxer shorts. No shoes. No pants.

"Hey, man," he yelled at a rookie waiting by the partition for his turn to be taped. "I'm in front of you and don't let nobody in. Get me?" The rookie waved and nodded.

"How you feeling?" I asked Huddle, as I stood behind him to knead the muscles at the base of his neck. "Ready?"

"Yeah, Bubba. How 'bout you?" He reached back and tried to grab my balls. I jumped and he roared his high-pitched bursting laugh.

"I was ready there for a minute," I said, brushing my hand across the top of his woolly head and sitting down. My knee banged against a table leg and water spilled out of one of the metal pitchers.

"You ain't lettin' the Man get you down?"

I shook my head, a silent lie.

"Just settle down." Huddle smiled but his eyes remained serious. "How's the leg?"

"Feeling better," I reported, squeezing the quadricep of my right leg absently. "Gets to feeling too good they'll want to cut it off."

Huddle laughed again in his peculiar high-pitched giggle.

A heavyset waitress in a dirty white smock set a plate of scrambled eggs and steaks in the middle of our table. The traditional pregame meal was precooked steak and powdered eggs, proven to be among the worst foods a man can put in his stomach before extensive physical activity. They just lie there and putrefy, pregame fear having shifted the blood from the stomach to other parts of the body.

"Look at that, Bubba," Huddle said, pointing to a plate of food. The scrambled eggs were a light green. Hotel kitchens put food coloring in the powdered eggs to make them look yellow. Green isn't too far removed on the color spectrum. In Pittsburgh, the hotel dyed our eggs so yellow that Huddle donned sunglasses to eat them.

The sweating waitress delivered the green eggs to each table, receiving treatment at the hands of Jo Bob and others similar to the harassing served up to the bus driver on the way in from the airport.

"Hey, lady," Jo Bob yelled, "was the chicken ready to lay these or did you go in after 'em? They don't look ripe to me."

The waitress kept her jaws clenched but moved her lips silently. Every so often she paused to wipe rivulets of sweat from her nose and forehead.

"Don't sweat in the scrambled eggs, Momma," Jo Bob sang out, stringing the words together like a song title. Several people across the room laughed.

When the last plate of eggs was deposited, there were murmurs and grumblings, but shortly the emerald eggs were consumed. They would lie quietly until the body could get around to digesting them. Or they would sit uneasily waiting for that incredibly tense moment just before game time when they would spout all over the locker room floor and any bystanders.

It was 9 A.M. I took the first of my day's dosage of codeine. I would take another at eleven and a third just before game time. Huddle watched me swallow the pills.

"Codeine?" he asked.

I nodded.

"Doesn't it make you sleepy?" Huddle asked, his eyes fixed on my face.

"No. Actually I feel pretty alert, just numb."

"You remember Jake?" Huddle asked.

I nodded again. Jacob Jacobs was a black running back who had come to Dallas in the middle sixties. When we got him he had been around nine years and was pretty beat up, but he still played hard if not too well.

"Jake used to take codeine and hearts," Huddle confided. "It made him feel nineteen and untouchable. He'd take five of each. He said it put ten panes of glass between him and everything else. The only thing was it made his eyes burn."

"Jesus, how strong were the hearts?" Hearts were Dexedrine or Dexamyl tablets.

"He didn't say. I think they were greenies, but I dunno. I don' mess with that shit, man."

"You were born perfect," I pointed out. "Some of us need to constantly make alterations or we don't make it." I smiled and threw my shoulders back. "I guess I'll have to try Jake's formula. I may have ten more years in me if I can just master the chemistry of this game."

"You shore are weird, Bubba."

"Hey," I said, the time just registering. "I thought we were meeting at nine."

"The Man has a special speaker for the devotional," Huddle explained, "and he can't get here till nine for breakfast."

"Who is it?"

Huddle's face opened into a ridiculous smile.

"Oh shit," I groaned. "Doctor Tom?"

Huddle toasted me with his coffee cup and nodded.

Doctor Tom Bennett was a enigmatic figure who had materialized in our training camp three years ago and had been haunting me ever since. Nattily dressed in cardigan sweaters and duck-billed golf hats he wandered around the dorm and was everybody's pal. He was a Doctor of Divinity and B.A. had invited him to address a team meeting on the miracles of God, Christ, salvation, and faith.

Using himself as an example, Doctor Tom explained the pitfalls of a lack of faith in the power of the Lord. He recounted how during his early ministry his modicum of faith caused him to be saddled with a tiny worthless congregation in northern Washington. Doctor Tom soon realized that to make it big he needed greater faith. He immediately got some. Rewards weren't long in coming. Soon our Doctor Tom commanded a large, wealthy congregation in Florida where he successfully led his flock in their struggle for salvation and security in the face of universal cynicism and ever-spiraling inflation. In return Doctor Tom received great personal satisfaction and a small percentage of a large oceanfront real estate deal.

Once a wealthy man, Doctor Tom set out to fulfill the bargain he had made with the Lord. In an even swap with God for salvation and its Puritan ethic ramifications, Doctor Tom swore an oath to the Lord Almighty on the blood of the crucified Christ that he would carry the mantle of Christianity without recompense to a congregation that desperately needed his divine guidance. He chose the National Football League.

B.A. and Doctor Tom became fast friends, Doctor Tom wanting to hang around football players and B.A. wanting to hang around God. B.A. took to wearing cardigan sweaters and golf hats and inviting Doctor Tom to give inspirational messages before important contests.

The Doc had tried several times to get me to attend the devotionals. In the first categorical rebuff, I explained there were other places God was needed more than in a hotel in Minneapolis, listening to some pompous fool refer to him as The Big Coach in the Sky. After that Doctor Tom took a chummier approach, directing the talk to young girls and drinking.

I always made it a point to talk as profanely as possible around the Doc. I would raise my eyebrows and wink at him, after making loud senseless denials of anything resembling a God, and I would always point out what a sucker Jesus was.

But in all fairness I must admit the Doc was a pretty good sport and quite fast on his feet. He had rescued me more than once when I was set upon in the middle of my mindless tirade by one or more of the larger and more pious members of the team.

B.A. stood up at the head table, a fragment of green egg in the corner of his mouth, and announced that Doctor Tom's schedule had required a slight shuffling on our part and that the meeting would begin at 9:35 with the devotional at 10.

I looked over at Maxwell, obviously struggling over the merits of Doctor Tom and the devotional versus the eternal verities of Bullwinkle and His Friends.

At ten o'clock, as the meeting ended, I walked out in my usual negative response to B.A.'s invitation "to those who would like to stay and hear the message." I gave the Doc a smile and a short wave as I crossed in front of the portable podium. Maxwell fell into step next to me.

"Jesus," Maxwell moaned, once we were in the hallway, "he really looked pissed."

"He'll probably let Art Hartman lead the Lord's Prayer. First, loss of grace, next, loss of position. It's a universal pattern, that's why the Commies are doomed."

Seth Maxwell walked to the elevator, his head down. "Why do I punish myself like this?" he asked himself over and over.

After "The Bullwinkle Show" I packed up, grabbed my record player, and caught a cab to the stadium. Maxwell stayed in the room and read the Sunday paper. He would ride out on the team bus at 11:30.

Because of serious injuries and the complexity of their treatment, nine players, myself included, were required to arrive at the stadium early so the trainers and team doctors could have enough time to effect repairs. A tenth player, Gino Machado, recently acquired from the Rams, came out early just to take his amphetamines and "get ready to kick ass." Machado would sit by his locker, his legs shaking uncontrollably from the speed surging through his brain, and talk like a top-forty disc jockey to anyone within earshot. I spent hours listening to him describe sex acts, fist fights, and ball games. His lips were white from constant nervous licking, his mouth stretched open from time to time in a grotesque, compulsive yawn, and his eyes rolled while he clenched and unclenched his fists. Every now and then, gripping his shoulders with his hands, he would hug himself and bend double as if trying to slow himself down. In the early season Texas heat, the trainers often had to pack Machado in ice after a game to cool down his incredibly overheated body.

On the first day of camp Machado took twenty milligrams of Dexamyl to run "B.A.'s Mile." The linemen had to finish the four laps around the track in six minutes and thirty seconds to prove they had come to camp in condition. Gino took four hearts before he left the locker room. He went blind on the third lap and fell down six times before he crossed the finish line. It took him over eight minutes but he finished. He lay in the dummy shack while everyone else went to lunch. He was still there when we returned for the afternoon workout.

The cab to the stadium took me through Central Park.

"You afraid you ain't gonna get a seat?" the driver asked. "You're goin' to the stadium pretty early."

"Yeah," I replied. "I know."

"I went to see them bums last week, when the Colts was here," he continued, alternating his attention between the road and the back seat. "The Giants stink. They ain't hadda good team since they got rid of Huff an' all them guys—remember? How can they run a football team and be so stupid?"

"The same way they run everything else, I guess."

"Well, them Texas boys'll kick their ass, I'll tell ya. I got twenty bucks on it."

"Invest your winnings in real estate," I advised.

Two cabs, doors open and trunk lids up, were parked at the players' entrance to Yankee Stadium. The trainers were unloading bags of tape and medication.

"Phil, grab a couple of these bags," Eddie Rand ordered as I stepped away from my cab.

"Sure." I shifted my flight bag to my left hand, tucked my record player up under my arm, and grabbed two black medical kits from the cluster stacked behind the cabs.

I started down the ramp toward the uniformed guard defending the entrance. As the distance closed between us he began to eye me nervously for some identification.

"Player," I said casually, looking him straight in the eye. He waved me past.

Just act like you belong. It was the advice my older brother had given me to get me into bars before my twenty-first birthday. It was the only thing he ever said that made sense. An All-American in high school and college, he graduated with honors and became a successful high school coach. Last spring he quit his job, left his wife and three girls and ran off with the senior-class valedictorian. She came back after three weeks. No one has heard from him since.

Instead of heading down the tunnel to the locker room, I turned up one of the ramps leading into the stadium seats. I walked down ten rows and sat. The ground crew was removing the tarpaulin covering the patches of green and brown that made up the playing field.

In a far corner of the stadium a high school band was counter-marching to the shallow sounds of "Raindrops Keep Fallin' on My Head" done in march time. The band members were in full uniform but wore coats and sweaters against the damp morning chill. A row of shiny silver sousaphones executed the gyrations of a routine that seemed to combine the techniques of a marine close-order drill team with the intricate moves of Smokey Robinson and the Miracles.

Several rows in front of me a television-camera crew was setting up. The camera operator was talking into his headset to the director in the mobile van, discussing just what America was going to see today.

Near the New York bench three men stood in a semicircle, chatting and pointing to different parts of the playing field. One of the men was Frank Gifford. I didn't recognize the other two.

I sat for several minutes trying to imagine how I would look and feel down there on the field in a few short hours.

Two concessionaires in aprons and tricornered paper hats walked up and stood two rows in front of me. They surveyed the field.

"Hey—" the shorter of the two, a man in his forties, nudged his companion, "—that's Frank Gifford over there."

"Where?"

"There, the guy in the trench coat." The shorter man leaned over and let his friend sight down his arm and out his pointing finger.

"Oh yeah," the taller responded. "Hey—hey—Frank . . . Frank Gifford." Both men waved and called frantically.

Gifford heard his name and turned toward the sound.

"Hey, Frank," the shorter man shouted, "we need you out there today. Whattaya say? Huh?"

The man who for more than a decade had lived this city's football fantasies waved back and returned to his conversation.

"What a great guy," the tall man said, as they turned back toward the tunnel entrance. "Just a great guy."

His partner seemed equally excited but a serious look chilled his eyes as the two passed me.

"You know," the taller huckster began, "somebody told me that he wears a hairpiece. Do you believe that?"

"Frank Gifford? Are you kidding?"

"I didn't believe it either."

"Not Frank Gifford."

They disappeared down the ramp.

I ran my eyes up and down the field, trying to fathom its condition. It looked soft, but I couldn't really tell anything until I got on it. I considered mud cleats, deciding to wait until the pregame warmup before making up my mind. Combination baseball and football fields like Yankee Stadium were difficult to gauge during wet weather, some parts being wet and soggy, others dry and quite hard. It had something to do with the drainage being set up for baseball.

Mud cleats, helpful on wet, loose ground because of their excessive length, were a danger in dry areas for the same reason. In Cleveland I sprained an ankle by hitting the dry clay of the infield at full speed wearing mud cleats. Suddenly the consideration of which cleats to wear struck me as foolish. I wasn't even sure I would get into the game, let alone cover all areas of the field.

Standing up, I felt a stitch in my back. I remained in the aisle for several minutes, rotating my trunk and rubbing my back, trying to work out the muscle spasm.

They say you should quit when you still hurt on Sunday from last Sunday. I wasn't sure I wasn't still hurting from exhibition season. I entered the tunnel and began winding my way through the catacombs to the dressing room.

Clusters of men in paper hats and change aprons stood around talking and laughing. Rubbing their hands together against the morning chill, some of the men nodded hello, but most just stopped what they were doing and stared at me as I passed.

"Where the hell have you been?" Eddie Rand screamed as I entered the dressing room. "You've got all the flesh-colored tape."

"Sorry, Eddie," I said, tossing the medical bags on top of a blue equipment trunk. I walked to my locker and sat down.

My nervous system was beginning to take over, trying to get my body and mind into the right chemical balance to survive the afternoon with a minimal amount of damage, whether it was to be a physical beating on the field or mental degeneration on the bench. I was becoming extremely tired and wanted to lie down and pull a blanket over my head. Stretching and yawning, I stood up and began to undress.

Hopping from foot to foot because of the cold concrete against my bare feet, I checked around to see who else had arrived. Tony Douglas stood naked on one of the wooden tables, the trainer tightly strapping the inside of the linebacker's right knee. The knee was missing both inside and outside cartilage, and the medial ligament had been totally reconstructed with tissue from his thigh. Without elastic tape, Tony wouldn't be able to set foot on the field. It was a great invention. I have been making it on elastic tape—and codeine—for years.

Gino Machado was sitting on a towel, leaning back against an equipment trunk. By the look of his eyes and his tapping feet, he was already well into his day's dosage of Dexamyl. We exchanged silent waves, though we were not more than twenty feet apart.

I walked to my locker to sort my equipment, already neatly arrayed according to tradition by the equipment manager. Shoulder pads turned upside-down on the top shelf of the metal cage, with my newly polished helmet sitting in the neck hole. Hanging from hooks inside the locker were my game pants and jersey.

On the floor of the locker were neatly shined and newly laced game shoes and a tidy stack of miscellaneous knee, thigh, forearm, elbow, and hip pads. The hip and knee pads were squares of half-inch sponge rubber. The thigh pads were quarter-inch thicknesses of molded white plastic. I made the pads myself and if I was injured in a spot protected by my homemade pads I could be fined as much as five hundred dollars. But they were lighter, more maneuverable pieces of equipment. As injuries slowed me, I made it up by cutting down on the weight of my pads, either paring them down or discarding them altogether. If things kept up as they had been, I would soon be hitting the old gridiron stark naked.

"Phil," Eddie Rand yelled, "you ready?"

"Yeah."

With practiced efficiency he quickly taped my ankles, locking my left and leaving my right free. He used a base of elastic tape to allow more flexibility, then put the final straps on with white adhesive tape for extra support. He finished the second ankle and slapped the bottom of my foot. I rolled over on my stomach and he began spreading analgesic on the backs of my legs. Lifting my shirt, he rubbed the hot cinnamon into my back. At the end of the rubdown he slapped my ass and I immediately stood up on the table while he wrapped both thighs with Ace Bandages to retain heat and give additional bracing. When he finished, I stepped down, pulled a new elastic knee brace over my right knee, grabbed a roll of white tape and walked to my locker.

I dug inside my coat and grabbed a cigar and lit it. I turned on my portable stereo and began sorting through my phonograph records, looking for one that, in addition to the various tapes, wraps, balms, drugs, and chemicals normally produced by the organs of my body under stress, might put me in an advantageous psychosomatic condition to which to endure the afternoon. I selected Country Joe and the Fish.

Gimme an F . . .

I turned my game pants inside out and inserted the knee and thigh pads into their respective pockets and turned the pants right side out again. The thigh pads were in the wrong pockets; it often happened because turning the pants inside out disoriented my already stricken mind. I changed the pads and pulled the pants on and slid my game jersey over my head.

> *Be the first one on your block*
> *To have your boy come home in a box. . . .*

The silver game pants had a satin front, but the backs of the legs were made of an elastic fabric similar to that used in ski pants. The pants fit snugly, like a glove, giving a strangely secure feeling, like being hugged by an old friend. They also gave my damaged legs the feeling or illusion of additional support.

> *Whoopee we're all gonna die. . . .*

I rummaged through the pads in the bottom of my locker and found the thin piece of molded plastic I had made to protect my crushed back. I slipped it into place beneath my jersey, securing it quickly with tape. No sense letting anybody see me do it. Country Joe and his pals blasted into the first of "The Streets of Your Town" as I spread a towel on the floor and lay down, my head resting on a pile of elbow pads.

> *As I walk around the streets of your town*
> *And try not to bring myself down. . . .*

I stared up at the ceiling and listened to the other people in the dressing room: trainers, teammates, equipment men, lower-echelon stadium maintenance people chattering nervously about a variety of topics ranging from the coming game to "nigger pussy" to "The Carol Burnett Show." Joe McDonald and the Fish tinned out of the cheap speakers.

> *The tears of the insane*
> *bounce like bullets off my brain . . .*

I closed my eyes and tried to rest, the chemicals in my blood flashing on my eyelids images of pass patterns, defensive backs, wobbly passes, angry linebackers, and Charlotte Caulder.

I finished the cigar and the record started over. Sitting up, I pulled on my blue-and-white striped knee socks and taped them at the tops of my calves. I folded two strips of white adhesive tape in half lengthwise, leaving the sticky side out, and wrapped them around my legs just above the ankles. Then I drew my wool sweat socks on and up over the tape, squeezing them tightly against the strips with my hands. The tape would anchor the socks neatly in place and keep them from falling down during the course of the game; not a necessity but a definite plus for one who wants to look well groomed in front of 56,000 attending people and untold millions of hypnotics watching at home. Nothing is more unsightly than sweat socks sliding down and bunching around one's ankles.

> *New York City good-bye*
> *New York City good-bye*
> *Good-bye New York City . . .*

The outside door banged open and shut and a rush of frothing athletes, thinly disguised in suits and sport coats, came crashing into the dressing room. The stream of players so neatly dressed and carrying attaché cases looked like five o'clock at State Farm Mutual.

The sights and sounds of my arriving teammates increased my anxiety. One thirty p.m. eastern standard time steadily approached. My mind wandered over the game plan checking to be sure I recalled all the adjustments that made B.A.'s multiple offense so deadly.

> *Normal people rush through the dawn*
> *with their normal people faces on . . .*

I shut off the record player before B.A. sent an assistant over with a directive, but the music still bounced around in my skull, mixing with roll-zone tendencies, man-to-man coverages, and the anticipation of good-looking women in the stands within eyeshot of the field.

"Kickers, quarterbacks, and receivers on the field in fifteen minutes."

Sliding the kangaroo game shoes around my tape-encased feet, I carefully laced one. I pushed the lace through the patented heel-lock strap that ran across my Achilles tendon and tugged the strings until the strap pulled taut along the top of my heel and the shoe closed snugly around my foot. I repeated the process with the other shoe, stood up and stamped a couple of times to seat the shoes, and then clacked back to the training tables. The conspicuous click and added height of the cleats further increased my awareness of the coming kickoff.

"Goddam, Doc," John Wilson moaned. He was standing at one end of a wooden table grimacing while the team doctor probed the point of his right hip with a three-inch needle. Wilson had a hip pointer.

The needle slid easily into a roll of flesh at the top of the afflicted hip. The doctor moved the stainless-steel spine around, changing the angle of insertion five or six times and simultaneously pumping in several cubic centimeters of Novocain. He succeeded in deadening a large portion of the muscle.

Alongside the doctor, the trainer lined up a row of syringes filled with local anesthesia. Several nervous players waiting their turns milled around behind Wilson.

"How's it feel?" the doctor asked the scowling safety man.

Wilson, keeping one hand on his hip and the other on the table for balance, flexed from the waist like a ballet dancer.

"Fine," Wilson nodded. "I can't feel a thing."

"Good," the doctor said. "Next." He reached out to take a prepared syringe from the trainer and caught sight of me standing to one side watching. "How about it?" He held up the syringe.

"No thanks, Doc," I said, recalling my previous bout with his needle. "I'm trying to quit."

The last time he tried to block my back with Novocain he had used three syringes of the opiate and I made it only half-way through warmup before collapsing. I rubbed the spot absently, feeling the dead skin and sore muscles beneath.

I watched while the doctor quickly jammed another needle into Monroe White's thigh. Monroe sported a slight cut under his eye, a result of his short and furious fight with Jo Bob during Thursday's practice. I turned to leave.

"Phil," the doctor called, "wait a minute." He handed the used needle to the trainer and grabbed me by the arm, walking me into a corner. His eyes were on Monroe White, limping out towards the lockers. "Goddam gold-brickin' nigger."

"What?" I had heard what he said.

"That White," he said, pointing at the wide black back as it moved back into the dressing room. "He ain't hurt, just like all them niggers. Only place you can hurt 'em is in the head."

I nodded.

"Listen," the doctor leaned close, "I don't think there's anything bad wrong with your leg. I know it hurts you but there ain't nothing worse you can do to it by playin' on it."

"That's what you said about my back."

"You're playing, ain't ya? Anyway I overheard the coaches talkin' and they're beginning to think you're doggin' it. Now you and I know better, but that's what they're saying, so go out and show 'em something today."

"Okay, Doc." I nodded, keeping my eyes fixed on the floor. He slapped me on the shoulder and walked back and grabbed a new needle. As I walked away he was shoving the shiny stainless-steel point into the top of Jo Bob Williams's shoulder. Jo Bob winced and screamed in pain.

I hopped up and sat on top of one of the equipment trunks and watched the eye blinking, jaw working, and lip licking that indicated several of my teammates were beginning to feel the effects of their amphetamines. O.W. Meadows was sitting on the floor rolling his head and jerking his shoulders, trying to loosen the speed-tightened neck muscles. Tony Douglas was sitting next to him rubbing his hands together as if they were cold. Both men's eyes were glassy.

Conrad Hunter walked in from outside, his cheeks rosy from the cold. He was smiling with anticipation. At his side was his friend, advisor, and constant companion Monsignor Twill of the Sacred Heart Catholic Church. The two men circulated rapidly around the room, slapping players on the back and giving smiles and words of encouragement. They missed me and continued to the training area, Monsignor Twill digging a Coca-Cola out of one of the ice chests and guzzling it down in one long swallow. Hot pipes, the sign of a long night of drinking.

Maxwell was sitting by his locker looking absently around the room, his mind already out in the stadium dealing with mud, wind, blitzes, zones, his teammates, and B.A.

I wandered into the bathroom to pee. All the commode stalls were closed. A row of stockinged feet with jockstraps and silver football pants hanging around the ankles testified to the effect of fear on the bowels. From the moment the team arrived at a stadium until we assembled for the pregame supplications, the commodes were occupied. The nauseating sounds and smell kept all but the most desperate at a safe distance. I held my breath, feeling the rise of panic as the capacity of my lungs threatened to be outstripped by the size of my bladder.

I clattered back into the dressing area and was hailed by Gino Machado.

"Elliott, gimme a hand."

Machado was trying to wind some tape around his forearm to secure a plastic forearm pad.

"Wind it for me, will ya?" he ordered, breathing heavy. He ground his teeth and tapped his toes rapidly.

"Tighter," he moaned, his huge pupils burning a hole in me. "Come on, asshole. Tighter."

"Jesus, Gino," I argued, "you're gonna get gangrene."

"Don't worry about it, fuckhead," he shot back. "Just wrap it tighter."

I complied, wrapping the tape so tightly around his forearm and pad that the veins on the back of his hand stood out half an inch. I hoped his fucking fingers fell off.

"Okay! First group on the field."

I fell in step next to Maxwell. We followed the tunnel to the dugout, both of us carrying blue warmup jackets over our shoulders.

"How you feelin'?" I inquired nervously, not really interested in how he felt.

"Awright," he answered absently, not bothering to look at me. "B.A. gave me shit on the bus about walking out of the devotional."

"Did you explain to him about Bullwinkle?"

Maxwell gave me a blank stare, his lips curling with a hint of disgust. He shook his head.

Reaching the dugout, we stepped over a pool of stagnant water and up onto the field. It was chilly and we both slipped our jackets on, then broke into a jog. There was a scattering of applause among the fans already in their seats. Maxwell was a New York favorite.

When we reached our bench, Doctor Tom Bennett was standing there holding a ball.

"Missed you boys at the devotional this morning," Doctor Tom sang out, tossing me the ball with the commissioner's autograph on it.

"We were getting head from the maid in the linen closet," I answered, gathering in the ball. Doctor Tom laughed good-naturedly and nodded.

Throwing the ball back and forth, Maxwell and I slowly backed away from each other to a distance of about fifteen yards, where we stood and played catch, Maxwell loosening up his arm while I practiced different catches.

The sounds of cadence numbers and the heavy thunk of foot against ball filled the stadium as the kicking specialists worked out, getting the wind and range from different parts of the field. Vendors were already hawking and the public address system kept crackling on and off.

The field was soft where we stood, but one of the kickers said the infield and the ground inside the twenties was pretty hard. I decided against mud cleats.

The assembled fans began to cheer and boo simultaneously as the Giant specialists, quarterbacks, and receivers took the field. Tarkenton and Maxwell exchanged waves and Bobby Joe Putnam, a wide receiver, trotted over to shake hands. Bobby Joe had gone to Texas Tech.

"Howdy, Seth. Phil," Bobby Joe said. "How ya'll doin'?"

"Passable, Bobby Joe. How 'bout yerself?" Maxwell answered. We started a game of three-cornered catch.

"How's the new coach?" Maxwell asked. The New York team had fired their coach at the start of the regular season and the owner had hired the new coach from his team "family." An ex-player and all-round nice guy, the new coach was having great difficulty winning any games.

"He's a good guy," Bobby Joe responded, tossing me the ball. "You know, dumb like most of 'em and scared to death of Jerele."

Jerele Sanford Davis was the owner of the New York franchise and ruled it with an iron hand. Tyrannical and religious, Davis ran his team by the same principles that ruled Conrad Hunter. He differed from Hunter by not giving his coaching and management personnel as wide a latitude in running the team as Conrad did.

I tossed the ball to Seth.

"You know what Leon did the day Jerele announced he was the new coach?" Bobby Joe asked, giggling. "He called a meeting of the team, Jerele was there too, and stood up in the front and told us he wasn't gonna be a hard ass and from Sunday night to Wednesday we could drink and chase pussy as much as we wanted. That's exactly what he said, we could drink and chase pussy as much as we wanted."

"Sounds like my kinda coach," Maxwell interjected, zinging the ball to Bobby Joe. It bounced off his hands.

"Goddam, Seth." Bobby Joe complained, shaking his hands and bending down to pick up the ball, "no wonder you get so many drops." Bobby Joe threw the ball to me as hard as he could.

"Hey. What the fuck are we playing," I asked, rubbing my palm where the laces had hit, "burn out?"

"Anyway," Bobby Joe continued his story, "Jerele stood up at the back of the room and said that was bullshit. Nobody on his team was drinking or chasing pussy ever. Leon retracted his statement."

Seth shot the ball to Bobby Joe again.

"Goddammit, Seth. Cut that shit out. The fate of New York rests on these babies." Bobby Joe held out his hands for inspection.

"The fingers look a little stubby to me, Seth," I said. "What do you think?"

"Looks like the forepaws on a momma 'coon," Seth drawled. "Probably can't catch but if he does he runs to the nearest stream and washes the ball."

Seth and I laughed insanely, while Bobby Joe stood glaring good-naturedly at us. Finally we recovered enough to resume our game of catch and Bobby started another story about his new coach.

"After we lost to the Jets," he went on, "Leon came in and tol' us that the reason we lost was that nobody was sittin' in the right place on the bench. Now he's painted numbers on the bench and we all have assigned seats. Can you believe that?"

"Yes," Maxwell and I said together.

Bobby Joe threw the ball ten feet over my head, wished us good luck, and trotted, laughing, back to the end zone where his teammates had assembled.

"Nice guy," I said, watching Bobby Joe jogging to the end of the field.

"There ain't no nice guys," Maxwell answered, sounding foolishly like Leo Durocher.

The rest of our team was coming out of the dugout and running onto the field. They passed Seth and me, and began breaking into ranks for exercises. Seth jogged to the front to lead, while I walked slowly to the twenty-yard line, where the other members of my file would shortly assemble.

I could feel Jim Johnson glaring at me from somewhere in the press box as I sauntered to my assigned position and began to stretch my aching legs and back. The soreness wasn't acute, the nerves dulled somewhat by the codeine, but they still seemed unusually painful. I decided to increase my codeine dosage when we went to the lockers for the ritual.

Maxwell led us quickly through exercises, finishing with the usual ten jumping jacks. I started to count, then caught myself and remained silent for the rest of the drill.

We broke into passing groups. The temperature was in the high forties and it took a while for everybody but the speed freaks to warm up. But soon we were running deep routes and Maxwell was hitting with amazing efficiency.

"Phil," Maxwell ordered, "gimme a deep square in. I'll drop it right on the six."

He called the snap number, backed up ten yards, and planted, gathering himself to throw. I drove at John Wilson full speed, moving slightly inside, forcing Wilson to adjust his outside position. He showed no sign of favoring his recently anesthetized hip. By fifteen yards downfield I had moved a couple of yards inside and Wilson had turned, ready to run deep. I broke the pattern off square inside and simply ran away from the defender. The ball came on a straight line, between linebackers, never getting more than six feet off the ground. I took it in the chest, feeling the solid thunk. It had traveled better than twenty-five yards in the air, slamming into the left side of my chest, right on the six of my jersey numeral 86.

"Great shot!" I exclaimed, charged with the thrill of a perfectly executed play.

Maxwell couldn't do it again on a bet. But that was Maxwell's secret. He always knew when he could do it.

After we ran a few team plays, B.A. herded us back into the dressing room for the final prekickoff preparations and pep talk. Inside, everybody moved around nervously, a few guys puffing on cigarettes, a couple of last-minute bowel movements. Finally, B.A. called us all together.

"Okay, listen up," B.A. droned. "Don't forget to take your helmets off during the national anthem. And it wouldn't hurt some of you guys to sing."

We used to stay in the locker room until after "The Star Spangled Banner," then would come player introductions, toss of the coin and all that. But now the national anthem was last and we got typed instructions from the commissioner on how to stand and on what we should not do, such as picking our noses, or scratching our nuts. I tried to do at least one at every game.

It was part of the television package, the cameras moving with deliberate slowness down rows of players, faces contorted with fear, speed, and attempts at remembering the words.

> . . . *Uncle Sam needs your help again*
> *He's got himself in a terrible jam*
> *Way down yonder in Vietnam* . . .

The Blue Angels fly by, while Anita Bryant smiles. Flags waving, color guards standing, and men sitting in their living rooms trying not to raise their beer cans until the end, usually starting toward their lips on "home of the brave."

> . . . *There ain't no time to wonder why*
> *Whoopee we're all gonna die* . . .

Sometimes when we were all lined up, neatly in a row, helmets on our hips, I would have to fight the urge to put my arms around the men flanking me and do a fast series of high kicks.

"And Phil," B.A. called, his eyes searching me out. My heart accelerated at the sound of my name. "You stay close. I may need you to run plays."

I glanced at Billy Gill and watched his face fall. B.A. hadn't bothered to tell him. It was okay with me, I couldn't stand Gill.

"Okay, boys. Let's bow our heads," B.A. ordered.

Immediately half of the team fell to one knee, resting the bridges of their noses on curled fingers in a classical meditative pose. The rest remained sitting or standing with heads bowed and eyes closed.

"Well, boys," Monsignor Twill's voice bounced around the silent concrete room. "This morning you heard Doctor Tom Bennett, now how about a word from the competition?"

A titter of laughter flitted through the ranks.

"Dear Lord, please be with these boys as they go out today to do battle." The priest was dressed in the standard black smock and he seemed to glide around the room as if on roller skates. He had his eyes closed and his head raised. His face seemed to glow. Every now and then as he floated around the room, he would squeeze one eye open to plot his course and to avoid stumbling over one of the kneelers.

I looked at B.A. He had his eyes closed, his hands clasped, his head bowed, and his hat on. His pants legs were rolled up a couple of turns to reveal crepe-soled shoes and white sweat socks. I wasn't sure whether it was the cold or emotion, but his cheeks were flushed.

The prayer thanked the Good Lord for giving us the chance to play football in the United States of America, and asked his protection, reminding him that none of us care about winning or about ourselves (a little reverse psychology on the old Master Workman). I almost laughed at the mention of our sound minds and bodies. Finally the Monsignor blessed the whole Hunter family and invited us to join in the Lord's Prayer.

I kept my eyes open, looking around, to make sure I didn't get caught not praying. A curl of smoke ascended from behind an equipment trunk. It was Maxwell sitting on the floor, smoking a cigarette and watching the smoke drift aimlessly upward into the maze of concrete supports and electrical conduits.

". . . the kingdom and the power and the glory forever. Aaamen."

The supplicants rose to their feet and broke into a long animal roar, preparing for battle, as the Monsignor had so eloquently put it.

"Let's kill those cocksuckers!" Tony Douglas screamed, leaping up from his knees. He caught himself and glanced sideways at the Monsignor, who was standing near him. "Sorry, Monsignor."

"That's all right, Tony," the Monsignor replied. "I know how you feel."

"Okay," B.A. yelled. "Defensive team out first." We had lost the coin toss, so the defense would be introduced.

The starting players elbowed their way to the front of the crowd milling by the door. When O.W. Meadows reached the door he jerked it open and the team filed out and down the tunnel to the dugout entrance.

A fat bald man with bad breath and a walkie-talkie lined up the defensive starters according to the list he had on his clipboard. He belched loudly, then said something into the walkie-talkie. Moments later an electronic voice introduced our starting team to a chorus of boos.

After the introductions the rest of us climbed through the dugout and trotted to the bench to join the wild-eyed defense, already busily banging the shit out of each other in a last-minute frenzy to ready themselves.

Maxwell picked up a ball and waved me behind the bench, where we played catch during the fraudulent coin toss. As the crowd roared over New York's good fortune, the public address system announced that a National Guard unit from New Jersey would guard the colors and a nightclub singer from Stamford, Connecticut, would sing the national anthem. I thought momentarily about Charlotte and the late John Caulder.

While the teams lined up on the sidelines for the anthem, Maxwell and I stayed behind the bench. I began to toss the ball nervously from hand to hand, dropping it twice. I couldn't remember any of the plays, and I was beginning to regret not wearing mud cleats. The field would certainly get soggier as the day progressed.

I dropped the ball again and when I bent to pick it up, a twinge of pain in my lower back reminded me I had forgotten my codeine. I panicked and walked several strides toward the rigid trainers (standing like seabees on parade in their white duck pants and shirts) before I realized the crowd was only at "ramparts' red glare." I was the only person in the stadium not at attention. I flinched and expected the color guard to open fire on me at any moment. I continued on to the end of the bench and stood behind the trainers, waiting for the anthem to end.

There was a general uneasiness in the stands as the crowd finished a full line ahead of the Stamford songster. The noise of the crowd erased the last four words from his lips and threw countless beer drinkers across the country out of sync.

I smiled at the confusion, scored two codeine, washed them down with Gatorade and went back to our game of catch.

The team was huddling on the sidelines, the coach giving last-minute encouragement, and everybody stacking their hands on top of other guys. It was a tradition I avoided since discovering in high school that the coach said the same thing every week.

"Hey man," I said, tossing the ball to Maxwell, "have a good one."

"Uh-huh," he responded, tossing the ball back.

The crowd bellowed as our kicker bore down on the ball, the roar increasing as the ball sailed through the air. It sounded as if they were surprised he hit it. They apparently knew about our kicker. The sounds of the crowd, although having a definite pattern, don't seem to coincide with their wishes. The clamor rose again as the New York receiver caught the ball and moved upfield. The noise reached its peak as our coverage team knocked the shit out of him.

As the eleven men on the New York offense huddled in the middle of the field, I watched the other twenty-nine men walk to the bench to find their numbers and sit down. I pointed this out to Maxwell. He didn't seem interested.

On first down, New York ran an unsuccessful trap for a loss of two yards. Maxwell quit playing catch, picked up his helmet, and walked to the sideline. I moved close to B.A. by the phone table and watched Meadows bat away a second down pass. On third, New York lost two on a draw when the back fumbled the handoff in the backfield. The crowd booed their offense to the bench.

New York lined up to punt. Alan Claridge and Delma Huddle were back to receive as Bobby Joe Putnam lofted the ball from his twenty-five. Alan caught it and started back upfield. He was turning the corner, trying to get behind his blocking wall, when a New York tackler hit him head on. The ball popped straight up, hanging in the air an eternity, and then dropping straight into the arms of another New York player. He looked around startled and then ran the thirty yards to our end zone unmolested. B.A. threw his hat down and glared Claridge to the bench.

After the official time-out to sell beer and shaving lotion, the crowd settled down. B.A. put his hat back on, and New York kicked off. The kick was short and Huddle raced forward to grab it. Misjudging his stride and the condition of the field, he overran the ball, tried to stop, and slipped down. The ball bounced off his shoulder. New York recovered on our nineteen. B.A. hit himself in the forehead with the palm of his hand and walked to the phone table. He picked up a headset and screamed at one of the assistants in the press box.

New York quickly lined up at scrimmage, snapped the ball, and ran a reverse, handing off to the split end. Nineteen yards later the split end slammed the ball onto the end zone grass. He was so excited, he raced to the bench and leaped on Tarkenton's back. They both fell in a heap on the sidelines. New York 14–Dallas 0.

Maxwell stood at the far end of our bench. He stared at the scoreboard. The kickoff went out of the end zone and Maxwell walked slowly toward the forming huddle.

"Elliott." B.A. called me to his side as the huddle broke. He put his arm around my shoulder and leaned close to my ear, ready to send me in with instructions.

Stepping quickly under the center, Maxwell went on a quick count, not bothering to set the line. He caught the defense in the middle of a shift.

Both backs faked into the line, while Maxwell kept and rolled to the weak side, laying the ball out in front of Delma Huddle five yards behind the New York secondary. Delma stepped out of bounds on the five.

Seeing the completion, B.A. pushed me away and strode down the sideline yelling encouragement.

A dive play didn't fool anybody. On second and goal, a picture pass over the middle hit Billy Gill in the face and fell harmlessly to the ground. Maxwell had barely gotten the ball off ahead of a blitz and sat on the ground watching Gill walk back to the huddle.

I could tell by the third down formation it would be another pass to Gill. It was like Maxwell to come fight back to a receiver who had just dropped a pass. He did it for me often enough. I tried not to hope Gill would drop the difficult outside throw, but I did, and he did.

The field goal team passed Gill and Maxwell as they left the field. Gill extended his arms to show Seth how far he thought the ball was off target.

The field goal was blocked and New York recovered on their own fourteen.

Tarkenton was unsuccessful in moving the Giants the first two downs, and on third and nine his deep post was intercepted by safetyman John Wilson and returned to the New York twenty.

Maxwell took the offense back on the field, turning back to yell at B.A. and point at me. The first play was a strongside pitch to Andy Crawford trying to sweep the end. Morris, New York's strong safety, came up fast behind his linebacker and quickly forced the play, dodging the tackle's block and stopping Crawford at the line of scrimmage.

"Elliott. Elliott." B.A. was motioning for me. "Get in there and tell Seth to watch for a sara blitz."

Gill saw me coming, dropped his head, and trotted off the field. Neither of us said a word as we passed.

I stepped into the circle of heavily breathing men. Maxwell was down on one knee looking up at me expectantly.

"All he said was to watch for that strongside blitz." I shrugged.

"Okay," he said. "Fire ninety T pull pass. Wing zig out."

It was a good call, faking the fullback into the line while Crawford flared wide from the halfback spot with the tackle pulling and leading, faking a run. If Morris, the strong safety, forced the run fake, I would be man to man against Ely, the cornerback. Ely's tendency to look constantly into the backfield should set him up perfectly for Maxwell's pump fake on the inside move of the zig out.

Schmidt, the center, snapped the ball. The tackle, the two backs, and Maxwell executed their fakes, forcing the strongside linebacker and safety to play the run and leaving me one on one against Ely.

I drove down hard slightly to the cornerback's inside, making him adjust his outside position. He was inching in, afraid of the quick-breaking post route. The play fake had robbed him of any inside help. At six yards I made my inside break. Ely went with me driving strong toward me trying to close the distance between us. He was covering the quick post well. I swiveled my head looking into our backfield. Maxwell brought the ball up high and made a strong pump fake at me. I planted my left foot and drove back outside, passing under Ely, still covering the inside move.

"Goddammit," Ely said as I slid beneath him and headed at a forty-five degree angle for the sideline.

As he released the ball, Maxwell was hit from the blind side and the pass took off. I turned quickly back to my left, diving for the ball as it wobbled toward the ground. I caught it with my right hand and bounced into the end zone on my head and left shoulder. Sitting up, I checked for flags. Seeing the official with his hands up, I slowly got to my feet and started toward the bench, where Maxwell stood smiling with his hands on his hips.

B.A. would leave me in until I made a mistake. I would try not to make any.

The defense held New York again on the next series, and, after a fair catch by Delma Huddle, we took over on our thirty-five.

There was an official television time-out as we were forming our huddle on the twenty-five. Maxwell stood back on the twenty alone looking toward the other end zone. The rest of us milled around giving each other encouragement. The whistle blew and Schmidt, the center, raised his hands and called the huddle on him. We were all waiting expectantly when Maxwell stepped back into the circle. He was singing.

"It wasn't God that made honky-tonk angels . . . I shoulda knowed that you'd never make a wiiiife . . ." He stopped, looked around the huddle smiling, and called a play.

During that series of downs Maxwell was superb, mixing his passes and runs, and in ten plays completed the drive with an audible pass to Delma Huddle. The split end stole the ball from the hands of Davey Waite, New York's right cornerback, for fifteen yards and the score. I had two catches during the drive, for eight and fifteen yards. The fifteen yarder was a good catch, going over the top of two defenders. Both catches were third downs. I was having a good day.

We went to the locker room tied 14–14.

The tops of the equipment trunks were covered with cans of Coca-Cola and Dr. Pepper. The Cokes were disappearing quickly. As far as I knew, Maxwell, Jo Bob, and Meadows were the only Dr. Pepper drinkers.

I sat in front of my locker wiping the sweat from my eyes and trying to catch my breath. Ever since I had been benched, I had trouble getting my second wind. Sometimes I thought it was conditioning, other times panic.

Several players were sprawled around the floor smoking cigarettes and coughing. Maxwell sat down next to me with a lighted cigarette and a Dr. Pepper.

"All I need now is a moon pie," he said, grinning and dropping his voice to a rasp, "and halftime would be hog heaven." He was confident and it was contagious. I felt my spirits rise.

On the blackboard was a list of the first-half Giant defenses. B.A. and Jim Johnson were standing beside the board studying them and listing the offensive formations we would use the second half to penetrate those defenses.

Our defense was huddled in the back of the dressing room considering the most systematic way to stop Tarkenton's scrambling. Except for that and the one end around, the New York offense had been powerless.

Over by the wooden tables, the trainers were patching a hole in the bridge of Jo Bob's nose. His helmet had smashed down and gouged out a quarter-sized hunk of flesh from between his eyes. Red rivulets had been running down both sides of his nose since the start of the second quarter. It looked as if he was crying blood. The doctor was bent over John Wilson, shooting his hip full of Novocain again. Three or four others were waiting their turn for treatment, blood pouring from torn flesh and joints swelling as body fluids pumped out of mutilated vessels.

The cigarette smoke began to get thick and I moved back to the showers to get some air. I took two more codeine.

Halftime was just long enough for muscles and ligaments to stiffen, while America sat and watched Dick Butkus shave without water. Many teams lost their momentum at the half, slowed by too many cigarettes and too much advice.

I watched O.W. Meadows down two fifteen-milligram Dexamyl Spansules. The pills wouldn't start working until the fourth quarter and maybe not until after the game. Dexamyl Spansules were one reason why Meadows never shut up all the way home after a road game. Spurred on by a goodly amount of bootlegged liquor, he would babble incredible shit at the top of his lungs about his personal philosophy of life, which fell somewhere between Spartacus and the Marquis de Sade.

I walked nervously into the bathroom and met John Wilson as he came out wiping his hands on the front of his silver pants.

"Pissed all over 'em," he said, holding the hands out for my inspection.

Most of the team was up and milling around. The coaches were still next to the blackboard talking over last-minute strategy that would be forgotten as soon as we hit the field.

Alan Claridge lay face down on a table while the doctor probed and prodded his right hamstring. Finding the knot, the doctor held his thumb on it and reached for a syringe. He drove the needle deep into Claridge's leg, moved it around, and emptied the syringe into the muscle. Repeating the procedure twice more, he deadened a large portion of the hamstring. If Claridge reinjured the leg in the second half, he wouldn't know until it was too late, but with luck he would finish the game with little problem.

The referee stuck his head in the door and signaled five minutes remaining in the halftime. As he opened the door, I could hear the distant strains of "Raindrops Keep Fallin' on My Head." I hoped everything was going off like clockwork for the boys with the sousaphones.

"Okay, listen up," B.A. said, walking to the middle of the room. "We've had some bad breaks out there, but we've come back and it's a brand-new game. We receive this half, so let's take it to 'em. The same team that started the game starts the second half."

Since Gill was the only starter on the bench, it would have been easier just to tell him and me. But B.A. didn't believe in dealing in personalities.

The crowd was back from the hot dog stand and America had returned safely, if somewhat confused, from CBS Control, when we took the field for the second half. The shadow of the stadium had moved almost halfway across the playing field, adding a dimension of time to the vacuum of fear. It was beginning to get cold and the sky was a fast-darkening gray.

The third quarter went quickly, with me alternating my attention from the field to the clock, hoping New York would get out ahead and I would get back into the game. The shadow steadily moved across the yardlines.

The Giants didn't move in the third quarter and Gill played a steady game, catching a nice turn in and a difficult sideline. I waited vainly for a signal from B.A. to carry in a play. Feeling powerless as my fate was being decided by twenty-two other men, I sat silently hating football, B.A., Conrad Hunter, Maxwell, my teammates, and the color guard from New Jersey. I could do nothing but wait and wish bad luck on my own team.

Near the end of the third quarter, Crawford fumbled a pitchout and my spirits rose. The Giants recovered on our thirty-five. Three plays later our defense had pushed them back to the forty. I could feel B.A.'s eyes searching me out as the ball hit the crossbar and bounced over. New York 17–Dallas 14.

"Elliott."

That familiar cry, cloud of dust, and a hearty hi-ho.

I turned my smile into a grimace and walked quickly to his side, trying my best to look as dedicated as I felt.

"Go in for Gill on the next series," he said, never taking his eyes off the field.

"Yes, sir," I said, immediately changing my allegiances and looking for Maxwell to discuss how we could salvage a victory. He was at the phones talking to a coach in the press box. His face was ashen and he was talking rapidly.

"Goddammit," he shouted into the phone, "I haven't had time to throw a deep zig out all day, maybe that's why they ain't coverin' it. Fuck you, don't tell me, you cocksucker, tell your fuckin' linemen."

Slamming down the earphones, Maxwell took a cup of water from one of the trainers. Looking over the rim of the cup, he watched me approach. The cup came away from his face.

"You in?" he asked, his breath coming in gasps. I nodded.

"Good. I wanna try and run wide and I want you cracking back on Whitman."

That news took the edge off the thrill of playing. It wasn't the fear of hitting the 235-pound linebacker, although that was substantial. It was the fear of missing him. If I missed and Maxwell didn't run me off the field, B.A. certainly would. The only way I could be sure of making the block was to spear him with my head; for me, it was the surest of open field blocks. I would dive headfirst at his knees, making it next to impossible to miss. The drawback was that I wouldn't have any control over where I took the blow—head, face, neck, back. It all depended on whether Whitman saw me sneaking back down the line at him and what kind of evasive technique he used if he did.

I watched Claridge bring the kickoff out from three yards deep in the end zone. Reaching the twenty-yard line, he suddenly straightened up and grabbed the back of his leg. He went rigid and as he fell forward Bobby Joe Putnam hit him full speed flush in the face with his headgear.

Seeing the ball torn loose elated me for an instant. Then guilt washed over me as I realized I was back in the game and had changed sides. I felt as if I had wished the fumble. I felt no better when Tarkenton scrambled to the five on the first play from scrimmage and the quarter ended.

The fourth quarter started. We were trailing 17–14 and New York had the ball, first and goal, on our five. Tarkenton tried to roll out, was trapped, and reversed his field back to the twenty-five, dancing around our exhausted defensive linemen for a full thirty seconds, finally making it back to the ten. New York was penalized for holding the next two plays in a row, and on second and goal from the forty Meadows trapped Tarkenton back at the New York forty-five. The next play we were called for pass interference and New York took the five-yard penalty and automatic first down.

They stayed on the ground the remainder of the drive, pushing out three first downs, getting the final yards on fourth down each time. They stalled on our eighteen and settled for a field goal. New York 20–Dallas 14.

I moved around the sidelines to loosen up, waiting for the network to return the slightly altered television audience so New York could kick off. Several people were standing over Claridge, who was stretched out face down on the bench. The doctor was digging his fingers in the hamstring he had anesthetized at halftime.

"See," the doctor said, "feel this. The hole? I can put my four fingers in it. It's torn pretty bad."

Claridge had his face turned away, into the back of the bench. He appeared to be in great pain, mumbling and crying apologies for the fumble. I knelt down next to him and put my hand on his shoulder. I shook him gently. I was going to explain that New York only got a field goal and we would get that back this series. I was again amazed at how quickly the team spirit possessed me when I was in the game.

Claridge turned to me; he was covered with blood. His double bar mask was shattered and his face was swollen and discolored a purplish-black. It seemed lopsided, twisted into a grotesque scowl, the running blood continually changing the expression. His nose was smashed flat and split open as if someone had sliced the length of it with a razor. The white cartilage shone brightly from the red-black maw that had been his nose. His eyes were wide and bright but seemed sightless. He tried to say something, raising his hand, but it was lost in a gurgle as black blood poured from his mouth.

"Goddam," I screamed. "Goddamm, somebody get over here and fix his face!"

Claridge had apparently gotten off the field under his own power and collapsed on the bench. Face down was the only way he could keep from strangling on the blood. I held his head up slightly, gripping his headgear through the earholes.

My cries brought several people and directed the doctor's attention from one end of Claridge to the other.

"Did he bite his tongue?" The doctor shoved a finger into Claridge's mouth and searched for his tongue, making sure he hadn't bitten it off or swallowed it. "We'd better get him to a hospital."

"What happened?" B.A. was peering over the huddle around Claridge.

"Smashed up his nose pretty bad," the doctor said. "Better take him to the hospital."

"Oh." B.A. nodded, and turned back to the field.

The crowd noises indicated America had returned to her living room and New York was about to kick off. Backing away from the mutilated man, I heard the kick but couldn't take my eyes off the black blood running through the slats in the bench and into the damp sand below.

The ball sailed out of the end zone and I walked slowly alongside Maxwell to the huddle at the ten-yard line.

"Jesus," I said, recalling the face that didn't resemble Claridge and the pitiful mindless eyes, "did you see Claridge's face?"

"I ain't got time to worry about that shit," he said, his mouth drawn and his eyes tired. "If you can't take it . . ." He broke into a trot and hurried to the huddle before he finished.

I followed a few steps behind.

The men in the huddle were tired and openly hostile to each other, the day's frustrations pushing several to the breaking point. The spirit and attitude had degenerated markedly from the first half.

"Goddammit, Andy. Hold onto the fuckin' ball this time."

"Fuck you, Schmidt. You just snap the ball, I'll take care of myself."

"All right, quiet down," Maxwell instructed angrily, kneeling into the huddle. "I'm the only one that talks in this huddle. All you guys shut up unless I ask you somethin'."

I looked around the huddle at the battered, bruised, and exhausted men, some already worrying about mistakes they would have to explain next Tuesday. Scared to death and angry, it would be a miracle if they could even get off on the same count, let alone outthink, outmaneuver, and outmuscle the men of similar talent across the line.

The shadows of the stadium had covered the field, adding further gloom to an already dismal afternoon.

"All right," Maxwell ordered. "Red right dive forty-one G pull. On two."

It was a simple trap up the middle. Jo Bob Williams jumped offsides. We walked back five yards.

"Goddammit, Jo Bob, pay attention to the count."

"Shove it up your ass, Schmidt. Who died and left you in charge?"

"Okay, I'm telling you guys," Maxwell shouted. "You better shut the fuck up in my huddle."

The huddle was silent as the quarterback scanned the grimy, sweaty faces. The gouge in Jo Bob's nose had opened up again and the blood was running into his mouth, turning his lips shiny red. He licked them nervously.

"Okay, Brown right dive forty-nine G take. On three."

It was a pitchout with a guard lead, coming off a fullback slant fake over the tackle. We ran it from a set backfield and the key block was our tight end against their defensive end Deyer. Deyer made the tackle for a two-yard loss.

"Jesus Christ," Crawford yelled, straightening his helmet as he regained his feet. "What the fuck is goin' on?" He wobbled back to the huddle, spitting out grass and mud.

"Sorry, Andy."

"Fuckin' sorry ain't gonna get it."

"Come on. Knock it off—"

"All right," Maxwell screamed. "This is the last time I'm gonna say it. Shut the fuck up in my huddle."

"If the dumb cocksuckers would do their jobs." Bill Schmidt, the center, was talking. Because he was a member of the original expansion family and worked for Conrad Hunter personally in the offseason, Schmidt considered himself a player–coach and the leader of the offensive line.

"Shut your mouth, Schmidt," Maxwell ordered, "or you're off the field."

"Bullshit, I am," Schmidt shot back, glaring at the quarterback.

Maxwell looked up, shocked, and returned Schmidt's gaze thoughtfully for a few seconds, then shook his head and stepped from the huddle. He walked in measured steps to the referee and then on to the sidelines.

The official signaled a Dallas time-out. The huddle dissolved into a group of pointless men, pulling off their helmets and kneeling down, or standing and looking around aimlessly, waiting for Maxwell to return. Nobody said a word. I looked over at Delma Huddle and he flashed a big smile and gave me the thumbs up sign. I smiled back. Looking up into the stands at the mass of gray dots that were faces, perched atop flashes of colors that expressed their egos, I suddenly realized how peculiar we must look. I thought of Al Capp shmoos paying six dollars a head to watch and scream while trained mice scurried around in panic.

Eddie Rand, his whites smudged and bloodied at the end of a long day, started out on the field with towels and water. Maxwell stopped him and sent him back to the sidelines.

B.A. walked a few steps onto the field to meet with Maxwell. Neither man looked at each other, Maxwell had turned almost away from his coach and seemed to be staring out at the milling, disorganized rabble that was his command. B.A. was looking down to one end zone and the scoreboard. The stadium band broke into a halting "Tea for Two Cha Cha." Maxwell suddenly whirled around and pointed his finger directly into B.A.'s face. The coach dropped his head momentarily, then nodded and turned back to the bench. Maxwell returned to the huddle.

"Schmidt," he said, matter-of-factly, "you're out."

Marion Konklin, a backup guard who doubled at center only in practice, lumbered onto the field.

Schmidt stared at Maxwell with pure animal hatred. Maxwell turned his back and stepped into the huddle already forming around Konklin. The veteran center turned and walked rapidly to the sidelines, throwing his helmet into a crowd of his teammates. The row of players lining the sidelines opened up slightly to dodge the helmet and let Schmidt pass, then closed as the furious man disappeared.

"All right, goddammit," Maxwell ordered. "This time we go. I wanted you out here, Konklin. Don't lemme down. You know what to do on a draw delay trap?"

It was third and fifteen.

"I'm not sure."

Several players coughed and moved uneasily.

"Just set for pass. Then fire out and get the middle linebacker. It's no sweat," Maxwell reassured the frightened substitute.

The whistle blew, signaling time back in.

"All right. Red right draw delay trap on two. Got it Marion? On two."

Maxwell stepped up behind Konklin and patted him reassuringly on the hip. The terrified center nearly leaped into New York's secondary. Maxwell shouted out the defensive alignment, set the line, and stood scanning the linebackers and deep backs. The middle linebacker moved up into the line showing blitz. I watched Maxwell as he considered an audible against the blitz. Konklin's legs started shaking slightly. Maxwell decided against the audible. Konklin would certainly miss it. Maxwell was gambling the linebacker was faking.

By the time Maxwell called the second hut, Konklin's legs were shaking noticeably. He slammed the ball up into Maxwell's hands and shot into the middle linebacker. He forgot about waiting to show pass set. It couldn't have worked better if it had been executed correctly. The straight power block caught the linebacker guessing. He had been expecting a pass or at least a pass set. The block caught him totally unprepared and he went right over backward with Konklin on top of him. Crawford carried for fourteen and the first down.

"That's a start. That's a start," Maxwell chattered confidently, clapping his hands and smiling broadly. He slipped into a heavy Texas drawl. "We're gonna run an' tho' this ball rat down their throats."

The huddle formed around Konklin, who was smiling broadly as everyone congratulated him. The energy was returning.

"All right. All right." Maxwell knelt back into the huddle. "Fire draw forty-one Y zig out on two. Now come on, you guys. I didn't leave them sand hills jest to come to the big city an' git beat." The huddle broke with a low grunt.

Maxwell hit Delma going out of bounds on the New York thirty-five. They had two men on him when he caught the ball. The sound waves from fifty thousand diaphragms blew through our bodies. It was innervating. My stomach started to churn violently. I needed to evacuate; the pressure was intense. I farted and felt better.

"Who the hell did that?"

"Goddam."

The huddle started to break up as players fanned at the air in front of their faces and scowled with disgust.

"All right, you guys. Get back in here," Maxwell ordered. "Jesus, who did that?" He looked around the huddle. I looked accusingly at Crawford next to me. "Okay," Maxwell began again. "Red right freeze protection. Wing out at six yards. You linemen on the strongside cut block to get their hands down."

I took long strides heading for Ely's outside shoulder forcing him back. On my fourth step I made a rounded cut with no fake and drove hard for the sideline. The ball was in the air when I looked back. I grabbed it and put it away quickly. I planted my right foot, dropped my shoulder, and turned upfield. Ely drilled me in the chest with his headgear and knocked me flat on my back at the twenty-five. The back of my head slammed into the ground, making my nose burn and my eyes water. The roof of my mouth hurt.

"All right. All right. Green right pitch twenty-nine wing T pull. On two."

My heart jumped and my mouth went dry at the call. I would have to crack back on Whitman, the outside linebacker on the right-hand side. Crawford would try to get outside of my block with the help of the strongside tackle.

Whitman moved toward the sideline in a low crouch, stringing the play out and watching Andy and the leading tackle. At the last second he felt me coming back down the line at him. I dove headlong as he turned. He tried to jump the block and his knees caught me in the forehead and the side of the neck. We went down in a jumble of arms and legs, my shoulder went numb, and a hot burn shot up my neck and into the back of my head. The play gained eight yards.

"All right. All right. Here we go." Maxwell looked up at me. I was shrugging my shoulders and rolling my neck, trying to ease the sting. "You okay?" he asked.

"Yeah, I'm fine."

"All right. All right. Here we go. Red right freeze. Wing out and go. You guys cut block just like the out but tie 'em up an' gimme some more time."

Just before the snap Ely moved up close to the line and played me tight, bumping me as I sprinted off the line. He covered the out move I had beaten him on earlier. I took three hard strides to the sideline, looking back for the ball, then planted hard and turned upfield past him.

"Son of a bitch!" he yelled when he realized Maxwell's pump was a fake and his interception had dissolved.

I caught the ball on the five and ran it into the end zone. Dallas 21–New York 20.

Our defense kept New York bottled up inside their own twenty and after a long punt by Bobby Joe Putnam we took over on our own thirty-five. There were less than two minutes to play.

An I-formation tackle slant was good for three yards and we were huddling up for the second and seven situation when Billy Gill raced in from the sidelines. He slapped me on the shoulder and delivered a play to Seth.

B.A. waved me to his side when I reached the bench. He put his arm around me, keeping his eyes on the field as our huddle broke and the team lined up to run the play. It was a draw delay trap. The fullback made it to the line of scrimmage.

It was third and ten.

"Tell him to roll weakside and hit Delma on a sideline. Or run with it himself."

I turned and raced to the already forming huddle.

I repeated the order, leaning into the huddle.

"Okay," Maxwell nodded. "Green left. Roll right Y sideline at twelve. Okay, Delma?"

"You get it there, Bubba, and I'll catch it."

The Giants rolled up into a zone against Delma. He dodged the cornerman's cut block and curled out to the sideline in front of the deep covering safety. Maxwell dropped the ball right in the hole to him. Delma dodged the fast-closing deep man and was cutting across the grain heading down the middle for the end zone. The middle linebacker made a desperate dive and hooked his arm. The ball popped free. Lewis, the Giant free safety, scooped up the crazily bouncing ball and returned it to our twenty. Gogolak kicked his third field goal of the day with fifteen seconds to play.

New York 23–Dallas 21.

The locker room was almost deserted. The equipment man was finishing packing the soiled and bloody uniforms into the blue trunks and was making a last-minute check of the lockers. He found Jo Bob's headgear. "Goddam Williams," he grumbled. "He'd ferget his ass if he wasn't always on it."

An aged black stadium custodian swept the used tape and gauze, the disposable syringes and needles, and the discarded paper cups and drink cans into a pile in the center of the room.

The last sportswriter had just left after listening to B.A. "reluctantly" place the blame on several players, most notably Delma Huddle and Alan Claridge.

The last bus to the airport was outside the stadium, its exhaust blowing white in the cold New York twilight. The first bus was well on its way to Kennedy.

The trainer had just given me a muscle-relaxant shot, had rubbed down and rewrapped my legs, and had strapped my arm to my chest. The taping gave protective support to the shoulder that had collided with Whitman.

I heard the sound of running water in the shower room. I pulled my coat on over my shoulders and walked back to investigate. Seth Maxwell was sitting in a steel folding chair, his head on his chest and a steady stream of water pounding on the back of his neck. His ankles were still taped. Every now and then he rotated his right arm at the shoulder and flexed his fingers. I watched him silently for several minutes. Finally I broke in.

"Hey, man, the last bus goes in about twenty minutes."

"Okay, okay," he responded instantly. "Throw me some tape cutters."

I borrowed cutters from the trainers and tossed them to Maxwell. He quickly sliced off the tape and slammed the water-soaked bandages against the shower floor.

"Cocksucker. Cocksucker," he shouted, punctuating the epithets by whacking the tape on the wet tile. "Cocksucker!"

"Shit," I said, smiling and trying to adjust my taped shoulder comfortably. "The way it went today, I'm surprised you hit the floor."

I ducked aside and the tape cutters clanged on the wall behind my head.

"That's more like it," I said, wincing slightly. Dodging the cutters had made my shoulder throb. I pushed up on my tightly bound forearm. "Come on, get dressed and let's find someplace to get high."

The trainers were taking their showers when we left the locker room. In the tunnel, the equipment man was loading the trunks into the back of an air-freight van for transport to Kennedy, where an orange Braniff 727 with a galley full of dry chicken sandwiches and eighty warm beers sat waiting.

"I sure could use me a Cutty and water," Maxwell rasped, his hands thrust deep in the pockets of his brown cashmere coat. His hair was slicked back and still slightly wet from his shower. Little beads of perspiration dotted his forehead.

"I mentioned it to Mary Jane on the way up. I'm sure she'll have us something."

The leather trench coat started slipping off my taped shoulder. I tried to pull it back on with my free hand but the twisting motion sent hot pains into my head. Maxwell noticed my struggle, grabbed the coat and reseated it on my shoulder.

As we reached the exit to the parking lot Maxwell went past and started up the ramp to the stadium seats. I followed, after making sure the bus was still waiting.

"We don't have much time," I called, as Maxwell disappeared into the stadium.

The covered seats were in such deep shadows that I had to stop for a moment to let my eyes adjust before I located Maxwell. He was sitting on the aisle four rows in front of me.

"You got a joint?" he asked.

There was a determination, a destructiveness, in his voice. He kept his eyes fixed on the field, almost totally lost in darkness. It looked cold and barren in the gray city dusk.

"Yeah, I think so. But we'll have to hurry." My caution drew a look of distaste.

"Sometimes I wonder about your manhood," he said.

The insult puzzled me, but I avoided his eyes and dug in my pocket for a joint. As long as I played well I was seldom upset by a loss. I looked at winning or losing as someone else's benefit, distantly removed from my daily struggles for existence. Maxwell took losses to heart, regardless of his personal performance.

I lit the joint and inhaled deeply; it made my shoulder hurt. I leaned over and passed to Maxwell, at the same time looking around the stadium for the police I knew were hiding behind every pillar. Maxwell pushed his cowboy hat down over his eyes, propped his feet on the seat in front, took a long, loud drag, and passed back to me. We smoked the whole joint in silence. Finally Maxwell stood up and flicked the glowing roach away.

"Well," he said, starting back down the ramp to the waiting bus, "she whipped me again."

Mary Jane had reserved the same seats for us and had filled the seatback pouches with tiny bottles of Cutty Sark and Jack Daniels. It took over an hour to get clearance out of New York and during the wait we consumed eight bottles apiece. I took two more codeine pills and Maxwell took one. The combination of codeine, marijuana, booze, and the heavy drone of the jet engines put Maxwell to sleep and me into a trance.

A short but furious pillow fight erupted between some members of the defense and several men who hadn't played in the course of the afternoon. As the tiny airline pillows sailed back and forth, it looked like a Michigan snow storm. A heavy-throated, official-sounding voice quoted some obscure FAA regulation over the intercom and brought the fight to a halt, although every now and then a white square would hum through the air and land with a thump.

Some players were up and moving around. Distinctive bulges and flashes of white under their clothing identified the wounded. My shoulder had become numb and I sat pleasantly stoned.

Alan Claridge, stitched up and sedated, arrived semiconscious by ambulance just before we taxied into line for takeoff. The doctor suggested placing him in the first-class section where he would have more room but his constant gagging and spitting blood disgusted Conrad Hunter's wife. He was carried back to the tourist section, both his eyes swollen shut. There were seventeen stitches in his lip.

I recalled B.A.'s postgame locker room press conference. "Undoubtedly," he had said, standing by the wooden taping table, "the two fumbles by Claridge and Huddle were costly. Nethertheless, that's no excuse for our all-around sloppy play."

B.A. would probably place Claridge on injured waivers for the remainder of the season, making certain to state it had no bearing on his performance against New York. He was merely a damaged player being replaced. And he was right, that was what was so infuriating. He was always right, analytically, scientifically, technically and psychocybernetically right. Football was technology and he was a master technician.

Andy Crawford sat across the aisle in his undershorts, ice packs on his right thigh to keep down the swelling of a bruise. He had been leg-whipped, just above the knee, in the first half. The Novocain had worn off John Wilson's hip, making it so painful he couldn't sit. He spent the entire flight in the aisle, watching Jo Bob and Tony Douglas play gin. Jo Bob set down his cards and, with great pain, made his way toward me and the bathroom beyond. As he passed he smiled weakly and congratulated my play. It was always surprising how sedate and friendly Jo Bob was after a game. I am sure it is the same principle that recommends masturbating circus lions to exhaustion before setting foot in their cages. The postgame Jo Bob was as calm and affable as the Dreyfus Lion after a couple of good whackoffs.

"Everything all right?" Mary Jane Woodley slipped into the pair of seats behind Maxwell and me.

The question was directed at me, but her attention seemed to be on the sleeping quarterback. Leaning on the back of his seat, she was looking wistfully at her fingers as they trailed gently through his thick brown hair.

"As good as can be expected, the quadruple amputee replied, trying to rise and shake hands," I said. "Thanks for the drinks."

She didn't reply and I looked back to see if she had heard me. Her eyes were still focused on the top of Maxwell's head as she combed the hair away from his eyes with her red-brown fingernails.

"How's he feeling?" she asked.

"Okay, I guess," I answered, without really considering the question. Besides, I never knew how Maxwell really felt. "A little depressed . . . and really smashed," I added, to give her something to work with.

"He played a great game," she said, disappointed but not surprised by the thought that Maxwell was despondent.

"We didn't win," I pointed out.

"Does it matter that much?"

"To him it does."

"Not to you?" She seemed surprised.

"A little, I suppose. Mostly I'm just trying to survive." I was a little embarrassed by the drama in my statement.

"I'm just trying to get the job done," I explained. "He worries about getting it done right, or what he thinks is right."

I paused for a minute and watched her fooling absently with his hair.

"You really like him, don't you?" I observed.

"I really do," she said, keeping her eyes on Maxwell. There was a tone of hopelessness in her voice.

"Why?"

"Because he's a man," she said. "What I thought all men were supposed to be like."

"What about me?" I asked with mock indignity.

"*You,*" she said, turning to look at me and smiling wryly. "You. You're what men really are. Like you said, just trying to survive."

I started to protest, but she was approximately right and my defense could, at best, be termed extenuating circumstances.

"I brung ya a drank." Seymour Scoop Zolinzowsky stood in the aisle in front of me holding out a styrofoam cup with the club insignia silk-screened on the side.

"What is it?" I asked, making no move to accept the drink.

"Vodka and Alka-Seltzer. They didn't have no tonic water." Scoop was weaving perceptibly and his face was ruddy. He called it his amphetamine flush.

I waved the drink off, not only nauseated by the idea of vodka and Alka-Seltzer but also knowing there were strings attached to almost any outright gift from this newspaperman.

"How 'bout you?" Scoop offered the drink to Mary Jane, who had stepped into the aisle and was trying to edge by him to get to the front. She shook her head and he stepped aside and bowed, waving her by with a flourish. He turned back to me.

"Well, what happened?" He tried vainly to focus his eyes on me.

"No comment, Scoop."

"Come on, man, quit movin' and tell me what happened. I missed the whole goddam thing."

"Didn't you even go to the game?" I was astonished that even Scoop would fail to attend at least part of the game.

"I went awright, I jus' don't 'member any of it." Suddenly he fell to the floor as if he had been struck dead by the hand of God. I leaned over to look at him. "Did you see that guy push me?" he said as he grabbed onto my chair arm and pulled himself rather shakily to his feet.

The seat in front of me was empty, so Scoop pushed the seat back forward until it lay flat, then crawled up on it and assumed the lotus position.

"C'mon, man, tell me what happened."

"We lost."

"Good," he said, nodding his head, then looking around absently. "I forgot my pencil 'n pad. You gotta pencil 'n pad?" I shook my head. "Never min', I'll 'member." He winked at me and tapped the side of his head. He offered me a drink from his cup. I leaned forward and peered into it. It looked like vodka and Alka-Seltzer. I shook my head and waved it away.

"Say," Scoop said, snapping his fingers soundlessly, "did the *nigger* really lose the game?" I winced at the volume that he used on the word nigger.

"What nigger?" I asked, too loudly. I looked around but didn't see any black faces or glaring eyes.

"I dunno," he continued, reeling and almost falling backward off the seat. "Clinton jes' said that the dumb nigger dropped the ball."

"I don't know anything about that."

Down the aisle Monsignor Twill made his way rather clumsily from first class back to tourist. He was quite drunk, as he always was on return flights, and stopped by various players to offer his condolences and pat them on the shoulder. Twice as he leaned over to talk to players the plane hit light air pockets and he sprawled into their laps. When he reached us, Scoop had noticed my gaze and was also watching him.

"I can't stan' drunks," Scoop said, as the Monsignor came to a halt beside us. The Monsignor was noticeably offended by the remark.

"Don't mind him, Father," I soothed. "He's upset by the loss."

"I can understand your feelings, Seymour," the Monsignor said, "but that is still no reason to be disrespectful."

"Don't call me Seymour."

"Should I call you Mr. Zolinzowsky?" The Monsignor straightened up, angry at Scoop's abrupt and rude manner. Scoop didn't answer and the Monsignor tried to calm himself and right the situation. "Isn't that a Polish name?"

"Why do you wanna know?" Scoop demanded, taking a long swig of his drink. "You selling bowling shirts?"

The Monsignor glared momentarily at Scoop, then shifted his eyes to me as if expecting an explanation. I shrugged. He shook his head and turned around to tell Andy Crawford he played a great game and he hoped the leg wasn't too long in the healing because "we" needed him next week. Then he moved on down the aisle and disappeared into one of the two restrooms.

"I hate Catholics," Scoop said.

"I thought you were Catholic."

"Tha's what I hate 'bout 'em."

Art Hartman slid into the seat next to Scoop.

"Hey, guys." He smiled. "Played a great game, Phil."

Scoop perked up at the comment.

"He did?" the reporter asked, grabbing at his ear for the nonexistent pencil. He turned to Hartman. "You gotta pencil 'n pad?" Hartman shook his head and then looked at me. His eyes wide, he rolled them in the direction of Scoop. I smiled and nodded.

"I gotta go talk to the losin' coach," Scoop announced, sliding from the seat back to a kneeling position on the floor. As he pulled himself upright, he sloshed his drink all over his hand. He saluted Hartman and me and moved back up toward the front.

"That oughta be a great interview," Hartman observed.

Scoop missed the doorway between sections by about six inches and banged his shoulders into the bulkhead. Backing away, the determined newsman made another run and shot through into first class only slightly scathed.

"How's the King feeling?" Hartman asked, looking around the seat at the sleeping Maxwell.

"Older, I think."

"He'll never get any older."

"That an observation or a complaint?"

"Just a statement, guy. I don't need him to grow old before I get that job. I'll get it when I deserve it."

"Some people thought you deserved it this year."

"Well, it just didn't work out."

"Doesn't that piss you off?"

"Naw." He shook his head. "I'd like to have started this year but B.A. doesn't think I'm ready and I can see his point. I need seasoning. And listen, guy, I love that man," he said, looking at the unconscious quarterback. "He's one of the best in the business. He's taught me a lot. We're good friends."

"You really believe that?"

"Sure, our friendship has nothing to do with competition on the field. We respect each other. When I'm playing, I work my butt off to beat him out, to take that job, but when we step off the field we're still friends."

"Don't you think you're better than he is?"

The question stopped the former All American and he chewed thoughtfully on his upper lip, his eyes squeezing into slits. He thought for a long time.

"Well," he finally said, hesitantly, "that's hard to say. I mean sure I think I'm better than he is. I have to if I ever hope to win the job. But it's B.A.'s decision as to who starts."

"What if B.A. makes the wrong decision. Or the right one and you don't start?"

"That won't happen."

"Why not?"

"Cause it just won't. I concentrate. I follow directions. I work hard. When my chance comes I'll be ready."

"What if it doesn't come?"

"It will come. It has to. I mean if I do everything right, it just has to."

"What if Maxwell's better than you?"

"He's not."

"Then why aren't you playing?"

"Look, I told you, that's B.A.'s decision. I wouldn't have done some of the things Maxwell did today and when my chance comes that'll be the difference between us."

"If you say so," I said, leaning back in my seat and closing my eyes.

"Whattaya mean by that? We lost, didn't we?"

"I don't think the loss was his fault."

"It's always the quarterback's fault when you lose."

"Okay," I said, pushing my feet against the floor, feeling the strangely delicious ache in the muscles. "If you say so." I dug my head into the seat back and fell asleep.

In a dream I was transported to the playing field at the Los Angeles Coliseum. The dream had something to do with being able to throw a football through an old tire. I don't know what the contest was, but I remember that I was scared to death that I couldn't do it. The guy in front of me had just missed and they were carrying him toward the tunnel. The crowd was yelling so loud I woke up. I opened my eyes to hear the sounds of an argument between O.W. Meadows and Jim Johnson. Apparently one, and most likely both, of the Dexamyl Spansules the giant defensive tackle had taken at halftime were beginning to work. The argument was typical postgame behavior for Meadows; he didn't quite grasp the chemistry of time capsules. Standing, screaming at Johnson and inspired by thirty milligrams of Dexedrine and Miltown, he gave vent to a new theory of football that had begun to take shape in his normally fallow brain.

Meadows's gestures were strangely exaggerated by the ice pack secured to his elbow with Ace Bandages and elastic tape. The elbow had been hyperextended in the second half. I was still in a dreamlike state, watching the ice bag wave in the air. I pictured the gruesome mechanics of Meadows's hyperextension. He had been knocked to the ground early in the third period and had extended his right arm to cushion the fall. His palm had dug into the soft ground and he had locked the elbow for support when the ball carrier slammed into the joint from the backside. The blow forced the bones the wrong way; ligaments and muscles stretched and tore. The two primary bones rode grinding over each other. For an instant the elbow dislocated, leaving a huge hole where the elbow point used to be. Somehow the remnants of the muscles and ligaments held and the bones popped back into place with a resounding snap.

He had run off the field, the injured arm hanging limply at his side, and had sat out the rest of that series while the doctor and trainers checked the arm and taped it into a half-flexed position. He returned to action the next se-ries and finished the game.

Tomorrow he would go to the hospital and get x-rayed for breaks. Tonight he was high on speed, adrenaline, codeine, and alcohol. He was feeling no pain if one could judge by the ease with which he whipped the arm around to add force to his argument with Johnson.

The defensive coach had the good sense to know that Meadows was too stoned to give obedience to the social nuances of player-coach relation-ships and might well use physical force to make his point. This left Johnson in a difficult position. Meadows was becoming louder and more specific in his the-orizing, dealing generally with the idea that responsibility for losing in the final seconds to an inferior team fell entirely on the coaching staff. Johnson had sev-eral choices: He could continue to suffer insults at the hands of this Hercules and have his reputation as a man, already seriously damaged by the Jo Bob–Monroe White fight, deteriorate further, or he could stand his ground and confront Meadows physically. He tried for a third alternative.

"Shit," Meadows was screaming. "You never give us anything to take into a game but fucking facts. I'm sick of goddam tendencies. It's a goddam business for you but it's still s'pose' to be a sport to us."

"You're a professional," Johnson protested. "You should—"

"Professional my ass," Meadows interrupted. "You mean under con-tract! Goddam, I'll work harder than anybody to win. But man, when I'm dead tired in the fourth quarter, winning's got to mean more than just money. I can make money selling real estate."

"You're hired to do a job. If—"

"Job! Job!" Meadows screamed into Johnson's face. "I don't want no fucking job, I wanna play football. If I wanted a job I'd go to work for Texas In-struments, you asshole! I want some feelings, some fucking team spirit."

Johnson's jaws tightened, but he remained calm out of respect for Meadows's size and rage.

"Listen," Johnson continued, "this ain't high school, you don't have to love each other for us to play."

"That's what I mean, you cocksucker," Meadows raged. "Every time I try and call it a business you say it's a game and every time I say it should be a game you call it a business. You and B.A. and the rest want us to be eleven total strangers out there thinkin' we was a team."

Johnson's eyes darted around the cabin. He knew he was in danger and only wanted out.

"Well, I'll tell you this." Meadows wagged his finger in the coach's face, his arm wobbling from the imbalance of the ice pack. "You and B.A. and all the rest are chickenshit cocksuckers, who couldn't really play and feel this game at all. Oh sure, you'll win, but what'll it mean? Just numbers on a scoreboard. Well, that ain't enough for me."

Meadows stood in the aisle, his face purple, clenching and unclenching his fists. His breath was coming in heavy gasps.

"I don't have to take this from you or anybody else," Johnson yelled and turned to leave.

"Oh, yes you do, you cocksucker," Meadows bellowed, grabbing the front of the coach's short-sleeved shirt. There was a loud rip and the front of Johnson's shirt split open. His clip-on tie came away in Meadows's hand as the coach quickly fled to the first-class section to tell B.A. about the episode. Johnson had lost two shirts and most of his self-respect in a few short days. It was a tough business.

"Chickenshit cocksuckers," Meadows screamed at the retreating figure. "Coaches are chickenshit cocksuckers. . . ."

Waving Johnson's tie around the cabin, he screamed at his teammates, "You're all chickenshit cocksuckers!"

I knew I was. I couldn't speak for the others.

I closed my eyes and sang a few lines from a Dylan song. The jet engines drowned the words from all ears but mine.

> . . . Some speak of the future
> My love she speaks softly
> She knows there's no success like failure
> And failure's no success at all . . .

The big 727 banked sharply and brought me out of my alcohol-and-codeine fog. I straightened up in my seat. I could see the lights of Dallas through the window. I shook Maxwell's shoulder gently.

We started losing altitude as we approached Love Field from the south, flying directly over downtown. I could see the flying red horse that someone had told me used to be the tallest point in town. Now it was dwarfed by bank buildings and insurance towers and, of course, the CRH Building, which tonight spelled out a reminder that Christmas wasn't too far off.

The pilot sighted down Lemmon Avenue and we skimmed the tops of franchised pizza parlors, hamburger stands, sandwich shops, beauty parlors, and car lots.

A large crowd of fans and friends was waiting when the plane pulled to the gate at the end of the Braniff terminal. As we filed down the ramp and across the concrete apron, Maxwell and I split off to avoid the crowd. Moving along the outside of the building, we made it to the baggage-claim area. We had finished off the remaining six bottles in the seatback pouches and were very drunk. Brushing past the baggage handlers, we climbed through an open bay into the terminal buildings, arriving simultaneously with the luggage off Continental 917 from Lubbock.

"How ya'll doin'?" Maxwell hollered, waving and smiling at the startled people as we climbed over their bags and jumped to the floor. Shaking hands on the way, the quarterback walked, with some difficulty, to Valet Parking to claim his car. I followed several feet behind, striding stiffly and frowning, trying my best to look like an FBI agent.

"You played a fine game out there today, Seth," the Valet attendant was saying as I stepped up with my stub in my hand. "Too bad that boy couldn't hold onto the ball."

"Jest wasn't in the cards," Maxwell explained.

"Well, when I played . . ." the attendant continued, stamping Maxwell's parking ticket and scribbling on it with a ballpoint pen. "That'll be seven fifty. When I played, if a boy fumbled like that he had to take five laps right then, during the game. You know what I mean?"

The attendant picked up his phone and called down to the lot.

"Number five four six eight. Blue Cadillac convertible, I think. That right, Seth?"

Maxwell nodded.

By now a line of people were behind us waiting to retrieve their machines. I handed my stub to the attendant as soon as he set down the receiver. A well-dressed man, who appeared in the middle forties or fifties, grabbed Seth on the shoulder.

"Seth?" the man said, smiling and shoving his hand into Seth's. "Harlen Quaid. From Tyler. We've got a couple of friends in common." His eyes twinkled with excitement.

"Oh yeah." Maxwell struggled to be courteous. His smile showed signs of strain.

"Yep." The man beamed. "Bibby and Gordon Mercer. I saw 'em just yesterday before I left Tyler. I had to come down here for a board meeting. I'm in the oil business."

Bibby and Gordon Mercer were the parents of Francie Mercer, Seth's first wife.

"Why that's real fine," Maxwell said, slipping more and more into his Texas twang as he tried to figure out what this man wanted, if anything. "How's ol' Bibby and Gordon doin'?"

"Jes' fine." The man was beside himself with excitement. His smile split his face open. "Saw Francie, too. An' the little boy. Looks jest like you." The man's smile widened, which seemed physically impossible.

Seth's eyes clouded with pain. He opened his mouth to speak but no words came. His smile collapsed. His eyes flicked around the people assembled watching him and waiting for their cars.

"Hey, man," I said to the oil tycoon from Tyler, "why don't you fuck off before they send you back to Texas in a sponge."

An ambivalence crept into the man's expression but the grin remained stubbornly on his face as he tried to decide who I was and what I meant.

"I ain't joking, motherfucker." I was almost yelling. "Get the fuck out of here." I pointed aimlessly back up toward the main section of the terminal building. "Now!" I screamed.

The man looked at me and then at Seth, who had leaned against the Valet Parking counter and didn't look at all well.

"There's no need to get violent," the man protested, nervously fingering the knot of his tie. His smile remained strangely intact, although the glitter had left his eyes. "Seth and I were just . . ." His eyes suddenly became angry and he tightened his lips into a scowl. "Who are you anyway?" he demanded.

Maxwell's car pulled up in front. Seth was still leaning against the counter, his face white. I pointed to the car and gave him a slight push in its direction. He stumbled toward it, bending perceptibly in the middle. I turned around and kicked the man, Harlen Quaid, as hard as I could in the shins. I followed Seth outside.

As my car pulled behind the Cadillac, I walked to the driver's side of Maxwell's blue convertible. Seth was sitting on the seat, his head and feet still outside. He was doubled up with stomach cramps and trying to throw up.

With the help of the parking attendants, I got Maxwell into my car, returned the Cadillac to the lot, and drove him home. The ride to his house was punctuated by several stops for his stomach to disgorge itself of what seemed like gallons of a reddish-brown whiskey-smelling foam. By the time we had reached the rows of thirty-five-thousand-dollar boxes in far north Dallas, he was feeling much better and invited me to stop by his apartment for a joint.

When it seemed as though I had gone so far north that the next hill would fall away to reveal the Red River, Maxwell told me to turn right, and we were immediately lost in a jungle of apartments. The architecture ranged from Spanish to Swedish, with one set of units that might be described as early Maginot Line. Seth had just moved to these apartments and wasn't too familiar with the layout, but he soon recognized a yellow MG that belonged to one of

PETER GENT . **8 3**

his neighbors ("She only likes to suck cocks—and she swallows it"), and I pulled in next to it. I wanted to go see the neighbor but he insisted on just smoking a joint.

We were met at the door by Seth's friend, roommate, and constant companion, a black unclipped standard poodle named Billy Wayne. The dog's size and friendliness made entering the apartment a constant problem. He would leap joyfully at any visitor, driving his forepaws into their genitals. Billy Wayne was the only thing Maxwell retained from his now-defunct marriage to Judith Ann.

"Goddammit, Billy Wayne," Maxwell yelled, "giddown."

The dog danced around us with his tongue out, wagging his whole body, his nails clicking noisily on the tile floor.

While Maxwell changed his clothes I pulled off my coat, readjusted my shoulder, and moved around the apartment poking into cupboards and closets. It was a typical north Dallas $175-a-month one-bedroom furnished apartment. The furniture was early orthodontist and already showed signs of wear, although the whole complex was less than six months old. There were large stains on the red deep-pile living room carpeting and a couple of heaps of dried poodle shit scattered around.

The drawers and shelves in the kitchen were practically bare. Three monogrammed glasses from a service station giveaway sat dirty and molding in the sink. A Budweiser can opener lay on the drainboard. I couldn't find any glasses or plates. The refrigerator held nine cans of Coors and a half-empty bottle of apple wine. The whole place reeked of rotting food, stale cigarettes, and beer.

A cardboard box that had once held a dishwasher lay wedged in the corner of the breakfast nook. It was filled with trophies, plaques, government citations, autographed footballs, loving cups, and game balls. I rummaged through the results of a lifetime of hard work and dedication; two All American awards, a College All Star Game autographed ball, no fewer than five game balls awarded by his teammates in Dallas, three awards for Professional Athlete of the Year (two cups and a wall plaque), three Pro-Bowl and All-Pro selections and innumerable citations and rewards for jobs done outstandingly well. For all this metal, plastic, and rubber millions of Americans would give their right arm and both testicles (if we are to believe recent surveys about football and sexual sublimation).

"How 'bout that dope?" Maxwell walked into the kitchen, holding a foil package of antacid tablets. He tore the package open, popped the tablets into his mouth and crunched them up noisily, impatient for their promised relief.

"Aaahh," he moaned happily, rolling his eyes. "With Rolaids and ciga-rettes, I'm indestructible." He boosted himself onto the countertop and waited nervously while I fished a joint out of my shirt pocket.

Lighting the joint and inhaling deeply, I was almost struck uncon-scious by the stabbing throbs of an alcohol headache. Holding my breath in-creased the pounding to the point where I expected a loud pop inside my skull and everything to go black. I endured and passed to Maxwell. From some-where in the recesses of my ravaged brain, I recalled an early doping maxim bequeathed to me by a friend now doing two to life in Huntsville for posses-sion: No matter what happens, he had said, always pass the joint first. Unlike most of the rules by which I have tried somewhat unsuccessfully to get my ship safely into port, that rule given to me by a man who must now be endur-ing unspeakable assaults on his integrity has held up against time and the Texas sun. What else can I say?

As Maxwell snatched the joint from my outstretched fingers he no-ticed the rather large red blotches that spotted my forearm.

"What's that?" he asked.

I didn't know and held up both arms for further inspection. They were covered with them. I unbuttoned my shirt and found my stomach and chest covered also.

"Looks like I O.D.'d on the codeine and booze," I decided.

Maxwell had changed clothes and was wearing an old pair of faded Levi's and a red silk Western shirt coated with sequin wagon wheels and cactus plants. The front of the shirt, the two flap pockets, and the cuffs were riveted with white mother-of-pearl snaps. He was barefoot and looked like Porter Wagoner at the beach.

I considered driving out to Charlotte's; I was anxious to see her, but the headache and my overall physical condition dissuaded me. I would get a good sleep and drive out in the morning.

While we smoked the joint, I reflected on the day's work. I was pleased by my performance. Although we had lost, I had a total of five catches for two touchdowns, had not missed an assignment that I could recall, and had made several key blocks. It had been hard and frustrating, but things were looking up. I made a mental note to be more agreeable with the staff and my teammates. It couldn't hurt to bend a little.

"You played a helluva game today," I said, offering Maxwell the joint. He waved it away, inserted a Winston between his lips, lit it, and dragged deeply, throwing his head back as he exhaled.

"Not good enough," he said. He looked emptily at his bare feet. He stuck the tip of his tongue out and picked a piece of tobacco off the end. "Not good *e*-nough." He accented the *E* heavily.

"You can't take the blame, man," I argued. "There were a lotta mistakes out there. Christ, look at Claridge and Huddle. Besides, you and I both know we'll win the division. Shit, nobody can touch us—"

"That don't matter," Maxwell retorted. "My job is to win. Nothin' else is good enough."

"You and that Vince Lombardi no-second-place shit," I harangued. "You sound like Art Hartman." Maxwell's head came up at the mention of his competitor's name.

"You know," he said, "I used to think that that kid had it all." He shook his head and looked at the floor. "But he don't. He's got the size and the arm. He's conscientious and he works hard." Seth brought his eyes up to meet mine. "But he's simple, too simple. I'll get him. He just don't understand what it's all about." Maxwell paused and a smile trickled from cheek to cheek. "You know what I mean?"

I nodded.

"He thinks that he is destined to be number one," Maxwell said. A note of amazement edged his voice. "When I win he really seems pleased. He never seems to worry about it."

"He's a team man."

"I'm a team man," Maxwell said. "He just ain't on my team. Besides, a man that don't worry, don't win. And as long as I win for them they need me."

"Well, you can believe all that sport shit if you want to," I said. "But we're not the team, man, they are. B.A. and Conrad Hunter and Clinton Foote, and all those front office cocksuckers, they're the team. We're just the fucking equipment to be listed along with the shoulder pads and headgear and jockstraps. This is first and foremost a business, with antitrust exemptions, tax breaks, and depreciations. And all the first and tens, all the last-second touchdowns and 95-yard passes are just items on a ledger to be weighed along with the cost of precooked steak and green eggs. People don't talk about football teams anymore, they talk about football systems, and the control long ago moved off the field. Tell me who looks more pathetic against our defense than Johnny Unitas."

"He looked pretty bad," Maxwell admitted grudgingly. "But—"

"But nothing. He looked bad because B.A. had got old Johnny U. and Johnny U.'s system logged in those computer banks downtown and he knows what old high-tops is gonna do before old high-tops knows it."

"So?"

"So, everything you think is so swell and wonderful and unduplicat-able about you as a quarterback B.A. has on a tape downtown ready to be pumped into the next guy like he was pulling on headgear."

"You're wrong," Maxwell argued, "dead wrong. You're just pissed off because you can't get the starting job. And if you don't quit goofing off pretty soon you'll never get it."

"Probably so," I said, shaking my head slowly and wondering whatever possessed me to start the argument. "But what can I do? I'm too used to seeing myself on a list—a six-foot-four-inch two-hundred-fifteen-pound flankerback, right alongside the six and seven-eighths helmets and the size thirteen shoes. No, man, I *FEEL* like a piece of equipment. I *know* I'm a piece of equipment."

We both fell silent.

"Ya know," Maxwell began, "you just don't understand. You let things bother you too much. I learned a long time ago, you can't let things bother you."

"How do you keep from it?" I knelt down to rub on Billy Wayne, who had come over and was licking the back of my hand.

"It's easy, man. You just don't. When I was about six or seven, I don't remember too clear, my folks took me to the doctor to have my tonsils out. Only they didn't tell me what was goin' on . . . just that we was goin' to the doctor. It was a plan they'd worked out with the doctor to keep me from raisin' too much hell.

"Well, anyway," Maxwell continued, "I knew somethin' was up by the way my folks acted in the car, so by the time we got to the doctor's office, I was scared shitless, but I didn't let on. You know what I mean?"

I agreed, my mind swimming back twenty-odd years to a small doctor's office in Michigan.

"But even when they laid me out on the table I never let on I was scared. Even when they put the mask over my face and tol' me to count back-wards from ten, I knew they didn't think I could make it but I held my breath and counted real fast and got to zero just before everything went black.

"Do you know what I'm sayin'?" he continued. "Let 'em do what they want, I just keep foolin' 'em."

"Jesus," I said, finally. "That's almost the same thing that happened to me, except I thought they were killing me and I screamed bloody murder from start to finish."

"They still took your tonsils out, didn't they?"

I nodded.

"Well, that's my point. It don't do no good to fight. What you gotta do is fool 'em. I been foolin' 'em ever since."

"Yeah, man," I protested, "but if you spend all your time pretending you're something else, that's what you are—something else."

"That's what I love about sports, man," I continued, trying to explain. "There is a basic reality where it is just me and the job to be done, the game and all its skills. And the reward wasn't what other people thought or how much they paid me but how I felt at the moment I was exhibiting my special skill. How I felt about me. That's what's true. That's what I loved. All the rest is just a matter of opinion."

Maxwell's eyes brightened slightly and he nodded his head.

"I know what you're saying," he admitted. "I guess that's why we all start playing in the first place."

I nodded and smiled, pleased that we had an understanding.

"You still feel that way?" I asked, not really certain of my own answer.

"I dunno anymore, man. Back before we won it all, I used to always feel that way. Hell, there was hardly any other reason to play, you remember that. I used to fight with B.A. all the time, just like you do now. Shit," he laughed, "I not only wouldn't call the plays he sent in, I ran the guys that brought 'em in off the field. But, I do know this. B.A. is the winning side, and I may not have the fun that I used to, but I sure win a lot more and that's good enough for me.

"It's tougher now; maybe that's the price of winning," he conceded. "Now, it's all sort of mixed up with statistics, incentive money, and how much money I get if I win the division or lead the league. I still play for the thrill, but winning has its responsibilities and it gets a little confusing."

"You're totally obsessed with winning," I pointed out. "Don't you think that's wrong?"

"No. If you don't win, what's the sense of playing?"

"The game man," I argued. "The game. Not the end, the winning or losing, but the means: the game. That's the reason—the game, only the game."

"Well, all I know is what I have to do statistically to keep playing and that's what I try and do each week. If I enjoy playing, that's great, but I need those numbers first and have to do whatever is necessary to get 'em."

"It takes away a lot of the fun."

"What's fun?"

We fell silent while I continued to pat on Billy Wayne and think about what Seth had just said. Finally, I stood up and began to organize myself to leave.

"I guess it's whose opinion is the most important to you," I said. "I don't know whether it's really my keen judgment I respect or if I'm swayed by the fact that I'm the only one who thinks I'm any good."

Maxwell seemed no longer interested and called Billy Wayne to his side and they resumed their play. I picked up my coat and threw it over my shoulder.

"See you tomorrow or Tuesday," I called, heading for the door.

"Right," he answered without looking up. He was holding Billy Wayne's curly black head and looking into his brown eyes. He was whispering something to the dog but it was too soft for me to hear.

The wind was picking up as I walked slowly to the car, my head tilted back, searching vainly for the supernova I knew I would never see. If I can just get to zero before everything goes black.

The house looked dark and uninviting as I stopped the Riviera at the front curb. I let the engine idle and listened to Mick Jagger grind through "Jig-saw Puzzle."

I thought of the incredible confusion I had come through in just seven short days. My career had moved out of peril into an area of relative security and possible success. I always felt I had the ability to be a great receiver and now it could be working out. B.A. would have difficulty denying my performance today. The day seemed almost surreal. My legs and back still hurt, but I had a new energy, a force, that helped me endure and overcome the debilitating effects of constant pain. Amazingly I no longer worried about the pain, I accepted it.

Coming of Age on the 50-Yard Line

ROBERT ANDREW POWELL

Sports are often seen as a way to advance one's station in life, particularly for those who grow up poor—make it to the pros, and those days in the ghetto will be just a bad memory. Robert Andrew Powell's take on the emergence of a Pop Warner football program in a Miami housing project shows how youth football can affect a depressed community.

Neighborhood coaches and the Greater Miami Boys and Girls Club dedicate their own time and money to pull area youths from their decrepit surroundings and teach them the game. Some of the children take to the instruction, the teamwork, and the aggressive nature of football and make the league a positive experience. But others are as aimless on the field as off. Particularly telling is one coach's estimation that only about 30 percent of the children involved will become successful adults.

The political nature of the neighborhood organization is also an ugly reality. A local administrator is accused of embezzling funds from the organization and driven from his position. Is this Pop Warner or the NFL? The similarities between a league designed as a constructive outlet for kids and the unseemly aspects of big time sports programs are striking in "Coming of Age on the 50-Yard Line."

What politics is to the Cuban community, football is to the black community.

—RICHARD DUNN, former Miami city commissioner

On Friday, Gwen Cherry Park rests. An empty Doritos bag tumbles across the abandoned main football field, lodging itself in one of the hollow diamonds of a chainlink fence. With all the kids in school, no noise bounces off the steel roof of the new gymnasium, a gift from the National Football League. A low-riding Toyota glides down NW 71st Street past the Scott housing project, its muted bass groove cutting the silence, its metallic gold rims glittering in the light of a sun that burns hot at noon on an early autumn day.

Saturday the park comes alive. Hundreds of neighbors have turned out to watch the eight Gwen Cherry teams sponsored by the Greater Miami Boys and Girls Club—all nicknamed the Bulls—battle for Pop Warner football superiority. Right now the 80-pound Bulls (Pop Warner teams aren't divided according to age but by their weight, which ranges from 65 pounds to 140 pounds) hold a 10–0 lead over Palmetto. Ten-year-old Bulls wide receiver Sammie Bush, barely taller than a man's hip, snags a lateral and, finding himself free of any defenders, darts 45 yards for a touchdown. Six coaches dressed in matching blue and yellow shirts, caps, and sneakers gleefully trade high-fives and slap their clipboards. Twenty tiny cheerleaders shake pompons.

It's hot out here, it's hot out here
There must be a Bull in the atmosphere!

Beyond the yellow rope that separates the players from their followers, a half-dozen barbecue grills pump out a cloud of charcoal smoke and chicken fat that drifts over the field like a misty blimp. One young spectator parks his rear end on a bicycle seat. His neighbor rests his on a metal folding chair. Standing up in the fifth and highest row of the flimsy bleachers, the gits—local slang for gang members—puff on blunts while they berate the coaches. *Y'all better start throwing the ball!*

The Gwen Cherry Bulls 80-pounders have dispatched their first three opponents this season—South Dade, Richmond, and Tamiami—with relative ease. With a shutout against Palmetto an imminent possibility, Bulls players have already started celebrating. Sammie Bush choreographs Deion Sanders dance steps while linebacker Richard Dunn, son of the former Miami city commissioner, pushes his palms skyward, "raising the roof" on an impending 4–0 record.

"Every Saturday is a festival in this park," beams Charlie Brown, executive athletic director of the Boys and Girls Clubs. "With the inner city, there's basically nothing planned or organized on a weekly basis for people to do. Our football games are a day people can look forward to spending with their neighbors and their families, just enjoying the afternoon."

A fight breaks out on the sideline. Linebacker Steven Green's dad excoriates his son for a mental mistake. The critique is overheard by the boy's stepfather, who is standing not far off, talking on a cellular phone. "That's *my* motherfucking son!" shouts the stepfather, flashing a mouthful of gold teeth. He turns back to his phone: "Excuse me, I got to deal with this guy." Then: "I'll kick your ass right now, boy!"

The men lunge at one another but are quickly restrained by coaches. The natural father slips free and sprints across the field, hurdling the railroad tracks and disappearing into the Scott projects. "Is he getting a gun?" a spectator wonders aloud. Steven Green's mother grabs her son without wiping the tears from his smooth brown face, pulls him off the field, and incarcerates him in the passenger seat of her car.

"Pay attention! Pay attention!" head coach Andre "Dre" Greene shouts to his squad, most of whom have turned from the action on the field to watch the fracas. "Keep your head in the game, y'all! We still playing a game!"

Not for long. Only four minutes later a second fight erupts. The mothers of Tony Brown and Darrell "Dee" Samuel, both running backs, have been arguing throughout the game about their son's respective playing time. Both kids' teachers filed "unacceptable" progress reports earlier in the week, forcing the coach to bench the boys for at least part of the game. Yet (and apparently by accident) Dre put one of the boys into the game earlier than he was supposed to, and tempers flared.

"The mother of Tony starts ragging on Dee, saying he only has one finger," imparts defensive-back coach Tommy Streeter. (Nine-year-old Dee was born with a malformed left hand.) "You don't ever be saying that!" warns Streeter. "Not to a kid, and especially not to his mother. That's why they scrapped."

Two county police cruisers arrive after the second fight has died down. The officers stroll among the remaining participants of both altercations, calmly asking questions. When the game ends anticlimactically in another Bulls victory, no one cheers.

"We're 4–0, but I tell you, this has been the hardest season of my life," grumbles Dre's brother Darrell Greene, the team's offensive coordinator. "It's the worst season, so hard, so difficult. I mean, man, this team can go to the Super Bowl! If they just stay focused, they can *go.*"

The National Football League's annual Super Bowl has become an unofficial American holiday, watched by nearly 130 million people nation-wide. But in terms of pure passion, the Super Bowl of the Greater Miami Pop Warner football league may eclipse its grownup counterpart. Nearly 6,500 people turned out for the two days of last year's championships, held in Liberty City's Curtis Park. That's 6,500 people to watch kids as young as six (and as Lil-liputian as 65 pounds) play football.

When Darrell Greene says that "the Super Bowl is what it's all about," he's not referring to the professional game. "When I was a kid playing Opti-mists, we won a championship in 1975," Greene recalls. "I'll never forget that banquet afterward, how good we all felt from moving toward a goal and ac-complishing it together. I want these kids to understand that feeling."

To win the Super Bowl in Miami–Dade County is to beat the best young teams in the nation. The local Pop Warner leagues (also known as Opti-mist football, after the charity that sponsors several teams) are the breeding grounds for the county's superlative high school teams; local high schools have won four of the past six Class 6A state championships. In turn, many of the county's top high school players stay in-state to play for America's best college programs: the University of Miami, Florida State, and the University of Florida have won five of the past ten national championships.

"The success of the University of Miami a few years ago inspired a lot more inner-city kids to play Optimist football, which has really improved the overall quality of football in Dade County," affirms Billy Rolle, head football coach at Northwestern High, the 1995 Class 6A state champs. "Our high school teams are some of the best in the country, and I think that's due in large part to the strength of our Optimists."

The Boys and Girls Clubs' Daron Chiverton, commissioner of Gwen Cherry's football program, believes football is ideally suited for the kids who grow up in and around the Scott Homes. "Football is the most natural for them," says Chiverton. "Basketball puts limits on their aggression; baseball puts limits on their aggression. In football they had better well be aggressive. And with the background of these kids, where these kids come from, aggres-sion comes naturally."

Danny Dye, who coaches a 65-pound team and is the stepfather of the 80s' quarterback, offers another theory about why football dominates Miami's inner city. "I could sum that up in a couple of words: everybody wants to see their kid play in the NFL."

Indeed, despite brutally long odds, several parents who stalk the sidelines on game days see football as a legitimate career option for their progeny. The Boston-based Center for the Study of Sport and Society reports that only one in one hundred high school football and basketball players will earn a college scholarship and only one in ten thousand will play pro sports. Yet a few who have beaten those odds came from this very neighborhood; Miami Dolphins wide receiver Brett Perriman and New York Jets linebacker Marvin Jones both played for Northwestern in the late eighties. Coach Streeter, a former Northwestern linebacker, played college ball for the University of Colorado and professionally in the Canadian Football League. Such anecdotal evidence is hard for some parents to ignore. "It's realistic!" imparts Tim Torrence, a coach of the 105s and father of a linebacker who plays for the 80s.

"Somebody a long time ago came to the idea that this—football—was the very best way to show that we could make it out, that we could rise above the slave mentality, segregation, and really be what we want to be," theorizes Carlos Guy, an aide to County Commissioner James Burke and the uncle of a boy on the 65s. "With the generations that passed since then, over time, things have gotten stronger and stronger. It's not a *part* of the culture now. It *is* the culture."

And the culture reveals itself at the Super Bowl. Speedy wide receiver Sammie Bush played in last year's Super Bowl for one of the Liberty City Warriors' 65-pound teams. Now with the Bulls, he dreams of making it back. "We was 10–0," he says of last year's final against the Northwestern Boys Club Falcons. Time was running out as Liberty City marched toward the end zone in pursuit of a game-tying touchdown. "The clock was ticking, and the crowd was chanting 'three . . . two . . . one,' when their team intercepted the ball," Sammie remembers wistfully. "I hope to meet them this year in the Super Bowl. It'll be exciting to see them try to beat the Bulls."

Noon is the scheduled kickoff for today's home game against the Inner City Jaguars, based in M. Athalie Range Park across from Edison High School. At close to two o'clock, players and coaches still laze under a shade tree near the field, wondering where their opponents are. Eventually, and reluctantly, Charlie Brown calls the game. "All right, those niggas be scared of us. They forfeit," announces Coach Dre, prompting his players to cheer. "Listen, listen!" he instructs, hushing the celebration. "This don't mean we're off the hook. We don't want to win this way."

Even as Dre speaks, a yellow school bus rolls across the grass and comes to a stop near the football field. Teams of turquoise Jaguars spill out the door and onto the field. Inner City has arrived. "All right, it's showtime!" Coach Streeter shouts. "Get hyped, y'all!"

Nine-year-old Greg Finnie, sporting a Nike headband, Nike wristbands, and Nike cleats, leaps up to lead the cheers. "Everybody ready to throw down?" he hollers. "Yes we are!" the team shouts back. "Breakdown!" The Bulls peel off a series of rhythmic chants. "Bulls, Bulls, Bulls, no limit Bulls! . . . Undefeated, undefeated, undefeated! Can't be beaten, can't be beaten, can't be beaten! . . . Blue get ready to roll! Gold get ready to roll! . . ." They stomp their feet and slap twice on their thigh pads. "Blue and gold, rolling to the Super Bowl!"

Under Coach Dre's command, the players drop to one knee to say a prayer. The younger Richard Dunn cranes his neck to catch the attention of his father, standing among the spectators. "This is the part I like best," confides the older Dunn, a minister. "It's holistic, you know?"

When the amens have been said, Coach Dre wraps up his pep talk. "They made us wait. Get mad," he orders. "What are you going to do?"

"Punch them in the mouth!" one boy shouts.

"That's not the answer I was looking for," Dre responds. "No, you'all saying the wrong thing. Teamwork. Play as a team. Teamwork. Let's go! Get mad!"

Through the Second World War and into the 1950s, Gwen Cherry Park was a rock pit. From about 1954, when Scott Homes was built, until 1963, the pit was filled with trash and construction debris. The county park opened in 1980, on top of the landfill. But county, state, and federal environmental officials have recently discovered high levels of lead and arsenic in the park's soil. Although the environmentalists insist there's no danger to the kids who play there, further soil and water testing is under way to determine whether the park qualifies as a Superfund site, making it eligible for federal clean-up money.

"The state and the feds—the big wheels—are all here," reports Charlie Brown at a town meeting called in early October to address the contamination. "If it was just the Metro-Dade Parks, maybe this could have been swept under the rug. But for the NFL to spend all that money to find this out, they're not going to be pleased. Not at all."

Brown is referring to the National Football League's Youth Education Town Center, a gleaming year-old complex constructed with a million-dollar grant the NFL awarded in 1995 in conjunction with Super Bowl XXIX. Besides a new football field and a 9,000-square-foot gym, the center offers two computer labs, tutoring, and arts-and-crafts classes. NationsBank, the Miami

Dolphins, and other businesses covered the rest of the center's $3.1 million cost. The county maintains and protects the building, while the Boys and Girls Clubs provides the recreational programs.

"That center was the best thing to happen to this community, ever," states Danny Dye.

In the years before the YET center was built, Gwen Cherry youth football floundered. Coaches recall scrambling for cash to pay bus drivers to haul teams to away games. Although money had been set aside to purchase both practice and game uniforms, the game jerseys never appeared. Several coaches say the teams' former administrator Anthony Dawkins wore out his welcome in the community he served. "He was going to get himself hurt," asserts coach A. D. Williams, who has worked at the park for eight years. "I mean physically hurt. People were threatening him, driving by his house, accusing him of mismanaging the program and stealing funds. So he got out. He left before Charlie [Brown] and the other administrators asked him to leave."

Brown takes a diplomatic posture regarding his predecessor. "I commend Anthony Dawkins for coming in and trying to make it work," he offers calmly. "But with the Boys and Girls Clubs running the program, it gets a different respect. We came in with a forty-year history of being involved with youth. He was a single venture. Things just didn't work out for him. He wasn't prepared."

Dawkins admits he transferred money from one account to another, in violation of standard bookkeeping practices. And without a staff, he could provide only so much service. But he didn't break any laws and all the money went to the kids. "It was inexperience," he says. "Yes, I shouldn't have bought T-shirts for the kids with the money set aside to pay the refs. Yes, it was run inefficiently. If I had been doing this for forty years [like the Boys and Girls Clubs], I'd probably be doing it better."

The former administrator, who confirms that county police investigated him for embezzlement, points out that he was never charged with any crime. "Do you think if I took government money I'd still be walking around free?" he asks. His problems with the community, Dawkins theorizes, stem from the community itself. "I am a local boy," he argues. "Too local. I grew up in the Scott projects. The people there would see me get a grant from the county and they'd say, 'Why should he have the opportunity?'"

The Boys and Girls Clubs took over the football program in August 1996. One young player showed up for the first practice with a loaded pistol. At the second practice, when a coach scolded one of his players, a gang of young men watching from the sidelines stormed the field and physically attacked him. The park adopted the colors and nickname of the champion Northwestern Bulls. Not one Gwen Cherry team made the playoffs.

This year coaches and parents sport yellow T-shirts emblazoned with the team's new slogan: "From the bottom to the top, don't miss the climb, Gwen Cherry football."

Now, as the 80s prepare to storm the field after finishing their breakdowns, Charlie Brown pulls Coach Dre aside. Even though the Jaguars are here, the referees have already left. It's too late now to get a new crew, so Inner City must—officially, this time—forfeit. The Jaguars head coach explains that his administrator misread the schedule and wrote down the wrong starting time for the game. The administrator: Anthony Dawkins.

The play is a halfback pass. Keith Holmes is in at quarterback, Frankie Adams at halfback. For this practice drill, there are no defenders. "Hut one, hut two," barks Keith. "Hike!" As two wide receivers sprint down the sideline, Keith drops back two steps, turns, and hands the ball to the tiny halfback. Frankie carries it 5 yards toward the sideline, plants his foot, cocks his right arm, and throws.

"WHOOOOooooooooooeeee!" A whistle erupts in unison from three teenage spectators as the ball sails over their heads, the WHOOOO commencing the moment the ball leaves Frankie's fingertips, the last of the *eees* sounding as the tight spiral lands perfectly in Sammie Bush's arms, 45 yards down the field. "That git can *throw!*"

It's an amazing sight, Frankie throwing a football. It doesn't seem physically possible that a boy only 43 inches tall, encumbered by shoulder and elbow pads and a helmet looking as big as an apple crate, can chuck a ball so far. Yet he does, every time, effortlessly. Not only can he throw the ball, he can also kick accurate field goals of 35 yards, making him—at age 10—the only kicker in the entire park. Thanks to Frankie, the Bulls are the only team in their league that regularly kicks for an extra 2 points after touchdowns (which owing to their difficulty at this level are worth twice as much as a running play).

But it's the throwing that dazzles the sideline gits at this practice, one of the few that Frankie attends. When asked why Frankie isn't the team's regular quarterback, defensive coordinator Anthony Snelling twirls a finger around his ear. "That boy be messed up in the head," Snelling declares. "He's got all the talent in the world, *all* the talent in the *world,* yet he'd rather play on the train tracks with his boys than play with the real men over here. Ain't that right, Frankie?"

Frankie finds himself in constant trouble at school, where he often fails to complete his homework and acts up in class. "He's screwing up," declares Coach Streeter, who frequently visits his players' schools to check on their academic progress. Frankie's file at Lillie C. Evans Elementary is crammed with disciplinary reports. One of his fifth-grade teachers tells Streeter that it's the boy's boundless energy that gets him into so much trouble. He's a good-humored, smart kid, reports the teacher, but he needs to be less disruptive in the classroom.

Three out of every four children in the Scott Homes are raised by a single parent, usually a mother, says the Boys and Girls Clubs' Daron Chiverton. He believes that age eleven is the cutoff, the time when kids choose to work within the system or to reject it. This dismal vision, that Frankie is on the cusp of doom at age ten, is shared by many Bulls coaches.

"Society says you're a man when you turn eighteen," observes defensive line coach Gary Robinson. "But in real life, rites of passage come much earlier than eighteen. Especially for some of the kids in the Scott Homes. Many of them are the man of the house at age twelve or thirteen. Their parents might be at work, so they have to work in the house helping to raise their brothers and sisters. And some of them can't handle that."

Robinson scans the practice field, where Frankie continues to uncork bombs. "Hopefully, none of them will fail, in life, but if I had to tell you realistically, and generously, only maybe 30 percent will turn out to be full successes. The other 70 percent? Realistically? Forget about it."

Despite his talents, Frankie plays sparingly on game days. With the exception of kickoffs and extra points, he whiles away most quarters on the bench, absently flipping his kicking tee. In close games Coach Dre itches to insert his secret weapon to drop one of those bombs on the other team's unsuspecting defense. Sometimes he gets to, when Frankie has shown up for practice and stayed out of trouble in school. Usually he does not. "My wife [a teacher at Frankie's school] comes home every day telling me, 'Ain't no way that boy should be playing this Saturday. Ain't no way!'"

Frankie says he learned how to throw and kick by watching his three older brothers. "I was good at kicking kickballs, but I didn't know how to kick a football. I kept kicking from the top of the ball, but my brother Cecil taught me to kick from the bottom," he says, punctuating this recollection by spitting on the ground.

When asked what his favorite food is, Frankie unspools a verbal list that embraces the entire nutritional pyramid. "I like macaroni, chicken, rice, spinach, carrots, potato salad, hot dogs, cupcakes, hamburgers," he says, taking more than two minutes to end on crabcakes, which he apologizes for not putting first. He wishes he could have $5,000 to buy his mama a house and a pool and a car. "I'd buy myself a little fish, and I'd build a pond with big fishing poles." he also wishes he lived in Heaven.

Why isn't he playing quarterback? "'Cause Coach won't let me play," he responds, spitting again. Is it because of his schoolwork? No response. Why is he struggling so much in school? If the question makes Frankie uncomfortable, he tries not to show it. Instead he snakes his pink tongue around the rim of a can of strawberry soda, spitting out what he finds. His eyes fix on a man diving into a Dumpster in search of aluminum. Absently he rubs the shredded skin of his index finger into one of several infected, nickel-size scabs on his shins. When he realizes that an answer is expected, he continues to poke at his wounds. Eventually he just shrugs.

The Bulls squeak past South Miami 8–0, on a touchdown and Frankie's extra two points. Six games into the season, the team is undefeated, and the dream of a berth in the playoffs is inching closer to being a reality. All that stands in the team's way is next week's road trip to Goulds, which is also undefeated. "Coach told us whoever wins the Goulds game is going to the Super Bowl," relays linebacker Vincent Powell as he dons his helmet before practice.

Most of the spectators at the practices are women—mothers, usually, though a few men do drive up to the field to lean against their car doors and watch a son or nephew scrimmage. In greeting one another, the men invariably employ the same salutation: *coach*. "That's a thing that we do in this culture," explains Carlos Guy. "Whenever a man out here sees another man, and they don't know each other, they call each other 'coach.' It's a sign of respect for what they are doing out here, even if they aren't actually coaching."

Watching a practice, when all the Bulls' age groups share the same big field, is like watching a three-dimensional growth chart. The 65-pound 6-year-olds are so diminutive they look like a helmet with two cleats beneath it. The 80s are taller (if that's the right word), and appear more stable; their heads fit better into their helmets. The 110s are lanky, with long shins and athletic gaits. The 140s, growing into their adult bodies, are nothing less than smaller versions of the pros.

After stretching and running sprints as a team, the 80s split up for positional work. While Darrell Greene and his brother run the offense through a new pass play, Gary Robinson teaches the linebackers how to sack, and coach A.D. puts the offensive line through a blocking drill. "That's the definition of insanity," A.D. instructs a lineman who has dressed for practice in a Dallas Cowboys jersey. "You're doing exactly the same thing but expecting a different outcome. You got to crack it back, then come with some force. Some force! Crack it back, lose those zombie arms! Come on, man, you got to crack him!"

Like all the coaches, A.D. is out here Tuesday through Friday from 5:00 to 8:00 P.M. Like all the coaches, he has kids of his own waiting for him to trudge home worn-out from his volunteerism. And like all the coaches, he logs the hours in order to repay the debt he feels he owes the game.

"My friends and I were tight," the coach imparts during a short break. "We'd be together from as soon as we got up in the morning until we came home at night and went to sleep. We were *tight,* you know. So many of them grew up to be messed up with drugs and in jail and all sorts of problems, I look at them and I realize how lucky I was to be involved in Optimist football. If you can look at yourself, and at how you grew up to not be a total failure, it makes you want to give something back."

Dre, the 80s' head coach, puts in his three hours of practice before working the night shift at a Burger King warehouse, his job for the past decade. Gary Robinson replaces broken windshields for Charlie's Auto Glass. None of the coaches are paid for their time. All spend their own money on gas, on food after games, on team sleepovers and Halloween parties, and on the eight-dollar black neckrolls awarded each Thursday to the best defensive player from the previous game.

"These coaches are the best teachers these kids have," notes Carlos Guy. "Until they are 6, they're growing up with their mamas. They're waiting to find out what they're supposed to do as men. No one around them can show them, and the mamas know they can't show them, and the boys sure as hell can't know it. So they come out here and they see the coaches and they learn how to be men."

Gits who've dropped out of football still swing through the park on mountain bikes to scout for talent. Mothers sit in lawn chairs beneath the trees, idly chatting while they wait for practice to end. Across the park echoes a smack of plastic on plastic. "Tough!" someone cries out. "Oh baby, good hit!"

"Lil" Tim Torrence stands on a steel scale in a storage room at Goulds Park, hoping to make weight. Though a 10-year-old might play on a team with kids who are 12 if he's heavy enough, far more common is the phenomenon of "making weight"—shedding pounds to play against younger kids. Under the careful watch of his father, 9-year-old Tim maintains a strict diet.

"When they come home for dinner, I feed them a tuna salad and some water," the father elaborates as his son steps off the scale, having made weight. "That will fill them up and they'll get tired. They'll go to sleep. In the morning I give them breakfast. They need that, and then they'll burn it off anyway during the day. One of my boys, I'm telling you, he lost nine pounds."

During the first half of the Goulds game, the Bulls offense bogs down, blowing several gimmick plays. Frankie is in, but his halfback pass fails twice and he's sacked by the Goulds defense. Reverses, in which the halfback hands off the ball to a wide receiver, gain little. At the end of the first quarter the game is scoreless.

Goulds threatens early in the second quarter, breaking off a fourth-down run for 40 yards to the Bulls' 1-yard line. But penalties and the Bulls' inspired defense keep the Rams out of the end zone and force a turnover on downs. Still scoreless at the end of the first half.

"Let's play authenticity football," Darrell Greene urges at halftime. "This is just like the playoffs. This is when the big-time players step up. If you want to make a name for yourself in Optimist football, now is the time to do it."

The Bulls catch a break on a fluke at the start of the second half. Frankie's kickoff travels only twelve yards, transforming it into a de facto onside kick, which the Bulls manage to recover. Once again Darrell Greene calls for a trick play, but this time it works: quarterback Keith Holmes fakes a hand-off to his halfback, then hides the ball in his midsection before taking the defense by surprise. He throws 25 yards downfield to a wide-open Sammie Bush, who is brought down at the 7-yard line, not by a tackler from the opposing team but by an equipment failure of sorts. "I would have made a touchdown," Sammie later reports, "but my pants were all baggy. I had to stop to pull them up." Two plays later the Bulls score on a straightforward running play. Frankie's kick sails true for the extra two points, giving the team an 8–0 lead.

But as the Bulls offense continues to sputter into the fourth quarter, Goulds finally begins to click. The Rams' halfback gains good ground outside, and as the clock winds down his coaches keep calling for halfback sweeps, a strategy that pays off in a Rams touchdown with only twelve seconds remaining. Dre, Darrell, and Streeter muffle their curses while the parents let the profanity fly. Tie score, pending the point-after kick.

At this level of football, where it's against the rules to rush the kicker, distraction is the Bulls' only weapon. The defensive line commences jumping jacks. Sammie, at free safety, stares down the kicker, hoping to unnerve him. From the Bulls bleachers, parents chant, "Miss it! Miss it!"

The snap sails over the holder's head. Fetching the ball and running back to his place, the holder sets it down. The kicker hesitates, crossing fingers on both hands and clenching his eyes tight as if in prayer. "Please," he begs as he finally approaches the ball. His toe strikes the pigskin awkwardly, causing it to wobble wide left.

Bulls win.

The offense, the coaching staff, all the mothers, and everyone else in blue and yellow storms the field. "Yeah! Yeah! Yeah!" A.D. roars, flexing his muscles like a bodybuilder. Bulls players race to meet their coaches, hollering their own squeaky cheers. "I felt like I'd been touched by an angel!" cries an ecstatic Sammie. "It felt so good I jumped in the air higher than I've ever jumped in my life!"

Coaches hug players, players hug their mothers, mothers hug the coaches, cheerleaders frantically wave their pompons. The celebration subsides only for the handshakes at midfield. Cheerleaders on the right, players on the left, both teams march single-file toward the opposite sideline. Triumphant Bulls slap hands with sobbing Rams. Coach Streeter commands his team to gather at the end zone to usher in the next weight division by forming a human chute for the 90-pounders to run through. Coach Dre, chugging a can of orange soda, hovers around midfield, looking for more people to embrace.

"We're going to go all the way!" someone shouts. "We're going all . . . the . . . way!"

After the Goulds game, Frankie misses every practice. As punishment he sits on the bench while the Bulls trounce West Kendall, 26–0. A week later he's still sitting as Scott Lake, from north of the Palmetto Expressway, is blown out 36–0. Coach Dre lets him kick off and convert extra points, but that's it.

Linda Adams, Frankie's mother, says her boy missed the practices because he was in trouble at school.

In the regular-season finale, Frankie doesn't play a down as the team loses its first game, to the Northwest Boys Club, a league power. He doesn't even get in to attempt an extra point because the Bulls never score. "Keep your heads up and feel good about Gwen Cherry Park," Dre orders after the 26–0 drubbing. "It ain't nothing but one loss, baby. We're 9–1, we'll see them again." Despite the upbeat words, tears stream down the faces of tackle Lawrence Hook and several of his teammates.

The loss means little: with nine wins the Bulls had secured homefield advantage for the playoffs even before the kickoff. Still, Dre pulls Frankie aside afterward. "This is the playoffs now, Frankie. Do or die," says the head coach, grasping his kicker by the shoulder. "I need you to show up for practices this week. We need you in there at tight end. Can you show up for me? Can you do that for me, Frankie?" Frankie stares blankly at Dre, nodding slightly.

Frankie does not show up for a single practice in preparation for the first playoff game, against defending champion Liberty City. Coaches Dre, Streeter, and A.D. all pay separate visits to Frankie's row in Scott Homes to try to persuade his mother that practice is the best place for him to be. Sometimes she says Frankie is sick, other times that he's being punished for poor behavior in school. "She says that," spits Darrell Greene, "then we see him outside playing on the street. Man, I give up on Frankie."

At practice the Friday before the first round of playoffs, Dre cannot mask his disappointment at Frankie's absence. He recalls how he first saw the boy back in August, playing on the railroad tracks while the team practiced. Not knowing anything about Frankie's talents, the coach persuaded him to join the team and paid the entrance fee out of his own pocket. "Frankie breaks my heart," Dre laments, watching his offense run through a drill. "Every season I try to get through to all my players. But Frankie, I just can't get through to him. I tried to work with him. I tried to talk to him. But I can't break through."

Frankie doesn't show up for the contest against Liberty City, his first game-day absence all year. Before the coin toss, Dre gives the kicking duties to Ant Henderson, a wiry 9-year-old. To everyone's surprise, Ant converts after a Bulls touchdown, providing the winning margin in a close 8–6 game.

Needing just one more victory to reach the championship game, Gwen Cherry finally feels the loss of its regular kicker. This past Saturday morning, on a field slick with drizzle, Ant returns a punt 60 yards to give the Bulls a 6–0 first-quarter lead over the visiting Kendall Hammocks Chiefs. But his 2-point attempt sails wide left, and the missed conversion proves costly when Kendall scores its own touchdown minutes later and amazingly makes the kick, taking a lead it will carry into the last minute of the game.

Down by 2 and out of timeouts, Gwen Cherry manages to move the ball 70 yards to the Chiefs' 4-yard line. After Keith Holmes attempts a futile quarterback sneak up the middle, Dre frantically calls for a running play with less than ten seconds remaining.

Keith takes the snap and turns to hand off to Sammie Bush, but there's a miscommunication and the ball falls to the ground. As time expires, players on both teams scramble to recover the fumble, which squirts into the end zone. Somehow, amid the tangle of legs and shoulder pads, Sammie spies the bouncing pigskin and falls on top of it.

"Everyone on both teams was just standing there looking at him," Coach Dre will later recall. "Everybody was quiet. Finally, after maybe ten seconds, the ref threw up his hands."

Touchdown: Bulls win, 12–8.

Sammie, mobbed by frenzied Bulls, breaks into tears. Dre and A.D. leap onto the pile. As Charlie Brown tries in vain to keep fans from hopping the fence to join the fray, the Kendall Hammocks players slump off the field dragging their helmets on the grass. The 80s remain in the end zone to bring in the 110s, who are about to face Liberty City. Clapping, laughing, still crying with joy, the Bulls break it down. Blue and gold, rolling to the Super Bowl.

My Body, My Weapon, My Shame

ELWOOD REID

Elwood Reid vividly depicts the physical devastation caused to his body from a season of Big Ten college football in "My Body, My Weapon, My Shame."

The pressures placed on a young man first by his father, then by coaches and teammates, and eventually by himself were enough to justify risking his physical well-being. His body is both his greatest weapon and his biggest liability. He learns to use his size and physical gifts to their maximum potential while at the same time betraying his body in ways that will cause him pain for the rest of his life. In accepting the goals that others have set out for him, Reid accepts a physical pain and mental anguish that are usually hidden under a helmet and face mask. The greatest gift he receives is his body's eventual refusal to participate in the charade.

"My Body" is also a look at the unseemly byproducts of the entitlements given to the young men "lucky" enough to play big-time college football.

I did bad things for football. Because I could. Because I was 19 years old, weighed 270 pounds, had 5 percent body fat and had muscle to burn. Forget touchdowns, I played football for the chance to hit another man as hard as I could—to fuck him up, move through him like wind through a door. Anybody who tells you different is a liar.

There is the fear that any hit may be your last. That some bigger, stronger, better player will come along—take you down to the turf and end your career with the snap of bone or the pop of an anterior cruciate ligament.

The moment of impact goes like this: you slam helmet-first into another person's back until you can hear the air whoosh out of his lungs. Or better yet—you ram a forearm so hard into his throat that the crunch of cartilage and the fear in his eyes give you pause. Time stops. No pain, only a sucking sound as the physics of the impact sort themselves out—who hit whom first, angle, shoulder, mass, helmet, speed, forearm. Silence follows the cruel twist of limbs as the pain rushes in the way oxygen blows through the streets of a fire-bombed city, leaving flame in its wake. The pain is good. Both of you know it, and for a few precious seconds the world has order. Hitter and hittee. Motherfucker and motherfucked.

I came by football through my father. I played because if you were big, it was what you did in Cleveland. To do anything else was to be soft or queer. As long as I could hit and tackle, nobody made fun of my size. I played football, and that was all you needed to know about me. Then there were the men—the coaches who demanded a single-minded intensity from me each time I strapped on the pads. Even then I knew these were men who kept basements full of plaques and trophies from their glory days, collected beer steins and fell into deep depressions when the Cleveland Browns lost or their wives bore them daughters instead of sons. Their solution to everything was to hit harder. The word was forever on their lips. They scrawled it on chalkboards and spat it in my face: *Hit. Hit. Hit.* They knew how to infect eager minds with the desire to someday play in the pros. And when one of these potbellied men screamed at me to kick ass, act like a man or gut it out, I did, because I wanted to believe that a sport or even life could be boiled down to a few simple maxims. I was big, and I could hit; therefore I had purpose.

In high school, my scrawny body filled out as I moved from junior varsity to varsity and then to captain of a mediocre football team. College scouts came to time me in the forty-yard dash, watch me lift weights and eye me coming out of the shower as if I were a horse they might someday bid for at auction. I can't say I didn't enjoy the attention, but I began to realize that as a potential college-football recruit, I was expected to behave like one. I had to shake hands and look scouts in the eye and thank them for coming to see me. I had to talk sports, tell them who my favorite players were, what team I liked in the Super Bowl. I had to be smart but not too smart. Grades mattered only because colleges like "no risk" players, guys who can be recruited without the worry that they'll flunk out. I couldn't tell them that I didn't care who won the Super Bowl, that what really mattered to me was books. That when I finished *One Flew Over the Cuckoo's Nest* or *Heart of Darkness,* my heart beat faster than it ever had on the football field. I knew that I had to keep this part of me hidden and let the scouts and coaches see the bright-eyed athlete they wanted to see.

Pursuing a football scholarship became a full-time job. Everything I did was for my body. I ate well, went running at night, swallowed handfuls of vitamins, swilled gallons of protein shakes and fell asleep rubbing sore muscles. Everything fell away as I focused on using this body I'd nurtured and cared for, asking it to come back day after day, stronger, better. And it did. Even after the most tortuous practices, my body responded by snapping back, fresh and ready to go. If there were limits, I had yet to find them.

On the field, I plugged my heart in, throwing my body at tailbacks with reckless abandon. I went both ways and loved every minute of it—reveling in the sheer exhaustion that came every fourth quarter, when it was all I could do to hunker down into a three-point stance and fire out. To be better than the man lined up across from you was to summon your body to do what it didn't want to do—what it would normally resist doing off the gridiron. Great ballplayers are full of hate and a kind of love for what they are capable of inflicting on another man. And in between whistles, I hated.

When the first recruiting letter arrived, I had this feeling that I was standing on the cusp of what I imagined to be greatness. I saw television, cheerleaders and, I suppose even then, the endgame—the NFL.

"This is a great opportunity," my father said, holding the letter in his hands as if it were alive.

I nodded, knowing that the ante had been raised. I was no longer playing because I liked to hit but for the chance to get out of Cleveland and escape the factory-gray fate that awaited me.

I escaped by signing a letter of intent to play ball for one of those Big Ten colleges, where football is king, the coach is feared and anybody wearing a letterman's jacket is instantly revered. I felt important, my head swirling with the possibilities that seemed to shimmer before me. I had worked hard; my friends had gone out drinking or had sat around watching television, but I'd been running and lifting. Now I felt as if I had been rewarded and everything would be O.K.

That was ten years ago, and what I did both on and off the field for football is preserved forever in the aches, pains and injuries that haunt my body, lurking no matter how many aspirins I chew or how early I go to bed.

When I report to freshman summer camp, there are thirty or so other new recruits sitting around a huge indoor practice facility. Some of them are bigger and stronger than me, guys with no necks and triceps that hang off their arms like stapled-on hams. The speedsters and skill guys, mostly thick-legged black dudes with gold chains and shaved heads, pool over into their own corner, staring down at their feet as if the secret of their speed lay somewhere underground. The oddball white guys—quarterbacks, tight ends, and a few gangly-looking receivers—find one another and talk like bankers, in slow, measured tones.

I make my way over to the group of big guys who stand, shifting foot to foot, in a loose semicircle, until the coaches walk in and everybody snaps to attention. I am relieved to find that they look like all the other coaches who have ever yelled at me or offered arm-swinging praise. They are the very same gray/white-haired men, swaddled head to toe in loud polyester, I've been trying to impress my whole life.

Nobody says a word. Instead, the coaches stand there looking at us the way a mechanic eyes his socket wrenches, as tools to be picked up, used and thrown aside. There is only this simple equation: as a ballplayer, I am expected to do as I'm told, lay my body on the line or else get out of the way for somebody who will. Everybody in the room knows and understands this and, when asked, will put himself in harm's way with the dim, deluded hope that he will come out the other end a star.

The speech begins, and it's like every other coach's speech, only this time the coach spouting the platitudes owns our bodies and our minds for the next four years, five if we redshirt. He lays down the rules—the same rules I've heard all my life about what I can and can't do—about how we're here to win and anything less is simply unacceptable.

Then his theory of football: "Domination through hard work, men," he says, his short body quivering with anger. "More hard work until we come together as a team of men focused on one thing: *winning*. Am I understood?"

"Yes, sir," we answer.

"Good then," he says. "I'll accept nothing less than smash-mouth, cream-them-in-the-ear hole football. That is why you are here, and I will not tolerate softness or excuses. You are here because we think each of you will someday become a ballplayer. You are not yet ballplayers, but if you do what we ask, you will become ballplayers, and for that you are lucky."

All thirty of us grunt, "Yes, sir."

Then this no-neck guy, his face swollen with fear and desire, leans into me and says, "I wish we could skip the bullshit, strap on the pads and sort out who's who."

My first inclination is to laugh, to tell him to relax. Instead, I lid my eyes and clench my jaw and tell him that yes, that would be good, that I too like to hit.

Coach finishes his rah-rah speech, and the air is heavy with anticipation as the realization washes over everyone in the room that all of the lifting and running has come down to this—the chance to prove ourselves by putting our bodies on the line with guys who are every bit as strong and as fast.

Then we're marched off to the training room, where a team of doctors pokes and prods us as if we were cattle heading to market. By the time we're through, everybody has a nickname: Fuckhead, Slope, Rope, Sith, Crawdaddy, Pin Dick, Yo Joe, Hernia, Bible Boy, Vic, Napalm, Six-Four, Too Tall, Dead Fuck, Flat-Ass Phil, the Creeper, Revlon. Somebody tags me with Sweet Lou Reid because before every practice I listen to "Coney Island Baby."

On our first day of padded practice, the line coach, a man with steel blue and gray hair, cold eyes, and a hatchet nose, marches us over to a row of low metal cages. "Get into a three-point," Coach says as he lines us across from one another on opposite sides of the cages.

I hunker down, straddling one of the boards, and look out at the man in front of me.

"*Hit!*" Coach screams.

And with a blast of his whistle, my college football career begins. We hit and fall to the ground, fighting and spitting until he whistles us back to attention. We line up and do it over and over. After ten minutes, I am bleeding from three different places, my arms are numb, and my right thumb hangs from my hand at an angle I know is wrong. But to stop and go to the sideline is to pussy out. So I play through the pain, and after a few more hits I don't care what happens to my thumb.

The rest of practice takes place in five-second bursts, until our pads, wet with blood and sweat, hang on us like second skins. Everything is done harder and faster. Fights break out without warning. Two long-armed D-backs start swinging at each other, and the coaches let it go until the taller one splits his hand on a facemask. Blood flies from his smashed paw as he spins around like some shoulder-padded Tasmanian devil. One of the coaches finally grabs him by the facemask and drags him to the sideline, leaving his opponent alone and bewildered, with nothing to do except join the huddle. Guys suffer knee injuries, pop hamstrings, tear Achilles tendons, while others just go down with silent, allover injuries that are the same as quitting—telling the team you can no longer take it. During the first week, nine walk-ons clear out their lockers and quit.

We learn to live with injuries and spend what little free time we have complaining and scheming about our positions on the depth chart. Hernia has a bruise he can move up and down his forearm. Bible Boy's knee is fucked, and my shoulder slides in and out of place so much that I no longer notice it. All of us have scabbed-over noses and turf burns on our shins that crack and fill our shoes with warm blood the minute practice starts.

After practice and a shower, I stand in front of the mirror and stare at the road map of bruises, cuts, and mysterious pink swellings. I touch each bruise, scrape, and swelling until I feel something, and I know that my body is still there, capable of doing what I ask of it.

When the upperclassmen report to camp, we become their tackling dummies. Even the coaches forget about us and concentrate on the home opener four weeks off. I'm moved from defense to offense because my feet are too slow and my "opportunities," Coach says, are better on the other side of the ball. He tells me that offense is the thinking man's side of the ball, that it is about forward motion and scoring.

I adjust, and within a week I become an offensive lineman. Every day is the same grind—the same flesh-filled five yards on either side of the ball, where we grunt, shove, kick, and gouge at one another. In the trenches, success is measured in feet and inches, not long touchdown runs or head-over-ass catches that bring crowds to their feet.

After three weeks, I begin to root for injuries. Not only do I want the man in front of me on the depth chart to go down but I begin to look for ways to hasten his downfall. I am not the only one. More than once I see guys twisting knees in pileups, lowering helmets into exposed spines, gouging throats and faces with the hope that a few well-placed injuries will move them up the depth chart. The coaches seem to encourage this ballplayer-eat-ballplayer mentality, pitting starter against backup and watching as the two players wrestle and pump padded fists at each other long after the play has been blown dead.

But it is off the field that the real training happens, where I learn about how the team is not really a team. Offensive players hate defensive players. Linemen hate ball handlers because they get all the glory and half the aches and pains. It goes without saying that everybody hates the kickers because of their soft bodies and clean uniforms and the way they run warm-up laps out in front, making the rest of us look bad.

There is also a silent division between blacks and whites. Any white guy who hangs with the brothers and listens to their music is called a "whigger." Black guys who hang with the white guys are called "Oreo-cookie motherfuckers" or sellouts. In the locker room, when there are only white faces around, some guy will call a black guy who fumbles the ball or hits too hard in warm-ups a stupid nigger, and I know that I am supposed to nod in agreement or high-five the racist bastard. And when I don't, there is another line drawn.

But somehow it all comes together, and there are times when black and white, offense and defense, and even the kickers seem to be part of the same team, especially when practice is over and we're all glad to be walking off the field, happy to have seen our bodies through another day, united by our aches, pains, and fatigue.

I learn that among the linemen there are those who belong and those who don't. To belong means to go about the game of football grim-faced, cocksure of your ability to take any hit and keep moving. The guys who zone out on God, refuse the pack or are refused by it end up falling by the wayside, unnoticed by the coaching staff and their fellow players.

Then there are the guys who have already made it—broken out of the pack to start or platoon with another player in a starting position. Among the linemen, they are called "the fellas." Coaches love the fellas because they have proven themselves. But what really distinguishes a fella is not his success on the field but rather his ability to wallow in the easy gratification afforded any athlete at any university that is nuts for football. Everything is permitted—drinking, scoring chicks, fighting off the field—because he has survived the mayhem and the mindless drudgery of practices. I hear the stories over lunch or in the locker room after a workout: how to score with a woman nicknamed "the Dishwasher." How to persuade one of the brains or geeks to cheat for you. How to cop free meals at restaurants or free drinks at a bar. How to wrangle free T-shirts from the equipment manager. How to pass the drug test. And, most important, how to act like you don't give a shit, because you've got it coming to you.

We win our Big Ten opener, and for a few minutes in the locker room the air seems to vibrate with goodwill and camaraderie. Even I who have stood on the sideline getting rained on feel like a player as I listen to reporters question today's heroes. After the coaches leave, word that there will be a party at a fella's house percolates through the sweaty room.

When I enter the party, the room seems to be in some sort of drunken-action overload. Near the keg there is a makeshift wrestling pit, circled by grubby couches full of squealing teased-haired women who look at me briefly, decide that I am not a starter and look away. I am handed a beer and told to drink. My beertender is a huge, smiling defensive tackle named the Wall, who watches as I raise the cup to my lips and sip.

"What's a matter with you?" he says, pointing at the beer. "We've got beer and a roomful of chicks who want to fuck us 'cause we won the game. What more do you want?"

"I'm just a frosh," I tell him.

"Skip the *Leave It to Beaver* bullshit and drink," Wall says.

I nod, drain the cup and follow him to the kitchen, past heavily made-up groupies who stare at me now that I am with Wall. There are others, big guys mostly, and we keep pace with Wall, who tosses back beer as if it's water. After every round, somebody slops an arm around me or smacks me on the shoulder, and for a moment I feel the tug of the fella fraternity.

What happens next is what happens in varying degrees at every subsequent party. Fights erupt over women, favorite teams, etc. There is a girl in an upstairs bedroom handing out blow jobs or an underclassman who is too drunk and vomits before he is stripped naked and thrown out a window or tossed down the stairs.

I down half a bottle of Everclear grain alcohol when it is handed to me and let a sad-eyed chubby girl in tight jeans sit on my lap. As the liquor hits my brain, I realize that there are no victims here, even as I watch this girl get talked into going upstairs with three guys. Later I see her in the front yard, leaning against a lamppost crying, as several players throw empty beer cans at her and call her a whore. Everybody, including the skinny-shouldered engineering student and the jock-sniffing schlub with stars in his eyes whom we occasionally torture and torment, knows the deal and comes back for more. We have something they want, and they'll take anything we have—even the laughter and the cruel pranks—just to be near us, to wear one of our sweatshirts or to talk to us about the game. And it all seems so normal. When our starting defensive tackle rams a frat boy's head into a steel grate, not once but several times, there are no repercussions because he is a star and the team needs him. There are rules on the field and in the locker room when we are around the coaches, but off the field, anything goes.

And I do bad things because I want to belong. I hide the part of me that enjoys classes and reading in my room after practice. I know better, yet I find myself doing the same stupid shit I see others do, and nobody tells me that it's wrong. Nobody blinks when I walk into a party, pick up the first girl I see and pin her to the ceiling until her laughter turns to screams and then finally to tears. I put lit cigarettes out on the back of my hand to prove to the fellas that I don't give a fuck—that I am above pain, above caring what happens to my body, because I am young and I am a ballplayer and my body seems to have no limits.

At another party, I split a frat boy's nose for no particular reason other than that I am drunk and it feels like the right thing to do. He goes down, holding his nose, and I hop up on a thick oak banister, close my eyes and walk, not caring if I fall or if someone pushes me. When I do fall down two flights of stairs, I pop right back up, though my knee doesn't seem to be working, and there are several fraternity brothers closing in on me. Instead of running, I go outside and proceed to kick in the basement windows until I hear police sirens and escape into the snowy back yards. The next day, I am sober and ready to practice, and only at that point do I feel remorse. But then there is the first hit, and my body hurts, my joints crack, and I am absolved.

One night at a party during my sophomore year, I am asked by a fella if I want to help him videotape some girl giving head to a couple of guys in an upstairs room. I nod drunkenly and follow him through the forest of oversize flesh and dull-eyed groupies to the stairs, where he turns around and winks at me. For a moment, I'm not sure if he's joking or not. The music is loud—too loud. There are women playing quarters at a table to my right and guys staring at *Hustler* magazine on a couch in the corner, while several sophomores write their names with a permanent Magic Marker on the body of a passed-out frosh and discuss shaving his balls.

"You ready?" my guide asks. I can tell he's waiting for me to say no so he can call me a pussy or a Boy Scout. I look around at the monster bodies of ballplayers acting like children grabbing at boys, and I realize that I've finally become what the coaches and my fellow players have always expected me to become—a fella, a person living in a world of no consequence. I am not a star or even a starter; still, everything I do is acceptable, allowed and in the end . . . empty.

I look at the hulking player as he awaits my response. Part of me wants to go upstairs and rescue the girl, take her away. But I know she'd only be back next week, drunker and more willing, and I would be there, too, and maybe then, a few beers to the better, I'd say yes when asked if I wanted to help with the videotaping, because I could, because it is expected of me and because it is what a fella does.

I turn to go, but before I can get to the door, Fuckhead jumps on my back and screams, "Isn't this great?" I shake him off and toss him to the floor, tell him no and walk outside, feeling cold and hollow. But most of all, I feel simple and stupid, because I can't see a way out. if I quit, I lose my scholarship and go back home to Cleveland having failed. If I choose not to partake in the fun, there will be a line drawn and I will be exiled into the lonely world of those who practice but will never play or belong. That is my problem, that I want to belong at any cost. I still have the dream that someday I will become a starter, and the pro scouts will come to time me in the forty-yard dash and I will have a chance to go to the next level.

It starts with a tingling in my arm, one of a thousand jolts of pain that have run through my body that I no longer seem to notice. Only this time it doesn't go away.

I hear one of the coaches screaming, "Get up, Reid. Get the fuck up and get your ass back to the huddle."

Without thinking, I roll to my feet and try to shake it off. When I re-join the huddle, the coach glares at me and another play is called, and I line up, hit and do it again, the pain lingering in my spine. Then one morning I awake unable to raise my arms above my head. After swallowing a handful of Tylenol Threes and a few anti-inflammatories, I go to practice and hit. My arms dangle from my shoulders, bloodless and weak, forcing me to deliver the blows with my head and helmet. The coaches scream when I am slow to rise after the whistle. And when the pills wear off, the numbness is replaced by a hot poker of pain and a dull, crunching sound in my neck. After I miss a block, Coach sends me to the sideline and motions for the trainers to have a look. I explain and point to my neck as they walk me to the training room. It is the longest walk of my life, and no one even turns a helmet in my direction. In the train-ing room, I am told to lie still while the trainers pull my pads off and wrap ice bags around my neck.

I sit the sideline for a full week. No one except the trainers and the team doctor says a word to me, and it's all right, because for once I am outside looking in at the football machine as it whirs and clicks along without me. But by the end of the week, I want more than anything else to peel the ice bags off my neck and shoulders, strap on pads and prove that I'm still one of them. I think that this time it will be different, that I can hit and go about the game I've played and nursed my body for without acting like one of the fellas off the field.

So when the team doctor works his way up my arm with a safety pin, poking my flesh and asking, "Do you feel this?" I say, "Yes."

"And this?"

Yes, yes, and yes. Although I have no idea where or if he is poking me. He plays along with the charade. There are no X-rays, only ice and pills that make my head feel like it's stuffed with cotton. After the pain has subsided, I am put on a cycle of cervical steroids and must report to the training room twice a day to have my blood pressure monitored.

In a week, I am back on the field, and everything falls into place. My legs move and my body goes where it's directed, but the pain won't go away. I imagine a rotten spot in my spine, a cancer I want to cut out. My body learns to hit all over again, making small adjustments in some vain hope that the injury will go away and with it the nerve pain that seems to lurk after every collision.

Instead the pain gets worse, and most nights I'm back in the training room with the other gimps, begging for ice and more pills that I hope will somehow allow me to hit again. Nobody questions the toughness of the guys who are hauled off the field with their knees turned inside out or the players who are knocked cold and can't so much as wiggle a toe. But I look healthy. There is no blood, no bone poking through skin, no body cast, no evidence that I am injured. I can walk and talk and smile, and in the eyes of the team the real problem is that I can't stand the pain.

I go another month, practicing when my neck will allow, sitting the sideline when it won't. Finally, I'm referred to a neurologist. This time there are tests: X-rays, CAT scans, an MRI, and an EMG. When a nurse pumps two needles into each of my arms, telling me my mouth will taste like I have a spoon in it and that I'll feel nauseous, I smile, happy to have the pain and the sickness so controlled.

As I stare into the fluorescent lights with the taste of metal in my mouth, I know that something in my body has given out, that I somehow deserve this for not wanting to be a fella.

When the tests are over, I am not allowed to see the results. "We'll have them sent to the team doctor," the technician tells me.

"Am I O.K.?" I ask, wanting this guy in a white smock with his needles and nurses to tell me that I'm all right—that I'll have my body back. But I know that I'd only throw it away again, out on the field, to prove that I am one of them.

Instead, there are other tests, more pills, and a neck brace. I start going to the parties, watching the fellas go about their fun, envious of what their play and performance has earned them. To prove to the fellas and myself that I still matter, I get drunk, head-butt walls, and stick needles into my numb hands, despite rational thoughts that tell me what I am doing is stupid. I am careful to inflict this abuse only on myself, to show them that the injury they can't see is real and I can stand even more pain than they can imagine. So I let someone push a stapler into my biceps over and over until my shirt turns red, and for a few precious minutes the fellas pay attention to me—one even shakes his head and calls me a "sick dog motherfucker." And I'm proud. The pain leaves, and my body feels like it used to—large, powerful, and capable of great things.

Then there is the morning, the staples still scabbed into my arms, the cigarette burns on the backs of my hands. But worst of all, there is the silent crunching in my neck and the dead feeling in my fingers. I stand in front of the mirror, staring at the smooth outline of my neck muscles, the slope of my shoulders. I know one thing: I no longer want to play football the way the best of them do—dying between whistles as if you are born to it and there is no other option. Still, when I'm called into the head coach's office and told that I can no longer play, I walk out of the room despising my neck, my body, and the fact that it will no longer have the opportunity to hit another man.

Some guys go through life feeding the athlete inside with weekend-warrior games of touch football, season tickets, tailgate parties, and war stories about what it was like to play. Athletes don't, as they say, die twice; instead, part of them remains 19 years old forever, with the body ready and willing to prove itself all over again. I had to kill that 19-year-old, the one who enjoyed being able to prove himself to the world with sheer brute force: hitting, taking, and not thinking.

After college I headed for Alaska to get away from football. I became a frame carpenter and spent my days pounding nails and lifting twenty-foot sections of wall until my back and neck shivered with pain and my arms went numb. Every time I went home sore, bruised and full of splinters, it felt good—punishment for failing at football and at being a fella. Work helped to kill the jock in me. Falling off buildings and being crushed by two-by-fours dropped by stoned Hi-Lo operators finished what football had started. There were days and even weeks when I couldn't pull myself out of bed. And I liked it, because for once I could see the end—somewhere, sometime I would no longer be able to use my body, and what would be left would be the guy who loved reading and talking about books.

Later I would work as a bouncer, a bartender, a grunt laborer, a truck dispatcher, and a handyman. When I needed money, I rented out my body to schizophrenia-drug-testing programs at a VA hospital. The drugs left me with waking aural and visual hallucinations for days. I thought I was Miles Davis and that I could hear ants crawling in the grass. There were other tests with needles and electric current and more drugs. I didn't care. I got paid for all of it and never once questioned why I wanted to do this to myself. But somewhere along the line, the jock in me died.

Now I'm a guy who used to play. I rise out of bed each morning to a symphony of cracks and crunches. I have pain from football injuries I don't remember. My shoulders still slop around in their sockets if I don't sleep in exactly the same position every night. Sometimes my neck and back lock up without warning, and I fall, and I'm reminded that I did bad things for football and it did bad things to me. It left me with this clear-cut of a body, a burned-out village that I sacked for a sport.

I Hate the Dallas Cowboys

BILL CONLIN

The New York Yankees, the Los Angeles Lakers, and the Dallas Cowboys. In the world of pro sports, no teams engender as much hatred as these.

That they are marquee members of their respective leagues makes no difference to those who would just as soon see their charter flights face-plant into a grassy field somewhere. And that their consistent excellence and numerous championships have brought great pride to their fans only make them more distasteful. Their flamboyant stars, cocky owners, and apparent disdain for anything less than perfection set off the collective gag reflex in their less successful competitors—which, of course, is basically everyone else.

Bill Conlin's light-hearted "Why I Hate the Dallas Cowboys"—at least I think it's light-hearted—is the personification of the most well-cultivated of emotions: sports hatred. And it's all the more pertinent when considering Conlin has been a columnist for a hometown newspaper of the Cowboys' longtime division foe Philadelphia Eagles for over 30 years.

This short riff also cements a common sports theme—the blue collar challenger decrying the wealth of its overly polished nemesis. The visceral emotions this inequity engenders are the cornerstone of support from the overmatched hometown team's fans, and it's a formula that has proved popular on the fictional level as well. Without the ugly, arrogant, undeserving champ, another of Philly's favorite sons, Rocky Balboa, would have been just another Rico Suave.

In sports, hatred is passed down from one generation to the next. When the object of derision is a real, shiny-uniformed band of pompous, coddled jerks that shows up to trounce the home team once a year, sports hatred can blossom like no other emotion. And if it's possible for hatred to blossom into something beautiful, then a Philadelphia Eagles fan's hatred of the Dallas Cowboys is truly a beautiful thing.

Philadelphians hate Dallas in the springtime, when it drizzles. We hate Dallas in the summer, when it sizzles. We hate Dallas in the winter, when it freezes. And above all, Philly hates Dallas in the fall, when the football team breezes. Oh, Jesus!

How do we hate the Dallas Cowboys? Let me count the ways. And the hatred that people of the Philadelphia persuasion—most of them bleak-out-looking, blue-collar nihilists—have locked in their hearts is much more complex that that of, say, Metroplex postal workers. I have heard that deep in the bowels of the main post office in Dallas—not far from Lee Harvey Oswald's last, gut-clutching stand—there is a therapy room for postal employees who feel they are ready to do the McDonald's thing. Or hijack a school bus.

I hear there is a wall filled with Dallas Cowboy mug shots.

Uptight certified-letter clerks and harassed operators of the constantly jamming sorting machines may check out a paintball-firing automatic weapon and blaze away. Whoever can put the tightest pattern on Michael Irvin wins a free weekend with one of the wideout's covey of self-employed models.

In Philadelphia, we have more creative therapy. The throwing-snow-balls-at-Santa-Claus thing has been vastly overrated. Actually, on that almost forgotten day in Franklin Field, the jolly old elf had been commissioned to circle the track at halftime and peg miniature footballs into the stands. Some of the footballs contained choice tickets to the next season's games. Alas, St. Nick had an arm like a Phillies outfielder. And when his attempts to reach the Franklin Field upper deck fell far short, the drunken denizens seated there let loose with a furious salvo of frozen missiles made possible by a recent snowstorm.

It was nothing personal. Just business, as they say in the barber shops, pizza parlors, and cheesesteak emporiums of South Philly.

The folks who threw snowballs at Santa represent the sunny side of Philadelphia's outer self—the smiling, generous child in us. They are the grinning free spirits who say, "Yo . . . Michael Irvin and Jerry Jones are sitting on the bench in preseason at The Ranch. Two Dallas Cowboys cheerleaders walk by on their way to practice. Irvin nudges his owner. 'Wanna fuck 'em?' he asks. Jerry Jones replies, 'Out of what?'"

On the flip side of that good-natured bonhomie is Ben Franklin's evil twin. It seems that for every Marian Anderson, Stan Getz, and Rocky Balboa we produce, Philly also breeds a Gary Heidnick, the Duncan Hines of cannibalistic serial killers.

And the most egregious example of this dark side came on a bright May day in 1985, when Philadelphia made a perverse kind of military history. In 1812 British men-of-war bombarded Fort McHenry, a minor military annoyance, with the unhappy side effect of inspiring Baltimore's Francis Scott Key to compose an anthem that invites the kind of pregame mutilation it deserves and almost always receives.

That was one bombing of American soil.

In 1941 a Japanese submarine surfaced and lobbed a few harmless shells at a coastal oil refinery in Southern California. Uncle Sam responded to this miniscule annoyance by herding hundreds of thousands of Japanese Americans into concentration camps, where most of them languished four long years. Hollywood committed an even more heinous crime: It made the John Belushi movie titled *1941.*

That made two bombings of American soil.

But until May of 1985, no American city had been bombed from the air. Certainly, no American city had been bombed by its own police department.

So listen up, Dallas Cowboys fans, this will give you just a little better feel for what we're all about than does snowballing Santa or booing unwed mothers on Mother's Day. It speaks more to our "Fire up the *Enola Gay*" toughness than does booing orphans who fail to find an egg in the Easter egg hunt, or even the way we practice booing, which is to stand on a bridge over the Schuylkill River and boo also-rans in the Dad Vail Regatta.

When a long confrontation between police and a back-to-nature cult called MOVE escalated into gunfire, the Philadelphia Air Force roared into action. A police helicopter dropped what was euphemistically called "an explosive device" on the roof of the MOVE row house. A bomb! Hundreds of gallons of fuel were stored in containers there to run the cult's generators, the city having long since cut off the utilities.

The MOVE members were pinned in the cellar by intense police sniper fire. The flames moved faster than Citizen Jones when he fired Tom Landry and Tex Schramm. A dozen cult members died and fifty-six row houses—an entire city block—went up in a raging conflagration.

So . . . Now that you know who you're fucking with, Cowboys, let's turn to football.

Six months before the MOVE incident the Cowboys flogged the Eagles 34–17, starting a four-game losing streak that knocked them out of playoff contention. Before that grim season began, the Eagles were all but in Phoenix, as cash-strapped owner Leonard Tose fought an unsuccessful rearguard action against the banks that held the notes on the team. Then former Philadelphian and current Miami luxury auto dealer Norman Braman rode to the rescue. Before the final game of the 1985 season, Braman fired Marion Campbell. And when he failed to hire young David Shula, son of Don, Braman hired crusty, irascible Bears defensive specialist Buddy Ryan. He was the architect of the vastly overrated "46" defense that worked so well when manned by All-Pros from a Super Bowl defense.

Before Buddy, true hatred for the Cowboys was more regional and historical than based on any particular incidents. In fact, Philadelphia fans were split into two factions when Ryan came along. Fans who remembered Pearl Harbor were old enough to appreciate the brilliance of the Eagles teams that won NFL titles in 1948 and 1949 after losing the title game in 1947. That seminal era finally came to an end in 1960, when the Eagles beat Vince Lombardi's Green Bay Packers on the Jell-O pudding gridiron of Franklin Field.

As Buddy Ryan began his blustering career with a braying radio show on a new all-sports radio station, WIP, the graybeards were opposed by a new breed of "passionate" follower, to borrow a talk-radio buzzword. These people were destined to be the infantry in the one-way but bitter trench warfare against the hated Cowboys. They wore the ugly green apparel that the NFL had begun to market, tailgated relentlessly, and either puked or peed in every cranny of befouled Veterans Stadium.

And as the creativity of their delinquency matured, they would pelt the reviled Jimmy Johnson—not Santa Claus—with lethal iceballs, not fluffy snowballs.

Buddy Ryan's disdain for the enemy orchestrated their peevish ire just as surely as Eugene Ormandy's baton pulled soaring crescendos from the string section of the Philadelphia Orchestra.

For this younger, harder-drinking, decidedly blue-collar season ticket holder, there was no NFL before Super Bowl I. Nothing happened until the Voice of God, ubiquitous Philadelphia TV news personality John Facenda, turned the "frozen tundra" of Green Bay into a religious shrine. And looking at their beloved "Iggles" through that flawed prism, they agreed that the Eagles' modern era began on the great, getting-up afternoon of January 11, 1981.

Lined up on the other side of the ball on the Eagles' first possession of the NFC title game on a brutally cold 20-degree day were Landry's lordly Cowboys. They were favored to win the game even though the Eagles won the division and had the home field advantage throughout the playoffs. But Wilbert Montgomery, the Birds' popular workhorse, slashed through a gaping hole, cut back, and raced untouched for a long touchdown. The air rushed out of the benumbed Cowboys, who collapsed like an overbaked soufflé. The 20–7 victory took the Eagles to the Super Bowl. Few remember the flat effort that caused them to be gangplanked in New Orleans by the wild-card Oakland Raiders.

When today's character-assassinating WIP hosts ask callers to name Philadelphia's all-time sports moment, the inevitable winner, cleats down, is Wilbert Montgomery's run in a penultimate game.

That it happened against the Dallas Cowboys has come to mean everything.

By 1986 Landry's Cowboys were deep into their Decline and Fall of the Roman Empire imitation. Buddy Ryan split with the Fervent Fedora. Same result in 1987, but with a huge difference. . . .

There was the bitter players' strike. In Philly, Ryan remained loyal to his picketing players and treated the scabs like, uh, scabs. In Dallas, Landry signed the best replacement team available, looking for an edge. His strike-breakers flogged Ryan's brutally bad pseudo-Iggles, 44–21.

The luck of the schedule had the Eagles and the Cowboys playing again the first Sunday after the strike ended. With the game safely won and nothing more required of quarterback Randall Cunningham than to take a knee, Buddy orchestrated this: Cunningham faked taking a knee, sprang up, and threw a touchdown pass for a 37–20 victory.

That began an unprecedented run of Eagles victories over the Cowboys, who did not bottom out until Jimmy Johnson's 1–15 debut. Philadelphia beat the 'Pokes 24–23, 23–7, 27–0, 20–10, 21–20, 17–3, and 24–0. Ryan had been replaced by Rich Kotite in 1991. The highlight of his 24–0 victory were nine—count 'em—sacks of rookie coach Jimmy Johnson's quarterback, Troy Aikman.

In the 700 level of Veterans Stadium, life was good. The polyester green jackets felt like imported silk, the beer tasted like Dom Perignon, and the hoagies could have been croissants filled with wafer-thin carpaccio and brie.

And this became the new problem. As the Eagles' fortunes under Kotite slowly eroded and Johnson began leading the Cowboys to Super Bowls, the fans expected—no, demanded—Dallas to hate them back.

They thought the first thing that fans of America's Team did in the week leading up to an Eagles game was wake up and immediately reach for the phone to call Norm Hitzges and rip the hated Eagles. Instead, Cowboy fans reached for what they usually reached for. Then they smoked a cigarette and breakfasted on yogurt and Raisin Bran.

To this day it infuriates Iggles fans that no matter how hard they hate the Cowboys, their demented dudgeon is simply not shared in the town where, on a clear day, you can see the flames from the Branch Davidian's complex in Waco.

Philadelphians, so proud of their colonial heritage, Quaker thrift, and record of having lost more baseball games than any major league city in history, came up empty on the anorexic history of Dallas, Fort Worth, and Irving—named for 1897 deli owner Irving Crockett.

Were it not for the invention of air-conditioning, Dallas would have remained a dusty rail hub for the transport of cattle, a place for ranchers to sow their wild oats, barley, and other more nutritious seed at the kind of watering hole Jack Ruby was running when he avenged Jack.

Modern Dallas was settled by outsiders with clean fingernails. The image-conscious football team put together by Schramm and Landry, with help from a computer-pioneering personnel director named Gil Brandt, was perfect for a population on the move. They even needed the paradox of the pious Landry juxtaposed against the bawdy image set forth by former Cowboy wideout Peter Gent in *North Dallas Forty*. The real Cowboys were a lot closer to the transgressions of a wide range of sinners and the porn classic *Debbie Does Dallas*. Before Michael Irvin and Erik Williams, there were Lance Rentzel and Hollywood Henderson. And many, many others.

The hate of Iggles fans for their Cowboys counterparts has never been reciprocated. When the Iggles were enjoying their modest run of success under Buddy Ryan, the Cowboys were in a protracted down cycle. Everybody was whupping up on them. It is not as if Philadelphia was performing some great football feat.

Then when Jimmy Johnson turned it around, the Eagles were heading south under Rich Kotite.

WIP's mavens of misery keep flogging the dead horse, however. There is a morning drive-time zombie named Angelo Cataldi, a sterile Howard Stern who was once a solid football writer for the *Philadelphia Inquirer* before WIP part-owner and former Eagles great Tom Brookshier pointed him toward his $500,000-a-year destiny.

Twice more this year, and, hopefully, for the sake of the nineteen-to-forty-five male demographics, a third time in the playoffs, Cataldi and the spear-carriers who follow him through the day will fan the fires of hatred for America's Team. On a weekly TV panel show he moderates, Cataldi, who combines the gauntness of Ichabod Crane and the schnozz of Cyrano de Bergerac, will whip his T-shirted and green-jacketed audience to a frenzy, using all the communications skills that go with a master's degree from the Columbia School of Journalism.

In Dallas, however, where they killed our President with a magic bullet, the fans look beyond the Eagles. Or look back, depending on the schedule.

What concerns real Cowboys fans is not the dog-ass, canned-beer-swilling, cholesterol-mainlining, ugly-woman-marrying Iggles fans who keep calling Norm during the week.

No, it is the Washington Redskins that matter in Dallas. The Redskins and the annual game where they whip the Green Bay Packers' butts. Even the Giants are bigger than the ho-hum Eagles.

How 'bout them Iggles? Just more lumps of reeking roadkill on the freeway to Texas Stadium.

The Gipper and Other Whoppers

SALLY JENKINS

I've always found it funny when a stereotype proves to be a reality—the fat person inhaling a Big Mac, the person who looks like their dog, etc. In a world where the PC police have sanitized society, I still got a guilty laugh noticing that the pimp who worked the street corner by my old apartment wore an entire Zale's catalog worth of gold and constantly had some sort of dead animal draped over his shoulders, no matter how hot the oppressive Atlanta summers got. He may have broken the occasional law, but at least he's "keeping it real."

Sally Jenkins's take on the male football fan, "Men will be boys: the modern woman explains football and other amusing male rituals," is a romp through stereotypical male obsessions that have proved amusingly true for years. Her tongue-in-cheek exploration of the sociological development of the male psyche on the path to obsessive football fan is frighteningly funny in that it's frighteningly true.

That someone—and a female someone, at that—might be wary of these whoppers is disconcerting. And that she's willing to share her suspicions with other members of her gender is downright horrifying. It should be against the rules. I can't help thinking that such an unmasking might somehow lead to the downfall of society. Since I'm no longer required to hunt and gather, how can I assert my physical dominance? Stories, that's how. And since very few people can remember what happened in my distant past as an athlete, no one will notice if I embellish a little now and then for emphasis, right?

Well, Sally Jenkins has exposed us all, and it's apparent that I'm just another living, breathing, embellishing stereotype. It's just that I'm not so sure this one is all that funny . . .

Behind every major disappointment is an unreasonable expectation. And behind every unreasonable expectation is a fairy tale.

There's going to be a man, they tell you.

A man on a horse.

A white horse.

Not a tan one. White.

Not ivory, or bone, or ecru.

White.

If it's a tan one, don't go near it. Don't touch it, don't pet it, don't feed it.

As women grow older, we move into the more elaborately constructed illusions.

There will be a man in a uniform.

With a helmet.

And cleats.

He will have broad shoulders, a tapering waist. From fibula to scapula, perfection.

These fantasies, of course, lead to permanent disenchantment. They all go up in smoke the first time a charm boy holds his cigarette lighter to your heart in high school.

It turns out the guy on the horse won't commit. To anything. He might commit to breakfast or to the Jets game. But that's it. One thing he's definitely not going to commit to is reading you the love poems of John Donne.

He's going to read the paper.

And then he's going to the Y to play pickup.

There is a major misconception going around that women invented fairy tales. Wrong. Guys made them up for the specific purpose of sidetracking us. Guys invented Prince Charming fairy tales to preoccupy and subdue women, so that they could play football. Football is the male version of *The Slipper and the Rose,* a shameless exercise in athletic grandeur and other things that we strident feminist types call Gender Traps.

Guys think that if their team wins, then they've won the Big Contest. Win the game, and they drink the best beer. *All* the best beers. Also, they get the best girl. *All* the best girls.

They get a signing bonus. And they get a giant house on its own cul-de-sac. With a swimming pool, a water slide, a Nerf basketball hoop, a billiards table, a wet bar, several big-screen TVs, and not a single bookshelf. A big sign on the front lawn says: GAME OVER. I WON.

And that's just if they win the pickup game.

If they win the Orange Bowl, they get a million dollars, minimum, and if they win the Super Bowl, they get a million-trillion dollars.

Guys believe this, even when they are fifty-five. They still regale you with stories about their athletic feats in the park that afternoon, as if a recruiter is going to ring the doorbell at any moment and offer them scholarships to USC. The reason they are so fervent in their sports fantasies is because they, unlike women, have never been disenchanted.

Women are disabused of their fantasies early on in life. Shortly after our high school boyfriends turn out to be emotional arsonists, we learn that there are things called Domestic Chores, and every babe has to do them, not just Cinderella. No matter how successful a babe becomes, she still has to clean up after someone. Unless she is born with the last name of Radziwell, Grimaldi, Von Bulow, or Cushing. Women with Pamela for a first name also tend to get off.

Whereas guys go on to ever-higher stages of fairytaledom.

This is what all guys think: "I could have played this game if I hadn't blown out my knee."

A quick review of the Disney film library shows that guys made up fairy tales. Disney is how small boys and girls are indoctrinated in Western society. It is the first stage in their intellectual development.

Bambi No mother. Father stud of the forest.

Pinocchio No mother. Two father figures in Gepetto and Jiminy Cricket.

Peter Pan No mother. Doesn't want to grow up. Abducts young woman and makes her sew.

Aladdin No mother. Fortune-hunting tendencies. Likes Princess Jasmine's dough, castle.

The Lion King Has a mother, but he ditches her. Dad's ghost guides him.

Snow White Virgin beauty stalked by evil queen, freed by studly you know who.

Cinderella Evil stepmother. Evil stepsisters. Only hope is studly prince.

Beauty and the Beast No mother. Love interest is a beast, who beneath his beastly getup is a—that's right—studly prince of a guy.

The Little Mermaid No mother. Evil octopus Ursula. Only hope is a studly trans-species prince.

Pocahontas Largest-breasted active female on record.

The next stage in a young man's development is superhero cartoons with toy licensing tie-ins. One spin through Toys "R" Us and every four-year-old in America is certain that all men are built like Tron the Traitorous and are meant to participate in fiery extraterrestrial battles.

Take the Modern Woman's best friend, Missy. One day her seven-year-old, Max, was assigned to draw a picture of Jesus in Sunday school. He really went to work, scrawling with purple crayons all over construction paper.

Then he showed it to her. Jesus was built like something out of a Van Damme movie. Plus he had all this gear.

"What's that on Jesus' belt?" she asked.

"That's his gun, Mommy," he said.

Missy, thinking they were raising a postal office sniper, asked her husband, Bill the Thrill, to spend a little extra time with kid. So the Thrilling One did. And then she overheard this conversation.

"Dad, what's grosser, boogers or snot?"

"Boogers," Bill said.

"Why?" Max asked.

"Because you can throw them at people," Bill said.

After cartoons, guys graduate to buddy movies, war movies, and demolition flicks. At about six, Dad starts him with *The Fighting Seabees.* Women can't help noticing that there are no equivalent action-type movies for them. One thing that never changes in Hollywood's portrayals of active women is the lunatic sex element. Like Sharon Stone. How come she never plays an undercover agent freeing young American servicemen? Instead her character always has the moral sense of a light switch. She constantly plays kill-happy heiresses or harlots who keep their patience in their diaphrams. Nobody is getting it right, except for Susan Sarandon and sometimes Michelle Pfeiffer, who was pretty good as Catwoman in *Batman Returns,* a dark, sick girl with a body like a whip. "Batman threw me off a roof just when I was starting to feel good about myself," Pfeiffer said. Most active Hollywood females are just visions of nervous men. This is empowered? The convergence of taut muscle, spiritual numbness, and moral blindness?

It's not just Hollywood, either. There are exactly three statues of women in all of New York City: *Mother Goose, Alice in Wonderland,* and *Joan of Arc.*

Anyway, back to guys. A young man's education goes like this: 1) Disney; 2) Violent Weekend Cartoons; and 3) War and Demolition Flicks. Then comes the very last stage in a guy's intellectual development.

Lore.

A man is not fully grown until he has read all of the major sports biographies, as well as the Compleat Works of John R. Tunis and Tex Maule. Ask a guy how many Roosevelts have been President, and he will stare blankly ahead. Ask him how many Super Bowl rings Charles Haley has, and he will spring upright in his chair and say brightly, "Five!"

The Modern Woman has no interest in football lore. She's too busy holding her midlevel job with less pay and less chance of advancement than the modern guy, while also trying to raise two children and choking back her fear that Gilda the daycare center supervisor is a satanic cult worshipper who likes to smear naked little bodies with cat blood.

So when guys start humming fight songs and talking about what a model football is for good old American values and heritage, a siren sounds in the Modern Woman's head like the *"Dive! Dive! Dive!"* alarm on a submarine and a rage seeps into her brain.

Next thing you know, the guy is weeping while he sings the fight songs of schools he didn't even go to, like *On, Brave Old Army Team,* and *The Notre Dame Victory March.* He acts as though he personally sent in the game-winning call in the 1952 Rose Bowl.

A 1992 study at the University of Indiana showed that fans who heavily identify with sports teams regard the successes and failures of the teams as *personal* successes and failures.

Maybe that's why guys perpetuate so many tall tales around football. Heywood Broun noted in 1922 the similarity "between Harvard football and any story by O. Henry."

The problem with lore, as far as the Modern Woman is concerned, is that it is too easily co-opted by people like the Romans and the Nazis and the NCAA. Pretty soon everybody starts believing it and it takes the place of real history.

Give her the real goods.

The Modern Woman is always finding out fascinating little details guys have hidden from her while he was spouting lots of overblown pseudo-historical baloney. She wants a *true* story. For instance, what people from Penn State don't tell you about their famously plain uniforms is that the school colors used to be black and pink.

Their cheer was "Yah! Yah! Yah! Yah! Wish, Wack, Pink, Black!"

No one is more to blame than the Fighting Irish of Notre Dame for perpetuating several dangerous fables and outright whoppers when it comes to football. They are continually swamping the sport in sentiment and false idolatry. Former Fighting Irish linebacker Ned Bolcar used to get teary phone calls in his dorm room from distraught alumni, pleading for him to win for the Gipper. One night before a crucial game against Miami, the so-called outlaw school, Bolcar had to talk down a guy who was having a nervous breakdown right there on the phone. "Hey, man, stop crying," Bolcar said. "We'll win, okay? Just stop crying."

What confuses the Modern Woman is not that men are passionate about football, but that they translate their passions into such outrageous myths and then try to palm them off as truths. Perfectly intelligent men fall for the most obvious kinds of propaganda time and again. Women are more honest about the game. We don't fondly remember the lowest degenerate, simply because he could throw on the run.

Fabled football coach Bob Zuppke of Illinois admitted that a lot of the so-called heroes of the game were media creations. "Show me an All-American, and I'll show you a guy with weak opponents and a poet in the press box," he said. Even Walter Camp, father of modern football and the man who, along with Caspar Whitney, created the All-American team, regretted the hype that was beginning to swamp the game as early as the 1890s. "During the last two or three years, it has become overpopular with the public, and this craze has led it to assume an importance and prominence wholly unsought," Camp complained.

Women have an interesting immunity to the spin-doctoring that occurs around football. We have the capacity to be passionate fans without being fools about it. We do not idealize our sports heroes to nearly the extent that men do. You won't catch the Modern Woman bursting into tears just because she passes Chris Evert in the street. Joan Tisch notes that her husband, Bob Tisch, owns several business interests, the least of which is the New York Giants, but that's all his friends and associates want to talk about. "Not once has anyone said to us, 'How's the insurance business?'" she says.

Female memories are shorter. Not that that is always for the best. Recently, the Modern Woman called Gloria Steinem's office at *Ms.* magazine, hoping to talk to Steinem about the death of Bobby Riggs. A young woman answered the phone in her office.

"Who's Bobby Riggs?" the young woman asked.

Babes don't mind a certain amount of nostalgia. But they would prefer that the pedestals be lowered and the objects of reverence be the slightest bit deserving. When genuine character flaws are whitewashed as boyish foibles, it becomes impossible to tell the good guys from the bad.

When a myth gets busted, we're the ones who have to explain it to the kids.

So the next time the guy in the easy chair at home starts waxing lyrical about football, lay a few simple truths on him. Tell him to quit doctoring the past. We can't be spun.

A female reading of some of the taller tales in football:

the four horsemen of notre dame

The truth about Famine, Pestilence, Destruction, and Death is that they averaged five-foot-ten and at least one of them got somebody else to do his homework for him.

They should have been called Three Little Guys and a Real Scholar-Athlete. Their myth was popularized by sportswriter Grantland Rice of *The New York Herald Tribune,* who, after watching the Fighting Irish defeat Army by 13–7 on October 28, 1924, penned this outrageously overwritten paragraph:

"Outlined against a blue-gray October sky, the Four Horsemen rode again. In dramatic lore, they are known as famine, pestilence, destruction, and death. These are only aliases. Their real names are Stuhldreher, Miller, Crowley, and Layden."

Here's the real deal. Quarterback Harry Stuhldreher (five-seven, 151) of Massillon, Ohio, right halfback Don Miller (five-eleven, 160) of Defiance, Ohio, left halfback Jim Crowley (five-eleven, 162) of Green Bay, Wisconsin, and fullback Elmer Layden (six-even, 162) of Davenport, Iowa, were indeed great players, three of them consensus All-Americans, and the core of a national championship team. But they were also small even for the day and beneficiaries of Coach Knute Rockne's savvy public relations sense.

After reading Rice's story, Rockne had a student aide in charge of PR dredge up four plowhorses from the campus farm and pose the players aboard for a famed photograph that immortalized them.

Stuhldreher's classroom performance was recalled this way by Johnny Blood McNally, a star in the pros in the late 1920s and 1930s who spent a brief time at Notre Dame before he got kicked out for overindulging one St. Patrick's Day. "I always like to say that my one contribution at Notre Dame was that I used to write Harry Stuhldreher's English poetry papers for him," McNally said.

the gipper

Among the most famous inspirational speeches of all time was "Win one for the Gipper." Supposedly, when legendary halfback George Gipp of

Notre Dame was expiring of pneumonia in 1920, he made a dying request. According to that noted PR firm of Rockne and Rice, Gipp asked that he be baptized by a Notre Dame priest. After he took a communion wafer, he said, "Someday, Rock, sometime, when the going isn't so easy, when the odds are against us, ask a Notre Dame team to win a game for me—for the Gipper. I don't know where I'll be then, Rock, but I'll know about it, and I'll be happy."

According to Rockne, he used Gipp's words at halftime to inspire the Fighting Irish to break a 0–0 tie and go on to victory, 12–6.

But here's another account of the deathbed scene, told by *New York Daily news* writer Paul Gallico. Rockne held Gipp's hand and said, "It must be tough to go, George." To which Gipp replied, "What's tough about it?"

Gipp was a heavy drinker, womanizer, pool hustler, and inveterate gambler who wagered on Notre Dame games. At one point he was expelled, but Rockne pleaded his case to university officials to get Gipp readmitted.

Gallico claimed the truth about Rockne's halftime tearjerkers was that Gipp was no great fan of them. In 1920, when Notre Dame trailed Indiana by ten points at the half, Rockne tried to deliver a rousing speech, but about halfway through he realized Gipp was missing. Afterward, Rockne found Gipp standing at the back door.

Smoking a cigarette.

Gipp told Rockne not to worry, that he had $200 bet on the game. In the second half, Gipp scored two touchdowns.

walter camp

A bloodless, elitist Yalie and the game's first control freak. Walter Camp arrived at Yale as an undergraduate in 1876 and never really left. He dropped out of medical school in favor of a business career, rising to the presidency and board chairmanship of the New Haven Clock Company, which subsidized his passion: the formulating of arcane rules like the system of downs and set yardage and signal-calling. In three ponderous tomes, written in a relentlessly moralizing style, Camp was responsible for advancing the notion that football is a scientific game and based his coaching techniques on a corporate model. Men were cogs or "material" and coaches were autocrats. Camp said it was "entirely inadvisable" to let players know what the outcome of a play should be. He also advised "the whip and spur of continual, and in many cases extremely severe, criticism."

Michael Oriard points out that despite his cerebral posturings, Camp was hardly a civilizing influence. He championed the flying wedge, one of the more brutal tactics ever devised on a playing field. Football, Camp noted, was "an opportunity not afforded in any other sport for the big, overgrown fat boy."

A little-known fact about Walter Camp is that his wife, Allie, served as his de facto assistant coach. Camp had dropped out of Yale after a knee injury ended his football career in 1882 and spent most of his free time loitering around the Yale football field. When his bosses at the New Haven Clock Company objected to his spending afternoons at practice, Walter sent his wife instead.

Allie Camp would watch Yale workouts and scribble in a notebook. In the evenings, she would show them to her husband. Yale star Pudge Heffelfinger remembered that in the 1880s Allie Camp was an integral part of the Eli staff. (Heffelfinger was the first known pro football player, secretly receiving $500 on November 12, 1892, to play for the Allegheny A.A. against the Pittsburgh A.C.)

In John McCallum's book *Ivy League Football Since 1872,* Heffelfinger recalled: "In 1888, Yale actually had two coaches—Camp and his earnest young bride, Allie. They were newlyweds and Walter was sales manager in the New York office of the New Heaven Clock Company. His superiors wouldn't let him attend our afternoon practices, so he sent his wife to stand in for him. I can still see her pacing up and down the sideline, taking notes of our scrimmages. Walter kept in touch with our progress by reading her notebook. Then, several nights a week, some of the team would go over to the Camps' home in New Heaven for a review of strategy. Allie Camp could spot the good points and the weaknesses in each man's play."

the carlisle indians

The clapboard Indian school in Carlisle, Pennsylvania, was founded by a cavalry officer named R. H. Pratt in an abandoned military barracks as a supposed model of opportunity for young Native Americans. Its most famous graduate was Jim Thorpe. In fact, Carlisle offered only an eighth-grade education at best and its students were forced to hack off their hair, wear secondhand military surplus clothing, and work at menial jobs. "When it comes to educating the Indian, I am a Baptist," Pratt said. "I believe in holding them under until they're immersed." After a good cultural drowning, the Indian youths were then returned to the reservations, where their school experience became extremely problematic. They were shadowland people, not assimilated into either their native tribes or Anglo-Saxon society.

In 1891, a former Carlisle student named Plenty Horses murdered a U.S. cavalry officer, Lieutenant Edward Casey, during the ghost dance uprisings at the Pine Ridge reservation. At his trial, Plenty Horses explained that he committed the murder in an attempt to regain his standing with the Sioux people and "to wipe the stain of Carlisle" from him.

Despite its tiny student body, the Carlisle Indians managed to produce some of the greatest upsets in collegiate history, thanks to the coaching of Glenn "Pop" Warner. They had to fight not only the opponents, but referees who showed a decided bias and penchant for cheating them. In 1896, they lost three close games to Harvard, Princeton, and Yale on officiating calls. "We can beat eleven Yale men, but we can't beat eleven Yale men and a Yale referee," Warner complained.

the halftime pep talk

The uninspiring reality is that there is little opportunity for great oratory in the locker room. Rather, teams break up into squads and coaches make dozens of technical adjustments, drawing X's and O's on the chalkboard. "Speeches? Ha!" Dallas Cowboys coach Barry Switzer says. "You're too busy figuring out how to stop this, how to open up that. You're making all kinds of adjustments. Then it's time to go back out on the field. Nobody has *time* for speeches."

you have to be intelligent to play this game

Oh, yeah? Joe Theismann, a former Super Bowl quarterback for the Washington Redskins who is now a TV color commentator, was once asked what the level of intelligence in the NFL was. "There aren't a lot of Norman Einsteins out there," Theismann said.

And how to classify Joe Gibbs, Theismann's former coach? Joe Gibbs was a true football genius, winning Super Bowls with three different quarterbacks. "I considered college a waste of time, except for the people skills I learned," he said. "You learn more from competing in sports than you do sitting in class taking notes."

The author feels compelled to add this public service message to the male youth of America: Boys, only a minute percentage of all college players make it to the NFL. Joe Gibbs, who went to San Diego State, considered only one career alternative to football: stock car racing.

jesus loves you

Guys are always "God"-ing up football. They are always referring to the "cradle" of this and the "temple" of that when they mean Green Bay, Wisconsin, and South Bend, Indiana.

Women believe it is unseemly to apply religion to football. Frankly, such overdramatization is where all the trouble starts. The Modern Woman has been suspicious of prayer in the locker room ever since she read the following in a newspaper: "Gatherers of personal data claim they've found ways to determine what people pray for and that they now know that one out of every twenty-five prays for something bad to happen to somebody."

One year this sign appeared at the First Baptist Church in Fayetteville, Arkansas: FOOTBALL IS ONLY A GAME. SPIRITUAL THINGS ARE ETERNAL. NEVERTHELESS, BEAT TEXAS.

If the Modern Woman was God—a position she feels is not totally out of her range—and some guy took time out of her day to beg for a field goal when there were real wars and famines and such to attend to, it would make her want to wield her lightning bolts like cattle prods.

The Modern Woman feels she could get very good at smiting.

But here is what the Modern Woman really wants to know on the subject of religion and football, being a creature with natural leanings toward procreation: What does it mean to be born . . . again?

paul "bear" bryant

George Blanda once said of Bryant: "That must be what God looks like."

Actually, Bryant's means of winning were quite mortal. When he took over at Alabama, Bryant announced that he was on a five-year plan. "In the first year, a .500 season," he said. "Second year a conference championship. Third year unbeaten, and fourth year national champ."

"What about the fifth year?" someone asked.

"We'll be on probation, of course," Bryant said.

"winning isn't everything. it's the only thing."

Yes, Vince Lombardi said it. The Green Bay Packers coach became known as the General George Patton of football for that statement. But the truth is, he regretted it.

Later Lombardi remarked, "I wish to hell I'd never said that damn thing. I sure as hell didn't mean for people to crush human values and morality."

A Civil War: Army vs. Navy

JOHN FEINSTEIN

Feinstein recounts the pageantry and passion involved in the 96th annual Army-Navy football game in "A Civil War." Players attending America's military schools have not challenged the college football powerhouses for years, but the annual meeting between Army and Navy is seen by many as the epitome of amateur athletics.

A Civil War

S aturday dawned clear and sunny, the temperature climbing toward the mid-forties. Army–Navy games are often played in frigid, close-to-unbearable conditions. That would not be the case for this game, and the 12:08 kickoff meant there would be none of the torturous waiting around the hotel, counting the minutes, watching the clock.

This would be the last Army–Navy game on ABC for at least six years. CBS had won the rights to the next five games, and ABC had responded by scheduling not one but two other games to follow Army–Navy that day: Texas–Texas A&M and the Southeast Conference championship game (or as the ABC flaks liked to say: "The Dr Pepper SEC Championship Game").

And, just to show Army and Navy how they felt about their game, they assigned not their number one broadcast team, not their number two broadcast team, but their number three broadcast team to the game. The shame of that decision was that the number two team, Brent Musburger and Dick Vermeil, loved doing the game.

Musburger was often criticized for his hyperbolic nature and Vermeil tended to talk in coach-speak a lot. But they were the right duo for this game. Musburger had opened the broadcast two years ago this way: "There is no bowl at stake here. There is no coalition poll, no number one ranking. No Heisman Trophy is at stake either. This is bigger than all of that."

Exactly.

Vermeil had described the game in one sentence: "It's the only game you'll watch all year where eighteen guys will be on the ground on the opening kickoff."

Mark Jones would do the play-by-play and Todd Blackledge the color, with Dean Blevins on the sidelines. All were solid, professional announcers. All were working their first Army–Navy game. Each would come away wishing they could have the chance to do a second.

The teams' pregame routines were the same as they had been for ten weeks, except that Paul Johnson asked the seniors on the offensive unit to get up and speak to their teammates one last time during the offense's morning meeting.

Everyone talked about how much playing football at Navy had meant to them and how much they would miss being part of the team. Shaun Stephenson thanked everyone for making him feel part of the team even though his knee had limited him and he still hadn't caught a single pass. Brian Schrum thanked everyone for keeping him less busy. "Last year I punted seventy-two times," he said. "This year, I've only punted fifty-three. That shows how much you guys have improved."

The most impassioned speech came from John Moe, an offensive tackle who hadn't played a single down as a sophomore or a junior because of injuries and had come back to play a limited role as a senior. He would only play in this game if it turned into a rout.

"I am sick and tired of losing to these guys," he said. "I know I'm not really going to play a role today, so I'm asking all you guys to win the game so we'll all be able to walk away from all this as winners. I can't even stand the thought of losing to them again. Please, please go out and play like mother-------. It's the only way to win."

Moe was crying by the time he finished. He wasn't alone. Even Johnson, everyone's favorite curmudgeon, was a little bit misty-eyed. "I just want to find out about ringing this damn bell," he said, referring to the bell of the USS *Enterprise*—known on the Yard as the E-bell. Navy players get to ring the E-bell after a win over Army. No one in the room had ever had that pleasure. The room was quiet when Johnson finished. They all seemed to know that, unless they went to war someday, they would never again feel as close to a group of people as they all did that day.

The coaches spent a good portion of their pregame meeting talking about—what else?—the kicking game. Weatherbie asked everyone who they thought should kick. Wright went first, again saying he thought Vanderhorst could handle the pressure; that he had dealt with everything thrown at him during the week. He had gone to talk to Schrum again the previous evening to see how he felt since he was the one holding the ball for each of the kickers. Schrum said he liked Vanderhorst's mental approach, that it seemed as if none of this was a big deal each time he was asked to make a kick.

"It's going to be a lot bigger deal with 70,000 people watching than it was on that practice field," Weatherbie said.

A couple of the coaches pointed out that Covarrubias had kicked better near the end of the week. "Only after he thought he'd lost the job," Wright said. "The pressure was off."

Weatherbie nodded. "I agree with that."

It was the first time he had let his feelings show. All week he had been thinking that Vanderhorst should kick, but he didn't want to let anyone—even the coaches—know he felt that way because he didn't want their opinions swayed by knowing his.

They went through all the usual questions and answers. Johnson said he again planned to get McCoy into the game when the time was right but that Fay would play for at least the first few series because "I want to throw the ball around a little, loosen them up some." They had decided to go back to using Scornavacchi on punt returns. Mill might have more potential to break a long return, but being a plebe, he also had more potential for fumbling. "Can't give the ball up," Weatherbie said softly. "Not in this game."

Had he finally come around to the notion that this game was special? He shook his head and laughed. "It's special," he said. "But I still don't think it's as special as people want to make it out to be."

There was one other change that had to be dealt with. Scott Runyan, the receivers coach, hadn't been with the team all week because of the death of his father. Weatherbie had told him not to rush back for the game, to stay with his family as long as he was needed. That meant that Damon Dixon, who had been with the team all season as a graduate assistant coach, would be in charge of the receivers.

"Just stay with the regular rotation," Weatherbie told him. "I'll help you out whenever necessary."

Weatherbie was concerned about Stephenson. Even though the doctors had said it was OK for him to play, he was concerned about his ability to play on artificial turf, which has so much less give than real grass.

They broke up to go talk to their players one last time before boarding the buses. Todd Wright lingered in the doorway. "My gut really tells me it's Vanderhorst," he said one last time.

Weatherbie nodded. "So does mine," he said. Wright breathed a sigh of relief.

"I just hope," Weatherbie said as Wright left, "that both our guts are right."

The team buses arrived at the stadium at almost the same time that the march-ons were beginning. Navy, as the designated visiting team, went first, filling the playing field with blue and white. It was not yet 10 o'clock in the morning, but already the stands were beginning to fill up and a full-blown traffic jam was under way outside. Only at Army–Navy, because of the march-ons, is there more traffic two hours before kickoff than ten minutes before kickoff.

Many of the players on both teams walked down their respective tunnels—Veterans Stadium's locker rooms are set up so that the teams do not have to share a tunnel—to watch the march-ons. Some of them had participated in the past, some had not. It was an impressive sight, the entire student bodies—minus the football teams—marching onto the playing field in perfect precision, reaching their positions and then offering cheers: first one for the opposition, then one for themselves. The cheers for the opponent were just a little bit louder than a TV set sounds with the mute button on. The cheers for their own schools boomed through the stadium, off the empty seats, and back around again.

Weatherbie's pregame talk was similar to the other ten he had already given. He reminded them that this was their chance to do something special—produce a winning season—and told them that he had never seen a team more ready to play a football game than this one.

"All I want," he said, "is everything you got. Come back in here with nothing left."

Sutton's approach was a little different. He talked about desperation. "The most desperate team wins Army–Navy games," he said. "The effort will be there on both sides, we all know that. The question is, which team will be more desperate to win when it comes time to decide the game? I think this is the more desperate team."

Both teams were still in the locker room when the national anthem was played. Even though the sounds of the song were muted by the walls and the distance, they all stood and listened. In the Navy locker room, Mark Hammond felt himself choking up, knowing he wouldn't ever again listen to the anthem in a football uniform.

The Cadets came down the tunnel with Jimi Hendrix blaring in their eardrums, the music that last year's captains had chosen. Cantelupe and Davis had decided to stick with it. Conroy, who was more of a Sinatra fan when it came to music, loved hearing Hendrix on his way to the field. "There are times for Sinatra," he said. "And times for Hendrix. Football is Hendrix."

There was no music in the Navy tunnel. But as the players made their way to the field, they could hear their band at the far end of the stadium playing "Anchors Aweigh."

For some of the seniors, this was their last football game—but their first Army–Navy game in uniform. Stephenson and Ramon Vasquez had been on the lightweight team until this year. Moe had battled injuries. Billy Butler had played basketball for three years and Brad Snodgrass had played baseball before each came out for football as a senior. On the Army side, Conroy, Graves, and Tom Burrell—all of whom would start—had never played a down against Navy.

For Burrell, who had worked so hard to keep his head above water academically and as a football player, the whole scene when he got to the field—the packed house, the Corps of Cadets on one side, the Brigade of Midshipmen on the other—was overwhelming. "I had to get ahold of myself," he said. "It all hit me at once, that finally, after four years, I was living my dream to play in this game. I almost lost it before we even started playing."

Navy had one clear advantage right from the beginning: its sideline was bathed in sunshine; the Army sideline was already in shadows, and it was at least ten degrees colder as a result. Cantelupe and Davis walked to midfield to meet Thompson and Smith. The handshakes were warm, but there was no small talk. There would be time for that later. Smith, who always called the toss for Navy, called heads. It came up heads. It was the eleventh straight time Navy had won the coin toss in 1995. For the eleventh straight time, they elected to defer receiving the kickoff until the second half. Army would receive the kick and defend the west goal—the one at the locker room end of the field.

It was forty-one degrees in Philadelphia as Covarrubias teed the ball up to kick off. Veterans Stadium was completely full; not a ticket had gone unsold. On the message board, in the corner of the stadium, where the brigade was located, the series history was neatly summed up:

The 96th Meeting
Army—45 wins
Navy—43 wins
Seven ties

The only thing it didn't mention was that through those 95 games, the total point differential was a grand total of 54—Navy had the edge there. Fifty-four points apart after 95 games—a virtual deadlock.

Covarrubias's kick floated to Jeff Brizic at the five yard line. He got as far as the 16 before he was buried by a group of flying white shirts. Good start for Navy; poor field position for Army.

Army went into its grinding routine: Carpenter picked up three; Conroy went up the middle for four. That set up third-and-three at the 23. In the huddle, McAda called 54 option. He could give the ball to Conroy or pull it out and keep it himself. He took the snap and turned toward Conroy.

All the players had noticed during the practices the day before that the field was saturated after a week filled with rain. When they arrived on Saturday, the conditions were much better, but the field was still wet in spots—especially where the bases from the baseball field had been removed and covered over with new dirt that the turf was then placed over.

Coming out of his stance, Conroy slipped on one of those spots. As he fell forward, trying to catch himself, his helmet hit the ball, knocking it loose from McAda before he knew what had happened. In the blink of an eye, Andy Person, who had penetrated the backfield on the play, was on top of the ball.

The game was 71 seconds old and Navy had the first big break. It was first down on the Army 22. True to his word, Johnson came out "throwing the ball around." On first down, Fay looked deep for Cory Schemm in the end zone but just missed him. Undeterred, he ran a fake option on second down, dropped back, and found LeBron Butts wide open behind all the Army defenders in the end zone.

Touchdown. Vanderhorst trotted onto the field for the extra point. On the Army sideline, a lot of people wondered who number 78 was. They had never heard the name before. Vanderhorst easily kicked the point. No sign of jitters. Navy led, 7–0. The game was less than two minutes old.

"I thought, 'We're going to blow these guys out,'" Person said. "I really thought we were that much better than they were, that we were going to move the ball all day and the D would stuff them. It was probably a mistake thinking that. No one ever blows anybody out in the Army–Navy game."

Cantelupe was furious. This was exactly the kind of start he had worried about. They *had* gotten too laid back the day before and they had been sloppy, first on the fumble, then biting too easily on Fay's fake.

"That's it!" he screamed at his teammates. "That's all they get!"

The Army offense managed to pick up a first down on the next series but had to punt from the 39. Hughes calmly sailed a 41-yard punt to Scornavacchi on the 20. He tried to cut back to pick up yardage and was swarmed under by Al Roberts and Landis Maddox, two seniors willingly playing on special teams and playing as if their lives depended on it.

This time, the Army defense held and Schrum's punt was downed at the Army 48. With good field position, the Cadet offense finally got rolling. Abel Young picked up 19 yards on an option play to the 23. Then, on third-and-eight, McAda went back and looked, and looked. No one was open. Navy's coverage was perfect. Finally, just as he was about to be sacked by Hammond, he tossed a desperation knuckleball toward Young. Young reached for the ball, but it was over his head. He got a hand on it, deflecting it back to the middle of the field.

Graves had been running his route on the other side of the field. When he saw McAda in trouble, he broke his pattern and began looking for an open spot on the field. "When I saw Ronnie throw the ball, I thought, 'Oh boy, that's an interception,'" Graves said. "I just started towards it, hoping I could break it up and get the ball on the ground."

Instead, Graves saw the ball change direction and suddenly come right at him. He dove for it, just getting his hands underneath it as he fell, stretched across the six yard line.

The Navy bench couldn't believe it. They had played perfect defense and the result was a 15-yard Army pickup. On the Army side, Jack Hecker shook his head. "Can you believe that kid?" he said as Graves flipped the ball to the referee. "He always finds a way."

Not bad for the worst wide receiver in Army football history.

Three running plays later, Conroy pounded into the end zone from the one, and with 3:20 left in the first quarter, it was 7–7. The Navy defense came off the field angry, but not discouraged. "They needed a lucky play," Thompson screamed at his teammates. "Don't worry about it. It can't happen all day."

Inside, his thoughts were churning. Why, he wondered, did it seem the lucky bounces always went Army's way? When would Navy's lucky bounce come?

Neither team did much bouncing one way or the other until late in the first half. The most action was in the stands, where the corps, reacting to the news that twenty-four mids had been charged as a result of the NCIS drug investigation done after the LSD arrests in October, began chanting "Just Say No" in the direction of the brigade. The spirit leaders eventually convinced them to return to the more standard cheers.

Slowly, Army seemed to be taking control of the line of scrimmage on both sides of the ball. The Fat Men were opening holes for the backs and the defense wasn't giving up very much. When Johnson brought McCoy in, hoping for a spark, he carried on three straight plays and netted four yards. Schrum's fourth punt of the half was caught by Cantelupe at the Army 34. He picked up two yards before Galloway brought him down. There were no conversations about E-mail messages.

On the second play of the Army drive, Conroy blasted up the middle for 10 yards before Sean Andrews stopped him. As he was going down, Conroy felt someone come in from behind to finish the tackle and heard the dull "thwack" of a helmet hitting bone. A sharp pain raced through him and he came up holding his rib cage.

He walked slowly back to the huddle. "You OK?" McAda asked.

"Fine," he said. "Just a little stiff."

Two plays later, Conroy carried again, this time for a yard. Once again as he was going down, he felt a sharp pain. This time he had been nailed in the ribs on the other side. It wasn't as bad as the first hit, but now he felt stiff on both sides. Still, he played in the game. "It wasn't like I couldn't breathe," he said.

The ball was now at midfield and it was third and nine. On the next play, McAda, finding no one open, somehow scrambled away from what looked like a sure sack and took off down the sideline for 23 yards. First down at the Navy 27.

"Wrap him up!" Weatherbie screamed. McAda had dodged four different potential tacklers.

They picked up another first down at the 17. The clock was under three minutes. Conroy, sore ribs and all, got seven more on second down to set up first-and-goal at the six. But now Navy dug in. Hammond and Person, Bruce and Harris. They could all hear Dick Bumpas's voice in their heads: "You do *not* let their ass run the ball into the end zone."

Conroy got two before Harris wrestled him down. They tried Carpenter as a change-up and Hammond stepped into the hole and knocked him down at the line of scrimmage. Person, Hammond, and Bruce were all over the field throughout the game. Bruce, who had played against McAda in high school, would end up with 16 tackles. Hammond was double-teamed constantly, but still made plays. He had even engaged in the first—and last—trash talking of his college career.

When the Army offense came on the field early in the second quarter with excellent field position at the 40-yard line, Joel Davis was screaming at his teammates: "Here we go, right now, we're rolling them!"

Three plays later as the Army punt team trotted on, Hammond couldn't resist yelling at Davis as he and the Fat Men left, "Guess you aren't going just yet!"

Hammond shook his head later at the memory. "I don't know what got into me," he said. "Usually, I don't say a word. But there was nothing usual about this game."

His tackle of Carpenter for no gain brought up third-and-goal from the four. With 1:29 left in the half, Sutton wanted to talk before calling the next play. He called time and McAda trotted over. The call was 59 Volvo, a play-action fake to Conroy with tight end Ron Leshinski as the primary receiver in the corner of the end zone.

As McAda turned to go back into the game, Sutton grabbed his arm. "Don't force anything," he said. "If it's not there, throw it away or take the sack and we'll get three."

McAda nodded. Bumpas was thinking Army would pass and no one on the defense bought the play-fake. Joe Speed was blitzing from the left side and came charging right at McAda, who could see that Sean Andrews had Leshinski well covered. There was no time to look for a secondary receiver.

Throw it away or take the sack. McAda could still hear Sutton's last words, but he wasn't listening. Instinct had taken over. "I have a tendency at times to force things," he said. "That's why Coach reminded me the way he did. I just think I can get the play done somehow and I throw it up there. Sometimes I get away with it."

This time he didn't. Andrews had been outjumped for a ball only once all season—by Derrick Mayes at Notre Dame. This time he was in perfect position, and he grabbed the ball without Leshinski ever getting a hand on it. Navy had the ball back. Army had no points. Sutton had a headache.

"What in the world were you thinking?" he demanded of McAda as he came to the sideline. McAda's sheepish look was the only available answer. There wasn't much more Sutton could say. The damage was done.

"I was thinking we could lead 14–7 and at worst we'd be up 10–7," Sutton said. "The second quarter had gone all our way. The next thing I know, I'm scared to death we're going to be *behind* at halftime."

They almost were behind. With 1:24 left, Fay came back in and, just as he had done at Notre Dame, pieced together an excellent last-minute drive. He hit Astor Heaven for 10. Then Tim Cannada took a screen, picked up 15 yards, *and* got out-of-bounds at the Navy 47. There were still 29 seconds left. Schemm got seven over the middle and they spent a time-out. Two incomplete passes and it was fourth-and-three with 15 seconds left. Johnson crossed Army up, calling an option on fourth down, and Cannada went up the middle for nine to the 37. First down. They used their last time-out.

Fay, under heavy pressure from new dad Bill Doutt, threw a pass over Scornavacchi's head. Six seconds left. Time for one last play. Scornavacchi went straight down the left side on a streak pattern with cornerback Garland Gay step for step with him. Fay threw the ball up and both players looked back for it. Ever so gently, Scornavacchi bumped Gay, getting him off balance just enough that he suddenly had enough room from the defender to reach out for the ball as it came down into his arms.

But the bump had also knocked Scornavacchi a little off balance. His hands were turned just a little bit sideways. Instead of being able to cradle the ball, he had to reach for it. With Gay desperately trying to knock him off balance, Scornavacchi felt the ball brush his hands and roll off. He made one last lunge for it, but it was too late. The ball hit the ground. The half was over.

Army 7, Navy 7.

"NO!" Scornavacchi screamed in frustration. He had done everything right. The official hadn't even seen his push—there was no flag on the play. A touchdown pass, one that would have given his team a huge boost while knocking Army for a loop, had literally been in his hands. And he had dropped it.

In the stands many members of the brigade shook their heads and said "PIF."

It wasn't that simple. If Scornavacchi had made the play, it would have been both brilliant and controversial. Army would have screamed—justifiably—

for pass interference. If the flag hadn't been thrown and Scornavacchi had held on, it would have gone down as one of the great plays in Army–Navy history.

Scornavacchi wasn't thinking about any of that, going up the tunnel. He was furious with himself. "Don't feel bad, Scorno," Tommy Raye said, putting an arm around him. "If you'da caught it, they'da flagged you."

Scornavacchi appreciated the encouragement. But he spent most of halftime pacing the locker room angrily while his teammates told him to forget it and get ready for the second half.

The feeling in each locker room was almost identical: *they're* lucky the score is tied. The Army players and coaches were convinced they had taken control of the game in the second quarter and that only McAda's misjudgment had prevented them from being in the lead. The Navy players and coaches were furious that they hadn't been more assertive, especially on the offensive line, and disappointed that they hadn't stolen a last-second touchdown.

Brian Dreschler, the sophomore center who rarely said anything during a game, screamed at his linemates as they left the field: "Saying you want to win is one thing, doing it is another. This is embarrassing!"

Johnson said roughly the same thing when he spoke to the offense. "In a way, we're lucky as hell to be tied because you can't possibly play any worse. I mean, fellas, why would you play scared in *this* game? Do you think they want it more than you? I can't believe that. You guys have let number 60 [Stephen King] run around in the backfield as if he was on our team."

He paused and looked around. At the other end of the locker room, Bumpas had paused in his talk to the defense, so everyone was listening. Weatherbie stood right in the middle of the room, hands on hips, listening with everyone else.

"Against a running team, you've got to make every possession count," Johnson continued. "*We're running out of NEXT TIMES,* guys. This is all that's left now—thirty minutes. They've given us two turnovers and we've got seven points. Not good enough. But you know what the good news is? If we win the game, 110 percent of the people won't care or remember the first half."

Andrew Thompson's knee was killing him. He kept trying to stretch it out, hoping it would loosen up for him one last time. He hadn't slept a wink the night before but that didn't matter. He would worry about sleep later.

Down the hallway, the Army coaches were convinced they didn't need to make any major changes on either side of the ball, although they were frustrated by what had happened in the last 90 seconds. They had dominated the statistics: 186 total yards to 102 for Navy—only 59 of them before the Mids' last drive against the prevent defense. They had 166 yards rushing, Navy 35.

They had kept the ball almost 20 of the 30 minutes. But it was still 7–7. The two turnovers had hurt a lot. Sutton and Greg Gregory both reminded McAda to stay patient and not try to win the game on every play.

Conroy spent most of the break in the training room. Bob Arciero looked at his ribs and checked to make sure he wasn't having any trouble breathing. His breathing was fine, he was just having trouble moving around. Tim Kelly offered a pad that would cushion the ribs but might slow him down a little bit. Conroy said no. He was upset.

"My last game and I feel like I can't get the job done," he said. "I gave up the first touchdown"—causing the fumble by slipping—"and now I don't know what I'm going to feel like in the second half."

Sutton's message was the same as it had been before the game: stay desperate. "Thirty minutes, men," he said. "These games always come down to one or two plays. There's just no way to know what those plays will be. Let's go out and be the ones to make them happen."

Weatherbie still felt that the game was his team's to win or lose. "Hey, men, this game doesn't *have* to be close," he said. "Let's go out in this second half and show 'em what Navy football is all about. Turn it up a notch now and let's take care of business just like we did in the second half against Tulane. Thirty more minutes and then we'll really have some fun!"

And so they came back to the field: one team confident, the other team desperate. Navy's confidence seemed justified at the start of the third quarter. The Midshipmen took the kickoff and, as Weatherbie and Johnson had been convinced could happen, they went right down the field with it.

Not that it was easy. The Army defense gave ground—but grudgingly. Every time the Cadets seemed to have Navy stopped, the Mids came up with a big play. And the player who came up with the most big plays was Matt Scornavacchi.

First, he went over the middle on third-and-14 at the Army 47 and made a fingertip catch of a Fay pass just as cornerback Bobby Brown slammed into him. Scorno hung on. First down at the Army 33. Three plays after that, it was fourth-and-seven at the 30. Too far to try a field goal, so the Mids went for it. Again, Scornavacchi went over the middle. Fay found him, and this time it was Cantelupe trying to knock his head off. Scorno's head stayed on and the ball stayed in his hands. Another first down at the 21. Two plays later, it was Fay to Scorno again—over the middle one more time. Three passes, three tough catches. No PIF, just hard-nosed, clutch receiving.

Scornavacchi's third catch set up third-and-three at the 14. Fay tried the quarterback draw that had worked so well against both Villanova and

Delaware. But this wasn't Villanova or Delaware. The Army coaches had seen the play on tape and were ready for it. Defensive tackle Scott Eichelberger nailed Fay for a three-yard loss. Fourth-and-six. Did they go for it again or bring in Vanderhorst to try a 34-yard field goal?

Everyone crowded around listening as the coaches decided. Finally, they sent the kicking team in. Lestor Fortney snapped the ball, Brian Schrum put it down, and Vanderhorst coolly sailed it through the uprights. There was just one problem. With all the hemming and hawing about what to do, the play clock had run out. The kick didn't count. Vanderhorst would have to move back five yards and try again. Everyone on the Navy sideline had the same thought: Here we go again.

This time, though, they were wrong. Calm as could be, Vanderhorst actually kicked the ball higher and farther from 39 yards than he had from 34. It was good. The Navy sideline was bedlam. The lead was just 10–7, but they had made a field goal!

"We made one!" Scornavacchi screamed as the ball sailed through the uprights. Like everyone else, he was amazed. What's more, they had eaten 7:31 off the clock, keeping the Army offense off the field.

In fact, the Army offense, sitting on the shaded south side of the stadium, had gotten cold during Navy's extended drive. Although McAda did pick up two first downs on option runs, the offense was stopped at the 40 and Hughes was forced to punt. They exchanged punts again, each defense controlling the other offense, and when Army punted the ball back to Navy with 1:20 left in the quarter, Johnson decided it was time to bring McCoy back in at quarterback.

He immediately picked up a first down, going from the 17 to the 28 on an option keeper that brought back memories of SMU as he ducked tackles. Then, with Army thinking run since McCoy was in the game, he rose up on second-and-seven and found Neal Plaskanos open on the sideline at the 48. Seventeen yards and another first down. As Plaskanos stepped out-of-bounds, the quarter ended. It was 10–7, Navy.

Fifteen minutes to play. As always, the Army–Navy game would be decided in the fourth quarter.

Throughout the game, the atmosphere in the stadium had been wild. The relatively warm weather meant that people didn't have to huddle to keep warm. The tight nature of the game made every possession and every play seem important. Both the brigade and the corps were convinced their school was going to win. The sense on the Navy side was that it was their turn. Army had escaped for three straight years. Now, with the new coaching staff, this was a different Navy team with a different attitude. They were gradually taking control. On the Army side, although the breaks had gone their way in Navy games, they certainly hadn't in other games during this season. Maybe this was the game that was going to make up for all those earlier disappointments.

Both sides thought they deserved to win. Both were probably right.

The fourth quarter started with another Navy explosion. McCoy, dashing and darting, picked his way for 42 yards, all the way to the Army 10 yard line. If it wasn't for Cantelupe, fighting off a blocker to get to him, McCoy would have scored.

By now, Cantelupe was exhausted. The defense had been on the field almost the entire third quarter and he had been all over the field all day. Just as Hammond, Harris, and Person were playing heroically for Navy's defense in their last game, Cantelupe, Burrell, King, Al Roberts, and nose guard Colin Kearns were coming up big for Army.

But Navy was rolling now. A touchdown could put them up 10 points, and even this early in the fourth quarter that could be a tough margin to overcome. Close to the goal line, though, McCoy's tendency to hang on to the ball and not pitch it made him less effective. Three times he ran the ball himself. Roberts got him the first time; Burrell and Cantelupe the second; King and Kearns the third when he had to scramble because of good pass coverage. The last run put the ball on the four—fourth down.

Vanderhorst had become the Mids man of the hour. He trotted on and made the 22-yard field goal. Nothing to this game when you're 18 and haven't missed a kick yet. There was 12:33 left to play and Navy now led, 13–7.

There was no panic on the Army sideline. Being behind in the fourth quarter against Navy was hardly unusual. The only game in the last three in which they had led throughout the fourth quarter was the Bucchianeri game—and that was the one they had come closest to losing.

The Navy players were convinced that was ancient history. Irrelevant ancient history. They were moving the ball. The defense was stuffing Army's offense. The vaunted Army running attack was doing very little damage. The Fat Men were no longer opening holes the way they had in the first half. With Sutton keeping the ball on the ground most of the time, Bumpas kept moving the defensive backs closer and closer to the line, calling more blitzes.

Covarrubias kicked off to Brizic, who for the first time all day got a good return, taking the ball to the 32. But Army was caught holding and the ball moved back ten yards to the 22.

It moved back another four yards on the first down. McAda pitched to Ron Thomas, who had been held in check all day. This play was no different. Keith Galloway, having talked the talk, was walking the walk. He brought Thomas down for a four-yard loss.

More important than the lost yardage was the lost player—McAda was hit hard as he pitched the ball and didn't get up. He had landed squarely on his tail-bone and felt pain shoot through him. He had to be helped off the field. Army's sideline was starting to look like a MASH unit. Conroy was hurting and so was Al Roberts, who had a hip-pointer. Eichelberger had a sore knee. Now, most impor-tant of all, McAda. Arciero and Kelly began checking him immediately.

In the meantime, Adam Thompson, who had been a spectator for two and a half hours, had to rush into the game without the benefit of taking even one warm-up snap. By now, the entire field was in shadows, and the Army bench had been cold all day anyway. All year long, Thompson had been superb when forced to come in for McAda on the spur of the moment.

But this time, with cold hands—cold *small* hands—and in the cauldron of the fourth quarter of Army–Navy, he tried to get away from center just a little too quickly. Kyle Scott's snap never quite made it into his hands and the ball was lying on the turf. Fernando Harris, the quickest player Navy had, dove into the scrum for the ball, and when they picked all the players apart, he was clutching it.

The Navy bench was jubilant. They had the ball on the Army 17. Time to move into the end zone for the kill. As Garrett Smith grabbed his helmet and ran onto the field with the offense, he thought: "Score here and we can blow them out. We can get John Moe into this game."

For the first time on the Army sideline, the thought of losing began to creep into people's minds. When McCoy picked up 13 yards on two straight option plays to set up first-and-goal on the three, Sutton was screaming at the officials, convinced that his players were being held. He came all the way down to the 15 yard line, yelling, then realized he was risking a penalty and retreated.

The clock had ticked under 10 minutes. The only reason McCoy hadn't scored on the second option run was Cantelupe, who had come from the far side of the field to bring him down. Cantelupe talked often about Pat Work being the unsung hero of the Bucchianeri game because he had come from nowhere to trip Brad Stramanak up on the goal line just before the ill-fated kick. This play was reminiscent of Work's, Cantelupe refusing to give up on the play when it looked like McCoy was bound to score.

Now, though, it would take a miracle from the defense to keep Navy out of the end zone. Cannada got nothing on first down. On second down, McCoy ran left and Kearns and Cantelupe pulled him down for a loss of one.

The Army bench was imploring the defense to dig in and force Navy to kick a field goal. By now, everyone in the stadium was standing, sensing that the game was about to reach a turning point.

Third down. Ball on the four. McCoy started backwards and to the right, then cut left. The Army defense had bought his first move to the right and had overrun the play. As McCoy started left, he appeared to have a clear path to the end zone. In complete desperation, Tom Burrell reached out and back with his right arm, hoping to get a hand on any part of McCoy's body.

Instead, he got his hand on his face mask. Since McCoy was going toward the goal line and Burrell was off balance, Burrell's grab didn't stop him, but it did slow him. As McCoy struggled to pull free, linebacker Ben Kotwica, who had initially been blocked, managed to pull himself loose just long enough to get his body between McCoy and the goal line. Still driving forward, McCoy was finally stopped no more than six inches away.

Lying on the ground, Burrell looked around for the flag that he knew had to come. He hadn't intentionally grabbed McCoy's face mask, but that didn't matter. He had grabbed it and that would mean the officials would move the ball half the distance to the goal line—in this case three inches—and, far more important, Navy would have an automatic first down. The Mids would have four cracks from three inches away to score.

But there was no flag. Later, looking at the play on tape, the Cadets—Burrell most of all—would be amazed to see one of the officials standing on the goal line, hands on his knees, looking right at the play. Or so it seemed. Somehow, he didn't pull his flag.

"To this day, I'll never know why he didn't throw the flag," Burrell said. "I just got lucky on the play, very lucky."

Navy's view of it was a little bit different. When he saw the tape, Weatherbie angrily sent it to the Big East office (the officials were from the Big East), but at that point it didn't matter.

What did matter was that, thanks to the non-whistle, Navy now had fourth down and inches. Weatherbie called time with 8:26 left in the game.

On the Army sideline, there wasn't any doubt in anybody's mind about what Navy was going to do. With Vanderhorst already two-for-two and the fourth quarter almost half over, putting Army in a nine-point hole would be huge. "At that point, nine was about as good as thirteen for them," Cantelupe said. "It was two scores. That wouldn't be impossible, but it would be tough."

By now McAda was on his feet. He was sore, but OK. Arciero had told him he could go back in the game. He was standing with John Graves, watching as the Navy coaches huddled on the sideline.

"They gotta kick it," McAda said to Graves.

"We need a good return on the kickoff," Graves said, already thinking ahead to what the offense would have to do with a nine-point deficit.

Weatherbie was on his handset, talking to Johnson in the press box. "We can score with A-pop," Johnson told him. "They'll have so many people on the line it'll be wide open."

Weatherbie's mind was racing. The field goal would be 18 yards. Somewhere, in the deep recesses of his brain, he remembered that Bucchianeri's miss had been 18 yards. That close, the angle could be a factor. They could take a delay-of-game penalty and move the ball back five yards, making it a little easier angle from 23 yards. Vanderhorst had been solid all day. But this was the fourth quarter; this was that moment with 70,000 people screaming that Weatherbie had wondered about in the pregame coaches meeting.

He looked at his offensive coaches, who were all nodding as Johnson explained how they could score. There was only one dissenting voice: defensive backs coach Gary Patterson. He knew it was none of his business telling the offense what to do, but Patterson thought going for anything but three was crazy. "It's all we need," he said. "They can't score twice, they just can't."

On the field, the offense waited. Smith and Bryce Minamyer, the two seniors on the offensive line, wanted to go for it; they wanted to explode off the ball one more time, push the Army defense back on its heels, and run the ball in for the score. "I'm thinking, 'Six inches. Come on, we can move the ball six inches,'" Smith said.

On the other side of the huddle, Matt Scornavacchi nudged Scott Zimmerman. "Zim," he said, "we gotta kick the field goal."

Zimmerman shook his head. "We're not. Look, Tom's not even standing up there near Coach."

A chill ran through Scornavacchi. He was reckless enough to appreciate the nature of the gamble, but a bit unnerved by what would now be at stake on this play.

Weatherbie put his arm around McCoy. "Three twenty-eight A-pop," he said.

It was a quick pass play, a pop pass to the A-back, in this case Schemm. It was designed to take advantage of a defense lined up to stop the run at all costs. McCoy would take the snap, drop back a step, and throw the ball quickly to Schemm, who only had to take two or three steps to be open.

When the Army players saw McCoy trotting back onto the field, they were amazed. Cantelupe and Klein were both on the sidelines, since the "heavy," goal-line defense was in the game. "Has to be a fake," Cantelupe said. "They'll take the penalty, then kick."

As soon as he saw McCoy come back to the huddle, offensive line coach Ed Warriner began screaming for the O-line to get ready. "We're gonna stop 'em and get the ball back!"

No one was sitting on either sideline or in the stands. McCoy walked to the line and saw the entire Army defense pinching the middle to stop what they all thought would be a quarterback sneak or a fullback dive. "The play was wide open," he said. "No one was even on Cory."

Schemm was linked up on the right side, just behind the line. As soon as he stepped outside, toward the sideline, he would be all alone. On the other side, Scornavacchi noticed that no one was on Schemm and he took a deep breath. "It's right there," he thought.

McCoy got under Dreschler, and, to the surprise of the Army sideline, went on a quick count. No delay of game penalty coming here. He dropped quickly and saw Schemm all alone.

"I got too excited," he said later. "I rushed it and I didn't have to. I never quite got my arm back right or the ball off the way I wanted to."

The ball wobbled off McCoy's hand. Seeing that it was low, Schemm dove, got his hands on it, bobbled it a little as he hit the turf, and then watched helplessly as it just rolled off his fingertips. He lay there for a moment, pounding the ground in frustration.

For a split second it was as if no one was quite sure what had happened. Then everyone understood. The Army bench exploded as if it had just scored the winning touchdown. People were jumping into one another's arms.

The Navy defensive players sagged for a split second, then gathered themselves. "Come on!" Thompson screamed. "It's our game now! Let's go out there and stuff them like we have all day!"

Across the way, Cantelupe grabbed Klein by both shoulders. "Guess what!" he yelled. "We just won this goddamn game. You watch. We just won the goddamn game."

The Drive

As Cantelupe spoke, the football was sitting 99 yards, two feet, and six inches from where it had to be for Army to win the game. And yet, there was no doubt that all the emotion in the stadium, all the adrenaline, all the momentum, was now on Army's side.

Before the offense took the field, McAda gathered everyone around him. Even though there was still 8:23 left in the game, there was a sense of urgency. They all knew that if they gave the football back now, they might not see it again. The defense was exhausted and it was entirely possible that, given another possession, Navy might run out the clock with two or three first downs.

"Listen up," McAda commanded. None of the Fat Men told him to shut up. They listened. "The D did its job, now we have to do ours. Right now!"

As they huddled up, deep in the end zone, waiting for the TV time-out to end, Davis turned to the other Fat Men. "This is our destiny," he said. "Ninety-nine yards to win. This is what the whole thing is all about."

The Navy defense was rested and ready. Everyone knew if they could hold Army without a first down and force a Hughes punt from the end zone, they would get great field position. "It was as if someone had decided that we were supposed to win the game," Person said. "There was part of me that liked that idea. I had no doubt we would get the job done."

Thompson, who had been frustrated all day because Army had consistently run the option away from him, didn't care anymore about where the plays went. All he wanted was a stop right now to get the damn game under control once and for all. He looked at Joe Speed, who just nodded his head as if reading Thompson's mind. "Now's the time," Speed said.

McAda knew what the first call was going to be even before Heath Bates trotted into the huddle carrying it: 60 short. It was a basic, straight-ahead fullback dive designed to create a little bit of room when the offense was backed up. They would never be more backed up than they were at that moment. McAda handed the ball to Conroy, the Fat Men pushed as hard as they could, and the Navy line pushed back. Conroy burrowed for almost two yards—putting the ball squarely on the two. His ribs were sore, but felt better than they had earlier.

Second down. Now McAda was at least standing on the playing field and not in the end zone as he called signals. The call was 204 option, meaning he would read the defense and decide whether to give to Conroy again or keep the ball himself. If he kept the ball and got trapped, a safety was possible. Turning to hand the ball to Conroy, McAda could see that Stover and Blair had blasted off the ball so hard that they had wedged a hole in the right side of the line. He stuck the ball in Conroy's gut and Conroy slid through the hole, broke a tackle at the five, and was finally brought down at the 14.

First down. A roar went up from the corps. At the very least they had now given Hughes some breathing room if he had to punt. Conroy was slow getting up. The ribs had gotten banged again. He was hobbling as he tried to go back to the huddle. "I couldn't take a step without pain," he said. "I knew I had to come out."

With a little more room to operate, McAda kept the ball on the first-down play and pitched it to Abel Young. He got six. Steve Carpenter got three more on a counter play, again running behind Stover. It was third-and-one at the 23. Now the noise was coming from the brigade, urging the defense to dig in and hold right now.

Conroy had taken his helmet off when he came to the sideline. The pain was almost unbearable. Kelly told him to take it easy and sit down. The message was: you're done, kid.

The third-down call was 46 stack reach. The fullback—now Demetrius Perry—was the decoy and the give would again be to Carpenter going over the right side. This time, though, Navy read the play and Clint Bruce had ahold of Carpenter two yards behind the line of scrimmage. Bruce was probably Navy's best tackler. But Carpenter somehow found some extra surge in his legs and pulled loose from Bruce just enough to dive past the line of scrimmage and land a foot beyond the first-down marker.

Bruce came up screaming in anger at himself. Carpenter, who always seemed to be the other guy during his four years at Army, had just become *the* guy. First down again. The ball was at the 24. The clock was now down to 6:25. Army's grind-it-out attack ate up the time quickly. More and more it looked like this drive would be now or never.

Sutton and Gregory knew they couldn't run the ball on every play. Navy was putting 10 men on the line to deny the option room. And so, on first down, Gregory suggested 29 Volvo, a three-man pass route with Leshinski as the primary pass receiver. McAda dropped and saw that Leshinski was covered.

Graves, coming from the right side, had gone about 15 yards when he saw Speed coming up to meet him. "If I ran the route just the way I was supposed to, the guy would have been right there," he said. "I looked up and figured I better flatten it out some and make sure I was open."

McAda saw him make his cut early and hit him on the numbers. Speed brought him down immediately on the 41. First down again. They went back to the option, but this time McAda dropped the ball as he turned away from the line. He picked it up before anyone from Navy could make a move at it, but Bruce was all over him. The gain was one. On second down, Perry, still in the game for Conroy, got two up the middle.

It was third-and-seven. The drive had now lasted seven plays and, more important, had eaten up almost four minutes. Sutton called for the fullback screen, a play Conroy had run very well all season. Only now he wasn't in the game. Bumpas, sensing a chance to make a big play, had both safeties, Thompson and Speed, blitzing. McAda dropped, and before he even had a chance to set up, Thompson and Speed were on him. Somehow, using every bit of his six feet four inches, he managed to get his arm up and loft the ball just over the hands of the diving Thompson. Perry caught it, dodged a tackler, and crossed midfield. Michael Ogden got him down at the 47, but again, it was a yard late. Another first down.

Back behind the line of scrimmage, Thompson and Speed could not believe how close they had come to the sack. Thompson stood up and went to help Speed up. But Speed wasn't getting up. Diving for McAda he had felt a sharp pain in his legs. Both of them had cramped on him at the same time.

"I didn't adjust for the weather being warmer," he said. "I should have been drinking more fluids. The legs just went."

Speed had to come off. He didn't know it then, but his football career had just ended. Sophomore Kevin Lewis, who often came in on passing downs anyway, took his place.

Watching all this, Conroy still felt pain in his ribs. But it was duller now. He walked a few yards and felt all right. He looked at the clock and saw that he had less than five minutes to be a football player. "I've got the rest of my life to heal," he thought. "I have to get back in the game."

He went to get his helmet, but it was gone. "Hey!" he screamed. "Where's my helmet?" Everyone looked at him blankly. What was he raving about his helmet for? He didn't need it to watch the rest of the game. "Where's my helmet?" Conroy screamed again.

From behind the bench, someone was trying to get his attention. "Hey, Conroy," the man said. "It's under the bench, down at the end there."

Conroy had no idea who the man was. Maybe his guardian angel. He grabbed the helmet, stuck it on, and headed back to the field. He didn't bother to check with any doctors, trainers, or coaches. He just ran in and told Perry, "Hey D, Coach wants to see you."

Perry nodded and ran off. McAda grabbed his shoulder. "You sure you're OK?" The noise in the stadium was so loud now that everyone had to scream to be heard.

"I'm fine," Conroy yelled back. "Call the play."

McAda called Carpenter's number again and the little halfback picked up three to the Navy 44. Then, using Conroy as the decoy, McAda faked the dive handoff, started right as if to run the option, then handed to Jeff Brizic on the counter. Davis and Wells opened a gaping hole and Brizic roared to the 26. Three and a half minutes left. There was now no doubt that this was it for both teams. The game would be decided on this possession.

Army went back to basics, McAda leaving the ball in Conroy's stomach on the option. He picked up six more to the 20. Then Brizic got five to the 15 for another first down. The Navy players were screaming at each other to dig in the way the Army players had done on the goal line a few minutes earlier.

Sutton called 54 option, the play that they had fumbled on way back in the first quarter. This time Conroy didn't slip, and McAda pulled the ball out of his stomach and started right. But Fernando Harris had read the play and he caught McAda from behind and pulled him down at the 17. The loss was two yards. The clock was at 2:03. Army took its second time-out.

Sutton and Gregory talked on the headsets while McAda waited. During the week they had worked on a play called 96 solid-suzy, a fake screen pass that ended up being a deep pass to one of the half-backs. They had used the screen effectively all game, so a screen look might suck Navy in. They all agreed it was the right play. Coby Short, the best receiver among the halfbacks, went into the game.

McAda dropped, made his fake, and looked deep for Short. Kevin Lewis hadn't bought the fake even for a second. He was all over Short as they streaked to the left corner of the end zone together. A little voice was telling McAda to throw the ball away, but his gut was telling him there wasn't anymore time to waste plays. He tossed the ball in the direction of Short and Lewis and hoped for a miracle.

In a sense, he got it. Only one person had a chance to catch the ball: Lewis. He turned and saw it coming right at him. Short was reaching back to try and pull him away from the ball. Even so, Lewis had a clean shot at it. But he was a split second slow getting his hands up and the ball slid through them and hit him on the helmet. It bounced away harmlessly.

McAda's heart started beating again. "I thought for a second it was over," he said. "That I had lost the game. I got away with that one."

It was third-and-12. Sutton and Gregory were deep into their bag of tricks now. They called 28 willie-cross, a post pattern for Graves. Bumpas knew the Cadets had to pass and he called a full blitz. Again, Thompson came in clean. McAda saw him and spun to try and clear room. But Thompson was too close to him, and as he spun he tripped and fell, 12 yards behind the line of scrimmage.

Thompson jumped to his feet, screaming at the top of his lungs. The Navy players were in full celebration. It was fourth-and-24 at the 29. The clock was at 1:46. Army used its last time-out to try and regroup. All Navy had to do was stop this play and the game would be over. Army wouldn't be able to stop the clock again.

McAda trotted over to Sutton, who was talking again to Gregory. They were convinced that Navy would come with a full blitz package again, trying to make sure that McAda didn't have time to pick out a receiver down the field. They had little choice but to call a play that would commit McAda to throwing the ball to one receiver in one spot, do or die. There wouldn't be time for anything else. There was no doubt in Sutton's mind that Graves was the man to throw the ball to.

He looked at Graves, who was standing next to McAda. "Which do you want to run, post or corner," he said.

Graves thought for a split second. "Corner," he said, thinking he felt more comfortable running toward the sideline than over the middle. That was the answer Sutton wanted to hear. He thought Graves would have a better chance to get open running the corner route than the post if only because there was less chance for the defense to get help near the sideline.

"OK then," Sutton said. "Four-ninety-six, steve-key."

That meant there would only be two receivers in the pattern—Graves and Thomas—and Thomas was strictly a decoy. Everyone else would stay in to give McAda maximum protection against the blitz they all expected.

McAda and Graves returned to the huddle. Before McAda called the play, Joel Davis stepped in and pointed a finger around the circle of 11 players. "Who is going to step up?" he demanded. "Who steps up right now and makes the play?"

McAda's voice was much softer. "Just give me time," he said, looking into the eyes of the Fat Men. "Give me time, we'll make it work."

The look he got back told him all he needed to know: they would give him time, one way or the other. The rest would be up to him and to Graves.

It took the Navy sideline a full minute to get a collective hold of itself after Thompson's sack. The offensive players and second-teamers were still hugging and screaming when Thompson and Bruce came to the sideline.

"Hey," Thompson yelled. "No celebrating yet. We still need one more play."

It was at that moment that Charlie Weatherbie came back into the football game. From the moment that the ball had rolled off Schemm's hands until the moment he heard Thompson's voice, he had mentally checked out. As soon as he saw McCoy's fourth-down pass fall incomplete, a wave of dread swept over him.

"What have I done?" he kept thinking over and over. *"What was I thinking? All we needed was a field goal."*

"I was in an absolute state of shock," he said later. "I did the one thing I always tell the players not to do: I turned one mistake into two. Because I was standing there beating myself up and not thinking about the football game."

Bumpas was calling the defensive signals and Weatherbie heard them in his headset. But he wasn't listening. All he could see was Army moving down the field and the clock ticking down. He had a vague sense that there were moments when the defense had a chance to put him out of his misery by getting the ball back, but it didn't happen. Then he heard Thompson's voice and he snapped back to reality.

"I looked up and realized we were one play from winning," he said. "The kids were still battling, still trying to win the game after I had just put them in a position to lose it."

No one was thinking about the goal-line incompletion now, not even Weatherbie. They were thinking only about making one more play and getting almost everything they had wanted from the season. Bumpas was calling the play—full blitz with coverage in the defensive backfield backed off to give up a short pass. The key was to make McAda get rid of the ball (or sack him) before any of his receivers had the chance to get anywhere near the five yard line, which was where they had to get to pick up the first down.

Everyone was in agreement. Thompson looked at Speed, who was trying to stand up straight, the pain still biting at his legs. "Can't go?" he asked. Speed shook his head. There were tears in his eyes. Thompson reached out and grabbed Speed's mouthpiece out of his hand. He took his own mouthpiece, handed it to Speed, and stuck Speed's in his mouth. "You're out there with me, Joe," he said. "This is for you."

He ran back to the huddle. In the Army huddle, McAda calmly called "496 steve-key," and brought them up to the line. On the Navy side, Ben Fay and Lester Fortney kneeled, helmet-to-helmet, praying.

Sutton watched Graves trot out to the left side and saw that Kevin Lewis was alone out there with him. Sean Andrews was with Thomas on the other side. Everyone else was bunched in the middle of the field. Sutton's heart leapt. Graves was one-on-one with Lewis! If the protection would hold up long enough . . . "Greg," he said into his headset, "I think we've got a shot at this."

McAda took the snap and dropped and nine Navy players came at him. Hammond made a twist move coming up the middle and had a lane, but Carpenter stepped in his way. At the same time, Thompson was forced a step wider than he wanted to go and was still two steps from McAda when he saw the quarterback's arm come up.

Graves came off the line and ran straight at Lewis, who was back-pedaling to give him room, since anything caught short of the five yard line would be worthless to Army. Graves went down 15 yards and took a jab step toward the middle of the field. Lewis read post and took a tiny step in that direction.

As he did, Graves planted his right foot as hard as he could and spun to the outside. His heart was racing. He knew Lewis had bought the fake and he had a step on him. He looked back over his shoulder, hoping the ball would be dropping down toward him, because if it wasn't, that meant that McAda was in trouble.

McAda saw Carpenter pick up Hammond and saw Graves come open. His quarterback senses told him the ball had to be released right then because Thompson and Person and Bruce were bearing down on him. He stood up in the pocket as tall as he could and let the ball go. For one horrifying millisecond he thought he had put too much on it and thrown it too close to the sideline. Then he saw Graves race under it and he knew everything was OK.

Graves wasn't worried about the sideline, but he wasn't absolutely certain what *yard* line he was on. As the ball dropped through the air into his waiting arms, he was tempted to look down for a yard marker. But his gut told him he was where he should be and he had to make sure he made the catch. He gathered the ball safely into his arms just as Lewis, lunging for him, pushed him out-of-bounds. Graves looked down as he went out and saw the flag—the end zone flag—almost on top of him.

"For a second, I thought I might be in," he said.

He wasn't, but he was close. The official spotted the ball on the one yard line. It was first-and-goal. The play had taken six seconds. That meant the Fat Men, with considerable help from Scott and Conroy and Carpenter and Leshinski, had held the blitzing Navy defense out for close to four seconds— an eternity.

Now it was the Army bench going crazy; the Navy bench in shock. Weatherbie called *his* last time-out to give his players a chance to regroup. A three-minute time-out wasn't going to be long enough to do that. They had gone from one play away from having the game won to one yard away from losing it.

"I just couldn't believe it," Hammond said later. "Fourth-and-twenty-four, you've got them. You have to have them. Only we didn't."

"How many times," Andy Person asked, "do you see someone pick up fourth-and-twenty-four?"

The defense wasn't going to give up. They had simulated this situation in practice 100 times. Dig way down, get underneath the offensive linemen, and, as Bumpas always put it, "move the line of scrimmage backward."

Sutton called 72 diamond, the play off right tackle that Conroy had scored the first touchdown on. Blair and Stover were screaming for the ball to come that way. The only person who wasn't sure was Conroy. "They'll be looking for that play," he said to Steve Carpenter in the huddle. "We should run forty-six and I can block for you."

Carpenter looked at Conroy. "John," he said, "just shut up and put the ball in the end zone."

Conroy thought he would do just that. Blair and Stover created space, but as he hit the hole, Thompson was waiting. Conroy hadn't been brought down by one tackler very often during the season. Thompson stood him up and Conroy heard him screaming, "NO, NO, NO!" He tried to drive forward, but Thompson was a wall. He brought him down on the one.

The clock ticked toward a minute. "Actually," Jack Hecker said on the Army sideline, "it's probably better for us to take a couple of plays to get it in. Use up the clock."

Bob Arciero looked at him as if he were crazy. "Use up the clock!" he screamed. "Forget that! We've got to get the ball in the damn end zone!"

Cantelupe was already gathering the defense. "When we score, we've got to do our job one more time," he said. "Don't think the game is over when we score. Because it's not."

On second down, Sutton called 73 diamond: same play, only over the left side, behind Davis and Wells. This time, Conroy agreed with the call. "I figured *now* they would be looking for forty-six," he said.

As they broke the huddle, Davis looked back at him. "Just follow me, babe," he said.

McAda took the snap and handed the ball to Conroy for the 22d and last time of the afternoon. Conroy submarined to get his body as low as possible, and following orders, ran right behind Davis and Wells as they plowed open just enough space for him to squeeze through. Conroy heard the cannon go off and he knew he had scored. Lying on the ground, Davis pounded his fist on the turf joyfully. He was screaming to the heavens, "We did it, we did it, we did it!" Mike Wells was lying next to him, his eyes filling with tears.

"The last time my feet will ever touch a football field as a player," he thought, "and I was a part of *this.*"

This was as epic a drive as anyone in the stadium had ever seen: 19 plays, seven minutes and 20 seconds, 100 yards, minus those fateful six inches. When Graves made his catch, they had driven the ball 99 yards—and still weren't in the end zone yet. It was a monumental drive because it came against a defense that stood in on every play and pushed and shoved and scrambled trying desperately to stop them.

But Army was just a little more desperate. The Fat Men refused to be denied their destiny. J. Parker came in and kicked the extra point—putting it just a little closer to the right upright than anyone from Army cared for—and, after three hours, the Cadets led for the first time: Army 14, Navy 13.

But as Cantelupe had said, the game wasn't over. There were still 63 seconds left. Navy had one last chance.

There was nothing left to hold back on either side now. Neal Plaskanos took the kickoff at the eight and got as far as the 30 before Cantelupe and Maddox tackled him. It was Cantelupe's 13th tackle of the game.

Ben Fay came back at quarterback because Navy now had to throw the ball. The kickoff had taken six seconds. There were 57 seconds to play. On first down, Fay made an awful mistake. With no time-outs left, Johnson had called a pass play, but when he looked at the defense Fay thought he saw room in the middle. Going on instinct, rather than on the situation, he audibled to an option.

When Smith and Minamyer heard the check-off call they were shocked. But they couldn't turn around and call time to ask Fay what he was doing because there were no time-outs left. Having made a mistake by changing the play, Fay then made the wrong read on the option, handing the ball to Cannada on the fullback dive. He got nothing. Worse than that, the clock was running and Navy couldn't stop it. By the time Fay got them lined up so he could spike the ball to stop the clock there were only 36 seconds left.

They had wasted 21 critical seconds and faced third-and-ten. On third down, Fay dropped straight back and looked up to find Al Roberts in his face. Roberts would have taken him down 10 yards behind the line of scrimmage and Navy might not have gotten off another play if Fay hadn't smartly thrown the ball away just before Roberts piled into him.

It was fourth-and-ten and now *Army* was one play from winning. The Navy bench was almost silent. Fay took the snap and was again under heavy pressure. He rolled left, looking desperately for someone to throw to. "I knew I couldn't run with it because I probably wouldn't get the first down and if I didn't we were done," he said. "I was about out of room when I saw Astor."

Heaven had done the same thing Graves had done earlier, breaking his pattern when he saw his quarterback in trouble. Since Fay was running toward the sideline, Heaven ran in that direction, putting his hand up to get his attention. Fay spotted him and let go of the ball just as Roberts and Doutt were about to bury him.

For a moment it looked as if Jerrold Tyquiengco was in perfect position to intercept the ball or knock it down. But somehow the ball threaded its way past his arms and fell right into Heaven's hands. Heaven-sent, Heaven-*caught*, for Navy. Tyquiengco pushed him out-of-bounds on the Army 44, but it was a pickup of 26 yards.

Amazingly, with 26 seconds to go, the game still wasn't over. "I saw that and I thought, 'Oh my God, what's going on here?' " Graves said. "I thought maybe it was going to come down to another kick."

McAda's reaction was more direct: "Won't this damn game ever end?"

On the Navy sideline, the same thought went through everyone's mind: was the game going to come down to a kick? Again? Fortney, Schrum, and Vanderhorst went to the kicking area behind the bench to get ready, just in case . . .

The problem Navy had was that it was going into what had now become a strong wind. With no wind, getting the ball to the 35 yard line would have given Vanderhorst a fighting chance; anything closer than that would have been gravy. But because of the wind, they probably needed an extra 10 yards to have a chance.

Fay tried to pick up the 19 yards they probably needed on one play, looking again for Heaven, this time over the middle. The ball was on target, but as Heaven went down for it, Cantelupe dove in front of him and got both hands on it. Only Heaven wrestling with him and the impact of hitting the ground kept him from intercepting the ball.

Cantelupe picked himself up and looked at the clock. He didn't even pause to think about how close he had been to the interception. There was no time for that now. The clock was at 20 seconds.

Fay dropped once more and here came Al Roberts one more time. Navy simply couldn't keep him out of the backfield. The coverage downfield was perfect and Fay had no choice but to scramble. Desperately trying to get to the first-down marker since a first down would stop the clock, he was stopped three yards short by Ray Tomasits.

The clock was under 10 and running. Army was taking as much time as possible to unpile and line up. It looked as if the clock might run out, but Dreschler got the snap off with three ticks left and Fay spiked the ball to stop it with two seconds to go.

They had one play left. The ball was on the Army 36 yard line. If the wind had been the other way, their best chance probably would have been Vanderhorst. But 54 yards into a strong wind was an impossibility. They had no choice but to send everyone into the end zone, have Fay throw it up for grabs, and pray that this time the bounce would go their way.

Remarkably, they almost got lucky. In the bedlam that was the Army sideline, there was confusion about which defense they were supposed to be in. Some players thought the coaches wanted "prevent," others heard defensive coordinator Denny Doornbos screaming, "Victory, victory." The victory defense, used only on the last play of the game, consisted of nine defensive backs along with Roberts and Doutt.

Landis Maddox, who would have been one of the DBs, didn't hear Doornbos screaming "victory." As Navy lined up, Derek Klein thought they were a man short and started onto the field. But he was seized with panic: what if he had miscounted and he was the 12th man? He stopped and went back. Cantelupe *knew* they were a man short and started screaming for a time-out. But Army was out of time-outs so the officials ignored him.

Navy had an 11-on-10 advantage. Fay went back, and with Roberts again bearing down on him he lofted the ball as high and far as he could. Roberts crashed into him and the two of them went down together. Both of them listened to hear which direction the next roar would come from.

From the Army sideline, McAda thought briefly that Heaven had somehow gotten behind everyone. Then he saw a jumble of white and black uniforms converging on the spot where the ball was coming down. Everyone jumped, but no one from Navy made any kind of deflection. The ball somehow floated through everyone and into the hands of Donnie Augustus, in the game strictly for "victory." It was his only play of the game. Augustus clutched the ball safely in his chest as the corps screamed joyously.

Lying underneath Roberts, Fay heard the screams coming from his right and he knew no miracle had occurred. So did Roberts. He pulled Fay to his feet and offered him his hand.

The corps poured onto the field, everyone looking for their friends or company-mates. When Conroy looked up and saw half his company bearing down on him, he put his hands up and screamed, "Please, no hugging!" He was terrified at the thought of anyone crunching his ribs.

Sutton and Weatherbie found each other at midfield amid a crush of cameras. Both men were completely drained. "Your kids played a great game," Sutton said.

Weatherbie was still in a state of semi-shock. "I just hope," he said to Sutton, "that we at least helped your job situation."

He meant it. The only glimmer he could find in the whole thing was the thought that Sutton's job might have been saved by his mistake. Sutton thanked him. Then he went looking for Smith and Person and Thompson. He found Smith, who had tears rolling down his face, and hugged him. He did the same for Person. But he couldn't find Thompson.

Thompson and Speed were still on the sideline, locked in an embrace, their bodies racking with sobs. It just wasn't possible. How could this happen four years in a row? Four years, six points, impossible endings each time.

Cantelupe found Person and Smith just as Sutton had, but couldn't find Thompson in the crush of people on the field. Speed and Thompson didn't let go of one another until the teams were standing at attention in front of the Navy band for "Blue and Gold." Almost everyone in a Navy uniform—football or dress blue—was crying. A close-up shot of Mark Hammond on ABC said it all: Hammond stood at attention, hand on his heart, singing every word of "Blue and Gold," tears streaming down his face.

The Mids weren't alone. The Fat Men were all fighting tears, especially Eddie Stover. In the midst of the hugs and the cheers, it had occurred to him that this really was it, that he had played his last football game. As the players from both teams made their way to the Army side for the playing of "Alma Mater," Stover felt himself losing it. His knees started to quake. As the song ended, Stover began racing for the locker room. He didn't want to stay and celebrate. He couldn't think of a reason to celebrate. They had won, but so what? Football was over. How would he live without football? He couldn't imagine it.

The last Navy player off the field was Thompson, who stood staring at the scoreboard, crying, somehow hoping that if he stood there long enough he could blink the numbers away. Speed and Gary Patterson finally took him by the arm and guided him up the tunnel to the locker room.

Once the doors closed, they all surrounded Weatherbie and kneeled to pray together one more time.

"Heavenly Father," Weatherbie began, "we come to you with pain, with sorrow, with hurt. Help us to learn a lesson from this to help us in life. Help us to learn a lesson, Lord, in dealing with disappointment."

He paused. "I just want to apologize to this team, Lord, for a stupid mistake."

"NO!" The shouts came from all over the room.

Weatherbie continued, his voice beginning to crack. "I just pray that you'll always be with these seniors, Lord." When he said the word "seniors," the crack became a sob. He paused, head still down, his arms stretched across the shoulders of the players kneeling next to him. For a few seconds it seemed he wouldn't be able to finish. The only sound in the room was his quiet sobbing. Then he forced himself to go on.

"Help them, Lord, as they go out to defend our country. Lord, I just thank you for their leadership and the guidance they gave us this year. I know you do have a plan for us, Lord. A plan to prosper us, not to harm us; a plan to give us a hope and a future. Thank you, Lord, for all these young men. Please put your healing hand on all those that are hurt. Help these young men hold their heads high and be proud to be part of the Naval Academy; the navy and the Marine Corps."

He paused once more as if trying to think of something else to say. He couldn't. "Thank you, Lord Jesus, for dying on the cross and for eternal life. In your name we pray; in your name we play. Amen."

Slowly, everyone stood. Weatherbie put his cap back on and stood in the middle of the room, the players fanning out on both sides of him.

"Guys, I tell you what, I made a stupid tactical error."

Again, the chorus: "No, no you didn't."

"*Yes I did, men!*" He shouted it back. "I did, gang. Now listen up. That's horsecrap on my part—horsecrap. You deserved to win that football game, gang. You *won* that football game. I was the one that screwed it up and *lost* it.

"Men, I'll tell you what, though. That ain't gonna happen again. It ain't never gonna happen again. You played your butts off, guys. You played your hearts out. I apologize."

He paused and looked at all of them, most of them still crying. "Underclassmen: juniors, sophomores, freshmen. Remember this feeling. Remember the pain. Remember how it hurts.

"Seniors. I appreciate your leadership. I appreciate what you've done for this football team. I'll never forget you." He was crying again. "I'm sorry."

He turned and fled into the coaches' locker room because now the tears were coming in a flood. Garrett Smith followed him into the coaches' room and found him sitting on a bench, curled up almost in the fetal position, his head down, his entire body racking with sobs. Gently, he stood him up.

"Coach," he said. "You always tell us, we win as a team, we lose as a team. This is no different."

He guided Weatherbie back into the locker room, where everyone stood waiting. Weatherbie and Smith moved into the middle of the huddle, and Thompson, his voice almost gone from shouting and crying, joined them.

"We're still a family no matter what!" he shrieked. "On three—*Family!*" They pushed and shoved to get as close as possible to each other and did one last team cheer. "One, two, three," Thompson called out.

"Family!" they all yelled back.

They broke the huddle. Now came the hard part. Taking off their uniforms and going on with the rest of their lives.

At the other end of the hallway, the scene was as different as you might expect it to be. For several minutes, the players and coaches just circled the locker room, high-fiving and hugging and laughing and crying all at once.

The only person not joining in the celebration was Stover, who sat at his locker for a moment, then burst into the training room screaming at the top of his lungs, "I can't go on without football. How can I not play football anymore?"

It took considerable consoling and cajoling by the trainers and other players to get Stover to calm down and join the party. Davis and Cantelupe waited until all the big shots—General John M. Shalikashvili, the chairman of the Joint Chiefs of Staff; General Dennis Reimer, the army chief of staff; Joe Reeder, the Undersecretary of the Army; and Superintendent Graves all came into the room, followed by all their various functionaries.

"We wanted to be sure," Davis said later, "that all the stars"—generals—"were in the room before we did anything."

Once the "stars" were all in, Davis climbed on a chair, holding the game ball. "Coach, all the seniors got together last night and decided we wanted to win this game as a way to thank you for everything you've done for us for the last four years. You've helped make us better players and better people and we want to tell you how much we appreciate everything you've done for us.

"That's why we decided that this game ball is for you, from us."

The ball was for Sutton. The message was for the "stars."

They all cheered as Davis handed the ball to Sutton and then bear-hugged him. So did Cantelupe. Sutton was both surprised and touched. In all his years as a coach, he had never been given a game ball.

After that, the "stars" all gave their little speeches, telling the players how wonderful they were and how wonderful Army–Navy was and how this game proved again that both the academies were producing great future leaders. The players listened, or at least stayed quiet, until the speeches were done. There was still one thing left to do. As soon as Superintendent Graves was finished, Sutton jumped up on the chair.

"Everybody in here?" he asked.

They nodded.

"OK," he said. "On three . . ." And so, one more time, at the top of their lungs, they sang the Song:

> *The Army team's the pride and dream of every heart in gray;*
> *The Army line you'll ever find a terror in the fray;*
> *And when the team is fighting for the Black and Gray and Gold;*
> *We're always near the song and cheer and this is the tale we're told;*

> *The Army team—Rah! Rah! Rah! Boom! . . .*
> *On Brave Old Army Team!*
> *On to the fraaay;*
> *Fight on to victory;*
> *For that's the fearless Army way;*
> *Ray! Rah! Rah! . . .*

When the last notes of the second chorus died away, they fell into one last extended team huddle, filled with heartfelt handshakes, hugs, even a few kisses. In their final minutes of Fatness, the Fat Men never felt fatter.

In a corner of the room, Cantelupe and Klein gave one another a final victory hug, a mutual thank you for four years as teammates, four years of friendship. As they pulled apart, Cantelupe said, "I never found Andy Thompson on the field. I should go see him."

And so, as the party that would eventually move from the stadium to a downtown hotel and go on all night long continued, Cantelupe quietly slipped out of the locker room and walked down the hall to find and console his former foe, his future friend.

Friday Night Lights

H . G . B I S S I N G E R

H. G. Bissinger's great high school football book *Friday Night Lights* is a staple for the literate football fan. Following Odessa Permian's adolescent team through a season of trials and tribulations in their quest for the Texas state high school football championship shows the dependence a depressed community can develop on its sons.

Permian's players are truly the pride of their town, and the pressures they feel to uphold the school's traditions and realize their own dreams are as real as any others they will feel in their lifetimes.

The formula for the book has been recreated in movies and on television, but Bissinger's true story provides insights that can't be squeezed into a 90-minute film. For three months every fall, the young men who take the field for Permian and thousands of other high schools are at once brothers, warriors, and potential saviors for their community. That's a lot to live up to for a group of 17- and 18-year-olds.

If the season could ever have any salvation, if it could ever make sense again, it would have to come tonight under a flood of stars on the flatiron plains, before thousands of fans who had once anointed him the chosen son but now mostly thought of him as just another nigger.

He felt good when he woke up in the little room that was his, with the poster of Michael Jordan taped to the wall. He felt good as he ate breakfast and talked to his uncle, L.V., who had rescued him from a foster home when he had been a little boy, who had been the one to teach him the game and had shown him how to cut for the corner and swivel his hips and use the stiff arm.

L.V. still had inescapable visions of his nephew—Boobie Miles as the best running back in the history of Permian High School, Boobie as the best high school running back at Nebraska or Texas A & M or one of those other fantastic college casinos, Boobie as winner of the Heisman. He couldn't get those dreams out of his head, couldn't let go of them. And neither, of course, could Boobie.

There were still some questions about the knee, about how ready Boobie was after the injury two months earlier that had required arthroscopic surgery (they had a tape of it that L.V., who was out of work because of the slump in the oil field, sometimes watched in the afternoon darkness of the living room, just as he sometimes watched other pivotal moments of his nephew's football career).

The Cooper Cougars had thrashed Boobie pretty badly the previous week down in Abilene, headhunting for him to the point that he had to be restrained from getting into a fistfight. But he had held up under the physical punishment, two or three or four tacklers driving into him on many of the plays, the risk always there that they would take a sweet shot at his knee, smash into that still-tender mass of cartilage and ligament with all their might and see how tough the great Boobie Miles really was, see how quickly he got up off the ground after a jolting *thwack* that sounded like a head-on car collision, see how much he liked the game of football now as fear laced through him and the knee began to feel as tender to the touch as the cheek of a baby, see how the future winner of the Heisman felt as he lay there on the clumpy sod with those Cooper Cougars taunting through the slits in their helmets:

Com'on, Boobie, you tough motherfucker, com'on, let's see how tough you are!
Com'on, get up, get up!
You ain't nothin' but a pussy, a goddamn pussy!

He had made it through, he had survived, although it was clear to everyone that he wasn't the same runner of the year before, the instinct and the streak of meanness replaced by an almost sad tentativeness, a groping for feeling and moments and movements that before had always come as naturally as the muscles that rippled through his upper torso.

But there was a fire in his belly this morning, an intensity and sense of purpose. This game wasn't against a bunch of goody-two-shoes hacks from Abilene, the buckle of the West Texas Bible Belt. It was against Midland Lee— Permian's arch-rivals—the Rebels, those no-good son-of-a-bitch bastard Rebels—under the Friday night lights for the district championship before a crowd of fifteen thousand. If Permian won, it was guaranteed a trip to the most exciting sporting event in the entire world, the Texas high school football play-offs, and a chance to make it all the way, to go to State. Anybody who had ever been there knew what a magic feeling that was, how it forever ranked up there with the handful of other magic feelings you might be lucky enough to have in your life, like getting married or having your first child.

After tonight, Boobie knew the fans would be back in his corner extolling him once again, the young kids who were counting off the years until their own sun-kissed moment excitedly whispering to one another as he walked down the street or through the mall. *There he is! That's Boobie! There he is!* The big-time college recruiters would come charging back as well, the boys from Nebraska and Texas A & M and Arkansas and all the others who before the injury had come on to him as shamelessly as a street whore supporting a drug habit, telling him in letter after letter *what a fine-looking thing* he was with that six-foot, two-hundred-pound frame of his and that 4.6 speed in the forty and how sweet he would look in a uniform in Norman or College Station or Fayetteville and how he should just *stick with me, sugar, I'll take good care of you.* They would all be there pleading for him, just as they had before the knee injury, before his dreams had so horribly unraveled.

He felt good when he left the little white house that he lived in, where a green pickup truck sat in the bare, litter-strewn yard like a wrecked boat washed up on the shore. He felt good as he made his way out of the Southside part of town, the place where the low-income blacks and Mexicans lived, and crossed the railroad tracks as he headed for Permian over on the northeast side of town, the fancy side of town, the white side of town.

He felt good as he walked into the locker room of the Permian field house that morning and pulled on his jersey with the number 35 on it. He felt good at the pep rally as he and his teammates sat at the front of the gym in little metal chairs that were adorned with dozens of black and white balloons, the decorations making them look like little boys attending a gigantic birthday party. The wild cheering of the entire student body, two thousand strong, above him in the bleachers, the sweet hiss of the pom-poms from the cheerleaders, the sexy preening of the majorettes in their glittery black costumes with hair as intricately laced as frozen drizzles of ice and their tender Marilyn Monroe smiles, the way the lights dimmed during the playing of the alma mater, the little gifts of cookies and candy and cakes from the Pepettes, the pandemonium that broke loose when defensive back Coddi Dean gave the last lines of his verse—

> *The moral is obvious, it's plain to see*
> *Tonight at Ratliff Stadium, we're gonna stomp on Lee!*

—all these things only energized Boobie Miles even more. The feeling came back to him now, the cockiness, the "attitude" as his teammates liked to call it, the self-confidence that had caused him to gain 1,385 yards the previous season and knock vaunted linebackers semi-unconscious. As he sat there, surrounded by all that pulsating frenzy, he could envision sitting in this very same spot a week from now, acknowledging the cheers of the crowd as he picked up the Superstar of the Week award from one of the local television stations for his outstanding performance against the Rebels.

> *A person like me can't be stopped. If I put it in my mind, they can't stop*
> *   me . . . ain't gonna stop me.*
> *See if I can get a first down. Keep pumping my legs up, spin out of it, go*
> *   for a touchdown, go as far as I can.*

That's right. That's how it would feel again, getting that ball, tucking it under his arm, and going forever like someone in the euphoria of flight. Nothing in the world could ever be like it. No other thing could ever compare, running down that field in the glow of those Friday night lights with your legs pumping so high they seemed to touch the sky and thousands on their feet cheering wildly as the gap between you and everyone else just got wider and wider and wider.

After the pep rally he went to class, but it was impossible to concentrate. He sat there in a daze, the messages of algebra and biology and English lost to him. Like most of his other teammates on game day, he couldn't be bothered with classes. They were irrelevant, a sidelight to the true purpose of going to Permian High School: to play football for the Panthers. Only one thought crossed his mind as he sat in those antiseptic, whitewashed classrooms until the middle of the afternoon, and it didn't have anything to do with schoolwork. He desperately wanted to perform well against Midland Lee, to break tackle after tackle, to be Boobie once again.

He didn't seem like a high school football player at all, but an aging prizefighter who knew that if he didn't get a knockout tonight, if he didn't turn his opponent's face into a bloody pulp, if he didn't sting and jab and show the old footwork, he was done, washed up, haunted forever by the promise of what could have been. Could he regain his former footing as a star? Or at the age of eighteen, was he already a has-been?

He felt good as he left class for the day and had a few hours to kill before it was time to go to the field house to suit up.

He felt good.

After classes ended, Jerrod McDougal walked out of school into the parking lot. It didn't take him long to find his black Chevy pickup, perhaps the tallest object in all of Odessa with the thirty-three-inch Desert Dueler treads that made it hard to get into without a stepladder. He climbed inside the cab amid the clutter of cassettes and paper cups. He found what he was looking for and did the same thing he did every Friday afternoon in those lousy waning hours before game time.

The pounding of the drums came on first, then the scream of "Hey!", then the sound of a guitar like that of ten-inch fingernails sliding up and down a blackboard, then explosive sounds moving back and forth between the speakers. There were more guttural yells, more screeching snippets of guitar, then the sudden, ominous wail of an organ that kept building and building and made his heart beat a little faster.

The guitars dug into his ears and the lyrics poured into his veins like liquid fire, the louder the better, the angrier the better, every sound aimed to strike right at the top of the skull and just rattle up there for a little while, get trapped in there, like a ball bouncing repeatedly off a wall:

> *Lay your hands on me*
> *Lay your hands on me*
> *Lay your hands on me*
> *Lay your hands on me*
> *Lay your hands on me*

Thank God for Bon Jovi.

McDougal closed the tiny eyes of his face and leaned his head against the back of the seat. He waited to see if the feeling would be there, as it had been a couple of weeks ago when Permian had beaten the hell out of the Bulldogs, had taught them a thing or two about having the fucking nerve to step on the same field with the Panthers, the Boys in Black. And it was, yes it was, a series of chills shooting down his back straight to his spine like lightning splitting a tree, a tingling feeling that both reassured and excited him. And at that moment, at that very moment, he knew there was no way that Permian could lose to Midland Lee tonight, no fucking way, not as long as he was alive.

It was all that mattered to him, not because it was a ticket to anything or a way out of this town that held as many secrets as the back of his hand. Long before, when he had stopped growing at five nine, he had put away all lofty dreams of playing for the University of Texas, or anywhere else for that matter. He knew that all he was, when you got to the core of it, was an offensive tackle with a lot of heart but little natural ability.

After the season there would be plenty of time to think about college and careers and all that other stuff that a high school senior might want to start thinking about. But not now, not when the most important moment of his life was about to take place. Friday night is what he lived for, bled for, worked so hard for. It sure as hell wasn't school, where he shuffled from one creampuff course to another. It wasn't the prospect of going into the oil business either, where he had watched his father's company, built with sweat and tears, slide through the continued depression in oil prices.

> *I'm a fighter, I'm a poet*
> *I'm a preacher*
> *I've been to school and*
> *Baby, I've been the teacher*
> *If you show me how to get*
> *Up off the ground*
> *I can show you*
> *How to fly and never*
> *Ever come back down*

Thank God for Bon Jovi.

The tingling sensation stayed with him, and he knew that when he stepped on that field tonight he wouldn't feel like a football player at all but like someone much more powerful entering a glittering, barbaric arena.

"It's like the gladiators" was the way he once described it. "It's like the Christians and the lions, like Caesar standing up there and saying yay or nay.

There's nineteen thousand fans in the stands and they can't do what you're doing, and they're all cheering for one thing, they're cheering for you. Man, that's a high no drug or booze or woman can give you."

He pulled back into the school parking lot. He left his pickup and entered the locker room of the field house where everything had been laid out the night before with the meticulousness of a Christmas display window, the shoes and the shoulder pads and the socks and the pants all in their proper places, the helmets fresh and gleaming from the weekly hand cleaning by one of the student trainers.

Mike Winchell hated these moments in the field house, wandering around in his uniform as the minutes dripped away with excruciating slowness. Secretly he wished that he could be knocked out and not wake up until five minutes before game time when there was no longer any time to dwell on it. He was the quarterback and that gave him a certain status, because just about everybody in town knew who the quarterback was and the novelty of having his picture in the local paper had worn off long ago. But with all the responsibilities—learning the audible calls and the three-play packages, not getting fooled by that overshifted defense the Rebels liked to run—it was hard not to feel overwhelmed.

He awoke early that day, in the darkness of the shabby house on Texas Avenue that shamed him so much he wouldn't even let his girlfriend enter it. In silence he had carefully wrapped up some toast and bacon in paper towels so he would have something to eat when he got to school. Then he got his mother up so she could drive him there since, unlike most kids at Permian High School, he didn't have his own car. They barely said anything to each other, because he hated questions about the game. When she dropped him off she whispered, "Good luck," and then left.

Once he got to school he had to go to the pep rally, where his long, angular face, framed by balloons, had a look of delicate sadness as haunting as a Diane Arbus photograph. It was a fascinating face, Huck Finnish, high-cheek-boned, yet somehow devoid of expression, the eyes flat and deadened against the roar and tumult that surrounded him, impervious to it, unable to react.

He welcomed going to class afterward, finding relief in the equations spread across the blackboard in algebra II, glad to have something else filling his head besides the thousand and one things that were expected of him. But outside class the pressure intensified again, the Lee game hovering over him like a thundercloud, the incessant questions of the students as he walked through the halls driving him crazy and offering him no escape.

Everyone seemed uptight to him, even the teachers who always dressed up in black on game day. When he walked through the halls of school during the season it wasn't as a proud gladiator, but instead he seemed enveloped in an almost painful shyness, his head ducked to the side and his eyes shifting furtively, fending off questions with one-word answers, especially hating it when people came up to him and asked, "Do y'all think you're gonna win?"

He had first started as a junior, and back then he had been so nervous that the butterflies started on Tuesdays. In the huddle his hands shook. Teammates looked at him and wondered if he was going to make it. But this season he was leading the district in passing and had cut his interceptions down to almost none. A big game against the Rebels would be further vindication, further proof that he had what it took to be a college quarterback in the Southwest Conference.

There could have been other options for him. During the season he had gotten a letter from Brown expressing interest in him because he was not only a decent quarterback but a good student. But for Winchell, who had never been east of the Texas-Louisiana border, the mere idea scared him to death. Rhode Island? Where in God's name was *Rhode Island?* He looked on a map and there it was, halfway across the earth, so tiny it could move into West Texas overnight and no one would ever know it, taking its anonymous place beside Wink and Kermit and Notrees and Mentone.

"Hell, Brown, that might as well have been in India" was the way he put it. He had read about the Ivy League in the sports pages and seen a few of those games on ESPN where the caliber of play wasn't too bad but it sure as heck wasn't football the way he had grown up to understand football. He also got a nibble of interest from Yale, but when he tried to imagine what these schools were like, all he could think of was people standing around in goofy sweaters with little *Y*'s on the fronts yelling, "Go Yale, beat Brown."

A series of meetings was held in the field house, the five Permian coaches trying to pound in the game plan against Lee one more time. Afterward, as part of a long-standing tradition, all the lights were turned off. Some of the players lay on the floor or slumped against concrete posts. Some listened to music, the tinny sound from their headphones like violent whispering in a serious domestic spat. Winchell, who had gone over the audible calls in his mind yet again, agonized over the wait. It was the worst part of all, the very worst. After several minutes the lights came back on and he and his teammates boarded the yellow school buses waiting outside.

With the flashers of a police escort leading the way so there wouldn't be any wait at the traffic lights, the caravan made its way to Ratliff Stadium like a presidential motorcade.

The sound of vomiting echoed through the dressing room of the stadium, the retching, the physical embodiment of the ambivalence Ivory Christian felt about what he was doing and why he was there. Droplets of sweat trickled down his face as he lay in front of the porcelain. None of the other players paid much notice. They had heard it before and gave little half-smiles. It was just Ivory.

There was so much about football he hated—the practices, the conditioning, the expectations that because he was a captain he had to be Joe Rah-Rah. He wasn't sure if he cared about beating Midland Lee. He wasn't sure if he cared about winning the district championship and getting into the playoffs. Let other players dream their foolish dreams about getting recruited by a big-time school. It wasn't going to happen to him and he figured that after the year was over he would enlist in the Marines or something, maybe buy a Winnebago so he could get out of this place and drive around the country without a care in the world, where no one could get to him.

But the game had a funny hold on him. The elemental savagery of it appealed to him and he was good at it, damn good, strong, fast, quick, a gifted middle linebacker with a future potential he didn't begin to fathom. Severing from it, letting it go, was not going to be as easy as he thought it would be, particularly in Odessa, where if you were big and strong and fast and black it was difficult not to feel as if the whole world expected you to do one thing and one thing only and that was play football. And despite the grim detachment with which he seemed to approach almost everything, he seemed scared to death at the thought of failing at it. He loved it and he hated it and he hated it and he loved it.

After he had finished vomiting, he reappeared in the dressing room with a relieved smile on his face. He had gone through the catharsis. He had gotten it out of his system, the ambivalence, the fear.

Now he was ready to play.

Every sound in the dressing room in the final minutes seemed amplified a thousand times—the jagged, repeated rips of athletic tape, the clip of cleats on the concrete floor like that of tap shoes, the tumble of aspirin and Tylenol spilling from plastic bottles like the shaking of bones to ward off evil spirits.

The faces of the players were young, but the perfection of their equipment, the gleaming shoes and helmets and the immaculate pants and jerseys, the solemn ritual that was attached to almost everything, made them seem like boys going off to fight a war for the benefit of someone else, unwitting sacrifices to a strange and powerful god.

In the far corner of the dressing room Boobie Miles sat on a bench with his eyes closed, his face a mixture of seriousness and sadness, showing no trace of what this pivotal night would hold for him. Jerrod McDougal, pacing back and forth, went to the bathroom to wipe his face with paper towels. Staring into the mirror, he checked to make sure his shirt was tucked in and the sleeves were taped. He straightened his neck roll and then put on his gloves to protect his hands, the last touches of gladiatorial splendor. It looked good. It looked damn good. In the distance he could hear the Midland Lee band playing "Dixie," and it enraged him. He hated that song and the way those cocky bastards from Lee swaggered to it. His face became like that of an impulse killer, slitty-eyed, filled with anger. Mike Winchell lay on the floor, seduced by its coldness and how good it felt. His eyes closed, but the eyelids still fluttered and you could feel the nervousness churning inside him.

In the silence of that locker room it was hard not to admire these boys as well as fear for them, hard not to get caught up in the intoxicating craziness of it, hard not to whisper "My God!" at how important the game had become, not only to them, but to a town whose spirits crested and fell with each win and each loss. You wished for something to break that tension, a joke, a sigh, a burst of laughter, a simple phrase to convince them that if they lost to the Rebels tonight it wasn't the end of the world, that life would go on as it always had.

Gary Gaines, the coach of Permian, called the team to gather around him. He was a strikingly handsome man with a soft smile and rows of pearly white teeth somehow unstained, as if by divine intervention, from the toxic-looking thumbfuls of tobacco snuff that he snuck between front lip and gum when his wife wasn't around to catch him. He had beautiful eyes, not quite gray, not quite blue, filled with softness and reassurance. His message was short and sincere.

"Nobody rest a play, men. Don't coast on any play. You're on that field, you give it everything you got."

Across the field, in the visitor's dressing room, Earl Miller, the coach of the Rebels, gave similar advice in his thick Texas twang that made every syllable seem as long as a sentence.

"First time you step out on that field, you go down there as hard as you can and bust somebody."

Brian Chavez's eyes bulged as he made his way to the coin toss with the other captains. On one side was Ivory Christian, belching and hiccuping and trying to stop himself from retching again. On the other was Mike Winchell, lost in a trance of intensity. The three of them held hands as they walked down a ramp and then turned a corner to catch the first glimpse of a sheet of fans dressed in black that seemed to stretch forever into the desert night. The farther they moved into the stadium field, the more it felt as if they were entering a fantastic world, a world unlike any other.

The metamorphosis began to take hold of Chavez. When the game began and he took the field, his body would be vibrating and his heart would be beating fast and every muscle in his body would become taut. He knew he would try to hit his opponent as hard as he possibly could from his tight end position, to hurt him, to scare him with his 215-pound frame that was the strongest on the team, to make him think twice about getting back up again.

It was the whole reason he played football, for those hits, for those acts of physical violence that made him tingle and feel wonderful, for those quintessential shots that made him smile from ear to ear and earned him claps on the back from his teammates when he drove some defensive lineman to the sidelines and pinned him right on his butt. He knew he was an asshole when he played, but he figured it was better to be, as he saw it, an "asshole playin' football rather than in real life."

He had no other expectations beyond the physical thrill of it. He didn't have to rely on it or draw all his identity from it. "I played because I like it," he once said. "Others played because it was Permian football. It was their ticket to popularity. It was just a game to me, a high school game."

As the number-one student in his class, his aspirations extended far beyond the glimmer of expectation that a Texas school, any Texas school, might be willing to give him a football scholarship. He had set his sights differently, zeroing in on a target that seemed incomprehensible to his family, his friends, just about everyone. He wanted to go to Harvard.

When he tried to imagine it, he thought it would be like stepping into a different world, a world that was steeped in history and breathtaking and so utterly different from the finite world of Odessa, which spread over the endless horizon like the unshaven stubble of a beard. When he visited it his senior year, he sat by the window of his hotel and watched the towers along the Charles with their seemingly effortless grace, the strokes of their oars so delicate and perfectly timed as they skimmed along the water past the white domes and the red brick buildings and all those beautiful trees. It didn't seem real to him when he gazed out that window, but more like a painting, beautiful, unfathomable, unattainable.

But now he wasn't thinking about Harvard. Every bone in his body was focused on beating Midland Lee, and he felt so absolutely confident that he had already ordered a DISTRICT CHAMPS patch for his letter jacket. As the coin was being thrown into the air by one of the officials he stared across at Quincy White, Lee's bruising fullback. At that moment Brian felt hatred toward the Rebels, absolute hatred, and he wanted to prove he was the best there was on the damn field, the very best.

The team left the dressing room and gathered behind a huge banner that had been painstakingly made by the cheerleaders. It took up almost half the end zone and was fortified by the Pepettes with pieces of rope like in some scene of war from the Middle Ages. It became a curtain. The players congregated behind it in the liquid, fading light, yelling, screaming, pounding each other on the shoulder pads and the helmets, furious to be finally set loose onto the field, to revel in the thrilling roar of the crowd.

The fans couldn't see the players yet, but they could hear them bellowing behind that banner and they could see their arms and knees and helmets push against it and make it stretch. The buildup was infectious, making one's heart beat faster and faster. Suddenly, like a fantastic present coming unwrapped, the players burst through the sign, ripping it to shreds, little pieces of it floating into the air. They poured out in a steady stream, and the crowd rose to its feet.

The stillness was ruptured by a thousand different sounds smashing into each other in wonderful chaos—deep-throated yells, violent exhortations, giddy screams, hoarse whoops. The people in the stands lost all sight of who they were and what they were supposed to be like, all dignity and restraint thrown aside because of these high school boys in front of them, *their* boys, *their* heroes, upon whom they rested all their vicarious thrills, all their dreams. No connection in all of sports was more intimate than this one, the one between town and high school.

"MO-JO! MO-JO! MO-JO! MO-JO!"

Chants of the Permian moniker, which was taken from the title of an old Wilson Pickett song and stuck to the team after a bunch of drunken alumni had yelled the word for no apparent reason during a game in the late sixties, passed through the home side. The visitor's side answered back with equal ferocity:

"REB-ELS! REB-ELS! REB-ELS!"

Each wave of a Confederate flag by a Lee fan was answered by the waving of a white handkerchief by a Permian fan. Each rousing stanza of "Dixie" by the Lee band was answered by an equally rousing stanza of "Grandioso" by the Permian band, each cheer from the Rebelettes matched by one from the Pepettes. Nothing in the world made a difference on this October night except this game illuminating the plains like a three-hour Broadway finale.

Permian took the opening kickoff and moved down the field with the methodical precision that had made it a legend throughout the state of Texas. An easy touchdown, a quick and bloodless 7–0 lead. But Lee, a twenty-one-point underdog, came back with a touchdown of its own to tie the game. Early in the second quarter, a field goal gave the Rebels a 10–7 lead.

Permian responded with a seventy-seven-yard drive to make it 14–10. Chris Comer, the new great black hope who had replaced Boobie Miles in the backfield, carried the ball seven of nine plays and went over a thousand yards for the season.

Earlier in the season, Boobie had cheered on Comer's accomplishments with a proud smile. As the season progressed and Comer became a star while Boobie languished, the cheers stopped.

He made no acknowledgment of Comer's score. He sat on the bench, his eyes staring straight ahead, burning with a mixture of misery and anger as it became clear to him that the coaches had no intention of playing him tonight, that they were willing to test his knee out in meaningless runaways but not in games that counted. His helmet was off and he wore a black stocking cap over his head. The arm pads he liked still dangled from his jersey. The towel bearing the legend "TERMINATOR X" from the name of one of the members of the rap group Public Enemy, hung from his waist, spotless and unsullied. The stadium was lit up like a dance floor, its green surface shimmering and shining in the lights, and his uniform appeared like a glittering tuxedo loaded down with every conceivable extra. But it made him look silly, like one of those kids dressed to the nines to conceal the fact that they were unpopular and couldn't dance a lick. He sat on the bench and felt a coldness swirl through him, as if something sacred inside him was dying, as if every dream in his life was fleeing from him and all he could do was sit there and watch it disappear amid all those roars that had once been for him.

With 2:27 left in the half, Winchell threw the finest pass of his life, a sixty-yard bomb to Lloyd Hill, to make the score 21–10. But then, with less than ten seconds left, Lee scored after connecting on a forty-nine-yard Hail Mary pass that unfolded like a Rube Goldberg drawing, the ball fluttering off the hands and helmets and shoulder pads of several Permian defenders before somehow settling into the hands of a receiver who had never caught a varsity pass in his life. Lee's try for a two-point conversion failed.

The score was 21–16 at halftime.

The Permian players came off the field exhausted, in for a fight they had never quite expected. The gray shirts they wore underneath their jerseys were soaked. Winchell, who had taken a massive hit in the first half, felt dizzy and disoriented. They grabbed red cups of Coke and sat in front of their locker stalls trying to get their breath, the strange Lee touchdown at the end of the half a weird and scary omen. There was hardly a sound, hardly a movement. The players seemed more shell-shocked than frantic, and few even noticed when Boobie flung his shoulder pads against the wall.

In a furious rage he threw his equipment into a travel bag and started to walk out the door. He had had it. He was quitting at halftime of the biggest game of the year. He couldn't bear to watch it anymore, to be humiliated in those lights where everyone in the world could stare at him and know that he wasn't a star anymore, just some two-bit substitute who might get a chance to play if someone got hurt.

None of the varsity coaches made a move to stop him; it was clear that Boobie had become an expendable property. If he wanted to quit, let him go and good riddance. But Nate Hearne, a black junior varsity football coach whose primary responsibility was to handle the black players on the team, herded him into the trainer's room to try to calm him down, to somehow salvage what little of his psyche hadn't already been destroyed.

Boobie stood in the corner of the darkened room with his arms folded and his head turned down toward the floor, as if protecting himself from any more pain. "I quit, coach, they got a good season goin'," he said, his tone filled with the quiet hurt of a child who can't process the shame of what has happened except to run from it.

"Come on, man, don't do this."

"Why'd [Gaines] play me the last weekend and the weekend before that?"

"I know how hard it is. Don't quit now. Come on."

"That's why I'm gonna quit. They can do it without me."

"Everything's gonna be all right. Everybody knows how it feels to be on the sidelines when he should be out there."

"Could have hurt [my knee] last week, could have hurt it the week before. He didn't think about it then."

"You'll be all right. Just hang tough for now. The team needs you. You know we need you. Use your head. Don't let one night destroy everything."

"Why not just quit?"

"This is one game. We got six games down the line."

"Six games to sit on the sidelines."

"We're almost there and now you want to do this, don't do this."

"Next week it ain't gonna be a new story because I ain't gonna play. Just leave me alone, and I'll get out of here."

"You can't walk off now, in the middle of a game. You just can't walk off in the middle of a game."

"I'm just gonna leave because I ain't gonna sit on the sidelines for no one. I see what it's all about."

"What's it all about?"

"I'm a guinea pig."

It went on a little longer, Hearne's heartfelt understanding in contrast to the attitude of most of the other members of the Permian football staff who derided Boobie, who had grown weary of his emotional outbursts and privately called him lazy, and stupid, and shiftless, and selfish, and casually described him as just another "dumb nigger" if he couldn't carry a football under his arm.

Reluctantly, Boobie left the trainer's room and walked back out to the dressing room. Without emotion, he put on his hip pads and shoulder pads. Carefully, meticulously, he tucked his TERMINATOR X towel into the belt of his pants and put that ridiculous costume back on again because that's what it was now, a costume, a Halloween outfit. He went back out on the field, but it no longer had any promise. When players tried to talk to him, he said nothing. The Rebels scored early in the fourth quarter on a one-yard run to take a one-point lead, 22–21. The Lee band broke into "Dixie" and the taunting chant, now stronger than ever, resumed:

"REB-ELS! REB-ELS! REB-ELS!"

With about six minutes left Permian moved to a first and ten at the Lee 18, but the drive stalled and a thirty-yard field goal was blocked.

Permian got the ball back at its own 26 with 2:55 left in the game, but instead of confidence in the huddle there was fear. Chavez could see it in the eyes of the offensive linemen. He tapped them on the helmet and said, "Com'on, let's get it, this is it." But he could tell they weren't listening. The game was slipping away.

They were going to lose. They were goddamn going to lose and everything they had worked for for the past six years of their lives, everything they cared about, was about to be ruined.

Winchell, after the glorious touchdown pass he had thrown, now seemed hunted by failure. His face was etched in agony, the passes coming off his hand in a tentative, jerky motion, thrown desperately without rhythm. The Lee fans were on their feet. There was the incessant beat of the drums from the band. Both sides were screaming their hearts out.

"REB-ELS! REB-ELS!"

"MO-JO! MO-JO!"

How could a seventeen-year-old kid concentrate at a moment like this amid the frenzy of fifteen thousand fans? How could he possibly keep his poise?

With a third and ten at the Lee 41, flanker Robert Brown broke free down the left sideline after his defender fell down, but the ball was thrown away out of bounds.

"Fuck! Winchell!" screamed starting linebacker Chad Payne from the sidelines as the ball fluttered helplessly beyond Brown's grasp. With a fourth and ten, another pass fell incomplete.

It wasn't even close.

Jerrod McDougal watched as the Lee players fell all over each other on the field like kittens. He watched as they spit contemptuously on the field, *his* field, goddammit, his fucking field, defiling it, disgracing it, and never in his life had he felt such humiliation. Some gladiator he was, some heroic gladiator. In the dressing room he started to cry, his right hand draped tenderly around the bowed head of linebacker Greg Sweatt, who was sobbing also. With his other hand he punched a wall. Chavez and Winchell sat in silence, and Ivory Christian felt that creeping numbness. With a three-way tie for first and only one game left in the regular season, now Permian might not get into the state play-offs. But that wasn't potentially devastating to Ivory. There had to be something else in life, if only he could figure out what it was.

Boobie officially quit the team two days later. But no one paid much attention. There were a lot more important things to worry about than that pain-in-the-ass prima donna with a bad knee who couldn't cut worth a crap anymore anyway. There were plenty more on the Southside where he came from.

The loss to Lee sent Odessa into a tailspin, so unthinkable, so cata-strophic was it. As in a civil war, goodwill and love disintegrated and members of the town turned on each other.

Gaines himself was distraught, a year's worth of work wasted, the cho-rus against him only growing stronger that he was a very nice man who wasn't a very good coach when it counted. When he got back to the field house he stayed in the coaches' office long past midnight, still mulling over what had happened and why the eighteen-hour days he had spent preparing for the Rebels had not paid off. The idea of a team with this kind of talent not making the playoffs seemed impossible, but now it might happen. And if it did, he had to wonder if he would be in the same job next year.

When he went home late that night, several FOR SALE signs had been punched into his lawn, a not-so-subtle hint that maybe it would be best for everyone if he just got the hell out of town. He took them and dumped them in the garage along with the other ones he had already collected. He wasn't surprised by them.

After all, he was a high school football coach, and after all, this was Odessa, where Bob Rutherford, an affable realtor in town, might as well have been speaking for thousands when he casually said one day as if talking about the need for a rainstorm to settle the dust, "Life really wouldn't be worth livin' if you didn't have a high school football team to support."

Game Plan

DON DELILLO

The complicated schemes and technical verbiage that make up advanced football playbooks are gibberish to the untrained eye. The knowledge of said schemes can take hours, weeks, months to learn, and the speed at which they are referred to during a game is a blinding blur of seemingly incompatible words. The eleven men huddled on the field have Ph.Ds in a foreign dialect known only to them. Their only real unity comes from a shared mastery of the dialect and recognition of the shared purpose of organizing their actions to function as one.

Don DeLillo takes a witty look at the language of football in "Game Plan," which originally appeared in *The New Yorker.*

Of the game itself, a spectacle of high-shouldered men panting in the grass, I remember little or nothing. We played well that night or didn't play well; we won or lost. What I do recall are the names of plays and of players. Our opponent was West Centrex Biotechnical Institute. They were bigger than we were, a bit faster, possibly better trained, but as far as I could tell our plays had the better names.

At the kickoff, the receiving team dropped back and found its ground, holding a moment. Under the tumbling ball, the other team charged, verbs running into mammoth nouns, small wars commending here and there, exultation and first blood, a helmet bouncing brightly on the phosphorescent grass, the breathless impact of two destructive masses, quite pretty to watch.

We huddled at the thirty-one.

"Blue turk right," Hobbs said. "Double-slot, re-T chuck-and-go, gap-angle wide, near-in belly toss, counter-sad, middle-sift W, zero snag delay."

"You forgot the snap number," Onan Moley said.

"How about three?" Ed Jessup said.

"How about two?" I said.

"Two it is," Hobbs said.

Six plays later, we left the huddle with a sharp handclap and trotted up to the Centrex twenty, eager to move off the ball, sensing a faint anxiety on the other side of the line.

"How to hit!" George Dole shouted out to us from the bench. "Way to pop, way to go, way to move! How to sting them, big Jerry! Huh huh huh huh! How to play this game!"

We scored, and Bing Jackmin kicked the extra point. I went over to the sideline and got down on one knee, the chin strap of my helmet undone—material for a prize-winning sports photo. Commotion everywhere. Offensive Backfield Coach Oscar Veech was shouting into my left ear.

"On the 32-break I want you to catapult out of there. I want you to really bulldoze. I want to see you cascade into the secondary."

"Tremendous imagery," I said.

"But be sure you protect that ball."

"Right."

"Get fetal, get fetal."

"Fetal!" I shouted back.

Our defense rolled into a gut 4–3 with variable off-picks. Down at the end of the bench, Raymond Toon seemed to be talking into his right fist. I got up and went over there. When he saw me coming, he covered the fist with his other hand.

"What are you doing, Toonie?" I asked.

"Nothing."

"I know what you're doing."

"Broadcasting the game," he admitted.

Their quarterback, Artie Telcon, moved them on the ground past midfield. At the sideline, I listened to one of our backfield coaches lecturing Garland Hobbs: "Employ the aerial game to implement the running game whereby you force their defense to respect the run, which is what they won't do if they can anticipate pass and read pass and if our frequency, say on second and long, indicates pass. If they send their linebackers, you've been trained and briefed and you know how to counter this. You counter this by audibilizing. You've got your screen, your flare, your quick slant-in. Audibilize. Audibilize. Audibilize."

They tried a long field goal, wide, and we went out. Hobbs hit Ron Steeples for good yardage. Steeples was knocked cold on the play, and the ref called a time-out to get him off. Chuck Deering came running in to replace him, tripping and falling as he reached the huddle. His left ankle appeared to be broken, and the ref called time again to get him off.

When we rehuddled Hobbs said, "Stem left, L and R hitch and cross, F weak switch to strong. On hut."

"What?" Flanders said.

"On hut."

"No, the other thing, F something."

"F weak switch to strong."

"What kind of pattern is that?"

"Are you kidding? Are you serious?"

"What a bunch of turf-eaters," Co-Captain Moody Kimbrough said.

"When did they put that pattern in, Hobbsie?"

"Tuesday or Wednesday. Where were you?"

"It must have been Wednesday," Flanders said. "I was at the dentist Wednesday."

"Nobody told you about the weak switch to strong?"

"I don't think so, Hobbsie."

"Look, run out ten yards, put some moves on your man, and then wait for further instructions."

"I'm co-captain to a bunch of turf-eaters," Kimbrough said.

"On hut. Break."

Centrex sent their linebackers. Hobbs left the pocket and I had Mallon, their psychotic middle linebacker, by the jersey. He tripped and I released, moving into a passing plane for Hobbs. He saw me but threw low. I didn't bother diving for it. One of the coaches, Vern Feck, screamed into our chests as we came off. "What in the hell is going on here? What are you feebs doing out there? What in the goddam goat-smelling hell is the name of the game you people are playing?"

Head Coach said nothing.

Lenny Wells came off in pain—groin damage or hamstring. Telcon spotted a man absolutely alone in the end zone and hit him easily, and I looked around for my helmet.

"Our uniforms are green and white," Bing Jackmin said as we watched them kick off. "The field itself is green and white—grass and chalk markings. We melt into our environment. We are doubled in the primitive mirror."

Centrex called time because they had only seven men on the field. We assembled near our own forty-five while they got straightened out. Ed Jessup, our tight end, was bleeding from his mouth.

"That ass-belly 62 got his fist in," he said.

"You'd better go off," I said.

"I'm gonna hang in."

"A tough area to bandage, Ed. Looks like it's just under the skin-bridge running to the upper gum."

"I get that 62. I get that meat-man," he said.

"Let's ching those nancies," Flanders said.

"Maybe if you rinsed with warm water, Eddie."

Their left tackle was an immense and very geometric piece of work, about six-seven and two-seventy—an oblong monument to intimidation. It was the responsibility of our right guard, Cecil Rector, to contain this man. Offensive Line Coach Tweego had Cecil Rector by the pads as I crossed the sideline.

"I want you to fire out, boy," Tweego said. "You're not blowing them out. You're not popping. You're not putting any hurt on those people."

I sat on the bench next to Billy Mast as Telcon riddled our secondary with seam patterns. Billy was wearing his helmet. I leaned toward him and spoke in a monotonous intonation.

"Uh, this is Maxcom, Robomat."

Billy Mast looked at me.

"Robomat, this is Maxcom. Do you read?"

"Uh, Roger, Maxcom," he said.

"You're looking real good, Robomat. Is that affirm?"

"Uh, Roger. We're looking real good."

"What is your thermal passive mode control?"

"Vector five and locking."

"Uh, what is your inertial thrust correction on fourth and long?"

"We read circularize and non-adjust."

"That is affirm, Robomat. You are looking real super on the inset retro deployment thing. We read three one niner five niner. Twelve seconds to adapter vent circuit cutoff."

"Affirmative, Maxcom. Three one niner five niner. Twelve seconds to vent cut. There is God. We have just seen God. He is all around us."

"Uh, Roger, Robomat. Suggest braking burn and mid-course tracking profile. Blue and holding."

Hobbs faked a trigger pitch to Taft Robinson and handed to me, a variation off the KC draw. I was levelled by Mallon. He came down on top of me, chuffing like a train. In the huddle, Hobbs called the same play. For some reason, it seemed a very beautiful thing to do. More than the thoughtful gesture of a teammate—a near-philosophic statement. Hobbs received the snapback, Roy Yellin pulled, and there I was with the football, the pigskin, running to daylight, to starlight, and getting hit again by Mike Mallon, by No. 55, by five five. A lyrical moment, the sum of something doubled.

Three firecrackers went off in the stands. The crowd responded with prolonged applause. I flared to the left, taking Mallon with me. Taft Robinson held for a two-count and then swung over the middle. Hobbs threw high under pressure. Third and four, or maybe fourth and three. The gun sounded and we headed for the tunnel.

Here before our cubicles we sit quietly, content to suck the sweet flesh out of quartered oranges. We are preoccupied with conserving ourselves for the second half and do not make work by gesturing to each other, or taking more than the minimum number of steps from here to there. A park bench has somehow found its way into the dressing area.

From nearby, I hear Sam Trammel's voice: "Crackback. Crackback."

I get to my feet and take six steps to the water fountain. Cecil Rector stands against the wall. Tweego has him by the shoulder pads once again.

"Contain, contain, contain that man," Tweego says. "Rape him. Rayyape that sumbitch. Do not let that sumbitch infringe."

Slowly I swing my arms over my head. I see Jerry Fallon and approach him. He is standing in front of his cubicle, hands at his sides, headgear on the floor between his feet.

"Jerry boy, big Jerry," I said.

"Huh huh huh," he mutters.

George Owen, a line coach, stands on a chair. His gaze moves slowly across the room, then back again. He holds his clenched fists against the sides of his head. Slowly his knees begin to bend. "Footbawl!" he shouts. "This is footbawl. You thow it, you ketch it, you kick it. Footbawl! Footbawl! Footbawl!"

Bing Jackmin squib-kicked down the middle. Andy Chudko hit the ballcarrier at full force and skidded on his knees over the fallen player's body. I watched Head Coach assume his stance at the mid-field stripe. Dennis Smee, our middle linebacker, shouted down at the front four: "Tango-2. Reset red. Choke off that sweep!"

Garland Hobbs opened with a burn-7 hitch to his flanker off the fake picket. I moved into my frozen-insect pose, ready to pass-block. Their big tackle shed Cecil Rector and came dog-paddling in. I jammed my helmet into his chest and brought it up fast, striking his chin. He kept coming, kept mauling me, finally driving me down and putting an elbow into my neck. I couldn't think of anything to say.

Hobbs looked toward the head coach for guidance on a tough third-down call. Head Coach said nothing. His arms remained folded, his right foot tamping the grass. This was his power, to deny us the words we needed. He was the maker of plays, the namegiver. We were his chalkscrawls. Something like that.

Hobbs said, "Zone set, triple tex, delta-3 series, jumbo trap delay, cable blocking, double-D to right, shallow hinge reverse."

The crowd was up and screaming—a massive, sustained, but somehow vacuous roar. I slowed to a walk and watched Taft Robinson glide into the end zone. Touchdown. He executed a dainty little curl to the left and casually dropped the football. Moody Kimbrough lifted him up. Spurgeon Cole stood beneath the goalposts, repeating them, arms raised in the shape of a crossbar and uprights, his fists clenched.

Jessup to No. 62: "Suckmouth. Nipplenose. Bluefinger."

I walked down to the end of the bench. Raymond Toon was all alone, still broadcasting into his right fist.

"There it goes, end over end, a high spiral. The deep man avoids—or evades would be better. Down he goes, woof. First and ten at the twenty-six or thirty-one. Here they come and Andy Chudko, in now for Butler, goes in high, No. 61, Andy Chudko—Fumble! Fumble!—six feet even, about two-twenty-five, doubles at center on offense. Chudko, majoring in airport-commissary management, plays a guitar to relax, no other hobbies, fumbles after the whistle. College football—a pleasant and colorful way to spend an autumn afternoon."

"It's nighttime, Toonie," I said.

"There he goes—five, six, seven, eight, nine, ten, eleven yards, power sweep, *twelve* yards, from our vantage point here at the Orange Bowl in sun-drenched Miami, Florida. John Billy Small combined to bring him down. John Billy, as they break the huddle—what a story behind this boy, a message of hope and inspiration to all those likewise afflicted, and now look at him literally slicing through those big ball-carriers! Flag, flag, flag—a flag down. All the color and excitement here. Oh, he's got it with a yard to spare off a good block by 53 or 63. Three Rivers Stadium in Pittsburgh or Cincinnati. Perfect weather for football. He's a good one, that Telcon. Multi-talented. Woof! Plenty of hitting down there. I'm sure glad I'm up here. D.C. Stadium in the heart of the nation's capital. Crisp blue skies. A new wrinkle in that offense, or is it a broken play? Time-out on the field with the score all locked up at something–something. And now back to our studios for this message."

I watched Lloyd Philpot, Jr., come toward the bench. His jersey wasn't tucked into his pants. Tape was hanging from his left wrist and hand. He squatted down next to me on the sideline.

"I didn't infringe," he said sadly. "The coaches wanted optimum infringement. They insisted on that all week in practice. But I didn't do the job. I didn't infringe."

Centrex was running sweeps. I went over and sat with Garland Hobbs. Somebody in the stands behind us, way up high, was blowing into some kind of air horn. It sent a prehistoric cry across the night.

"String-in left, modified crossbow, quickside brake and swing, flow-and-go, dummy stitch, on two, on two," Hobbs said.

"You're always giving us on two, on two," Roy Yellin said. "All freaking night—'on two, on 'two.' What about four for a change? 'On four?' "

"Four it is," Hobbs said.

More firecrackers went off in the stands, and newspapers blew across the line of scrimmage. I ran a desultory curl pattern over the middle, putting moves on everybody I passed, including teammates. The stadium was emptying out. I returned to the huddle. We went to the line and set. The left side of our line was offside. The gun sounded, and we walked off the field and went through the tunnel into the locker room.

Onan Moley is already naked as we walk in. We sit before our cubicles and pound our cleated shoes on the stone floor ten times. One of the school's oldest traditions. The coaches gather at one end of the room. Onan's right arm is in a cast and he stands against a wall absently waving his left hand to keep a fly away from his face. There are blades of grass stuck to the dried blood on his cheekbone. Next to me, Garland Hobbs takes a long red box from the bottom of his cubicle. The label on it reads: "All-American Quarterback. A Mendelsohn-Topping Sports Motivation Concept." Hobbs opens the box and puts it on the bench between us. He arranges twenty-two figurines on a tiny gridiron and then spins a dial. His team moves smartly downfield. Before it gets to be my turn to spin, the coaches call for quiet, clapping their hands and whistling. Head Coach is standing before a blackboard at the front of the room. His arms are crossed over his chest and he holds his baseball cap in his right hand. We are all waiting. He looks at his watch and then nods to Rolf Hauptführer, his defensive backfield coach.

Hauptführer faces us, assuming a stance of sorts. "Be ready," he says.

We sit waiting, immobile in our soaked equipment, until Hauptführer begins to read our names from the team roster, pausing after each one to give us time to chant an answer.

In Football Season

JOHN UPDIKE

The cultural significance of sports in America is most often linked to the personalities of athletes or the corruption caused by money in sports. But sport's cultural impact exists on a simpler level, one I believe is more at the root of the country's sports fetish. During their careers, individual athletes become inextricably linked to particular teams, teams linked to cities, and sports linked to specific moments in life. As different leagues line up to play year after year, the sports also become linked to the passage of time, the change of seasons.

Baseball drones on during the dog days of summer, a perennial soap opera that conjures thoughts of sunny days, meals on a bun, and the experience of the American pastime. Basketball evokes images of small-town farmhands sinking free-throws on a barnside rim or sleek inner-city youths using elegant crossover dribbles as the dead of winter rolls slowly toward spring.

For me, football has always been about autumn. Football season has a smell, a feel, and a taste that all begin to percolate as the temperature starts to head south. When daylight becomes scarce and wind-swept fall afternoons become crisp and cool, the familiar feel of football is inevitably in the air. John Updike's recollection of a long-ago football season and the raw emotions dredged up from his adolescence are evidence of his own attachment to the football season. His vivid recollections of the smells, sounds, and feelings surrounding his football memories are an homage football's place in the passage of time.

o you remember a fragrance girls acquire in autumn? As you walk beside them after school, they tighten their arms about their books and bend their heads forward to give a more flattering attention to your words, and in the little intimate area thus formed, carved into the clear air by an implicit crescent, there is a complex fragrance woven of tobacco, powder, lipstick, rinsed hair, and that perhaps imaginary and certainly elusive scent that wool, whether in the lapels of a jacket or the nap of a sweater, seems to yield when the cloudless fall sky like the blue bell of a vacuum lifts toward itself the glad exhalations of all things. This fragrance, so faint and flirtatious on those afternoon walks through the dry leaves, would be banked a thousandfold and lie heavy as the perfume of a flower shop on the dark slope of the stadium when, Friday nights, we played football in the city.

"We"—we the school. A suburban school, we rented for some of our home games the stadium of a college in the city of Alton three miles away. My father, a teacher, was active in the Olinger High athletic department, and I, waiting for him beside half-open doors of varnished wood and frosted glass, overheard arguments and felt the wind of the worries that accompanied this bold and at that time unprecedented decision. Later, many of the other county high schools followed our lead; for the decision was vindicated. The stadium each Friday night when we played was filled. Not only students and parents came but spectators unconnected with either school, and the money left over when the stadium rent was paid supported our entire athletic program. I remember the smell of the grass crushed by footsteps behind the end zones. The smell was more vivid than that of a meadow, and in the blue electric glare the green vibrated as if excited, like a child, by being allowed up late. I remember my father taking tickets at the far corner of the wall, wedged into a tiny wooden booth that made him seem somewhat magical, like a troll. And of course I remember the way we, the students, with all of our jealousies and antipathies and deformities, would be—beauty and boob, sexpot and grind—crushed together like flowers pressed to yield to the black sky a concentrated homage, an incense, of cosmetics, cigarette smoke, warmed wool, hot dogs, and the tang, both animal and metallic, of clean hair. In a hoarse olfactory shout, these odors ascended. A dense haze gathered along the ceiling of brightness at the upper limit of the arc lights, whose glare blotted out the stars and made the sky seem romantically void and intimately near, like the death that now and then stooped and plucked one of us out of a crumpled automobile. If we went to the back row and stood on the bench there, we could look over the stone lip of the stadium down into the houses of the city, and feel the cold November air like the black presence of the ocean beyond the rail of a ship; and when we left after the game and from the hushed residential streets of this part of the city saw behind us a great vessel steaming with light, the arches of the colonnades blazing like portholes, the stadium seemed a great ship sinking and we the survivors of a celebrated disaster.

To keep our courage up, we sang songs, usually the same song, the one whose primal verse runs,

> Oh, you can't get to Heaven
> > (Oh, you can't get to Heaven)
> In a rocking chair,
> > (In a rocking chair)
> 'Cause the Lord don't want
> > ('Cause the Lord don't want)
> No lazy people there!
> > (No lazy people there!)

And then repeated, double time. It was a song for eternity; when we ran out of verses, I would make them up:

> Oh, you can't get to Heaven
> > (Oh, you can't get to Heaven)
> In Smokey's Ford
> > (In Smokey's Ford)
> 'Cause the cylinders
> > ('Cause the cylinders)
> Have to be rebored.
> > (Have to be rebored.)

Down through the nice residential section, on through the not-so-nice and the shopping district, past dark churches where stained-glass windows, facing inward, warned us with left-handed blessings, down Buchanan Street to the Running Horse Bridge, across the bridge, and two miles out the pike we walked. My invention would become reckless:

> Oh, you can't get to Heaven
> > (Oh, you can't get to Heaven)
> In a motel bed
> > (In a motel bed)
> 'Cause the sky is blue

('Cause the sky is blue)
And the sheets are red.
(And the sheets are red.)

Few of us had a license to drive and fewer still had visited a motel. We were at that innocent age, on the borderline of sixteen, when damnation seems a delicious promise. There was Mary Louise Hornberger, who was tall and held herself with such upright and defiant poise that she was Mother in both our class plays, and Alma Bidding, with her hook nose and her smug smile caricatured in cerise lipstick, and Joanne Hardt, whose father was a typesetter, and Marilyn Wenrich, who had a gray front tooth and in study hall liked to have the small of her back scratched, and Nanette Seifert, with her button nose and black wet eyes and peach-down cheeks framed in the white fur frilling the blue hood of her parka. And there were boys, Henny Gring, Leo Horst, Hawley Peters, Jack Lilli-jedahl, myself. Sometimes these, sometimes less or more. Once there was Billy Trupp on crutches. Billy played football and, though only a sophomore, had made the varsity that year, until he broke his ankle. He was dull and dogged and liked Alma, and she with her painted smile led him on lovingly. We offered for his sake to take the trolley, but he had already refused a car ride back to Olinger, and obstinately walked with us, loping his heavy body along on the crutches, his lifted foot a boulder of plaster. His heroism infected us all; we taunted the cold stars with song, one mile, two miles, three miles. How slowly we went! With what a luxurious sense of waste did we abuse this stretch of time! For as children we had lived in a tight world of ticking clocks and punctual bells, where every minute was an admonition to thrift and where tardiness, to a child running late down a street with his panicked stomach burning, seemed the most mysterious and awful of sins. Now, turning the corner into adulthood, we found time to be instead a black immensity endlessly supplied, like the wind.

We would arrive in Olinger after the drugstores, which had kept open for the first waves of people returning from the game, were shut. Except for the street lights, the town was dark like a town in a fable. We scattered, each escorting a girl to her door; and there, perhaps, for a moment, you bowed your face into that silent crescent of fragrance, and tasted it, and let it bite into you indelibly. The other day, in a town far from Olinger, I passed on the sidewalk two girls utterly unknown to me and half my age, and sensed, very faintly, that flavor from far-off carried in their bent arms like a bouquet. And I seemed, continuing to walk, to sink into a chasm deeper than the one inverted above us on those Friday nights during football season.

For after seeing the girl home, I would stride through the hushed streets, where the rustling leaves seemed torn scraps scattered in the wake of the game, and go to Mr. Lloyd Stephens' house. There, looking in the little square window of his front storm door, I could see down a dark hall into the lit kitchen where Mr. Stephens and my father and Mr. Jesse Honneger were counting money around a worn porcelain table. Stephens, a local contractor, was the school-board treasurer, and Honneger, who taught social science, the chairman of the high-school athletic department. They were still counting; the silver stacks slipped and glinted among their fingers and the gold of beer stood in cylinders beside their hairy wrists. Their sleeves were rolled up and smoke like a fourth presence, wings spread, hung over their heads. They were still counting, so it was all right. I was not late. We lived ten miles away, and I could not go home until my father was ready. Some nights it took until midnight. I would knock and pull open the storm door and push open the real door and it would be warm in the contractor's hall. I would accept a glass of ginger ale and sit in the kitchen with the men until they were done. It was late, very late, but I was not blamed; it was permitted. Silently counting and expertly tamping the coins into little cylindrical wrappers of colored paper, the men ordered and consecrated this realm of night into which my days had never extended before. The hour or more behind me, which I had spent so wastefully, in walking when a trolley would have been swifter, and so wickedly, in blasphemy and lust, was past and forgiven me; it had been necessary; it was permitted.

Now I peek into windows and open doors and do not find that air of permission. It has fled the world. Girls walk by me carrying their invisible bouquets from fields still steeped in grace, and I look up in the manner of one who follows with his eyes the passage of a hearse, and remembers what pierces him.

The St. Dominick's Game

JAY NEUGEBOREN

A fatherless young man fills a void in his life by joining the school football team in Jay Neugeboren's "The St. Dominick's Game." Playing football, he discovers skills and values that were previously unknown and might have been left unearthed had he not forsaken his mother's wishes and joined the school team.

The experience brings him closer to manhood and, while initially driving a wedge in his relationship with his mother, it eventually brings them closer. But seeing the changes in him, his mother realizes that he is growing up.

This story is an examination of how team sports can provide life lessons unavailable in almost any other arena.

Though I missed my father most at school football games, when the other boys' fathers were there, I never told Mother. I didn't feel I had the right. My father died over eight years ago, and I was too young then to remember him much, so I figured the best thing was not to bother Mother about what I was feeling. It wasn't even as if I ever knew him well enough to miss him, I'd tell myself. It was more that at things such as football games, I was aware of his absence.

Mother didn't attend any of our football games and I could understand that. Ever since Father died, any kind of violence upsets her terribly. There are some days when she can't bear to look at raw meat or raw fish. Maybe if I'd been there when he died I'd feel the same. Mother has never told me what it was like, but it seems they were both sitting up in bed and reading that night, when he suddenly grabbed her and then blood started spilling from his mouth. She screamed and locked the door and wouldn't let me into the room until others had arrived, so I never got to see my father again until the funeral. He lived through the frozen hills of Korea, I heard her say to her sister, but he died in our bed in New Jersey. Go figure.

I used to try to picture what the scene was like, and I always imagined that his eyes must have been as wide and round as they could be—as if somebody had just surprised him—and then I'd find myself picturing Mother scrambling back and forth across the bed and the floor, trying to wipe things up, and the look I'd see in her eyes would be awful—so frantic and helpless and dazed that I'd just clench my fists and get more and more angry. Sometimes, trying to feel what she must have felt. I used to wonder if it was possible to love another person too much.

What I couldn't understand, though, was the way she acted when I told her I was trying out for the Fowler football team. Mother had been teaching French at the Fowler School since before Father died, and sometimes she worried that I was too quiet or too much of a loner, and I thought she'd be glad to hear that I wanted to participate in a team sport. But the first thing she did when I gave her my news was to threaten to get Dr. Hunter, our headmaster, to remove me from the squad. If she didn't receive satisfaction from him, she declared, she would go straight to Mr. Marcus, our coach.

I liked Mr. Marcus and I didn't want him to think I was a sissy, so what I did the next morning, despite her threat, was to talk with Dr. Hunter myself, before she could get to him. I told him about going out for the team and about how Mother was against it and about how I didn't want to disobey her, but that I was continuing to play anyway, and he sat in his big leather chair for a while, just thinking. I looked right at him, trying hard not to stare at his left arm, even though it fascinated me. It was shorter than his right one, and sort of hung from his shoulders, swinging gently to and fro whenever he walked, as if it were made of foam rubber. Most of us at school figured that, given his age, he'd maimed it in World War II, but nobody ever asked him, or knew for sure.

"You know," he said, "that your mother has not had the easiest life."

"I know," I said.

"Still, you can't be expected to sacrifice your boyhood because of the misfortunes she has endured, can you?"

I shrugged and said I didn't know. He nodded then and asked me a few more questions, all of which made me feel very uncomfortable, and then, after making some remarks about how contact sports build character, he said he would speak to her for me. The next evening he stopped by our house. Mother was upstairs grading papers, and when I told her who was there, she didn't seem to know what to do first. Finally, after starting down the stairs and coming back up two separate times, she sent me to entertain Dr. Hunter while she changed clothes.

My mother is a very attractive woman, with reddish-brown hair and very beautiful eyes. People tell me that I inherited her eyes. They're blue, but not pale blue—slate-blue, I would call them. She's tall and she makes a lot of her own clothing. When she's upstairs working at her sewing machine, which her mother used when my mother was a girl, and looking out the window, she always hums to herself in an easy way that lets me know she's feeling very peaceful. She's thirty-eight years old now, but people are never certain of her age. Sometimes she looks as if she's in her twenties, and other times, especially when she wears her hair up, she can look as if she's in her forties. It may sound strange, but one of the reasons I was sorriest that she objected to me playing football was that I'd always hoped I'd see her at a football game. She has the kind of face and coloring that's just perfect for a football game—what I would call an autumn kind of face.

When she came down the stairs that evening, she looked absolutely gorgeous. It wasn't what she was wearing—it was more the proud way she carried herself and the high color in her cheeks. Dr. Hunter must have noticed also, because he seemed a bit awkward when he stood up and shook her hand and said hello.

I went upstairs and tried to do my homework, but I couldn't. I put on the radio so they wouldn't think I was eavesdropping, and then I took out the sheets of plays that Mr. Marcus had passed out and I studied my assignments. At about ten-thirty, when I closed my door to go to bed, Dr. Hunter was still downstairs.

The next morning at breakfast Mother said that she'd decided it was all right for me to be on the football team. She warned me not to get hurt, and I said I'd be careful, and then she changed the subject. I tried not to smile too much, but I felt really good, and at practice that afternoon I nearly killed myself trying to impress Mr. Marcus. I dove for fumbles like a maniac, I was a tiger on defense, I wore myself out on wind sprints, and somehow I managed to intercept two passes. That was the day Mr. Marcus began using me as an example. At first I liked the idea. I wasn't an especially good athlete and I knew it. So did Mr. Marcus. But he kept pointing out to the other guys and telling them that if they would only try as hard as I did, they *might* have a good team.

Mr. Marcus wasn't very tall—maybe five-foot-seven—but there was something powerful about him and, like the other guys, I used to be scared sometimes that he would get so angry at us that he would pick us up, one by one, and smash our heads against each other. He yelled and screamed and never stopped moving. "My Aunt Tillie could do better——" he'd shout. Then, when the guys laughed, he'd counter with, "What are you laughing at?—Get in there and drive. What do you guys think this is—a church social? Put your shoulder in there and drive. Come on, girls—let's hustle. *Hustle!* Watch Eddie—there's guts for you! Watch that little guy give it his heart——" He could keep up patter like this for the entire two-hour practice, and at first I was thrilled with the way he praised me so much. After a while, however, I saw how it made the other guys resent me. Still, even though I didn't want them to, I kept giving it everything I had. I couldn't do anything else. I'd be as calm as could be during the day, or when I was standing on the sidelines watching—but the minute I was on the field and there were players opposite me, something inside me went click and I turned into a virtual madman. I didn't care what happened to me! It wasn't because I was angry or bitter or anything like that. In fact, whenever a fight broke out during a scrimmage or a game, I'd move back a step or two, instinctively, and stay away.

When I got home for supper, at about six-fifteen, I'd be totally beat. I'd stay in a hot tub for a long time, soaking my bruises, but when I came down for supper, Mother never asked me about practice or about Mr. Marcus or about any of my scratches or black-and-blue marks. As the weeks went by, it made me feel more and more depressed to sit with her each night and talk about the weather or her classes or my homework or our vacation plans, when all the time I was wanting to share the practices with her, and how great I was feeling just to be on a team with other guys. Finally one night, after a day on which a few of the guys had really had it with the way Mr. Marcus kept praising me and damning them, and they'd gotten me during a pile-up and given me some hard knuckles to the nose and eyes, I asked her straight out if, when he was young, my father had liked football.

She seemed surprised that I should ask, but when she answered, she didn't seem at all nervous. "I don't know," she said. "I suppose he did, but he never talked to me about it. Handball was your father's sport."

"Handball?" I asked.

She laughed then. "He grew up in a city, remember? Not out here with birds and trees. That came later—with me."

"Was he good?" I asked.

She wiped her lips, and when she sighed I could see that she was making a decision, to tell me something about him. "I suppose so," she said. "He was good at most things he tried. He was a very competitive man. He took me down to Brighton Beach once—this was when we were courting—and I stood behind the fence and watched him banging this little black ball against a brick wall on one of the hottest days of the year. He wore leather gloves." She brushed her hair back from her forehead and breathed heavily, almost as if she were feeling the heat of that summer day all over again. "I couldn't believe it, if you want the truth. And, as I recall things, it made him happy that I kept suggesting to him that it was too hot to play. I think he liked the idea of resisting my suggestions." She leaned forward then, her chin on her hands, looking very young. "Oh, Eddie," she said. "Your father was very special, did you know that? There was nobody quite like him. My parents couldn't understand for the life of them how a *cultivated* young woman like their daughter could be attracted to such a rough-and-tumble young man from the streets of Brooklyn, but there it was, wasn't it?" She smiled, as if dreaming, and I told myself I'd been right about why she always had such a hard time talking about him before— that it was because they'd loved each other too much, that for her it was always as if he'd died only a few weeks ago. "I mean, there was something about the way the sweat dripped along his chest and the ferocious look he got in his eyes whenever he slammed the ball, and then—the instant the game was over—that easy smile of his. Oh, he had a smile, Eddie! Bright and white in that dark surly face. And not just for me, I can assure you. Not just—"

She stopped and her smile became a straight line. "Not just what—?" I asked.

She looked away, and then stood and went to the sink. "Nothing," she said, and she changed the subject so abruptly—asking me about our Spanish class's magazine drive—that I knew there was nothing I could do to make her tell me any more.

Although our school went up to the twelfth grade, we fielded a team that represented only the seventh through the ninth grades. The Fowler School wasn't very large—four hundred students, including girls—and the other schools that were in our league were about the same size, so we played six-man football. We wore full uniforms and the rules were basically the same as in eleven-man football, except that no direct hand-offs were allowed and you had to go fifteen yards for a first down. The second week of practice Mr. Marcus made me a defensive end; I liked the position, especially when a blitz was on: this meant that instead of "boxing," and protecting my end against a run, I just crashed through the line and tried to knock over everybody I could until I got to the ballcarrier. Except for Charlie Gildea, who was the best player on our team, I seemed to be the only player who tried hard during practices. At games, when everyone's parents and girlfriends were there, the other guys would exert themselves, but it didn't matter much. "Games are won from Monday to Friday," Mr. Marcus would say, and he was right.

At the end of every practice session we would "run the gauntlet." We'd line up in a straight line, about three yards apart from each other, and Mr. Marcus would give the first man a football and he'd have to run through the entire team, one man at a time. When he finished he'd become the last man and the second man would get the football. The guys hated him for it. By the time you came to the fifth or sixth man you were usually dead, but Mr. Marcus wouldn't let you stop to get your wind back, either, so most of the guys would just fake the rest of the run, falling to the ground before they were tackled. What I'd do, though, would be to tuck the ball into my stomach, both hands around it, put my head down, and charge ahead, ramming as hard as I could into each guy I came to. I suppose it hurt me more than it did the others, but it made me feel so good! Mr. Marcus would tease me because I never tried to fake anybody out or even to sidestep. "Here comes Deion Sanders," he'd say. "Come on, girls, are you going to let this little runt bowl you over? Or is he too fast for you? Move toward the runner—*toward* him!" His voice kept me going, I think. "Way to drive, Eddie," he'd say, as I got up after each guy had rolled me to the ground. "Way to hang in there—"

Mr. Marcus wasn't very big, but we all knew he'd played halfback at a teacher's college in Pennsylvania, and once, on a hot day at the beginning of the season, he came to practice in short pants and I'd never seen such powerful legs. They weren't hairy, either. Just broad, smooth, and muscular. When he was teaching during the day, though, all his power seemed gone. He taught social studies and he could never control a class. I didn't have him for a teacher yet because he taught ninth and tenth grade and I was only in the eighth, but the guys on the team from the ninth grade would talk in the locker room about crazy things that went on in his classrooms. They said that some of the students actually smoked or made out right in front of him.

What seemed especially strange to me, though, wasn't anything Mr. Marcus said or did, but this look he had on his face when he walked through the halls. It was as if he were lost. The way my classes were arranged, I used to pass him in the halls three or four times a day and sometimes I'd say hello to him. He always said hello back to me, but I had the definite feeling that when I was out of my uniform, he didn't know who I was. He seemed to be thinking about something else, I thought, and when I was home remembering what his face had looked like as we passed each other, I'd start thinking that I'd been wrong: it wasn't as if he were lost, really it was more as if he had lost something.

He was never lost at practice, though. His eyes were all fire then. Especially when he began to get us ready for the big game against St. Dominick's on Parents Day.

St. Dominick's was an orphanage about twenty miles away, run by Jesuits, and we were playing them for the first time. Mr. Marcus told us that he'd seen them play the year before and that we would have to play more than perfectly if we expected to win. By this time we'd played six games, winning four of them, and I wasn't starting but I was getting in, usually near the end—at garbage time—when either victory or defeat seemed certain. I didn't expect to get into the St. Dominick's game, however, because even though I was hitting harder and playing better than ever before, so were the other guys. Dr. Hunter showed up at two of our practices that week, and once, when we were running through our kickoff return drill, I saw him pat Mr. Marcus on the shoulder in a friendly way. Until then I'd had the feeling Dr. Hunter didn't like him. It was nothing he ever said, but what he didn't say. He'd stopped by our house twice after that first time, and both times I'd tried to entertain him while Mother got ready to come downstairs, by telling him about our team. But whenever I said something nice about Mr. Marcus, and waited for him to say something back, he either changed the subject or agreed with me. He never added anything.

"You certainly are a quiet lad," he said to me one night, when, as usual, I'd run out of things to say. I shrugged. Nobody else I knew ever used a word like "lad," I thought to myself, looking down at the rug. But then he added something that made me look up fast. "Not at all like your father was, are you?"

"I don't know," I said. "I—I don't really remember him much . . ."

"Of course," he replied, but before I could get up the courage to ask him for more information, Mother had come down.

I went upstairs to my room, so they could talk. After the first time he came by, I'd begun to think of the fact that he might eventually marry Mother. The thing was, though, that every time I began to imagine what it would be like to have a man like Dr. Hunter for a father, I'd wind up by thinking of what it would be like to have Mr. Marcus as one. I knew this was foolish, especially since Mr. Marcus was seven or eight years younger than Mother, but I thought about it anyway and I wondered a lot about what he did after he went home from practice. I kept thinking what a waste it was that a man like him wasn't married, and how sad it would be if he somehow went the rest of his life without a son or daughter of his own.

I tried hard, a few times that week, to get Mother to talk about my father again, but she wasn't very interested. She did bring down a box of photos for me to look at one night—and after going through the first few, of them before they were married, going to Coney Island and Jones Beach and to her parents' home in Connecticut together, she got up and told me to come to her if I had any questions. All the photos were marked on the back, she said. Then she went upstairs.

I looked at the photos for as long as I could, but without Mother next to me, to give me stories about what wasn't in the photos, I got depressed. I closed my eyes tight a few times, and tried to force myself to remember things I'd done with my father, but it was hard, and the only clear pictures that came into my head were one of him laughing and giving me a ring for my thumb that he'd made out of a folded dollar bill—and another of him tossing me into the air and of how scared I was until I fell back down and he caught me and rubbed his rough beard against my cheek. I went upstairs and gave my mother each of these memories—asking her if he'd ever told her how to make a ring out of a dollar bill, and if he used to toss me in the air a lot or just once in a while, and if his beard had been very thick—but even though she answered my questions, she didn't add things to her answers, and she made me feel I was intruding on a part of her life I didn't have any right to.

The day before the St. Dominick's game, Dr. Hunter made a speech in our assembly about how we should be as friendly as possible toward the boys from the other school. They were less fortunate than we were, and he hoped we would all learn something from watching them and meeting them. The speech made me squirm. Words weren't going to do any tackling for us, I said to myself. But there was something else that was making me uneasy, and that was the way Mother was acting. When I turned to look at her in the back of the assembly hall, her cheeks were flushed, and this annoyed me. A lot of things annoyed me about her during this period, I know—the way she walked down the halls, the way she stopped to look in mirrors so much at home, the way she smiled at Dr. Hunter and the other teachers, the kind of clothing she wore—and the best way I can explain is to say that during this period, for the first time in my life, I was unhappy that Mother was pretty.

I certainly felt this way when we went to Parents Day together. Very few of the mothers came up to her to ask her questions about their children, but a lot of the fathers did, and the way she smiled, and the way they tried to impress her or make her laugh, bothered me. I kept wanting to go over to her and order her to stop—or to grab her and take her far away—and at the same time I kept wishing she would just pay a little more attention to me, and that she'd ask me about the game and about what our chances were and if I thought I'd get to play.

We were going through our passing drills when the St. Dominick's team arrived. They came in a pale yellow school bus, and they already had their uniforms and cleats on when they stepped down from the bus onto the field. Mr. Marcus went over to their coach, who wore a priest's black shirt and white collar, and shook hands with him, and while they talked we kept going through our drills, trying to act indifferent to their arrival. Their uniforms were black and gold, and I think we were all surprised at how new and clean they were.

I noticed, too, how serious they were about everything they did, even their jumping jacks. The other thing I noticed, of course, was the blacks on their team. Almost half their squad was black and there were also a few Puerto Rican-looking players. Although we had seven or eight at our school, and a few of the other teams in our league had one or two black players, I felt certain we were terrified by the sheer *percentage* of blacks on their team. One of the players standing near me confirmed my suspicion by saying that he wished we had "a few of those" on our team. "Can they run!" he exclaimed. I turned to him, wanting to contradict him, but I didn't say anything because I had to admit that my reaction had been pretty much the same. I assumed that black athletes were faster than whites, and that a team full of blacks would be almost impossible to beat.

By the time the whistle blew for the kickoff, our spirits were high, though, and the guys were all patting each other on the rear end and everybody was giving everybody else encouragement. On the sidelines the students and the parents were watching and clapping for us, and the girls stood together and did cheers most of the guys pretended to be annoyed by. I looked for my mother, but she wasn't there. We huddled around Mr. Marcus. "They look fast," he said, "but they're not very big. If you hit hard on the opening play, the game is ours. Is that clear? Hit hard and keep hitting. Drive, drive drive! Let the man opposite you know you're the boss, okay? I think we can win this game. What do you think—?" We yelled back that we would kill them, smash them, obliterate them, and then Mr. Marcus put his hand into the middle of the circle and we thrust our own hands in, pyramiding them until he shouted, *"Let's go!"* and then we all let out a big roar and the starting team ran out onto the field.

We kicked off and St. Dominick's ran the ball back to the twenty-five-yard line, but on the first play from scrimmage, Charlie Gildea red-dogged into their backfield and smashed this little black kid. The ball skittered out of his arms and John Weldon, our left end, fell on it. I threw my helmet into the air and raced down the sideline with the others to get closer to the play. Mr. Marcus tried not to seem excited, but I could tell he was just as thrilled as we were. Charlie Gildea went around right end on the first play after that and gained three yards. Mr. Marcus yelled at our guys to hit hard and I believe they were hitting as hard as they could, but on the next play I watched the way the St. Dominick's team dug in on defense. They dumped Guy Leonard to the ground for no gain. As I expected, Charlie Gildea went back to pass on the next play. I didn't watch him, though. I watched the line. The three St. Dominick's linemen charged through our men as if they weren't there. Charlie sidestepped one of them but the other two smashed him for a ten-yard loss.

Going back to pass again, on fourth down, Charlie was pulled down on the forty-two-yard line. It was their ball, first and fifteen to go, and it took them exactly four running plays to cover the fifty-eight yards they needed for a touchdown. The crowd was quiet. The St. Dominick's coach was yelling at his boys, and none of them were even smiling. Mr. Marcus was angry. "X–15!" he called. "And stop looking at the ground—look into their eyes. I want them to know they're in a ball game! Pick out a man on the kickoff and lay him flat!" X–15 was a reverse play, and it worked. The St. Dominick's team charged too quickly, and before they knew it, Charlie Gildea was in the clear, along the far sideline. Their safety man pulled him down on their own thirty-yard line, and we went wild. The thrill was short-lived. After the first play, when Guy Leonard gained four, our guys seemed to die again. As soon as the ball was snapped, the first thing you noticed was that our linemen seemed to move back a step, in unison. I could tell that Mr. Marcus noticed also because he started calling our guys girls, and right in front of the parents.

A few of us were still shouting encouragement to the guys on the field, but it didn't make much difference. After we gave up the ball, St. Dominick's began chewing up yardage again. "What's the matter?" Mister Marcus yelled. "Didn't you ever see a straightarm before? Christ!" He smacked his head with the palm of his hand and looked to either side of him. "Eddie," he called. "Where's Eddie?"

I ran to him, my heart pounding. "Go in for Shattuck. Show these girls something, okay? You show 'em, Eddie."

I dashed onto the field, pulling my helmet on and snapping the chin strap. "You're out, Shattuck," I said in the huddle. St. Dominick's was on our thirty-yard line. The other guys stared at me and none of them said anything, but I knew they were probably thinking that Mr. Marcus had put me in for spite. I didn't care. The first quarter wasn't even over and I was getting a chance to play. I lined up at right end, and when the ball was snapped, something went click inside my head. I took a step back, so as not to be taken in, and then I saw men moving toward me with the ballcarrier behind them. I charged forward, hand-fighting past the first man. The second man hit me with a cross-body block and laid me flat, however, and all I could do as the ballcarrier went by was to reach out with my hand, snatching for his ankle. I missed, and looking up I saw that he was laughing as he chugged by, his white teeth gleaming inside his brown face. Charlie Gildea came up from the secondary and made the tackle. He helped me up. "Good try," he said.

"I'll get him next time," I said. I heard my name and I looked sideways. Mr. Marcus was having fits. "Eddie! *Eddie!*" he was wailing. "How many times do I have to tell you? When you see men coming at you like that, don't try to fight them all—roll up the play and leave the tackle for somebody else. Is that clear? Roll it up!" I nodded and set myself for the next play. They ran the other end and made a first down. On the following play, though, they came my way again, and I did what Mr. Marcus wanted. Instead of trying to fight my way to the ballcarrier, I faked at the first blocker and then threw myself into him, low and sideways. It worked. He toppled over me and the other blocker tripped over him and the ballcarrier was slowed down long enough for Guy Leonard to bring him down for no gain.

The first half ended with the score 28 to 0, in favor of St. Dominick's. Between halves I lay under this big apple tree in back of the school, alongside the players, sucking on oranges. The St. Dominick's team stayed on the field, under the goalposts. Nobody said much. Mr. Marcus paced up and down, and it seemed to me that he had a million things he wanted to tell us and felt frustrated because he'd get to say only a few of them. In the distance I could see some of the fathers playing catch with a football. Beyond the football field I thought I spotted my mother, near where they were serving coffee and hot chocolate. I wanted her to look at me—to watch me sitting with the other guys and to be proud of me. I wanted her to know what it meant to me to have gotten into the game so early, and I wished too that I could just hear her voice—even if she was only laughing at some stupid joke one of the fathers was telling her—but, at such a distance, I couldn't be sure it was her.

"Do you know what the trouble is?" Mr. Marcus asked, his hands on his hips. "Do you?"

John Weldon shrugged. "They're too fast," he said. Some of the players covered their mouths and giggled.

"I see," Mr. Marcus said, nodding up and down. "I see. They're too fast. They're too fast. What else?"

Somebody to his left mumbled something. Mr. Marcus whirled toward him, then seemed to catch hold of himself, and when he spoke he did so firmly. "Would you mind repeating that for the other boys, Phil?"

Phil Siegel looked at the ground. "They got all those jigs on their team," he said. Everybody laughed.

"Do you know what the trouble is?" Mr. Marcus said again, ignoring Phil and the laughing. "Do you know what the trouble is?—You're not hungry ballplayers." He sighed, as if he knew how useless his words were. "Damn it, pay attention!" he snapped, and he grabbed John Weldon by his shoulder pad, yanked him from the ground, and then shoved him back down.

"In your little fingers you guys don't have—you don't have . . . Oh, what's the difference—" He looked around and his eyes flicked from one side to the other. He took a deep breath, concentrating hard, and then he spoke again. "Do you want to know what else? Do you? I'm glad you're getting beaten. How's that? This is probably the last time any of those boys will ever beat you at anything. When you're coming back here someday, watching your pansy children run around the field against the latest group of orphans or deprived kids, the boys you're playing against will be, will be . . ." He threw up his hands. "—God knows where! And while you and you and you," he said, pointing, "will be reminiscing about that time those jigs slaughtered you, none of them will even remember what the Fowler School was." He stopped. He seemed very tired suddenly, and I wished more than anything that I could help him. "Okay," he said, blinking. "This is the way it's going to be. I'm giving every one of you a chance to play, because I want every one of you, for once in your lives, to know what it is to get hit and to get hurt. Is that clear?" Nobody said anything. I was angry, and I wondered for a second if this was really what Mr. Marcus intended—if he'd only wanted to get us angry enough to go out and play hard-nosed football during the second half.

"That was a most interesting speech, Mr. Marcus." Some of the boys started to stand up. "Sit, boys. Please. Sit—" Dr. Hunter said. "You've been playing hard and you need the rest." He smiled, and when he did I looked at Mr. Marcus and the anger in his eyes made me imagine for a split second what my father's eyes might have looked like when he was moving in for a ball on the handball court, moving in to kill it. "I just wanted to wish you luck for the second half, boys. I know you'll do your best."

Mr. Marcus muttered something under his breath.

"What was that?" Dr. Hunter asked.

"Nothing I haven't said in other words," Mr. Marcus answered.

"Fine, fine—well. I'll leave you to your discussion."

Dr. Hunter left. Mr. Marcus waited a few seconds, then started off toward the playing field. "Follow me, girls," he said. "Don't be scared, now—"

The guys really hated him then, and during the second half they showed it. By the fourth quarter, when almost all the parents had stopped watching, they'd called their girlfriends over and were standing with them, wisecracking and showing off. One or two of them even took drags on cigarettes and necked with their girlfriends. It hardly affected Mr. Marcus. He just kept yelling at us and mocking us and he was true to his word about putting everybody into the game. For their part, the St. Dominick's team kept coming. At the time I would have given anything, I think, to have been one of them.

And I kept hoping, all through the second half, that before the end of the game one of them would speak to me—would say something about how hard I was playing, about how I was hanging in there—would make some gesture toward me. None of them did.

When the game was over, Charlie Gildea and I were the only players who stayed on the field and shook hands with them. I shook hands with as many of them as I could, even though they hardly seemed interested. They huddled at the far end of the field, gave us a 2–4–6–8 cheer, then walked to their bus and left. The final score was 54 to 0.

After I got dressed in my regular clothes, my gray flannel slacks and blue Fowler blazer, I went back to the field to look for my mother. Most of the parents were gone by now, and I couldn't find Mother anywhere. I walked over to the school building, and went inside, but it was deserted and her homeroom was locked. I came back outside—the sky was starting to turn orange from the sun—and, scared suddenly of being left alone, I found myself wondering for a second if she'd gone off with some other guy's father, if maybe one of them was divorced or a widower and if they were already sitting together in some plush lounge, having cocktails. I kicked at the ground and then got angry with her for not having told me where she'd gone, and for making me think such stupid thoughts and see such stupid pictures in my head. Didn't it ever occur to you that I might think things like that if you went off and left me alone? I wanted to shout at her. Didn't it? *Didn't* it . . . ?

Mr. Marcus saw me walking across the field, and he called to me and asked if I wanted a ride home with him. he had an old 1966 green Dodge Dart, and when I sat next to him we didn't say anything to each other. He smoked one cigarette after another, and since I'd never seen him smoke at school or practice, I was surprised. I gave him directions to our house, and when we got there I was relieved to see Mother's car in the driveway, and lights on in the kitchen. I asked Mr. Marcus if he wanted to come inside. I told him Mother could make us some coffee or hot chocolate.

"Some other time, Eddie. Okay?" He put his hand on my head and he stared at me for what seemed like ages, his mouth slightly open and a cigarette stuck to his lower lip. His eyes didn't shift or blink at all. Then he seemed to wake up. He looked at his hand as if he were puzzled to find it resting on my head. "Christ!" he said, ruffling my hair. "You're a sweet kid, Eddie. Now get inside, take a nice hot shower, and stay warm."

"Thanks for the ride home, sir," I said, when I was out of the car.

"Sure," he said. He backed the car out of the driveway and I started toward the house. Then he honked and I turned toward him. He looked out of the window and waved to me. "You played a good game, Eddie," he called.

On Monday I looked for him at school but he wasn't there. He didn't show up all week, and in assembly on Friday morning, Dr. Hunter announced that owing to illness in his immediate family, Mr. Marcus had been forced to leave the school for the remainder of the term. He said he hoped Mr. Marcus would be returning for the spring semester. When the spring semester began, Mr. Marcus didn't return. No announcements were made, and I was probably the only student in the school who even remembered what Dr. Hunter had said. I was feeling pretty upset, and when, on the evening after the first day of classes for the new term, Mother told me that Dr. Hunter was calling for her and that she'd have to leave me alone in the house for the evening, something inside me went click.

I stalked off, but while she was dressing, I walked straight into her room and asked her if she was going to marry Dr. Hunter.

"You should knock before you come in, Eddie. I might have been undressed." She looked into her mirror and fastened an earring.

"*Are* you?" I asked again. "I'm serious. I have a right to know!"

She kept working at her earring, as if I hadn't said a thing, but then I saw her mouth open slightly. I didn't give her a chance and I spoke before I even thought about what I was going to say. "How—how could you ever marry a man with a gimpy arm?" I demanded. "How could you—?"

She turned toward me and looked at me sternly for a second or two. Then her face broke into a big smile. "Oh, Eddie," she laughed. "Of course I'm not getting married." She stood and came to me and hugged me. Her perfume was strong, and I struggled to get loose. "You know you're the only man in my life."

"I'm not," I said, freeing myself. "I'm your son. You should get a husband while you're still young and pretty."

She backed off and looked at me for a long time after I said that, and I kept having these alternate feelings—that I shouldn't have said it and that I should have. I think she wanted to kiss me and hug me again, but for some reason she seemed afraid to do it now. She simply closed her eyes, nodded once, and then opened them. She turned back to her mirror. "Will you finish the dishes while I'm gone?" she asked.

"Sure," I said. And then: "How come Mr. Marcus didn't come back this term?"

"You're full of questions, aren't you?"

"Can I ask Dr. Hunter why Mr. Marcus didn't come back.?"

She sighed, then smiled again, but in a much easier way than she had a few minutes before. "I don't think that would get us anywhere, do you?"

"No," I admitted.

"Well, then?"

"I guess I ask too many questions."

When Dr. Hunter called for her, I didn't go out to say hello to him. After they left, though, still feeling worried about what I'd said to Mother, I kept walking around our house, going from room to room, upstairs and downstairs. It seemed terribly large to me, and I wondered if Mother was afraid when she stayed in it by herself sometimes. I tried hard to remember what things had been like when Father was there, but I couldn't. I went into Mother's room and took out her box of photos again and looked at the pictures of him, but that didn't help either. Not even when I found a picture of him with his arms around some other guys in sweatshirts, and a football on the ground in front of them.

But looking at the pictures of him, and seeing the way he smiled, reminded me of Mother being alone with Dr. Hunter, and when I saw that picture in my head, for the first time I asked myself if she could actually *enjoy* going out with him. Then I closed the box of photos and went downstairs to watch television.

I must have fallen asleep on the living room couch, because the next thing I knew, Mother was sitting next to me, stroking my forehead with her fingertips. The television set was still on.

"Hi, Eddie," she said. She bent over and kissed me. She held me for a long time, pressing her lips against my forehead in a very gentle way. Then she sat up.

"Did you have a good time tonight?" I asked.

She seemed surprised that I should ask her, but when she answered me I saw that I'd said the right thing. "Thrilling," she whispered. "I talked about irregular French verbs, and he told me about his eating club at Princeton."

"His *what?*" I asked.

"Never mind," she said, laughing. "At any rate, there was one interesting thing that occurred tonight. I couldn't stop thinking about our conversation, and about how much, when you get angry, you remind me of your father. You made good sense, you know . . ." I looked away from her then. She stood up, turned off the television, and sat down across from me, letting her shoes drop to the rug. "All right," she said. "Let me ask you something, Eddie. What would you think of our leaving the Fowler School and moving somewhere else? Maybe back to New York City, where—"

"Do you really mean it?" I exclaimed. My face must have registered how happy I was at the idea, and when she smiled and said that she did mean it, I tried to check myself, to hold back my enthusiasm. "Well, don't do it because of me," I said.

"You?" she laughed. "If we do it—and I'm not promising anything yet—we'll do it for the two of us." She leaned forward, and bit her lower lip before she spoke again. "I think we could both benefit by giving ourselves the chance to meet new people, don't you?"

"I suppose," I said, trying not to appear too excited. I didn't fool her, of course, and soon I stopped pretending and we were both talking about what it would be like to live in a place like Manhattan and of all the things we might do there together, and all the interesting people we might meet.

When she spoke about selling our house, though, I began to feel sad, and when she began talking about my going away to college someday and beginning a life of my own, what I wanted to do was to cry out that I would *never* leave her. *Never!* I didn't say anything, though. Because I guess I knew she was right, about my leaving her someday, and what I was hoping was that by the time I did she would be married again. But I knew that she might not be. I guess she knew it too, even though you never would have guessed it from the sweet way she kept smiling at me.

A Quarterback Speaks to His God

No man wants to contemplate his mortality, least of all one who has depended on his body for his livelihood. When the vessel that brought him all the success he ever knew—his body—begins to give out prematurely, Bobby Kraft is forced to confront his own vitality in Herbert Wilner's "A Quarterback Speaks to His God."

Successful football players who endure brutal punishment on the field are often described as having "heart." Kraft's reality is that the heart that served him so well on the field is not strong enough to keep him alive. He must overcome his insecurities about allowing others—his doctor, his God—take control of his body and his heart.

The physical and mental travails Kraft faces are even more personal knowing that Wilner, himself a former quarterback, endured illness and died at a young age. As Kraft transforms the real-life deterioration of his body into a game in his mind, one wonders if Wilner didn't fall back on a similar technique.

Bobby Kraft, the heroic old pro, lies in his bed in the grip of medicines relieving his ailing heart. Sometimes he tells his doctor your pills beat my ass, and the doctor says it's still Kraft's choice: medicine or open heart surgery. Kraft shuts up.

He wasn't five years out of pro football, retired at thirty-six after fourteen years, when he got the rare viral blood infection. Whatever they were, the damn things ate through his heart like termites, leaving him with pericarditis, valve dysfunction, murmurs, arrhythmia, and finally, congestive failure. The physiology has been explained to him, but he prefers not to understand it. Fascinated in the past by his strained ligaments, sprained ankles, torn cartilage, tendinitis, he now feels betrayed by his heart's disease.

"You want to hear it?" Dr. Felton once asked, offering the earpieces of the stethoscope.

Kraft recoiled.

"You don't want to hear the sound of your own heart?"

Sitting on the examining table, Kraft was as tall as the short doctor, whose mustache hid a crooked mouth.

"Why should I?" Kraft said. "Would you smile in the mirror after your teeth got knocked out?"

This morning in bed, as with almost every third morning of the past two years, Kraft begins to endure the therapeutic power of his drugs. He takes diuretics: Edecrin, or Lasix, or Dyazide, or combinations. They make him piss and piss, relieving for a day or two the worst effects of the congesting fluids that swamp his lungs and gut. He's been told the washout dumps potassium, an unfortunate consequence. The depletions cramp his muscles, give him headaches, sometimes trigger arrhythmias. They always drive him into depressions as deep as comas. He blames himself.

"It has nothing to do with will power," Dr. Felton explained. "If you ran five miles in Death Valley in August, you'd get about the same results as you do from a very successful diuresis."

To replenish some of his losses, Kraft stuffs himself with bananas, drinks orange juice by the pint, and takes two tablespoons a day of potassium chloride solution. To prevent and arrest the arrhythmia, he takes quinidine, eight pills a day, 200 mg per pill. To strengthen the enlarged and weakened muscle of his heart wall, he takes digoxin. Together they make him nauseous, gassy, and distressed. He takes anti-nausea pills and chews antacids as though they were Life Savers. Some nights he takes Valium to fall asleep. If one doesn't work, he takes two.

"I can't believe it's me," he protests to his wife, Elfi. "I never took pills, I wouldn't even touch aspirins. There were guys on coke, amphetamines, Novocaine. I wouldn't touch anything. Now look at me, I'm living in a drugstore."

His blurred eyes sweep the squads of large and small dark labeled bottles massed on his chest of drawers. His wife offers little sympathy.

"Again and again the same thing with you," she'll answer in her German accent. "So go have the surgery already, you coward ox."

Coward? Him? Bobby Kraft?

"I have to keep recommending against surgery," said Dr. Felton, named by the team physician as the best cardiologist in the city for Kraft's problems. "I'm not certain it can provide the help worth the risk. Meanwhile, we buy time. Every month these hotshot surgeons get better at their work. Our equipment for telling us precisely what's wrong with your heart gets better. In the meantime, since you don't need to work for a living, wait it out. Sit in the sun. Read. Watch television. Talk about the old games. Wait."

What does coward have to do with it?

This morning, in his bed, three hours after the double dose of Lasix with a Dyazide thrown in, Kraft has been to the toilet bowl fourteen times. His breathing is easier, his gut is relieved; and now he has to survive the payments of his good results.

He's dry as a stone, exhausted, and has a headache. The base of his skull feels kicked. The muscles of his neck are wrenched and pulled, as if they'd been wound on a spindle. His hips ache. So do his shoulder joints. His calves are heavy. They're tightening into cramps. His ankles feel as though tissue is dissolving in them, flaking off into small crystals, eroding gradually by bumping each other in slight, swirling collisions before they dissolve altogether in a bath of serum. His ankles feel absent.

He's cold. Under the turned up electric blanket, he has chills. His heart feels soaked.

He wants to stay awake, but he can't help sleeping. By the sixth of his returns from the bowl, he was collapsing into the bed. Falling asleep was more like fainting, like going under, like his knee surgery—some imperfect form of death. He needs to stay awake. His will is all that's left him for proving himself, but his will is shot by the depression he can't control.

By tomorrow he'll be mostly out of bed. He'll have reduced the Lasix to one pill, no Dyazide, piss just a little, and by the day after, with luck guarding against salt in his food, he'll have balanced out. He'll sit on the deck in his shorts when the sun starts to burn a little at noon. He'll squeeze the rubber ball in his right hand. He'll take a shower afterwards and oil himself down to rub the flaking off. He'll look at himself in the full-length mirror and stare at the part of his chest where the injured heart is supposed to be. He'll see little difference from what he saw five years ago when he was still playing. The shoulders sloping and wide, a little less full but not bony, the chest a little less deep but still broad and tapered, the right arm still flat-muscled and whip-hanging, same as it was ten years ago when he could throw a football sixty yards with better than fair accuracy. What he'll see in the mirror can infuriate him.

He once got angry enough to put on his sweat suit, go through the gate at the back fence and start to run in the foot-wide level dirt beside the creek bed in the shade of the laurels. After five cautious strides, he lengthened into ten hard ones. Then he was on his knees gasping for air, his heart arrhythmic, his throat congested. He couldn't move for five minutes. By the next day he'd gained six pounds. He told Elfi what he'd done.

"Imbecile!" She called the doctor. Kraft, his ankles swollen, was into heart failure. It was touch and go about sending him to the hospital for intravenous diuretics and relief oxygen.

It took a month to recover, he never made another effort to run, but he knew even today, that after all this pissing and depression, exhaustion and failure, when he balanced out the day after tomorrow and he was on the deck and the sun hit, nothing could keep the impulse out of his legs. He'd want to run. He'd feel the running in his legs. And he'd settle for a few belittling house chores, then all day imagine he'd have a go at screwing Elfi. But at night he didn't dare try.

When she gets home from her day with the retards, she fixes her Campari on ice, throws the dinner together, at which, as always, she pecks like a bird and he shovels what he can, making faces to advertise his nausea, rubbing his abdomen to soothe his distress and belching to release the gas. After dinner he'll report his day, shooting her combative looks to challenge the boredom glazing her face. They move to the living room. Standing, he towers over her. He's six foot two inches and she's tiny. His hand, large even for his size, would cover the top of her skull the way an ordinary man's might encapsulate an egg. She stretches full length on the couch; he slouches in the club chair. She wears a tweed skirt and buttoned blouse, he's in his pajamas and terry cloth robe. He still has a headache. His voice drones monotonously in his own ears, but he's obsessed with accounting for his symptoms as though they were football statistics. When he at last finishes, she sits up and nods.

"So all in all today is a little better. Nothing with the bad rhythm."

He gets sullen, then angry. No one has ever annoyed him as effectively as she. He'd married her six years ago, just before his retirement, as he'd always planned. He knew the stewardesses, models, second-rate actresses, and just plain hotel whores, would no longer do. He'd need children, a son. And this tiny woman's German accent and malicious tongue had knocked him out. And sometimes he caught her reciting prayers in French (she said for religion it was the perfect language), which seemed to him—a man without religion—unexplainably peculiar and right.

Now, offended by her flint heart (calling *this* a better day!), he goes to the den for TV. He has another den with shelves full of his history—plaques, cups, trophies, photos (one with the President of the United States), footballs, medals, albums, video tapes—but he no longer enters this room. After an hour, she comes in after him. She wants to purr. He wants to be left alone. His headache is worse, his chest tingles. She recounts events of her day, one of the two during the week when she drives to the city and consults at a school for what she calls learning-problem children. He doesn't even pretend to listen. She sulks.

Words go back and forth. He didn't think he could do it, but he tells her. In roundabout fashion, the TV jabbering, he finally makes her understand his latest attack of anxiety: the feel of his not feeling it. His prick.

She looked amazed, as if she were still not understanding him, then her eyes widen and she taps herself on the temple.

"You I don't understand," she sputters. "To me your head is something for doctors. Every day I worry sick about your heart, and you give me this big soap opera about your prick. Coward. You should go for the surgery. Every week you get worse, whatever that Dr. Felton says. You let all those oxes fall on you and knock you black and blue, then a little cutting with a knife, and you shiver. When they took away your football, they broke your baby's heart. So now, sew it up again. Let a surgeon do it. You don't know how. You think your heart can get better by itself? In you, Bobby, never."

When it suits her, she exaggerates her mispronunciation of his name. "*Beaubee. Beaubee.* What kind of name is this for a grown man your size, Beaubee?"

He heads to the bedroom to slam the door behind him. After ten minutes, the door opens cautiously. She sits at the edge of the bed near his feet. She strokes the part of the blanket covering his feet, puts her cheek to it, then straightens, stands, says it to him.

"I love you better than my own life. I swear it. How else could I stay with you?"

He hardly hears her. His attention concentrates on the first signs of his arrhythmia. He tells her, "It's beginning." She says she'll fetch the quinidine. She carries his low sodium milk for him to drink it with. He glances at her woefully through what used to be ice-blue eyes fixed in his head like crystals. He stares at the pills before he swallows them. He can identify any of them by color, shape and size. He doesn't trust her. She can't nurse, she always panics.

His heart is fluttering, subsiding, fluttering. Finally it levels off at the irregularity of the slightly felt extra beat which Felton has told him is an auricular fibrillation. Elfi finds an excuse to leave the room. He sits up in bed, his eyes closed, his thick back rammed against the sliding pillows, his head arched over them, the crown drilling into the headboard.

The flurries have advanced to a continuously altering input of extra beats. They are light and rapid, like the scurryings under his breastbone of a tiny creature with scrawny limbs. After ten minutes, the superfluous beats intensify and ride over the regular heartbeats.

There's chaos in his heart. Following a wild will of its own, it has nothing to do with him, nor can he do anything with it. Moderate pain begins in his upper left arm, and though the doctor has assured him it's nothing significant, and he knows it will last only through the arrhythmia, Kraft begins to sweat.

The heart goes wilder. He rubs his chest, runs his hands across the protruding bones of his cheeks and jaw. Ten minutes later the heart begins to yank as well as thump. It feels as if the heart's apex is stitched into tissues near the bottom of his chest, and the yanking of the bulk of the heart will tear the threads loose. Again and again he tries to will himself into the cool accommodation he can't command. Then at last it seems that for a few minutes the force of the intrusive beats is diminishing. He dares to hope it's now the beginning of the end of the episode.

Immediately a new sequence of light and differently irregular flurries resumes. The thumpings are now also on his back. He turns to his right side, flicks the control for the television, tries to lose himself with it, hears Elfi come in. She whispers, "Still?" and leaves again.

The thumpings deepen. They are really pounding. The headache is drilled in his forehead. It throbs. He thinks the heart is making sounds that can be heard in the room. He claws his long fingers into the tough flesh over the heart. It goes on for another hour. He waits, and waits. Then, indeed, in mo-

ments, they fade into the flutter with which they began. After a while the flutter is hard to pick out, slips under the regular beating of his heart, and gives
way at last to an occasional extra beat which pokes at his chest with the feel of
a mild bubbling of thick pudding at a slow boil. Then that's gone.

His heart has had its day's event.

Kraft tells himself: nothing's worth this. He's told it to himself often.
He tells himself he'll see Felton tomorrow. He'll insist on the surgery.

Afraid of surgery? Coward? She wasn't even in his life when he had his
knee done after being blindsided in Chicago. He came out of the anesthesia on
a cloud. The bandage on his leg went from thigh to ankle, but the girl who
came to visit him—stewardess, model; the cocktail waitress—he couldn't remember now, she was the one whose eyes changed colors—she had to fight
him off because he kept rubbing his hand under her skirt up the soft inside of
her thigh. She ended on his bed on top of him. He was almost instantaneous.
He had to throw her off, remembering his leg, his career. But was it really that
Felton runt who was keeping him from surgery?

In despair now, could he really arrange for the surgery tomorrow? Not
on a knee, but on his opened heart?

Bobby Kraft's heart?

"That's crap," he once said to a young reporter. "Any quarterback can throw.
We all start from there. Some of us do it a little better. That's not what it's all
about. Throwing aint passing, sonny, and passing aint all of quarterbacking
anyway."

"You mean picking your plays. Using your head. Reading defenses?"

"That's important. It's not all of it."

"What's the mystique?" the youth asked shyly, fearful of ignorance.
"Not in your arm; not in your head. I know you all have guts or wouldn't play
in such a violent game. If it's a special gift, where do you keep it?"

"In your godddamn chest, sonny. Where the blood comes." He smiled
and stared icily at the reporter until the young man turned away.

Actually, Kraft worked hard mastering the technical side of his skills. If
he needed to, for instance, if the wind wasn't strong against him, he could hang
the ball out fifty yards without putting too much arc in it. It should've been a
heavy ball to catch for a receiver running better than ten yards to the second.
But Kraft, in any practice, could get it out there inches ahead of the outstretched arms and have the forward end of the ball, as it was coming down,
begin to point up slightly over its spiralling axis. That way it fell with almost no

weight at all. The streaking receiver could palm it in one hand, as if he were snatching a fruit from a tree he ran by. It took Kraft years to get it right and do it in games.

There were ways of taking the ball from the center, places on it for each of his fingers, ways of wrist-cradling the ball before he threw if he had to break his pocket, and there was the rhythm set up between his right arm and the planting of his feet before he released the ball through the picket of huge, upraised arms.

He watched the films. He studied the game book. He worked with the coaches and his receivers for any coming Sunday. What the other team did every other time they played you, and what they did all season was something you had to remember. You also had to be free of it. You had to yield to the life of the particular game, build it, master it, improvise. And always you not only had to stand up to their cries of "Kill Kraft," you had to make them eat it. The sonsabitches!

That's what Kraft did most of the week waiting for his Sunday game. He worked the "sonsabitches" into a heat. Then he slid outside himself and watched it. It was like looking at a fire he'd taken out of his chest to hold before eyes. Tense all week, his eyes grew colder and colder as they gazed at the flame. By game time he was thoroughly impersonal.

Sunday on the field in the game, though he weighed 203, he looked between plays somewhat on the slender side, like someone who could get busted like a stick by most of those he played among. He stood out of the huddle a long time before he entered it through the horseshoe's slot to call the play. Outside the huddle, except in the last minutes when they might be fighting the clock, his pose was invariable. His right foot was anchored with the toe toward the opening for him in his huddle about nine feet away, the left angled toward where the referee had placed the ball. It threw his torso on a rakish slant toward the enormous opposing linemen, as though he'd tight-rigged himself against a headland. He kept the knuckles of his right hand high on his right ass, the fingers limp. His left hand hung motionless on his left side. Under his helmet, his head turned slowly and his eyes darted. He wasn't seeing anything that would matter. They'd change it all around when he got behind the center. He was emptying himself for his concentration. It was on the three strides back to the huddle that he picked his play and barked it to them in a toneless, commanding fierceness just short of rage.

Then the glory began for Kraft. What happened, what he lived for never got into the papers; it wasn't seen on television. What he saw was only part of what he knew. He would watch the free safety or the outside lineback-ers for giveaway cues on the blitz. He might detect from jumping linemen some of the signs of looping. The split second before he had the ball he might spot assignment against his receivers and automatically register the little habits and capacities of the defending sonsabitches. He could "feel" the defenses.

But none of it really began until, after barking the cadence of his signals, he ac-tually did have the ball in his hand. Then, for the fraction of a second before he gave it away to a runner, or for the maximum three seconds in the pocket be-fore he passed, there was nothing but grunting and roaring and cursing, the crashing of helmets and pads, the oofs of air going out of brutish men and the whisk of legs in tight pants cutting air like a scythe in tall grass and the soft suck of cleats in the grassy sod, and the actual vibration of the earth itself stampeded by that tonnage of sometimes gigantic, always fast, cruel, lethal bodies. And if Kraft kept the ball, if he dropped his three paces back into his protective pocket, he'd inch forward before he released it and turn his shoulders or his hips to slip past the bodies clashing at his sides. He would always sense and sometimes never see the spot to which he had to throw the ball through the nests of the raised arms of men two to five inches taller than himself and twice as broad and sixty, eighty pounds heavier. One of their swinging arms could, if he didn't see it coming, knock him off his feet as though he were a matchstick. He was often on his back or side, a pile of the sonsabitches taking every gouge and kick and swipe at him they could get away with. That was the sweetness for him.

To have his ass beaten and not even know it. To have that rush inside him mounting all through the game, and getting himself more and more under control as he heated up, regarding himself without awareness of it, his heart given to the fury, and his mind to a sly and joyous watching of his heart, stor-ing up images that went beyond the choral roaring of any huge crowd and that he would feed on through the week waiting for the next game, aching through the week but never knowing in the game any particular blow that would make him hurt. Not after the first time he got belted. They said he had rubber in his joints, springs in his ass, and a whip for an arm.

The combination of his fierce combativeness and laid back detach-ment infuriated the sonsabitches he played against. They hated him; it made them lose their heads. It was all the advantage Kraft ever needed. His own teammates, of course, went crazy with the game. They wound themselves up for it in the hours before it, and some of them didn't come down until the day after, regardless of who won.

Kraft depended on their lunacy. He loved them for needing it. And he loved them most during the game because no one ever thought of him as being like them. He was too distant. Too cunning. Too cold. But on the sideline, among them, waiting for his defensive team to get him back into the game, he might run his tongue over his lips, taste the salty blood he didn't know was there, and swallow. Then he'd rub his tongue across his gums and over the inside of a cheek, and an expression of wonder might flicker across his face, as if he were a boy with his first lick at the new candy, tasting the sweetness of his gratified desires, not on his tongue but in his own heart.

Three more months passed with Kraft delivered up to the cycles of his illness and medicines and waiting and brooding. Then he was sitting in his sweat socks and trunks at the side of the pool one late afternoon. He gazed vacantly at the water. His chest had caved a little; and his long head seemed larger, his wide neck thicker. Elfi had been reading on a mat near the fence under the shade of a laurel.

"So how long are you going to live like this?" she asked. Immediately he thought she was talking sex. "Two more years? Five? Ten?" She crossed her arms over her slender, fragile chest. "Maybe even fifteen, hah? But sooner or later you'll beg them for the surgery. On your knees. So why do you wait? Look how you lose all the time you could be better in."

His answer was pat.

"I told you. They can cut up my gut. They can monkey with my head. They can cut off my right arm even, how's that? But they're not going to cut up my heart. That's all. They're not putting plastic valves in my heart."

"Again with this plastic. Listen, I am reading a lot about it. There are times they can put in a valve from a sheep, or a pig."

He looked at her in amazement. He stood up. She came to his collarbone; he cast a shade over all of her.

"Sheep and pig!"

He looked like he might slam her, then he turned away and headed for the glass door to the bedroom.

"Your heart," she said. "You have such a special heart?"

When he turned she looked up at him and backed off a step.

"Yeah, it's special. My heart's me." He stabbed his chest with the long thumb of his right hand.

"You think I don't understand that? With my own heart I understand that. But this is the country where surgeons make miracles. You are lucky. It happens to you here, where you are such a famous ox. And here they have the surgeon who's also so famous. For him, what you have is a—is a—a blister."

He glared. She backed off another step. He turned and dove suddenly into the pool, touched bottom, came up slowly and thought he could live a long time in a chilly, blue, chlorinated water in which he would, suspended, always hold his breath. He rose slowly, broke the water at the nearer wall, hoisted himself at the coping and emerged from the water, with his back and shoulders glistening. He was breathless, but he moved on to the bedroom. He didn't double over until he had closed the glass door behind him. While he waited for his throat to empty and his chest to fill, he hurt. He got dizzy. Bent, he moved to the bed and fell on it. He stretched out.

He napped, or thought he did. When he woke, or his mind cleared, words filled him. He clasped his hands behind his neck, closed his eyes and tried to shut the words out. He got off the bed and stood before the full-length mirror. He put his hands to his thighs, bent his weight forward, clamped the heels of his hands together, dropped his left palm to make a nest for the ball the center would snap. Numbers barked in his head. When he heard the hup–hup he moved back the two swift steps, planted his feet, brought his right arm high behind his head, the elbow at his ear, then released the shoulder and snapped the wrist. He did it twice more. He was grinning. When he started it the fourth time, he was into arrhythmia.

Kraft consults Dr. Felton. Felton examines him, sits, glances at him, gazes at the ceiling, puts the tips of his index fingers to a pyramid point on his mustache, and says, "I'm still opposed, but I'll call him." He means the heart surgeon, Dr. Gottfried. They arrange for Kraft to take preliminary tests. He has already had some of them, but the heart catheterization will be new. A week later Kraft enters the hospital.

An hour after he's in his room, a parade of doctors begin the listening and thumping on Kraft's chest and back. A bearded doctor in his early thirties who will assist in the morning's catheterization briefs him on what to expect. He speaks rapidly.

"You'll be awake of course. You'll find it a painless procedure. We'll use a local on your arm where we insert the catheter. When it touches a wall of the heart, you might have a little flurry of heartbeats. Don't worry about it. Somewhere in the process we'll ask you to exercise a little. We need some measurements of the heart under physical stress. You won't have to do more than you can. Toward the end we'll inject a purple dye. We get very precise films that way. You'll probably get some burning sensations while the dye circulates. A couple of minutes or so. Otherwise you'll be quite comfortable. Do you have any questions?"

Kraft has a hundred and asks none.

The doctor starts out of the room, stops, comes back a little haltingly. He has his pen in his hand and his prescription pad out.

"Mr. Kraft, I have a nephew. He'd get a big kick out of . . ."

Kraft takes the extended pad and pen. "What's his name?"

"Oh, just sign yours."

He writes: "For the doc and his nephew for good luck from Bobby Kraft." He returns the items. He feels dead.

In the morning they move him on a gurney to a thick walled room in the basement. He's asked to slide onto an X-ray table. They cover him with a sheet. He raises himself on his elbows to see people busy at tasks he can't understand. There are two women and two men. All of them wear white. One of the women sits before a console full of knobs and meters on a table near his feet. Above and behind his head is a machine he'll know later is a fluoroscope. In a corner of the room there's a concrete alcove, the kind X-ray technicians hide behind. One of the men keeps popping in and out of its opening on his way to and from the fluoroscope. The ceiling is full of beams and grids on which X-ray equipment slides back and forth and is lowered and raised. The other man plays with it, and with film plates he slides under the table. A nurse attaches EKG bands to his ankles.

The two doctors come in. They are already masked, rubber-gloved, and dressed in green. The bearded one introduces the other, who has graying hair and brown eyes. A nurse fits Kraft's right arm into a metal rest draped with towels. "I'm going to tie your wrist," she says. She ties it and tucks the towels over his hand and wrist and over his shoulder and biceps. She washes the inside of his shaved arm with alcohol, rubbing hard at the crook of his elbow. The bearded doctor ties his arm tightly with a rubber strap, just above the elbow, then feels with his fingers in the crook of the elbow for the raised vessels. He swabs the skin with the yellow Xylocaine and waits. The other doctor asks the nurse at the console if she is ready. She says, "Not yet." He looks at Kraft, and Kraft looks up at the rails and grids.

In a few minutes the bearded doctor injects the anesthetic into several spots high on the inside of Kraft's forearm. It takes ten more minutes before the woman at the console is ready. She gets up twice to check with the man in the alcove. The older doctor goes there once. When the woman finally signals she's ready, Dr. Kahl says, "OK." Kraft looks. The older doctor stands alongside Kahl. The scalpel goes quickly into Kraft's flesh in a short cut. He doesn't feel it. Kahl removes the scalpel, and a little blood seeps. The doctor switches instruments and goes quickly into the small wound. Blood spurts. It comes in a few pumps about six inches over Kraft's arm, a thick, rich red blood. Kraft is astonished. Then the blood stops. The towels are soaked with it.

"I'm putting the cath in."

The older doctor nods. He turns toward the fluoroscope. Kraft watches again. The catheter is black and silky and no thicker than a cocktail straw. Still Kraft feels nothing. Kahl's brow creases. He's manipulating the black, slender thing with his rubbered fingers. He rolls his thumb along it as he moves it. Kraft waits to feel something. There is no feeling. He can't see where the loose end of the catheter is coming from. He turns his head away and takes a deep breath. He takes another deep one. He wants to relax. He wants to know how the hell he got into all this. What really happened to him? When? What for?

"You're in," the older doctor says.

The thing is in his heart.

It couldn't have taken more than ten seconds. They are in his heart with a black silky tube and he can't feel it.

"Hold it," the nurse at the console says. She begins calling out numbers.

"How are you feeling?" Dr. Kahl asks. Kraft nods.

"You feeling all right?" the older doctor repeats, walking toward the fluoroscope.

"Yeah."

They go on and on. He feels nothing. He hears the older doctor instructing the younger one: "Try the ventricle . . . Hold it . . . What's your reading now . . . There's the flutter . . . Don't worry about that, Mr. Kraft . . . Watch the pulmonary artery . . . He's irritable in there . . . Withdraw! . . . Fine, you're through the cusps . . . Try the mitral . . . You're on the wall again . . . How are you feeling, Mr. Kraft?"

Kraft nods. He licks his lips. He tries not to listen to them. When the flutter goes off in his chest, he thinks it will start an arrhythmia. It doesn't. It feels like a hummingbird hovering in his chest for a second. Something catches it. Occasionally the other doctor comes beside Kahl and plays for a moment with the catheter while he watches the fluoroscope. The bearded doctor chats sometimes, saying he's sorry Kraft has to lie so flat for so long, it must be uncomfortable. Does he use many pillows at home? Would he like to raise up for a while?

The arm hurts where the catheter enters it. Kraft feels a firm growing lump under the flesh, as if a golf ball is being forced into the wound. Kraft concentrates on the pain. He thinks of grass.

"How much longer?" he asks.

"We're more than half way."

In a while the nurse tells him they are going to have him do the exercises now. Something presses against his feet. The brown-eyed doctor talks.

"We have an apparatus here with bicycle pedals. Just push on them as you would on a bike. We'll adjust the pedals to keep making you push with more force. If it gets to be too much work, tell us. We want you to exert yourself, but not tire yourself."

What's he talking about, Kraft asks himself. He begins to pump. There's no resistance. He pumps faster, harder.

"That's fine. Keep it going. You're doing real fine."

He gets a rhythm to it quickly, thrusting his legs as rapidly as he can. He expects to get winded, but he doesn't. He's doing fine. He almost enjoys it. He concentrates. He feels the pain in his arm and pumps harder, faster. He imagines he's racing. For a moment it gets more difficult to pump. He presses harder, feels his calves stretch and harden. He gets his rhythm back. They encourage him. He licks his lips and clasps the edge of the table with his left hand and drives his legs. He forgets about any race. He knows he's doing well with this exercise. It will show on their computation. They'll tell him his heart is getting better. The resistance to his pumping gets stronger. He pumps harder.

"That was very good. We're taking the apparatus away now. You feel all right?"

"Fine."

Kraft closes his eyes. There's the pain in his arm again. His forearm is going to pop. It's too strong a pain now. They are moving in the room. He grinds his teeth.

"We're going to inject the dye now," the older doctor says.

Kraft turns his head and sees the metal cylinder of the syringe catch glinting light for a moment in Kahl's raised hand. He sees the rubbered thumb move; a blackish fluid spurts from the needle's tip. The needle goes toward his arm—into the wound or the catheter, he can't tell. He turns away.

"You'll feel some heat in your head very soon. That's just the effect of the dye. It'll wear off. You'll feel heat at the sphincter too. Are you all right?"

Kraft nods. He turns away. Why do they keep asking him? He sees the man from the alcove hurrying with X-ray plates that he slides into the slot under the table just below Kraft's shoulder blades. He hurries back to the alcove. The doctors call instructions. The voice from the alcove calls some words back and numbers. Kraft closes his eyes and tries to think of something to think of. He thinks if Elfi could—then Kraft feels the rush. It comes in way over the pain in his arm. It raises him off the table. He feels the heat racing through him. A terrific pounding at his forehead. It doesn't go away. He tries to think of the pain in his arm, but he feels the heat rushing through him in a rising fever. Then it hits his asshole and he rises off the table again. It burns tremendously. They have lit a candle in his asshole and the burned flesh is going to drop through.

"Wow!"

"That's all right. It'll go away soon."

It does, but not the headache. It burns and throbs in his forehead. He hears metal dropping under the table. The man runs out and removes film plates. Someone else inserts others. They call numbers. The plates fall again. They repeat the process. He closes his eyes. The rush is fading, but the headache remains, throbbing.

"How you doing?"

"All right. My head aches."

"It'll pass."

"How was the exercise part?"

"You did fine. We'll be through soon. How's the arm?"

"Hurts."

"No problem. More Novocaine."

"No. Leave it."

They hurry again. Words are exchanged about the films. Someone leaves the room. Someone enters it later. Kraft keeps his eyes closed. The ache is still in his forehead, but he thinks he might sleep.

"Well, that's it," the bearded Kahl says. Kraft looks toward him, then down at his arm. The wound is stitched. He hasn't felt it. The doctor covers it with a gauze pad and two strips of tape. The catheter's gone. Kraft sees no sign of it. They wash his arm of blood and get him onto the gurney. He hears someone say "I think we got good results." The older doctor tells Kraft they'll know some things tomorrow. "It looks good."

Back in his room Elfi is waiting for him. He gets into bed, and they leave. She throws herself on him. She's breathless. Her cheeks are streaked, her eyes are red. She's been crying. She's almost crying now.

"I don't want to talk about it now," he says when she begins to speak. "I don't want to hear it. That's the truth. Listen, I'm going home. Beaubee, I'm not good here."

She rushes from the room. He contemplates the increasing pain in his arm. It reaches into his biceps now. He keeps thinking about his heart. They had their black tube in *his* heart. The sonsabitches.

On the next day, just before lunch, reading a magazine in the chair in his room, he sees Dr. Gottfried for the first time. With him, in his white coat, is the gray-haired doctor from the catheterization. Dr. Gottfried is in the short-sleeved green shirt and the green baggy cotton trousers of the operating room. He has scuffed sneakers, and the stethoscope—like a metal and rubber noose, hangs from his neck. He looks tired. He has the sad eyes of a spaniel. And yet the man—in build neither here nor there, just a man—introduced by his colleague, stares and stares at Kraft before he moves or speaks, like a man before a fight. He keeps looking into Kraft's eyes, as if through his patient's eyes he could find the as yet untested condition of his true heart. He keeps on staring; Kraft stares back. Then the great famous doctor nods; a corner of his mouth flickers. He has apparently seen what he has needed to—and judged. He leans over Kraft and listens with the stethoscope to Kraft's chest. He could not have heard more than three heartbeats when he removes the earpieces, steps back, and speaks.

"Under it all, you've got a strong heart. I can tell by the snap."

Kraft, the heroic old pro, begins to smile. He beams. The doctor speaks in a slow, subdued voice; Kraft's smile fades.

"There's no real rush with your situation. However, the sooner the better, and there's a cancelled procedure two weeks from today. We can do you then. I'll operate. Right now I want to study more of the material in your folder. We've got several base lines. I'll be back soon. Dr. Pritchett will fill you in and answer any questions you have. He knows more than anyone in the world about pulmonary valve disease."

Leaving, Dr. Gottfried moves without a sound, his head tilted and the shoulder on that side sagging. When he closes the door, Kraft turns on Dr. Pritchett.

"What operation? He said my heart's good. You said you got good results on that catheter. The fat one yesterday said he got good results on his machine."

The doctor explains. The "good" results meant they were finding what they needed to know. They are all agreed now the linings of the heart should be removed. A simple procedure for Dr. Gottfried—"he's the best you could find"—even if the endocardium is scarred enough to be adhesive. They are also agreed about the pulmonary valve. It will be removed and replaced by an artificial device made of a flexible steel alloy. "Dr. Gottfried will just pop it right in. We're not, however, certain of the aortic valve. Dr. Gottfried will make that decision during surgery." Positive results are expected. There's the strong probability of the heart restored to ninety percent efficiency and a good possibility of total cure. Of course, you'll be on daily anticoagulant medicines for the rest of your life. No big affair. The important point, as Dr. Gottfried said, is the heart is essentially strong. Surgery, done now, while Kraft is young and before the heart is irreparably weakened, is the determining factor. Of course, as in any surgery, there's risk.

"Have I made it clear? Can I answer any questions, Mr. Kraft? I know we get too technical at times."

"I'm not stupid."

"No one implied you were."

Emptying with dread, Kraft slips his hands under the blanket to hide their trembling. "Will I still need pissing pills, after the operation?"

"Diuretics? No. I wouldn't think so."

"No more arrhythmia?"

"We can't be sure of that. Sometimes the—"

"Then what kind of total cure, man?"

"I can't explain all the physics and chemistry of the heart rhythm, Mr. Kraft. If you'd continue to have the arrhythmia, it would be benign. A mechanical thing. We have medicine to control it."

"You said I did great with the exercises."

"Yes. We got the results we needed."

Dr. Gottfried returns, still in his operating clothes, holding the manila folder, looking now a little bored as well as fatigued, his voice slow, quiet.

"Any questions for me?"

"The risk? Dr. What'shisname here said . . ."

"There's ten percent mortality risk. That covers all open heart surgery. A lot of it relates to heart disease more advanced than yours, where general health isn't as good as yours. There's risk however, for you too. You know that."

Kraft nods. He suddenly detests this man he needs, who'll have the power of life over him. He closes his eyes.

"As I said, there's no emergency. But I can fit you in two weeks from now. You could have it over with. Decide in a day or two. I'd appreciate that. Talk it over with your wife. With Dr. Felton. Let us know through him."

Home again, Kraft, on his medicines, pissed, grew depressed, endured his headaches and lassitude, the arrhythmias, the miscellaneous pains, his sense of dissolution, the nausea; and, as before, continued to blame himself as well as feel betrayed. He submitted, and he waited. He never looked in the mirror anymore. While he shaved, he never saw himself. Sometimes he felt tearful. On the few days that he came around, he no longer went out to the sun and the pool but stayed indoors. He called no one, but answered the phone on his better days and kept up his end of the bullshit with old buddies and some writers who still remembered. No one but Elfi knew his despair.

When he passed the closed door to the den of his heroic history, his trophy room, he wasn't even aware that he kept himself from going in. The door might as well have been the wall. What he kept seeing now was behind his eyes: The face of Dr. Gottfried. It flashed like a blurred, tired, boneless, powerful shape, producing a quality before which Kraft felt weak. He began to exalt the quality and despise the man and groped for a way by which he could begin to tell Elfi.

One night, in bed with her, a week after he'd made the decision to go for the surgery, which was now less than a week away, with the lights out and her figure illumined only by a small glow of clouded moonlight entering through the cracked drapes, he thought her asleep and ventured to loop his hand over her head where he could easily reach her outside shoulder. He touched it gently. It was the first time since his discovery of his impotence that he'd touched her in bed.

Immediately she moved across the space, nestled her head in his armpit, and pressed against his side. He resisted his desire to pull away. He was truly pleased by the way she fit.

"Every day now I pray," she said. "Oh, not for you, don't worry. You are going to be fine. I swear it, how much I believe that. You don't need me to pray for you. I need it. I do it for myself. Selfishly. Entirely."

He spoke of what was on his mind. "That surgeon's freaking me."

"You couldn't find anyone better. I have the utmost confidence. To me that is what you call a man. You should see in his clinic. What the patients say about him. The eyes they have when they look at him. He walks through like a god. And I tell you something else. He has a vast understanding."

He moved his hand from her arm. "It's *my* heart, not yours." His voice fell to despair. "It's a man thing. You can't understand. A sonofabitch puts his hand in Bobby Kraft's heart. He pops in some goddamned metal valve. He's flaky. He freaks me."

"I tell you, I feel sorry for you. Too bad. For any man I feel sorry who doesn't know who are his real enemies. Not to know that, that's your freak. That's the terrible thing can happen to a man in his life. Not to know who his enemies are."

"That's what *he* is," Kraft declaimed in the darkness. "He's my enemy. If there's one thing I've always known, that's it. The sonsabitches. Now Gottfried is. And there aint no game. I don't even get to play."

"You baby. Play. Play. It's because all your life you played a game for a boy. That's why you can't know. Precisely. I always knew that."

He pulled away from her. He got out of bed and loomed over her threateningly.

"Go on back home, Kraut. I don't need you for the operation. To hell with the operation. I'll call it off. How's that?"

"Here is home, with you. Try and make me leave. I am not a man. I don't need enemies."

He got out of bed to get away. The bitch. She'd caught him at a time when there was nothing left of him.

Kraft enters the hospital trying to imagine it's a stadium. The act lasts as long as his first smell of the antiseptics and the rubbery sound of a wheeled gurney. He tastes old metal in his mouth. He refuses the tranquilizers they keep pushing at him. He wants wakefulness. Elfi keeps visiting and fleeing.

He has nothing to say to her. She wants his buddies to come, she says he needs them. He says if one of them comes, that's it. He clears out of the hospital, period. He wants to talk, but he can't imagine a proper listener. For two years he endured what he never could have believed would've befallen him. There was no way to understand it, and this has left him now with loose ends. He can't think of any arrangement of his mind that could gather them. They simply fall out.

It occurs to him he doesn't know enough people who are dead.

It occurs to him he isn't sick enough.

He thinks he will be all right. He thinks he will be able to brag about it afterwards. Then he sees his heart and Gottfried's hand, and he wants the man there at once to ask him what right he thinks he has.

It occurs to him he never really liked football. It was just an excuse for something else.

It occurs to him he just made that up. It can't be so.

He wonders if he has ever really slept *with* Elfi. With any woman.

He laments his development of a double chin.

Sleep is a measure of defeat. Before games he never slept well.

Here, even at night, he keeps trying not to sleep. Most of the time he doesn't. He asks one of the doctors if it will matter in the outcome that he isn't sleeping now. The doctor says, Nope.

On the morning of the surgery, a nurse comes in. She sneaks up on him: She jabs a needle in his arm before he can say: What are you doing? She leaves before he can say: What the hell'd you do? I told you I aint taking anything will make me sleep. He begins to fight the fuzzy flaking in his head. He thinks he will talk to himself to keep awake and get it said. Say what?

Say it's only me here to go alone if there's no one going with me when he comes down like that from my apple to my gut to open where my heart is with a band of blood just before the saw goes off and rips from the apple to the gut down the middle of the bone while they pull the ribs wide the way mine under the center's balls when I made the signals to my blood and was from the time it ever was until they saw the goddamned Bobby Kraft slip a shoulder and fake it once and fade back and let it go uncorked up there the way it spirals against the blue of it, the point of it, leather brown spiralling on the jolted blue to the banging on me that was no use to them. You sonsabitches. Cause the ball's gone and hearing the roar of them with Jeffer getting it on his tips on the zig and in and streak that was going all the way cause I read the free safe blitz and called it on the line and faded against his looping where Copper picked him up and I let it go before the rest caved me with their hands pulling my ribs now and cranking on some ratchet bar to keep me spread and oh my God his rubbered hand on. Gottfried down with his knife in my heart's like a jelly sack the way he cuts through it with my blood in a plastic tube with the flow of it into some machine that cleans it for going back into me with blades like wipers on cars in the rain when I played in mud to my ankles and in the snows and over ninety in the Coliseum like in hell before the roar my God. Keep this my heart or let me die you sonsabitches. Pray for me again Elfi that I didn't love you the way such a little thing you are, and it was to do and I couldn't, but what could you know of me and what I had to and what it was for me, born to be a thing in the lot and the park, and in the school too with all of them calling me cold as ice bastard, and I wasn't any of that or how would I come to them in the pros out of a dink pussey college and be as good as any of them and better than most of all those that run the show on the field that are Quarterbacks. Godbacks goddammit. The way he's supposed to, this Gottfried with that stare and not any loser. Me? A loser? Because I cry in the dread I feel now of the what?

The Best Years of His Life

Athletes who come to the end of their sports careers are often tormented by the idea that they have left a portion of their identity behind. John Ed Bradley examines his own sense of loss in the *Sports Illustrated* piece "The Best Years of His Life."

The dedicated athlete spends his early life chiseling his body and his mind into a performance machine. Those lucky enough and good enough are awarded the chance to play sports at higher levels in front of larger crowds for bigger stakes. Bradley was skilled enough to play college football in front of one of the most rabid fan bases in the country at Louisiana State University in the late 1970s. College football is religion in the Deep South, and players in that football-crazed atmosphere were revered and worshipped.

Wary of giving in to the lure of droning on about his football exploits, Bradley's decision to turn his back on the former athlete in his adult life was brave, but unrealistic. Pushing all memory of his LSU experiences out of his mind left him conflicted and unfulfilled and no doubt fueled his career as a writer.

I t ends for everybody. It ends for the pro who makes $5 million a year and has his face on magazine covers and his name in the record books. It ends for the kid on the high school team who never comes off the bench except to congratulate his teammates as they file past him on their way to the Gatorade bucket.

In my case it ended on Dec. 22, 1979, at the Tangerine Bowl in Orlando. We beat Wake Forest that night 34–10, in a game I barely remember but for the fact that it was my last one. When it was over, a teammate and I grabbed our heroic old coach, hoisted him on our shoulders and carried him out to the midfield crest. It was ending that day for Charles McClendon, too, after 18 years as head coach at LSU and a superb 69% career winning percentage. The next day newspapers would run photos of Coach Mac's last victory ride, with Big Eddie Stanton and me, smeared with mud, serving as his chariot. Coach had a hand raised above his head as he waved goodbye, but it would strike me that his expression showed little joy at all. He looked tired and sad. More than anything, though, he looked like he didn't want it to end.

We were quiet on the flight back to Baton Rouge, and when the plane touched down at Ryan Field, no cheers went up and nobody said anything. A week or so later, done with the Christmas holidays, I went to Tiger Stadium to clean out my locker. I brought a big travel bag with me, and I stuffed it with pads, shoes, gym trunks, jockstraps, T-shirts and practice jerseys. I removed my nametag from the locker. Then I studied the purple stenciling against the gold matte. In one corner someone had scribbled the words TRAMPLE THE DEAD, HURDLE THE WEAK. The source of the legend eludes me now, but it had been a rallying cry for the team that year, especially for my mates on the offensive line.

The last thing I packed was my helmet. I'd been an offensive center, and the helmet's back and sides were covered with the little Tigers decals the coaches had given out as merit badges for big plays. I ran my fingertips over the surface, feeling the scars in the hard plastic crown. There were paint smudges and streaks from helmets I'd butted over the years. Was the gold Vanderbilt or Florida State? The red Alabama or Georgia, Indiana or USC?

When I finished packing, I walked down the chute that led to the playing field, pushed open the big metal door and squinted against the sudden blast of sunlight. I meant to have one last look at the old stadium where I'd played the last four years. Death Valley was quiet now under a blue winter sky. I could point to virtually any spot on the field and tell you about some incident that had happened there. I knew where teammates had blown out knees, dropped passes, made key blocks and tackles, thrown interceptions and recovered game-saving fumbles. I knew where we'd vomited in spring scrimmages under a brutal Louisiana sun and where we'd celebrated on autumn Saturday nights to the roar of maniacal Tigers fans and the roar of a real tiger, Mike IV, prowling in a cage on the sideline. We'd performed to a full house at most every home game, the crowds routinely in excess of 75,000, but today there was no one in sight, the bleachers running in silver ribbons around the gray cement bowl. It seemed the loneliest place on earth.

I was only 21 years old, yet I believed that nothing I did for the rest of my life would rise up to those days when I wore the Purple and Gold. I might go on to a satisfying career and make a lot of money, I might marry a beautiful woman and fill a house with perfect kids, I might make a mark that would be of some significance in other people's eyes. But I would never have it better than when I was playing football for LSU.

Despite this belief, I was determined to walk away from that place and that life and never look back. You wouldn't catch me 20 years later crowing about how it had been back in the day, when as a college kid I'd heard the cheers. I knew the type who couldn't give it up, and I didn't want to be him. He keeps going to the games and reminding anyone who'll listen of how things used to be. His wife and kids roll their eyes as he describes big plays, quotes from halftime speeches and embellishes a "career" that no one else seems to remember with any specificity. He stalks the memory until the memory reduces him to pathetic self-parody. To listen to him, he never screwed up a snap count or busted an assignment or had a coach berate him for dogging it or getting beat. In his mind he is forever young, forever strong, forever golden.

Standing there in Tiger Stadium, I squeezed my eyes closed and lowered my head. Then I wept.

Hell no, I said to myself. That wasn't going to be me.

I still remember their names and hometowns. And I can tell you, almost to a man, the high schools they went to. I remember how tall they were and how much they weighed. I remember their strengths and weaknesses, both as men and as football players. I remember the kinds of cars they drove, what religions they practiced, the music they favored, the hair color of their girlfriends, how many letters they earned, their injuries, their dreams, their times in the 40-yard dash. In many instances I remember their jersey numbers. On the day last August that I turned 43, I wondered what had happened to Robert DeLee. DeLee, a tight end from the small town of Clinton, La., wore number 43 on his jersey when I was a senior. During my freshman year a running back named Jack Clark had worn the number. Jack Clark, too, I thought to my-self—where on earth has he slipped off to? I had seen neither of them in more than two decades.

That was the case with almost all of my teammates. Last summer I at-tended a wedding reception for Barry Rubin, a former fullback at LSU who is a strength coach with the Green Bay Packers. It had been about eight years since I'd last had a face-to-face conversation with a teammate, and even that meeting had come purely by chance. One day I was waiting in the checkout line at a store in suburban New Orleans when someone standing behind me called out my name. I wheeled around, and there stood Charlie McDuff, an ex-offensive tackle who'd arrived at LSU at the same time I did, as a member of the celebrated 1976 freshman class. A couple of shoppers separated Charlie and me, and I couldn't reach past them to shake his hand. "How are things going?" he said.

"Things are good," I said. "How 'bout with you?"

I felt uncomfortable seeing him again, even though we'd always gotten along well back in school. The media guide had listed him at 6'6" and 263 pounds, but in actual fact he was a shade taller and closer to 275. Even after all these years away from the game he had a bull neck and arms thick with mus-cle. His hair was as sun-bleached as ever, his skin as darkly tanned.

I paid what I owed and started to leave. Then I turned back around and looked at him again. "You ever see anybody anymore, Charlie?" I said.

"Yeah. Sure, I see them. Some of them. You?"

"Not really."

He nodded as if he understood, and we parted without saying any-thing more, and two years later Charlie McDuff was dead. My sister called, cry-ing with the news. Charlie had suffered a pulmonary embolism while vacationing with his family at a Gulf Coast resort. He left behind a wife and three young sons. I wanted to call someone and talk about him, and I knew it had to be a player, one of our teammates, and preferably an offensive lineman. But I could-n't do it, I couldn't make the call. Nobody wanted to remember anymore, I tried to convince myself. It was too long ago. So instead I pulled some card-board boxes out of a closet and went through them. There were trophies and plaques wrapped in paper, letters tied with kite string, a short stack of souvenir programs and a couple of plastic-bound photo albums crowded with news clippings and yellowing images of boys who actually were capable of dying. If Charlie McDuff could die, it occurred to me, we all could.

At the bottom of the box I found a worn, gray T-shirt with purple lettering that said NOBODY WORKS HARDER THAN THE OFFENSIVE LINE. Charlie had had that shirt made, along with about a dozen others, and handed them out to the linemen on the '79 squad. The year before, we'd lost some outstanding players to graduation, and Charlie had hoped the shirts would inspire us to pull together as a unit. We wore the shirts at every opportunity, generally under our shoulder pads at practice and games. It seems crazy now, but there was a time when I considered stipulating in my will that I be buried in that ratty thing. I was never more proud than when I had it on.

I learned about Charlie's funeral arrangements, and I got dressed intending to go. I started down the road for Baton Rouge, rehearsing the lines I'd speak to his widow and children, and those I'd tell my old teammates to explain why I didn't come around anymore. I drove as far as the outskirts of Baton Rouge before turning around and heading back home.

Are there others out there like me? I've often wondered. Does the loss of a game they played in their youth haunt them as it's haunted me? Do others wake up from afternoon naps and bolt for the door, certain that they're late for practice even though their last practice was half a lifetime ago? My nightmares don't contain images of monsters or plane crashes or Boo Radley hiding behind the bedroom door. Mine have me jumping offside or muffing the center-quarterback exchange. They have me forgetting where I placed my helmet when the defense is coming off the field and it's time for me to go back in the game.

If it really ends, I wonder, then why doesn't it just end?

I suppose I was doomed from the start, having been sired by a Louisiana high school football coach. The year of my birth, 1958, was the same year LSU won its one and only national championship in football, and the month of my birth, August, was when two-a-day practices began for that season. Although my parents couldn't afford to take their five kids to the LSU games, we always listened to the radio broadcasts, usually while my father was outside barbecuing on the patio. He'd sit there in a lawn chair, lost in concentration, a purple-and-gold cap tipped back on his head. Not far away on the lawn I acted out big plays with friends from the neighborhood, some of us dressed in little Tigers uniforms. We played in the dark until someone ran into a tree or a clothesline and got hurt, then my dad would have me sit next to him and listen to the rest of the game, the real one. "Settle down now," I remember him saying. "LSU's on."

When I was a kid I always gave the same answer to adults who asked me what I wanted to be when I grew up. "I want to play football for LSU," I answered. Beyond that I had no clear picture of myself.

Nor could I fathom a future without the game when it ended for me 23 years ago. One day I was on the team, the next I was a guy with a pile of memories and a feeling in his gut that his best days were behind him. I shuffled around in my purple letter jacket wondering what to do with myself, and wondering who I was. Suddenly there were no afternoon workouts or meetings to attend. I didn't have to visit the training room for whirlpool or hot-wax baths or ultrasound treatments or massages or complicated ankle tapings or shots to kill the never-ending pain. If I wanted to, I could sit in a Tigerland bar and get drunk without fear of being booted from the team; I didn't have a team anymore. Every day for four years I'd stepped on a scale and recorded my weight on a chart for the coaches. But no one cared any longer how thin I got, or how fat.

That last year I served as captain of the offense, and either by some miracle or by a rigged ballot I was named to the second team All-Southeastern Conference squad. The first-team player, Alabama's Dwight Stephenson, went on to become a star with the Miami Dolphins and a member of the Pro Football Hall of Fame, and I'd seen enough film of the guy to know I was nowhere in his league. At the end of April, in the hours after the 1980 NFL draft, a scout for the Dallas Cowboys called and asked me to consider signing with the club as a free agent, but by then I'd already shed 30 pounds along with any notion of myself as an athlete. I gave some excuse and hung up. "You don't even want to try?" my father said.

I could've yelled at him for asking, but there was genuine compassion in his eyes. He and my mother were losing something, too. One of their sons had played football for LSU, and where I come from nothing topped that. "It's over," I said.

My father nodded and walked away.

Number 50 was Jay Whitley, the pride of Baton Rouge's Lee High. Fifty-one was Lou deLauney, then Albert Richardson; 52, Kevin Lair, then Leigh Shepard; 53, Steve Estes and Jim Holsombake; 54, Rocky Guillot. Fifty-five was linebacker S.J. Saia; then after my freshman year the number went to Marty Defrene, probably the toughest offensive lineman ever to come out of Lafourche Parish. My number was 56. When we left the stadium after games, fans were waiting outside under the streetlamps, some of them with programs and slips of paper to sign. Even a lowly offensive lineman was asked for an autograph. "Number 56 in your program, Number 1 in your heart," I'd write, disgracing myself for all eternity but way too ignorant at the time to know it.

I don't recall how I first learned about what happened to Marty. Maybe it was from a news story about efforts to raise money to help pay his medical bills. Or maybe it was another tearful call from a relative. But one day I found myself punching numbers on a telephone keypad, desperate to talk to him again. Marty was living in LaRose, his hometown in the heart of Cajun country, or "down the bayou," as the natives like to say. His wife, Lynne, answered. "Lynne, do you remember me?" I said, after introducing myself.

"Yes, I remember you," she answered. "You want to talk to Marty? Hold on, John Ed. It's going to take a few minutes, because I have to put him on the speakerphone."

A speakerphone? When he finally came on he sounded as though he was trapped at the bottom of a well.

"Marty, is it true you got hurt?" I said.

"Yeah," he said.

"You're paralyzed, man?"

"Yeah," he said, raising his voice to make sure I could hear. "I broke my neck. Can you believe it?"

It had happened in July 1986, some five years before my call. While in his second year of studies at a chiropractic college then based in Irving, Texas, Marty was injured in a freak accident at a pool party to welcome the incoming freshman class. He and friends were horsing around when a pair of them decided to bring big, strong Marty down. One held him in a headlock, the other took a running start and plowed into him. Marty smashed through the water's surface of a shallow children's pool and struck his head on the bottom, shattering a vertebra. He floated in the water, unable to move or feel anything from his neck down, until his friends pulled him out.

As he told me about the accident I kept flashing back to the kid I'd known in school. Marty had been a lean, powerfully built 6'2" and 235 pounds, small by today's standards but about average for a center in our era. On the field he'd played with a kind of swagger, as if certain that he could dominate his opponent. The swagger extended to his life off the field. Marty liked to have a good time. He spoke with a heavy Cajun accent, the kind of accent that made girls crazy and immediately identified him as a pure Louisiana thoroughbred. Football schools from the Midwest featured humongous linemen brought up on corn and prime beef. At LSU we had guys like Marty, raised on crawfish from the mud flats and seafood from the Gulf of Mexico.

The son of an offshore oil field worker, Marty was an all-state high school center in 1976. He was a highly recruited blue-chipper coming out of South Lafourche High, just as I had been at Opelousas High the year before. Marty had vacillated between committing to West Point and to LSU before he realized there really was only one choice for him. Air Force was the military academy that had tried to lure me before I snapped out of it and understood what my destiny was.

The only problem I'd ever had with Marty Dufrene was that we played the same position, and he wanted my job. Going into my senior year I was listed on the first team, Marty on the second. One day after practice he told me he was going to beat me out. I couldn't believe his gall. "I want to play pro ball," he said.

I shook my head and walked off, thinking, Pro ball? To hell with that, Dufrene. I'm going to see to it you don't even play in college.

Now, on the telephone, I was telling him, "I'd like to come see you, Marty."

"Yeah," he said. "It would be great to see you again."

"I'll do it. I promise. Just give me some time."

"Sure, whatever you need. I'd like to catch up."

But then 11 years passed, and I didn't visit Marty or follow up with another call. Nor did I write to him to explain my silence. How could I tell the man that I was afraid to see him again? Afraid to see him as a quadriplegic, afraid to have to acknowledge that, but for the grace of God, I could be the one confined to a chair, afraid to face the reality that what we once were was now ancient history.

I might've played football, in another life. But in my present one I had no doubt as to the depths of my cowardice.

At some point I decided to turn my back on it all, rather than endure the feeling of loss any longer. Marty Dufrene wasn't the only one I avoided. There were years when I tried to stay clear of the entire town of Baton Rouge. Travelers can see Tiger Stadium as they cross the Mississippi River Bridge and enter the city from the west, and whenever I journeyed across that elevated span I made sure to look at the downtown office buildings and the State Capitol to the north, rather than to the south where the old bowl sits nestled in the trees. I struggled to watch LSU games on TV and generally abandoned the set after less than a quarter. Same for radio broadcasts: I tuned most of them out by halftime. On two occasions the school's athletic department invited me to attend home games as an honorary captain, and while I showed both times, I was such a nervous wreck at being in the stadium again that I could barely walk out on the field before kickoff to receive my award and raise an arm in salute to the crowd.

Love ends, too, and when the girl invites you over to meet her new beau, you don't have to like it, do you?

I received invitations to participate in charity golf tournaments featuring former Tigers players; I never went to them. Teammates invited me to tailgate parties, suppers and over events; I never made it to them. The lettermen's club invited me to maintain a membership; except for one year, I always failed to pay my dues. Even Coach Mac tried to get in touch with me a few times. I was somehow too busy to call him back.

It wasn't until December of last year that I finally saw him again, and by then he was dying. In fact, in only three days he would be dead. Cancer had left him bedridden at his home in Baton Rouge, but even at the worst of it he was receiving guests, most of them former players who came by to tell him goodbye. One day I received a call from an old college friend, urging me to see Coach Mac again. She said it didn't look good; if I wanted to talk to him and make my peace, I'd better come right away.

So that was how I ended up at his doorstep one breezy weekday morning last winter, my hand shaking as I lifted a finger to punch the bell. I wondered if anyone in the house had seen me park on the drive in front, and I seriously considered walking back to my truck and leaving. But then the door swung open and there standing a few feet away was Coach Mac's wife, Dorothy Faye. I could feel my heart squeeze tight in my chest and my breath go shallow. My friend had called ahead and told her I might be coming; otherwise she surely would've been alarmed by the sight of a weeping middle-aged man at her front door. "Why, John Ed Bradley," she said. "Come in. Come in, John Ed."

She put her arms around me and kissed the side of my face. Dorothy Faye was as beautiful as ever, and as kind and gracious, not once asking why it had taken her husband's impending death to get me to come see him again. She led me down a hall to a bedroom, and I could see him before I walked in the door. He was lying supine on a hospital bed. His head was bald, the hair lost to past regimens of chemotherapy, and, at age 78, wrapped up in bedsheets, he seemed so much smaller than I remembered him. His eyes were large and haunted from the battle, but it was Coach Mac, all right. I snapped to attention when he spoke my name. "Come over here and talk to me, buddy," he said.

I sat next to the bed and we held hands and told stories, every one about football. He was still the aw-shucks country boy who'd played for Bear Bryant at Kentucky before going on to build his own legend in Louisiana, and the sound of his rich drawl made the past suddenly come alive for me. I named former teammates and asked him what had become of them, and in every case he had an answer. "Your old position coach was here yesterday," he said.

"Coach McCarty?"

"He sat right there." And we both looked at the place, an empty chair.

"And you're a writer now," he said.

"Yes sir, I'm a writer."

"I'm proud of you, John Ed."

I didn't stay long, maybe 20 minutes, and shortly before I got up to leave he asked me if I ever remembered back to 1979 and the night that the top-ranked USC Trojans came to Baton Rouge and the fans stood on their feet for four quarters and watched one of the most exciting games ever played in Tiger Stadium. "I remember it all the time," I said. "I don't always want to remember it, because we lost, Coach, but I remember it."

"I remember it too," he said in a wistful sort of way.

The Trojans that year had one of the most talented teams in college football history, with standouts Ronnie Lott, Charles White, Marcus Allen, Brad Budde and Anthony Munoz. They would go on to an 11–0–1 season and finish ranked second nationally behind Alabama, and White would win the Heisman Trophy.

In his bed Coach Mac lifted a hand and ran it over the front of his face in a raking gesture. "They called face-masking against Benjy," he whispered.

"Sir?"

"That penalty. The one at the end."

"Yes, sir. They sure did call it. And it cost us the game."

He swallowed, and it seemed I could see that night being replayed in his eyes: the yellow flag going up, the 15 yards being marched off, the subsequent touchdown with less than a minute to play that gave USC the 17–12 win. "Benjy Thibodeaux didn't face-mask anybody," I said, the heat rising in my face as I started to argue against a referee's call that nothing would ever change.

Coach Mac was quiet now, and he eased his grip on my hand. I stood and started for the door, determined not to look back. His voice stopped me.

"Hey, buddy?" he said. I managed to face him again. "Always remember I'm with you. I'm with all you boys." He lifted a hand off the bed and held it up high, just as he had so many years ago after his last game.

"I know you are, Coach."

"And buddy?" A smile came to his face. He pointed at me. "Next time don't wait so long before you come see your old coach again."

Now it is summer, the season before the season, and Major Marty Dufrene, Civil Department Head of the Lafourche Parish Sheriff's Department, motors his wheelchair to the end of a cement drive and nods in the direction of a horse barn at the rear of his 38-acre estate. Five horses stand along a fence and wait for him, just as they do every day when he rolls out to see them after work. "I'm going to be riding before the end of the year," he tells me. "I've got a saddle I'm making with the back beefed up for support, so I can strap myself in. Of course I'm going to have to use a lift to put me in the saddle. But I'm going to do it."

By now I have been with him for a couple of hours, and already the force of his personality has made the chair invisible. After the injury his muscles began to atrophy, and over time his midsection grew large and outsized, his face swollen. But the fire in his eyes hasn't changed. Marty is exactly as I remembered him. "One thing about him," says his wife, "Marty might've broken his neck, he might be paralyzed and in that chair, but he is still a football player."

Their large Acadian-style house stands only a stone's throw from Bayou Lafourche, the place where they met and fell in love as teenagers. Lynne and their 17-year-old daughter, Amy, are inside preparing dinner, and outside Marty is giving me a tour of the spread when we come to rest in the shade of a carport. I reach to touch the top of his shoulder, because he still has some feeling there, but then I stop myself. "Marty, you must've resented the hell out of me," I say.

He looks up, surprise registering on his face. He bucks forward and then back in his chair, and it isn't necessary for me to explain which of my failures might've led me to make such a statement. "No, never," he says. "I saw you as my competition, but I always have a lot of respect for my competition, and I did for you, too. You were standing in my way, standing in the way of where I wanted to be. But even then I knew my role and accepted it. I was going to push you as hard as I could. That was my duty to you and to the team. I looked up to you as a teacher, just as you looked up to Jay Whitley as a teacher when he was playing ahead of you. We were teammates, John Ed. That was the most important thing."

Lynne and Amy serve lasagna, green salad and blueberry cheesecake in the dining room, and afterward Marty and I move to the living room and sit together as dusk darkens the windows. He revisits the nightmare of his accident and the rough years that followed, but it isn't until he talks about his days as an LSU football player that he becomes emotional. "Nothing I've ever experienced compares to it," he says. "That first time I ran out with the team as a freshman—out into Tiger Stadium? God, I was 15 feet off the ground and covered with frissons. You know what frissons are? They're goose bumps. It's the French word for goose bumps." He lowers his head, and tears fill his eyes and run down his face. He weeps as I have wept, at the memory of how beautiful it all was. "It was the biggest high you could have," he says. "No drugs could match it. The way it felt to run out there with the crowd yelling for you. I wish every kid could experience that."

"If every kid could," I say, "then it wouldn't be what it is. It's because so few ever get there that it has such power."

We were quiet, and then he says, "Whenever I have a down time, or whenever I'm feeling sorry for myself, or whenever life is more than I can bear at the moment, I always do the same thing. I put the Tiger fight song on the stereo, and all the memories come back and somehow it makes everything O.K. All right, I say to myself, I can do it. I can do it. Let's go."

Marty and I talk deep into the night, oblivious to the time, and finally I get up to leave. He wheels his chair as far as the door, and as I'm driving away I look back and see him sitting there, a bolt of yellow light around him, arm raised in goodbye.

I could seek out each one of them and apologize for the vanishing act, but, like me, most of them eventually elected to vanish, too, moving into whatever roles the world had reserved for them. Last I heard, Jay Blass had become a commercial pilot. Greg Raymond returned to New Orleans and was running his family's jewelry store. Tom Tully became a veterinarian specializing in exotic birds, of all things. And Jay Whitley, somebody told me, is an orthodontist now, the father of four kids. If they're anything like their old man, they're stouthearted and fearless, and they eat linebackers for lunch.

When the pregame prayer and pep talks were done, we'd come out of the chute to the screams of people who were counting on us. The band would begin to play; up ahead the cheerleaders were waiting. Under the crossbar of the goalpost we huddled, seniors in front. I was always afraid to trip and fall and embarrass myself, and for the first few steps I ran with a hand on the teammate next to me. Arms pumping, knees lifted high. The heat felt like a dense, blistering weight in your lungs. If you looked up above the rim of the bowl you couldn't see the stars; the light from the standards had washed out the sky. Always in the back of your mind was the knowledge of your supreme good fortune. Everyone else would travel a similar course of human experience, but you were different.

And so, chin straps buckled tight, we filed out onto the field as one, the gold and the white a single elongated blur, neatly trimmed in purple.

W.C. Heinz's "The Ghost of the Gridiron" and Arthur Kretchmer's "Butkus" explore the men behind the myths of two of the greatest football heroes in the history of the game. I was struck by the similarities between the two.

When thinking of Red Grange or Dick Butkus, it's easy to think of them only as football gods rather than as men. Often sports stars are depicted as having a "burning desire," or a "passion for the game" that exceeds that of their peers. This intense drive is what separates them from the merely serviceable players of modest mental toughness. In fact, these stories suggest that Grange and Butkus were actually no more impassioned than the rest of the players, just better.

Grange realized his immense talent only after a fraternity brother demanded that he try out for the University of Illinois football team. Once on the field, he surprised even himself with the physical gifts he possessed. Butkus was an unassuming man from a large, working-class Lithuanian family who happened to grow into a 245-tackling machine. His acumen at finding angles between blocking schemes and reaching and punishing ball-carriers was an innate skill that few before or since have mirrored.

The careers of these two Midwestern football stars belied their relatively calm off-field lives, and put into question the idea that desire is what separates the good men from the better men.

The Ghost of the Gridiron

W. C. HEINZ

When I was ten years old I paid ten cents to see Red Grange run with a football. That was the year when, one afternoon a week, after school was out for the day, they used to show us movies in the auditorium, and we would all troop up there clutching our dimes, nickels or pennies in our fists.

The movies were, I suppose, carefully selected for their educational value. They must have shown us, as the weeks went by, films of the Everglades, of Yosemite, of the Gettysburg battlefield, of Washington, D.C., but I remember only the one about Grange.

I remember, in fact, only one shot. Grange, the football cradled in one arm, started down the field toward us. As we sat there in the dim, flickering light of the movie projector, he grew larger and larger. I can still see the rows and rows of us, with our thin little necks and bony heads, all looking up at the screen and Grange, enormous now, rushing right at us, and I shall never forget it. That was thirty-three years ago.

"I haven't any idea what film that might have been," Grange was saying now. "My last year at Illinois was all confusion. I had no privacy. Newsreel men were staying at the fraternity house for two or three days at a time."

He paused. The thought of it seemed to bring pain to his face, even at this late date.

"I wasn't able to study or anything," he said. "I thought and I still do, that they built me up out of all proportion."

Red Grange was the most sensational, the most publicized, and, possibly, the most gifted football player and greatest broken field runner of all time. In high school, at Wheaton, Illinois, he averaged five touchdowns a game. In twenty games for the University of Illinois, he scored thirty-one touchdowns and ran for 3,637 yards, or, as it was translated at the time, 2 miles and 117

250

yards. His name and his pseudonyms—The Galloping Ghost and The Wheaton Iceman—became household words, and what he was may have been summarized best by Paul Sann in his book *The Lawless Decade.*

"Red Grange, No. 77, made Jack Dempsey move over," Sann wrote. "He put college football ahead of boxing as the Golden Age picked up momentum. He also made the ball yards obsolete; they couldn't handle the crowds. He made people buy more radios: how could you wait until Sunday morning to find out what deeds Red Grange had performed on Saturday? He was "The Galloping Ghost" and he made the sports historians torture their portables without mercy."

Grange is now 55 years old, his reddish brown hair marked with gray, but he was one with Babe Ruth, Jack Dempsey, Bobby Jones and Bill Tilden.

"I could carry a football well," Grange was saying now, "but I've met hundreds of people who could do their thing better than I. I mean engineers, and writers, scientists, doctors—whatever.

"I can't take much credit for what I did, running with a football, because I don't know what I did. Nobody ever taught me, and I can't teach anybody. You can teach a man how to block or tackle or kick or pass. The ability to run with a ball is something you have or you haven't. If you can't explain it, how can you take credit for it?"

This was last year, and we were sitting in a restaurant in Syracuse, New York. Grange was in town to do a telecast with Lindsey Nelson of the Syracuse–Penn State game. He lives now in Miami, Florida, coming out of there on weekends during the football season to handle telecasts of college games on Saturdays and the Chicago Bears' games on Sundays. He approaches this job as he approached every job, with honesty and dedication, and, as could be expected, he is good at it. As befits a man who put the pro game on the map and made the whole nation football conscious, he has been making fans out of people who never followed the game before. Never, perhaps, has any one man done more for the game. And it, of course, has been good to him.

"Football did everything for me," he was saying now, "but what people don't understand is that it hasn't been my whole life. When I was a freshman at Illinois, I wasn't even going to go out for football. My fraternity brothers made me do it."

He was three times All-American. Once the Illinois students carried him two miles on their backs. A football jersey, with the number 77 that he made famous and that was retired after him, is enshrined at Champaign. His fellow students wanted him to run for Congress. A Senator from Illinois led him into the White House to shake hands with Calvin Coolidge. Here, in its entirety, is what was said.

"Howdy," Coolidge said. "Where do you live?"

"In Wheaton, Illinois," Grange said.

"Well, young man," Coolidge said, "I wish you luck."

Grange had his luck, but it was coming to him because he did more to popularize professional football than any other player before or since. In his first three years out of school he grossed almost $1,000,000 from football motion pictures, vaudeville appearances and endorsements, and he could afford to turn down a Florida real estate firm that wanted to pay him $120,000 a year. Seven years ago the Associated Press, in selecting an All-Time All-American team in conjunction with the National Football Hall of Fame, polled one hundred leading sportswriters and Grange received more votes than any other player.

"They talk about the runs I made," he was saying, "but I can't tell you one thing I did on any run. That's the truth. During the depression, though, I took a licking. Finally I got into the insurance business. I almost starved to death for three years, but I never once tried to use my football reputation. I never once opened a University of Illinois year book and knowingly called on an alumnus. I think I was as good an insurance man as there was in Chicago. On the football field I had ten other men blocking for me, but I'm more proud of what I did in the insurance business, because I did it alone."

Recently I went down to Miami and visited Grange in the white colonial duplex house where he lives with his wife. They met eighteen years ago on a plane, flying between Chicago and Omaha, on which she was a stewardess, and they were married the following year.

"Without sounding like an amateur psychologist," I said, "I believe you derive more satisfaction from what you did in the insurance business, not only because you did it alone, but also because you know how you did it, and, if you had to, you could do it again. You could never find any security in what you did when you ran with a football because it was inspirational and creative, rather than calculated."

"Yes," Grange said, "you could call it that. The sportswriters used to try to explain it, and they used to ask me. I couldn't tell them anything."

I have read what many of those sportswriters wrote, and they had as much trouble trying to corner Grange on paper as his opponents had trying to tackle him on the field. . . .

Grange had blinding speed, amazing lateral mobility, and exceptional change of pace and a powerful straight-arm. He moved with high knee action, but seemed to glide, rather than run, and he was a master at using his blockers. What made him great, however, was his instinctive ability to size up a field and plot a run the way a great general can map not only a battle but a whole campaign.

"The sportswriters wrote that I had peripheral vision," Grange was saying. "I didn't even know what the word meant. I had to look it up. They asked me about my change of pace, and I didn't even know that I ran at different speeds. I had a cross-over step, but I couldn't spin. Some ball carriers can spin but if I tried that, I would have broken a leg."

Harold Edward Grange was born on June 13, 1903, in Forksville, Pennsylvania, the third of four children. His mother died when he was five, and his sister Norma died in her teens. The other sister, Mildred, lives in Binghamton, New York. His brother, Garland, two and a half years younger than Red, was a 165-pound freshman end at Illinois and was later with the Chicago Bears and is now a credit manager for a Florida department store chain. Their father died at the age of 86.

"My father," Grange said, "was the foreman of three lumber camps near Forksville, and if you had known him, you'd know why I could never get a swelled head. He stood six-one and weighed 210 pounds, and he was quick as a cat. He had three hundred men under him and he had to be able to lick any one of them. One day he had a fight that lasted four hours."

Grange's father, after the death of his wife, moved to Wheaton, Illinois, where he had relatives. Then he sent the two girls back to Pennsylvania to live with their maternal grandparents. With his sons, he moved into a five-room apartment over a store where they took turns cooking and keeping house.

"Can you recall," I said, "the first time you ever ran with a football?"

"I think it started," Grange said, "with a game we used to play without a football. Ten or twelve of us would line up in the street, along one curb. One guy would be in the middle of the road and the rest of us would run across the street to the curb on the other side. When the kid in the middle of the street tackled one of the runners, the one who was tackled had to stay in the middle of the street with the tackler. Finally, all of us, except one last runner, would be in the middle of the street. We only had about thirty yards to maneuver in and dodge the tackler. I got to be pretty good at that. Then somebody got a football and we played games with it on vacant lots."

In high school Grange won sixteen letters in football, basketball, track and baseball. In track he competed in the 100 and 220 yard dashes, low and high hurdles, broad jump and high jump and often won all six events. In his sophomore year on the football team, he scored 15 touchdowns, in his junior year 36—eight in one game—and in his senior year 23. Once he was kicked in the head and was incoherent for 48 hours.

"I went to Illinois," he was saying, "because some of my friends from Wheaton went there and all the kids in the state wanted to play football for Bob Zuppke and because there weren't any athletic scholarships in those days and that was the cheapest place for me to go to. In May of my senior year in high school I was there for the Interscholastic track meet, and I just got through broad jumping when Zup came over. He said, 'Is your name Grainche?' That's the way he always pronounced my name. I said 'Yes.' He said, 'Where are you going to college?' I said, 'I don't know.' He put his arm around my shoulders and he said, 'I hope here. You may have a chance to make the team here.' That was the greatest moment I'd known."

That September, Grange arrived at Champaign with a battered second-hand trunk, one suit, a couple of pairs of trousers and a sweater. He had been working for four summers on an ice wagon in Wheaton and saving some money, and his one luxury now that he was entering college was to pledge Zeta Phi fraternity.

"One day," he was saying, "they lined us pledges up in the living room of the fraternity house. I had wanted to go out for basketball and track—I thought there would be too much competition in football—but they started to point to each one of us and tell us what to go out for? 'You go out for cheerleader. You go out for football manager. You go out for the band.' When they came to me, they said, 'You go out for football.'

"That afternoon I went over to the gym. I looked out the window at the football practice field and they had about three hundred freshman candidates out there. I went back to the house and I said to one of the seniors, 'I can't go out for football. I'll never make that team.'

"So he lined me up near the wall, with my head down, and he hit me with this paddle. I could show you the dent in that wall where my head took a piece of plaster out—this big."

With the thumb and forefinger of his right hand, he made a circle the size of a half dollar.

"Do you remember the name of that senior?" I said.

"Johnny Hawks," Grange said. "He was from Goshen, Indiana, and I see him now and then. I say to him, 'Damn you. If it wasn't for you, I'd never have gone out for football.' He gets a great boot out of that."

"So what happened when you went out the next day?"

"We had all these athletes from Chicago I'd been reading about. What chance did I have, from a little farm town and a high school with three hundred students? I think they cut about forty that first night, but I happened to win the wind sprints and that got them at least to know my name."

It was a great freshman team. On it with Grange was Earl Britton, who blocked for Grange and did the kicking throughout their college careers, and Moon Baker and Frank Wickhorst, who transferred to Northwestern and Annapolis, respectively, where they both made All-American. After one week of practice, the freshman team played the varsity and were barely nosed out, 21–19, as Grange scored two touchdowns, one on a 60 yard punt return. From then on, the freshmen trimmed the varsity regularly and Zuppke began to give most of his time to the freshmen.

"That number 77," I said to Grange, "became the most famous number in football. Do you remember when you first got it?"

"It was just handed to me in my sophomore year," he said. "I guess anybody who has a number and does well with it gets a little superstitious about it, and I guess that began against Nebraska in my first varsity game."

That game started Grange to national fame. This was 1923, and the previous year Nebraska had beaten Notre Dame and they were to beat "The Four Horsemen" later this same season. In the first quarter Grange sprinted 35 yards for a touchdown. In the second quarter he ran 60 yards for another. In the third period he scored again on a 12 yard burst, and Illinois won, 24–7. The next day, over Walter Eckersall's story in the Chicago *Tribune,* the headline said: GRANGE SPRINTS TO FAME.

From the Nebraska game, Illinois went on to an undefeated season. Against Butler, Grange scored twice. Against Iowa, he scored the only touchdown as Illinois won, 9–6. In the first quarter against Northwestern, he intercepted a pass and ran 90 yards to score the first of his three touchdowns. He made the only touchdown in the game with the University of Chicago and the only one in the Ohio State game, this time on a 34 yard run.

"All Grange can do is run," Fielding Yost, the coach at Michigan, was quoted as saying.

"All Galli-Curci can do is sing," Zuppke said.

Grange had his greatest day in his first game against Michigan during his junior year. On that day Michigan came to the dedication of the new $1,700,000 Illinois Memorial Stadium. The Wolverines had been undefeated in twenty games and for months the nation's football fans had been waiting for this meeting. There were 67,000 spectators in the stands, then the largest crowd ever to see a football game in the Midwest.

Michigan kicked off. Grange was standing on his goal line, with Wally McIlwain, whom Zuppke was to call "the greatest open field blocker of all time" on his right, Harry Hall, the Illinois quarterback, on his left, and Earl Britton in front of him. Michigan attempted to aim the kickoff to McIlwain, but as the ball descended, Grange moved over under it.

"I've got it," he said to McIlwain.

He caught it on the 5 yard line. McIlwain turned and took out the first Michigan man to get near him. Britton cut down the next one, and Grange started underway. He ran to his left, reversed his field to avoid one would-be tackler, and, then, cutting back again to the left, ran diagonally across the field through the oncoming Michigan players. At the Michigan 40 yard line he was in the open and on the 20 yard line, Tod Rockwell, the Michigan safety man, made a futile dive for him. Grange scored standing up. Michigan never recovered.

In less than twelve minutes, Grange scored three more touchdowns on runs of 67, 56 and 44 yards. Zuppke took him out to rest him. In the third period, he re-entered the game, and circled right end for 15 yards and another touchdown. In the final quarter, he threw a pass for another score. Illinois won, 39–14. Against a powerful, seasoned and favored team, Grange had handled the ball twenty-one times, gained 402 yards running, scored five touchdowns and collaborated, as a passer, in a sixth.

"This was," Coach Amos Alonzo Stagg, the famous Chicago mentor, later wrote, "the most spectacular singlehanded performance ever made in a major game."

"Did Zuppke tell you that you should have scored another touchdown?" I asked Grange.

"That's right," Grange said. "After the fourth touchdown we called a time-out, and when Matt Bullock, our trainer, came with the water, I said to him, 'I'm dog tired. You'd better tell Zup to get me out of here.' When I got to the bench Zup said to me, 'You should have had five touchdowns. You didn't cut right on one play.' Nobody could get a swelled head around him."

"And you don't recall," I said, "one feint or cut that you made during any one of those runs?"

"I don't remember one thing I ever did on any run I made. I just remember one vision from that Michigan game. On that opening kickoff runback, as I got downfield I saw that the only man still in front of me was the safety man, Tod Rockwell. I remember thinking then, 'I'd better get by this guy, because after coming all this way, I'll sure look like a bum if he tackles me.' I can't tell you, though, how I did get by him.'"

When Grange started his senior year, Illinois had lost seven regulars by graduation and Harry Hall, its quarterback, who had a broken collarbone. Zuppke shifted Grange to quarterback. Illinois lost to Nebraska, Iowa and Michigan and barely beat Butler before they came to Franklin Field in Philadelphia on October 31, 1925, to play Pennsylvania.

The previous year Penn had been considered the champion of the East. They had now beaten Brown, Yale and Chicago, among others. Although Grange's exploits in the Midwest had been widely reported in Eastern papers, most of the 65,000 spectators and the Eastern sportswriters—Grantland Rice, Damon Runyon and Ford Frick among them—came to be convinced.

It had rained and snowed for 24 hours, with only straw covering the field. At the kickoff, the players stood in mud. On the third play of the game, the first time he carried the ball, Grange went 55 yards for his first touchdown. On the next kickoff he ran 55 yards again, to the Penn 25 yard line, and Illinois worked it over the goal line from there. In the second period, Grange twisted 12 yards for another score and in the third period he ran 20 yards to a touchdown. Illinois won, 24–2, with Grange carrying the ball 363 yards, and scoring three touchdowns and setting up another one, in thirty-six rushes.

Two days later when the train carrying the Illinois team arrived in Champaign, there were 20,000 students, faculty members and townspeople waiting at the station. Grange tried to sneak out of the last car but he was recognized and carried two miles to his fraternity house.

"Do you remember your feelings during those two miles?" I asked him.

"I remember that I was embarrassed," he said. "You wish people would understand that it takes eleven men to make a football team. Unless they've played it, I guess they'll never understand it, but I've never been impressed by individual performances in football, my own or anyone else's."

"Do you remember the last touchdown you scored in college?"

"To tell the truth, I don't," he said. "It must have been against Ohio State. I can't tell you the score. I can't tell you the score of more than three or four games I ever played in."

I looked it up. Grange's last college appearance, against Ohio State, attracted 85,500 spectators at Columbus. He was held to 153 yards on the ground but threw one touchdown pass as Illinois won, 14–9. The following afternoon, in the Morrison Hotel in Chicago, he signed with Charles C. (Cash and Carry) Pyle to play professional football with the Chicago Bears, starting immediately, and he quit college. Twenty-five years later, however, he was elected to the University of Illinois Board of Trustees for a six-year term.

"I had a half year to finish when I quit," he said. "I had this chance to make a lot of money and I couldn't figure where having a sheepskin would pull any more people into football games."

"How were your marks in college?"

"I was an average student. I got B's and C's. I flunked one course, economics, and I made that up in the summer at Wheaton College. I'd leave the ice wagon at 11 o'clock in the morning and come back to it at 1 o'clock. There was so much written about my job on the ice wagon, and so many pictures of me lugging ice, that people thought it was a publicity stunt. It wasn't. I did it for eight summers, starting at 5 o'clock every morning, for two reasons. The pay was good—$37.50 a week—and I needed money. I didn't even have any decent clothes until my junior year. Also, it kept me in shape. After carrying those blocks of ice up and down stairs six days a week, my legs were always in shape when the football season started. Too many football players have to play their legs into shape in the first four or five games."

Grange played professional football from 1925 through the 1934 season, first with the Bears, then with the New York Yankees in a rival pro league that Pyle and he started, and then back with the Bears again. He was immobilized during the 1928 season with arm and knee injuries, and after that he was never able to cut sharply while carrying the ball. He did, however, score 162 touchdowns as a professional and kicked 86 conversion points, for a total of 1,058 points.

What the statistics do not show, however, is what Grange, more than any other player, did to focus public attention and approval on the professional game. In 1925, when he signed with the Bears, professional football attracted little notice on the sports page and few paying customers. There was so little interest that the National Professional Football League did not even hold a championship playoff at the end of the season.

In ten days after he left college Grange played five games as a pro and changed all that. After only three practice sessions with the Bears, he made his pro debut against the Chicago Cardinals on Thanksgiving Day, November 26. The game ended 0–0 but 36,000 people crowded into Wrigley Field to see Grange. Three days later, on a Sunday, 28,000 defied a snowstorm to watch him perform at the same field. On the next Wednesday, freezing weather in St.

Louis held the attendance down to 8,000 but on Saturday 40,000 Philadelphians watched him in the rain at Shibe Park. The next day the Bears played in the Polo Grounds against the New York Giants.

It had been raining for almost a week, and, although advance sales were almost unknown in pro football in those days, the Giants sold almost 60,000 before Sunday dawned. It turned out to be a beautiful day. Cautious fans who had not bought seats in advance stormed the ticket booths. Thousands of people were turned away but 73,651 crammed into the park. Grange did not score but the Bears won, 19–7.

That was the beginning of professional football's rise to its present popularity. At the end of those first ten days, Grange picked up a check for $50,000. He got another $50,000 when the season ended a month later.

"Can you remember," I asked him now, "the last time you ever carried a football?"

"It was in a game against the Giants in Gilmore Stadium in Hollywood in January of 1935. It was the last period, and we had a safe lead and I was sitting on the bench. George Halas said to me, 'Would you like to go in, Red?' I said, 'No, thanks.' Everybody knew this was my last year. He said, 'Go ahead. Why don't you run it just once more?'

"So I went in, and we lined up and they called a play for me. As soon as I got the ball and started to go I knew that they had it framed with the Giants to let me run. The line just opened up for me and I went through and started down the field. The farther I ran, the heavier my legs got and the farther those goal posts seemed to move away. I was thinking, 'When I make that end zone, I'm going to take off these shoes and shoulder pads for the last time.' With that something hit me from behind and down I went on about the 10 yard line. It was Cecil Irvin, a 230-pound tackle. He was so slow that, I guess, they never bothered to let him in on the plan. But when he caught me from behind, I knew I was finished."

Grange, who is 5 feet 11 and ¾ inches, weighed 180 in college and 185 in his last game with the Bears. Now he weighs 200. On December 15, 1951, he suffered a heart attack. This motivated him to give up his insurance business and to move to Florida where he and his wife own, in addition to their own home in Miami, land in Orlando and Melbourne and property at Indian Lake.

"Red," I said, "I'll bet there are some men still around whose greatest claim to fame is that they played football with you or against you. I imagine there are guys whose proudest boast is that they once tackled you. Have you ever run into a guy who thought he knew everything about football and didn't know he was talking with Red Grange?"

"Yes," he said. "Once about fifteen years ago, on my way home from work, I dropped into a tavern in Chicago for a beer. Two guys next to me and the bartender were arguing about Bronco Nagurski and Carl Brumbaugh. On the Bears, of course, I played in the backfield with both of them. One guy doesn't like Nagurski and he's talking against him. I happen to think Nagurski was the greatest football player I ever saw, and a wonderful guy. This fellow who is knocking him says to me, 'Do you know anything about football? Did you ever see Nagurski play?' I said, 'Yes, and I think he was great.' The guy gets mad and says, 'What was so great about him? What do you know about it?' I could see it was time to leave, but the guy kept at me. He said, 'Now wait a minute. What makes you think you know something about it? Who are you, anyway?' I reached into my wallet and took out my business card and handed it to him and started for the door. When I got to the door, I looked back at him. You should have seen his face."

Mrs. Grange, who had been listening to our talk, left the room and came back with a small, gold-plated medal that Grange had won in the broad jump at the Interscholastic track meet on the day when he first met Zuppke.

"A friend of mine just sent that to me," Grange said. "He wrote: 'You gave me this away back in 1921. I thought you might want it.' Just the other day I got a letter from a man in the Midwest who told me that his son just found a good football inscribed, 'University of Illinois, 1924' with the initials H. G. on it. I was the only H. G. on that squad so it must have been mine. I guess I gave it to somebody and he lost it. I wrote the man back and said: 'If your son would like it, I'd be happy to have him keep it.'"

Mrs. Grange said, "We have a friend who can't understand why Grange doesn't keep his souvenirs. He has his trophies in another friend's storage locker in Chicago. The clipping books are nailed up in a box in the garage here and Grange hasn't looked at them in years."

"I don't like to look back," Grange said. "You have to look ahead."

I remembered that night when we ate in the restaurant in Syracuse. As we stood in line to get our hats and coats, Grange nudged me and showed me his hat check. In the middle of the yellow cardboard disk was the number 77.

"Has this ever happened to you before?" I said.

"Never," he said, "as far as I know."

We walked out into the cold night air. A few flakes of snow were falling.

"That jersey with the 77 on it that's preserved at Illinois," I said, "is that your last game jersey?"

"I don't know," Grange said. "It was probably a new jersey."

"Do you have any piece of equipment that you wore on the football field?"

"No," he said. "I don't have anything."

The traffic light changed, and we started across the street. "I don't even have an I-sweater," he said.

We walked about three paces.

"You know," Grange said, "I'd kind of like to have an I-sweater now."

Butkus

ARTHUR KRETCHMER

Dick Butkus slowly unraveled his mass from the confines of a white Toronado and walked into the Golden Ox Restaurant on Chicago's North Side. He is built large and hard, big enough to make John Wayne look like his loyal sidekick. When he walks, he leads with his shoulders, and the slight forward hunch gives him an aura of barely restrained power. He always seems to be ready.

As he walked through the restaurant, he was recognized by most of the men sitting at lunch. But the expression on their faces was not the one of childlike surprise usually produced by celebrities. It was of frightened awe. It read: "Holy Christ! He really *is* an ape. He could tear me apart and he might *love* it."

Ten rolling steps into the restaurant, with all eyes fixed on him, he was stopped by an ebullient lady with a thick German accent, a member of the staff. "Mr. Boot-kuss!" she scolded him. "What have you done to yourself? You look so thin."

He smiled shyly. Not even the ferocious Dick Butkus can handle a rampant maternal instinct. "Aw," he said. "I'm just down to my playing weight."

Butkus chose a table in a far corner of the restaurant. It was a Friday afternoon, two days before the Chicago Bears were to meet the Minnesota Vikings in the first of two games the teams would play in 1970. The Vikings had won the NFL championship the year before and seemed likely to repeat. The Bears were presenting their usual combination of erratic offense and brutal defense and appeared to be on the verge of another undistinguished season. Butkus was joined at the table by a business associate and a journalist. He ordered a sandwich and a liter of dark beer. He doesn't like journalists and is cautious to the point of hostility with them. But he fields the questions, because it's part of his business.

"Do you think you can beat the Vikings?"

Butkus answers, "Yeah, the defense can beat them. I don't know if the offense can score any points. But we can take it to those guys."

"Have you ever been scared on a football field?"

"Scared?" he repeats, puzzled. "Of what?"

Then he smiled, knowing the effect he's had on his questioner. "Just injuries," he says. "That's the only thing to be afraid of. I'm always hurt, never been healthy. If I ever felt really great and could play a hundred percent, shit, nobody'd know what was going on, it would be so amazing."

"Does anybody play to intentionally hurt other guys?"

"Some assholes do. The really good ones don't."

"Dave Meggyesy, the ex-Cardinal, says that football is so brutal he was taught to use his hands to force a man's cleats into the turf and then drive his shoulder into the man's knee to rip his leg apart. That ever happen to you?"

"Hell, no! All you'd have to do is roll with the block and step on the guy's face."

That's my man. Richard Marvin Butkus, 28 years old, 245 pounds, six feet, three inches tall, middle linebacker for the Chicago Bears football team, possibly the best man to ever play the position. To a fan, the story on Butkus is very simple. He's the meanest, angriest, toughest, dirtiest son of a bitch in football. An animal, a savage, subhuman. But as good at his game as Ty Cobb was at his, or Don Budge at his, or Joe Louis at his.

As one of the Bear linemen said to me, "When you try to pick the best offensive guard, there are about five guys who are really close; it's hard to pick one. The same thing's true about most positions. But Butkus is the best. He's superman. He's the greatest thing since popcorn."

The Minnesota game is being played on a warm, sunny autumn day at Chicago's Wrigley Field before a capacity crowd. Both teams have come out to warm up, but Butkus is late, because his right knee is being shot up with cortisone. It was injured three weeks before in a game with the New York Giants. Butkus was caught from the blind side while moving sideways and the knee collapsed. Until then, the Giants had been playing away from him. When they realized he was hurt, they tried to play at him and he simply stuffed them. Giant quarterback Fran Tarkenton said afterward, "Butkus has the most concentration of any man in the game. He's fantastic. And after he was hurt, he dragged that leg around the whole field. He was better after the injury than before—better on that one damn leg than with two."

When Butkus finally comes out, his steps are hesitant, like he is trying to walk off a cramp. You notice immediately that he looks even bigger in pads and helmet—bigger than anyone else on the field, bigger than players listed in the program as outweighing him. He has the widest shoulders on earth. His name seems too small for him; the entire alphabet could be printed on the back of his uniform and there'd be room left over.

Both teams withdraw after warm-ups and the stadium announcer reads the line-ups. The biggest hand from the restless fans comes when Butkus' name is announced. In the quiet that follows the applause, a raucous voice from high in the stands shouts, "Get Butkus' ass."

The players return to the field and string out along the side line. Both team benches at Wrigley Field are on the same side of the field, the Bears to the north and the Vikings to the south. Near midfield, opposing players and coaches stand quite close to each other, but there is almost no conversation between them, abusive or otherwise. As the Vikings arrange themselves for the national anthem, linebacker Wally Hilgenberg roars in on tight end John Beasley, a teammate, and delivers a series of resounding two-fisted hammer blows to Beasley's shoulder pads, exhaling loud whoops as his fists land. Beasley then smashes Hilgenberg. Everyone is snarling and hissing as the seconds tick away before the kickoff. Butkus is one of the few who show no signs of nervousness. That is true off the field and on. He does not fidget nor pace. Mostly, he just stands rather loosely and stares.

After the anthem, the tempo on the side line increases. The Bears will be kicking off. Howard Mudd, an offensive guard who was all-pro when the Bears obtained him in a trade from San Francisco, is screaming, "KICKOFF KICK-OFF KICKOFF," trying to get everyone else up as well as discharge some of his own energy. Mudd is a gap-toothed, blue-eyed 29-year-old with a bald spot at his crown who arrives at the field about 8:30 A.M.—fully four and a half hours before the game. He spends a lot of that time throwing up.

As I watch the Vikings' first offensive series from the sideline, the sense of space and precision that the fan gets, either up in the stadium or at home on television, is destroyed. The careful delineation of plays done by the TV experts becomes absurd. At ground level, all is mayhem; sophistication and artistry are destroyed by the sheer velocity of the game. Each snap of the ball sets off 21 crazed men dueling with one another for some kind of edge—the 22nd, the quarterback, is the only one trying to maintain calm and seek some sense of order in the asylum.

It's the sudden, isolated noise that gets you. There is little sound just before each play begins—the crowd is usually quiet. At the snap, the tense vacuum is broken by sharp grunts and curses from the linemen as they slam into one another. The sudden smash of a forearm is sickening; and then there is the most chilling sound of all: the hollow thud as a launched, reckless body drives a shoulder pad into a ball carrier's head—a sound more lonely and terrifying than a gunshot.

After receiving the kickoff, the Vikings are forced to punt when a third-down pass from Gary Cuozzo, the Viking quarterback, to Gene Washington falls incomplete. As the Bears come off the field, Butkus is screaming at left linebacker Doug Buffone and cornerback Joe Taylor, because Washington was open for the throw. Luckily, he dropped it. They are having a problem with the signals. There is something comical about Butkus screaming with his helmet on. His face is so large that it seems to be trying to get *around* the helmet, as if the face were stuffed into it against its will.

That third-down play was marked by a lapse in execution by both offense and defense. It was one of those plays where all the neatly drawn lines in the playbook are meaningless. The truth about football is that, rather than being a game of incredible precision, it is a game of breakdowns, of entropy. If all plays happened as conceived, it would be too easy a sport. But the reality is that the timing is usually destroyed by a mental error, by a misstep, by a defenseman getting a bigger piece of a man than he was expected to, by the mere pace of the action being beyond a man's ability to think clearly when he's under pressure. Or by his being belted in the neck and knee simultaneously while he's supposed to be running nine steps down and four steps in.

The Bears don't get anywhere against the Viking defense and Butkus is back out quickly. On the field, his presence is commanding. He doesn't take a stance so much as install himself a few feet from the offensive center, screwing his heels down and hunching forward, hands on knees. His aura is total belligerence. As Cuozzo calls the signals, all of Butkus goes into motion. His mouth is usually calling signals of his own, his hands come off his knees, making preliminary pawing motions, and his legs begin to drive in place. No one in football has a better sense of where the ball will go, and Butkus moves instantly with the snap.

Two Cuozzo passes under pressure set up a Viking touchdown. On the Bears next set of offensive plays, they can't get anything going, and the defense is back out. On the second play from scrimmage, the Vikings set up a perfect sweep, a play that looks great each time you put it on the blackboard but works right one time in ten. This is one of those times. Guards Milt Sunde and Ed White lead Clint Jones around the left side with no one in front of them except Butkus, who is moving over from his position in the middle. All four bodies are accelerating rapidly. The play happens right in front of me and Butkus launches himself around Sunde and smashes both forearms into White, clawing his way over the guard to bring Jones down for no gain. He has beaten three men.

The Vikings are forced to punt after that and the Bears get their first first down. Then, on first and ten, Bear quarterback Jack Concannon lobs a perfect pass to halfback Craig Baynham; who is open in the Viking secondary. Baynham drops it. And that is about as much as the Bear offense will show this day.

With 56 seconds left in the half, the Vikings have the ball again. Cuozzo is trapped in the backfield trying to pass; and as he sets to throw, the ball falls to the ground and the Bears pick it up. The officials rule that Cuozzo was in the act of throwing and therefore the Vikings maintain possession on an incomplete pass. The Bears and all of Wrigley Field think it's a fumble and are expressing themselves accordingly. Butkus is enraged and is ranting at all the officials at once. But the Vikings keep the ball and a few seconds later try a field goal from the Bear 15. Butkus is stunting in the line, looking for a place to get through to block the kick. At the snap, he charges over tackle Ron Yary but is savagely triple-teamed and stopped. The field goal is good. When Yary comes off the field, he is bleeding heavily from the bridge of his nose but doesn't seem to notice it.

As the half ends, a ruddy-looking gray-haired man who had been enthusiastically jeering the officials on the Cuozzo call slumps forward in his seat. Oxygen and a stretcher are dispatched immediately and the early diagnosis is a heart attack. He is rushed from the stadium, but the betting among the side-line spectators—an elite group of photographers, friends of the athletes and hangers-on—is that he won't make it. They are right; the man is taken to a hospital and pronounced dead on arrival. A spectator, watching the game from behind a ground-level barricade, says, "If he had a season ticket, I'd like to buy it."

The second half is more of the same for the Bears' offense. Concannon throws another perfect touchdown pass, but it's dropped; and the Vikings maintain their edge. The surprising thing is that the Bears never give up. With the score 24–0, the Bear offensive line is still hitting and, God knows, so is the defense. The Bears have a reputation as a physical team, and it's justified. They have often given the impression, especially in the days when George Halas was coaching them, of being a bunch of guys who thought the best thing you could do on a Sunday afternoon was go out and kick a little ass. Winning was a possible but not necessary adjunct to playing football.

As Butkus comes off the field at the end of the third quarter, he's limping noticeably, but it hasn't affected his play. Cuozzo has had most of his success throwing short passes to the outside, but he continues to run plays in Butkus's area. The plays begin to take on a hypnotic pattern for me. Every three downs or so, there is this paradigm running play: Tingelhoff, the center, charges at Butkus, who fends him off with his forearms. Then Butkus moves to the hole that Osborn or Brown has committed himself to. Butkus, legs driving, arms outstretched, seems to simply step forward and embrace the largest amount of space he can. And he smothers everything in it—an offensive lineman, possibly one of his own defensive linemen and the ball carrier. Then he simply hangs on and bulls it all to the ground.

Finally, the game ends with a sense of stupefying boredom, because everyone seems to realize at once that there was never any hope. As the fans file out, one leans over a guardrail and screams at Bear head coach Jim Dooley. "Hey, Dooley! Whydoncha give Butkus a break? Trade him!" This is met with approval from his friends.

A few days after the Viking game, Butkus is in another North Side German restaurant. He is quiet, reserved and unhappy, because he feels that the Vikings didn't show the Bears much, didn't beat them physically nor with any great show of proficiency. I can't help thinking that a man of his talent would get tired of this kind of second-rate football.

"Don't you ever get bored? Don't you think of retiring from this grind?"

"No way!"

"But what do you get from it? It's got to be very frustrating. Why do you play?"

"Hell. That's like asking a guy why he fucks."

The following Sunday, the Bears are flat and lose badly to an amazing passing display from the San Diego Chargers. But they have been pointing toward their next big game—a rematch with an old and hated rival, the Detroit Lions. Earlier in the year, on national television, the Bears led the Lions for a half but ended up losing. After that game, Lion head coach Joe Schmidt said that his middle linebacker, Mike Lucci, was the best in football and that Butkus was overrated. The Lions generally said that Butkus was dirty rather than good. It added a little spice to a game that didn't need any.

The question of linebacking is an interesting one to consider. To play that position, a man must be strong enough in the arms and shoulders to fight off offensive linemen who often outweigh him, fast enough to cover receivers coming out of the backfield and rangy enough to move laterally with speed. But the real key to the position is an instantaneous ferocity—the ability to burst rather than run. And the man must function in the face of offenses that have been specifically designed to influence his actions away from the ball. Butkus is regarded as the strongest of middle linebackers, the very best at stopping running plays.

I once asked Howard Mudd if the 49ers, his previous team, had a special game plan for Butkus. "Sure," he said. "The plan was to not run between the tackles; always ensure that you block Dick. Once the game started, the plan changed, though. It became, 'Don't run. Just pass.'"

Mudd also pointed out something that belies Butkus' reputation for viciousness. "He doesn't try to punish the blockers," Mudd said. "He doesn't hit you in the head, like a lot of guys. The first time I played against him, I was—well—almost disappointed. It wasn't like hitting a wall or anything. He didn't mess with me, he went *by* me. All he wants is the ball. When he gets to the ball carrier, he really rings that man's bell."

In the Bear defense, Butkus is responsible for calling the signals and for smelling out the ball. If he has a weakness, it's that he sometimes seems to wallow a bit on his pass drops, allowing a man to catch a pass in front of him and assuming that the force of his tackle will have an effect on the man's confidence. It often does.

The night before the Lions game, Butkus was at his home in a suburb about 40 minutes' drive from Wrigley Field. It's an attractive ranch-style brick house. In front of the garage is a white pickup truck with the initials D. B. unobtrusively hand-lettered on the door. Inside the garage is a motorcycle. These are Butkus' toys. The main floor of the house is charmingly furnished and reflects the taste of his wife, Helen, an attractive auburn-haired woman who is expecting their third child early in 1971. She is a lively but reserved woman who runs the domestic side of their lives and attempts to keep track of Nikki, a four-year-old girl, and Ricky, a three-year-old boy—two golden-haired and rugged children.

The basement of the house belongs mostly to Butkus. Its finished paneled area contains a covered pool table—he doesn't enjoy the game very much nor play it well—and a bar. Along the walls are as many trophies and glory photos as a man could ever hope for. The only photograph he calls to a visitor's attention is an evocative one from *Sports Illustrated* that shows him in profile, looking grimy and tired, draining the contents of a soft-drink cup.

At the far end of the basement is Butkus' workroom. The area is dominated by a large apparatus of steel posts and appendages that looks like some futuristic torture chamber. It's called a Universal Gym and its various protrusions allow him to exercise every part of his body. There is other exercise equipment about and in a far corner is a sauna. Butkus works out regularly but not to build strength. His objective is to keep his weight down and his muscles loose.

After an early dinner with the family, Butkus secluded himself in the bedroom with his playbooks and .16 mm projector for a last look at the Lions' offense in its shadowy screen incarnation. Just after ten o'clock, he went to sleep. He woke early the next morning and went to early Mass, at 6:30, so that he didn't have to dress up. He and the priest were the only ones there. He returned home to eat a big steak and, after breakfast, he spent some more time with the playbooks. About ten o'clock he left the house for the drive to the ball park.

"He's real quiet before a game," Mrs. Butkus says, "but he's usually quiet. When he was dating me, my mother used to ask, 'Can't he talk?' I don't think he gets nervous before a game. I think it's just anticipation. He really wants to get at them."

She is remarkably cheerful about football and likes to talk about her husband's prowess. Her favorite story is one that she learned when she met Fuzzy Thurston, one of the great offensive linemen from Vince Lombardi's years at Green Bay. "Fuzzy told me," she says, "that when Dick played against the Packers the first time, Lombardi growled, 'Let's smear this kid's face.' But Fuzzy says they just couldn't touch him. After the game, Lombardi said, 'He's the best who ever played the position.'"

The day of the Lions game is cool and clear. When Butkus comes out, his expression is blank. The Bears are quieter and more fidgety than before the Viking game. It's immediately apparent that this game will be played at a higher pitch than the previous ones, nearly off the scale that measures human rage. People who play football and who write about it like to talk about finesse, about a lineman's "moves." But when the game is really on, the finesse gets very basic. The shoulder dip and slip is replaced by the clenched fist to the head, the forearm chop to the knee and the helmet in the face.

From the opening play, the fans show they are in a wild mood. They have begun to call Mike Lucci (pronounced Loo*chee*) Lucy. And when Lucci is on the field, they taunt him mercilessly. "Hey, Lucy! You're not big enough to carry Butkus' shoes."

The Lions are stopped on their first offensive series, and punt. As the ball sails downfield, Butkus and Ed Flanagan, the Detroit center, trade punches at midfield. They are both completely out of the play.

Soon enough, the Bear defense is back out. Butkus seems to be in a frenzy. He stunts constantly, pointing, shouting, trying to rattle Lion quarterback Bill Munson. On first down at the Lions' 20, he stuns Flanagan, who is trying to block him, with his forearm and knifes through on the left side to bring down Mel Farr for a five-yard loss.

On second down, Munson hands off to Farr going to his left. The left tackle, Roger Shoals, has gotten position on defensive end Ed O'Bradovich, as Farr cuts to the side line. Butkus, coming from the middle, lunges around the upright Shoals–O'Bradovich combination like a snake slithering around a tree and slashes at the runner's knees with his outstretched forearm. Farr crumbles.

On third down, Munson tries to pass to Altie Taylor in front of right linebacker Lee Roy Caffey. Caffey cocks his arm to ram it down Taylor's throat as he catches the ball, but Taylor drops the pass and Caffey relaxes the arm and pats him on the helmet.

The Lions set to punt and Butkus lurches up and down the line, looking for a gap. He finds one and gets a piece of the ball with his hand. The punt is short and the Bears have good position at midfield. On the first play from scrimmage, Concannon drops back and drills a pass to Dick Gordon, who has gotten behind two defenders. Gordon goes in standing up for a touchdown and pandemonium takes over Wrigley Field.

The game settles down a bit after that and the only other score for a while is a Lion field goal. Munson is trying to get a running game going to the outside, but Butkus is having an incredible day. He is getting outside as fast as Farr and Taylor. The runner and Butkus are in some strange *pas de deux*. Both seem to move to the same place at the same time, the runner driving fiercely with his legs, trying to set his blocks and find daylight. Butkus seems, by comparison, oddly graceful, his legs taking long lateral strides, his arms outstretched, fending off would-be blockers. But it's all happening at dervish speed and each impact has a jarring effect on the runner. Lucci, when he's on the field, just doesn't dominate the action and is taking abuse from the fans. He's neither as strong nor as quick. He's good on the pass drops, possibly better than Butkus, but he's not the same kind of destructive tackler.

Midway in the second quarter, Detroit cornerback Dick LeBeau intercepts a Concannon pass intended for Gordon. Gordon had gone inside and Concannon had thrown outside. Entropy again. The half ends with the score 7–3, Bears. On the side line after the half-time break, the Bears are back at high pitch. Concannon is yelling, "Go, defense," and Abe Gibron, the Bears' defensive coach, is offering, "Hit 'em to hurt 'em!" A wide man of medium height, Gibron was an all-pro tackle for many years in pro football's earlier era. He is a coach in the Lombardi mold, full of venom and fire—abusive to foe and friend. He is sometimes comical to watch as he walks the side line hurling imprecations for the entire football game: but his defenses are solid and brutal.

The intensity of the hitting seems to be increasing. Butkus makes successive resounding tackles, once on Farr and once on Taylor. He does not tackle so much as explode his shoulder into a man, as if he were trying to drive him under the ground. The effect is enhanced by his preference for hitting high, for getting as big a piece as he can. Butkus once told a television sports announcer, "I sometimes have a dream where I hit a man so hard his head pops off and rolls downfield." On a third-down play, Munson passes deep and Butkus, far downfield, breaks up the pass with his hand. The fans are overjoyed and have a few choice things to say about Lucci's parentage.

The Bears get the ball, but Concannon is intercepted again and the defense gets ready to go back in. As Butkus and the others stand tensely on the side line, it's clear to everyone that they are Chicago's only chance to win; the offense is just too sluggish. The "Ds," as they are called, have all the charisma on this team, and as they prepare to guts it out some more, I am overcome by a strange emotion. Stoop-shouldered and sunken-chested, weighing all of 177 pounds rather meagerly spread over a six-foot, three-inch frame, I want to join them. Not merely want but feel compelled to go out there and get my shoulder in—smash my body against the invaders. At this moment, those 11 men—frustrated, mean and near exhaustion—are the only possibility for gallantry and heroism that I know. The urge to be out there wells up in me the way it does in a kid reacting to a field sergeant who asks for the impossible—because to not volunteer involves a potential loss of manhood that is too great to face.

The defenses dominate the game for a while, but a short Bear punt gives the Lions good position and they get a field goal. A bit later, Munson passes for a touchdown and the Lions take the lead, 13–7. The Lions were favored in the betting before the game by as much as 16 points, and after the touchdown, the side-liners are murmuring things like, "I'm still all right, I got thirteen and a half."

With four minutes left in the game and the score 16–10 after each team has added a field goal, coach Dooley pulls Concannon in favor of the younger, less experienced but strong-armed Bobby Douglass, his second-string quarterback. A clumsy hand-off on a fourth and one convinced Dooley that Concannon was tired, although Concannon will indicate afterward that he wasn't. Pulling him at this point in the game, when the Bears obviously have only one chance to score and when a touchdown and point after would win, is an unusual thing to do, and Concannon is upset. He is a dark, scraggly-haired Irishman, very high strung, a ballplayer who stares at the fans when they're abusing him. He never feigns indifference. Now he is standing on the side line, head slightly bowed, pawing the ground with his cleats while someone else runs his team. His hands are firmly thrust into his warm-up jacket and all the time he stands there, intently watching the game, he repeats venomously over and over, "Stuff 'em! Stuff 'em! Fuck you, Lions! Goddamn it! Goddamn it! Fuck you, Lions!"

Douglass doesn't move the team and the Lions take over. Gibron is screaming that there's plenty of time. There is one minute, 36 seconds on the clock. Altie Taylor gets a crucial, time-consuming first down. Butkus tackles him viciously from behind, nearly bisecting him with his helmet; but the Bears are losers again.

The Bear defense had played tough football, and Butkus had played a great game. I said as much to him and he replied, "Hell, we're just losin' games again. It don't matter what else happened." But he didn't deny the ferocity of the Bear defense: "You didn't see a lot of that second effort out there," he said, referring to the Lion backs. "They weren't running as hard as they might."

"Do you think you intimidated them?"

"They knew they were getting hit. And when you know you're getting in there, then you really lay it on them."

"What was the reason for the punches with Flanagan?"

"I wanted to let him know he was going to be in a game."

Butkus seemed to talk all the time on the field. Was he calling signals to his own players or yelling at Detroit?

"Mostly it's signals for our side, but every once in a while, I'll say something to jag them a little."

"Like what?"

"Oh, you know. Call them a bunch of faggots or somethin'. Or I told sixty-three after a play when I got around him that he threw a horseshit block."

Butkus says these things in an emotionless voice—almost shrugging the words out rather than speaking them. His speech is filled with the nasal sounds of Chicago's Far South Side, and he is very much a neighborhood kid grown up. His tastes are simple—in food, in entertainment, in people. He doesn't run with a fast crowd. If you ask him what he does for kicks, he shrugs, "I don't know, just goof around, I guess." He has wanted to play football all his life, and one of his most disarming and embarrassing statements when he was graduated from college was, "I came here to play football. I knew they weren't going to make a genius out of me."

As a kid, Butkus loved to play baseball. Surprisingly, he couldn't hit but had all the other skills. He pitched, caught and played the infield. He had the grace of a "good little man," and that may be one key to his success. Unlike most big football players, who find it hard to walk and whistle at the same time, and have to be taught how to get around the field, Butkus has the moves of a quick, slippery small man who happens to have grown to 245 pounds.

By the time he got to high school, Butkus was committed to football. His high school coach wouldn't let him scrimmage in practice for fear that the overenthusiastic Butkus would hurt some of the kids on his own team.

He distrusts worldliness in most forms, except that he knows that his stardom can make money and he works at it. He has changed his hair style from the crewcut he wore in his early years to something a bit longer, but he's far from shaggy. His clothes are without style. He wears open-collar shirts, shapeless slacks and button-front cardigan sweaters that he never buttons. A floppy, unlined tan raincoat is his one concession to Chicago winters.

He is genuinely shy and deferential on all matters except football, and his façade is quiet cynicism. He especially dislikes bravado and gunghoism when he has reason to believe they're false, as he does with many of the Bear offensive players. Although he has a reputation for grimness, he smiles rather easily. And his laugh is a genuine surprise; it's a small boy's giggle, thoroughly disconcerting in his huge frame.

His shyness comes out in odd ways. When asked if, as defensive captain, he ever chews out another player for a missed assignment, he says, "Nah. Who am I to tell somebody else that he isn't doing the job? After all, maybe I'm not doing my job so good." Butkus is serious.

That sort of resignation makes him an ideal employee—sometimes to his own detriment. Butkus thinks, for example, that his original contract with the Bears was for too little money—and he's been suffering financially ever since. But he refuses to consider holding out for a renegotiation or laying out his contract option in order to get a better deal with a new team. "I made my mistake," he says. "Now I gotta live with it." And, although you probably couldn't find a coach in the world who wouldn't trade his next dozen draft choices for him, Butkus thinks that if he did something so downright daring as leave the Bears, no other team would take him, because he'd have marked himself a renegade.

This is not so much naïveté on Butkus's part as it is a deeply conservative strain in the man. When he saw a quote from Alex Johnson, the troubled California Angels baseball player, suggesting that he wanted to be treated like a human being, not like an athlete, Butkus said, "Hell, if he doesn't want to be treated like an athlete, let him go work the line in a steel mill. Ask those guys if they're treated like human beings."

Yet Butkus is not a company man. If anything, he is brutally cynical about established authorities—especially the management of the Chicago Bears football club—but he abhors being in a position where he finds himself personally exposed, and distrusts anyone who would willingly place himself in that position.

He especially dislikes personal contact with the fans. He complains about being stared at and being interrupted in restaurants. He is also inclined to moan about the ephemeral nature of his career. "It could be over any time," he says. "An injury could do it tomorrow. And even if I stay healthy, hell, it's all gonna be over in ten years." I ask if he has any plans for the future. "Not as a hanger-on, trying to live off my name. When it's over, I'm gonna hang up the fifty-one and get out. I'm not gonna fool around as some comedian or public speaker."

For the present, Butkus determinedly, but with no joy, does as much off-field promotional activity as he can get. He attends awards dinners and other ceremonial functions and will appear at just about any sports-related event that comes along. He's done some television appearances and made one delightful commercial for Rise shaving cream. This year, International Merchandising Corporation (the president of IMC, Mark McCormack, is the man who merchandised Arnold Palmer, among others) contacted Butkus and now manages his finances. His name has begun to appear on an assortment of sports gear and may yet make its way to hair dressings and other such men's items. When I told Butkus that he had taken his place in the pantheon of great middle linebackers, along with Sam Huff and Ray Nitschke, he said, "Hell, I'm going to make more money this year than those guys ever thought about."

Over the following six weeks, the Bears played a lot of mediocre football; they won two, lost four—although two of those were very close.

The next time I saw Butkus was on a cold, damp Thursday—a practice day for the Bears' return match with the Packers. The numbing grayness of the Chicago winter day was matched only by the Bears' mood at practice. They were sluggish and disconnected and seemed to be going through motions to run out the string. The Packer game was the next-to-last one of the season. Butkus was working with the defense under coaches Gibron and Don Shinnick. Shinnick is the Bears' linebacker coach and a veteran of 13 years with the Baltimore Colts. He is an enthusiastic, straightforward man who doesn't hassle his players. He is Butkus's favorite coach, and the impression you get from talking to either of them is that they both think that Don Shinnick and Dick Butkus are the only two men in the world qualified to talk about football.

The defense was working on its pass coverage against some second-string receivers. Doug Buffone was bitching to Shinnick because they weren't practicing against the first string and couldn't get their timing right. They had practiced with the first string before their Baltimore game and Buffone said that it was directly responsible for five interceptions in the game. Shinnick agreed but gave Buffone an "I don't make the rules" look and they both went back to the drill.

Gibron was installing some new formations to defend against Green Bay. One was called Duck and the other Cora. They tried out some plays to see if everyone could pick up Butkus' signal. Butkus called "Duck" if he wanted one formation in the backfield and "Cora" for another and they relayed it to one another. Gibron was unhappy with the rhythm and said, "Listen. Don't say 'Duck.' It could be 'fuck' or 'suck' or anything. Say 'Quack quack' instead, OK?" For the next few minutes, the Bears shouted "Quack quack" as loud as they could. Butkus just stared at Gibron. Then they ran some patterns.

Shortly, the defense left the field so Concannon and the first-string receivers could work out without interference. Butkus stood morosely on the side line with Ed O'Bradovich, the only team member he is really close to.

O.B., as he is called, is a huge curly-haired man endowed with a nonchalant grace and good humor. He looks like he's never shown concern for anything, especially his own safety.

A visitor at the practice says to Butkus, "That quack-quack stuff sounds pretty good."

"It's not quack, quack," says Butkus, glowering. "It's Duck."

Butkus is about two weeks into a mustache. "It's for one of those Mexican cowboy movies," he says.

O'Bradovich says, "You're gonna look like an overgrown Mexican faggot."

"Yeah, who's gonna tell me?" At that minute, a burst of sharp, raucous howling rises up where the offensive linemen are working on their pass blocking. "Look at 'em," Butkus says. "Let's see how much noise they make against Green Bay on Sunday."

As I look around the practice field, there seems to be chaos among the players. If I were a betting man, I'd go very heavy against the Bears. They seem totally dispirited. "It's all horseshit," Butkus says. "Everybody wants it to be over."

Just before the practice breaks up, coach Dooley calls everyone together and says, "All right! Now, we've had these three good practices this week. And we're ready. Let's do a big job out here Sunday." All the players leave after a muffled shout—except for Concannon, who runs some laps, and Mac Percival, the place kicker, who has been waiting for a clear field to practice on. One of the coaches holds for Percival, and as I head for the stands, Percival makes nine field goals in a row from the 36-yard line before missing one.

Sunday is sunny, but three previous days of rain have left the side lines muddy, although the field itself is in good shape. The air is damp and cold; it's a day when the fingers and toes go numb quickly and the rest of the body follows. Bear-Packer games are usually brutal affairs, but this game is meaningless in terms of divisional standings: both teams are out of contention. There is speculation, however, that each head coach—Phil Bengston of the Packers and Dooley of the Bears—has his job on the line and that the one who loses the game will also lose his job.

When the line-ups for the game are announced, the biggest hand is not for Butkus but for Bart Starr, Green Bay's legendary quarterback. If Butkus is the symbol of the game's ferocity, then Starr is the symbol of its potential for innocence and glory. He is the third-string quarterback who made good—Lombardi's quarterback—an uncanny incarnation of skill, resourcefulness, dedication and humility. He is the Decent American, a man of restraint and self-discipline who would be tough only in the face of a tough job. But he is so much in awe of the game he plays that he wept unashamedly after scoring the *winning* touchdown in Green Bay's last-second victory over Dallas in minus-13-degree weather for the NFL championship in 1967.

The Packers receive and on the first two plays from scrimmage, Butkus bangs first Donny Anderson, then Dave Hampton to the ground. He has come out ferocious. A third-down play fails and the Packers punt. On the Bears' first play from scrimmage, Concannon throws a screen pass to running back Don Shy, who scampers 64 yards to the Packer 15. Concannon completes a pass to George Farmer and then throws a short touchdown pass to Dick Gordon. Bears lead, 7–0.

Green Bay's ball: Starr hands off to Hampton, who slips before he gets to the line of scrimmage. On second and ten, Butkus stunts a bit, then gets an angle inside as Starr goes back to pass. Butkus gets through untouched and slams Starr for an eight-yard loss. The Packers are stopped again, and punt. As Starr comes off the field, he heads for the man with the headset on to find out from the rooftop spotters just what the hell is going on.

On the Bears' next offensive play, Concannon drops back and arcs a pass to Farmer, who has gotten behind Bob Jeter. Touchdown, Bears lead, 14–0, and there is ecstasy in the air. It is a complete turnaround and my shock at the Bears today—after watching them on Thursday—is testimony to how difficult sports clichés are to overcome. I am obsessed with whether the team is up or down, as if that were the essence of the game. Actually, for all anyone knows, the Packers might have come to Wrigley Field "up" out of their minds. It doesn't matter. The Bears are just good this day; they are at a peak of physical skill as well as emotional drive. Concannon is very close to his finest potential and, for all it matters, might be depressed emotionally. What counts is that his passes are perhaps an eighth of an inch truer as he loops his arm, and that is enough to touch greatness.

All the Bears are teeing off from their heels. When the game began, Bob Brown, the Packers' best pass rusher, sneered at Jim Cadile, Bear guard, the man across the line from him, "I'm gonna kill you."

Cadile drawled, "I'll be here all day."

The Packers now have the ball, third down, on their own 19. Starr drops back to pass and, with no open receiver, starts to run the ball himself. As he gets to the line of scrimmage, he is tripped up with four Bears closing in on him, one of whom is Butkus. I'm watching the play from the side line right behind Starr. From that vantage point Butkus, looking for a piece of Starr, is all helmet and shoulders brutally launched. The piece of Starr that Butkus gets is his head. Starr lies on the ground as the Packer trainer comes to his aid. The crowd noise is deafening.

Starr is helped from the field and immediately examined by the team physician, who checks his eyes to see if there are signs of concussion. The doctor leaves him and Starr, who looks frail at six feet, one inch, 190 pounds in the land of giants, puts his helmet on and says that he's all right. When the Bears are stopped on a drive and punt, he returns and immediately goes to work completing some short, perfectly timed passes. He moves the Packers to the Bear 15. Then, on second down, he is smashed trying to pass and comes off the field again. He is replaced by a rookie named Frank Patrick, who can't get anything going, and the Packers kick a field goal. Starr is now seated on the bench, head in hands, sniffing smelling salts. He's out for the day.

The game turns into a blood-lust orgy for the Bears. O'Bradovich is playing across from offensive tackle Francis Peay. Vince Lombardi had obtained Peay from the New York Giants, predicting that the tackle was going to be one of the greats, and he is good, indeed. But on this day, O'Bradovich is looming very large in Peay's life. In fact, he is kicking the shit out of him, actually hurling Peay's body out of his way each time Patrick tries to set up to pass. The Packer rookie is in the worst possible position for an inexperienced quarterback. He has to pass and the defense knows it. The linemen don't have to protect against the running game and just keep on coming.

Lee Roy Caffey had been traded to Chicago by the Packers. After each set of violent exhibitions by the Bear defense, he comes off the field right in front of Packer coach Bengston, screaming, "You motherfucker. You traded me! And we're gonna kill you!"

One of the most impressive pass plays of the game comes in the second quarter, with the score 14–3 and the Bears driving. Concannon throws a short high pass down the side line that George Farmer has to go high in the air to catch. Farmer seems to hang for a moment, as if the football has been nailed in place and his body were suspended from it. In that vulnerable position, Ray Nitschke, the Packers' middle linebacker, crashes him with a rolling tackle that swings Farmer's body like a pendulum. As Farmer turns horizontal, still in the air, Willie Wood, the safety, crushes him and Farmer bounces on the ground. But he holds onto the football.

A few plays later, Concannon, looking for a receiver at the Packer 25-yard line, finds no one open and runs in for a touchdown. It is a day when he can do no wrong.

The hysteria on the field even works its way up to the usually cool stadium announcer. In the third quarter, when Dick Gordon beats Doug Hart for another touchdown pass from Concannon, the announcer, with his mike behind his back, screams in livid rage at the Packer defender, "You're shit, Hart! You're shit!" Then he puts the instrument to his mouth and announces to the fans in his best oratorical voice, "Concannon's pass complete to Gordon. Touchdown Bears."

At the Packer bench, Bart Starr is spending the day with his head bowed, pawing the turf with his cleats. It occurs to me that every quarterback I have watched this year has spent a lot of his time in that position: Concannon, Munson, Unitas when the Bears were leading Baltimore, and now Starr.

Behind Starr, Ray Nitschke has just come off the field after the Bear touchdown. Nitschke is one of the great figures from Green Bay's irrepressible teams of the Sixties, and his face looks like he gave up any claims on the sanctity of his body when he decided to play football. He is gnarled, bald and has lost his front teeth. He constantly flexes his face muscles, opening and clamping his jaw in a set of grotesque expressions. He has put on a long Packer cape and is prowling the side line, exhaling plumes of vapor from his nostrils, the cape flowing gracefully behind him. There is something sublime in the image. Nitschke is the caped crusader; had there ever really been a Batman, he could not have been a pretty-boy millionaire—he'd have been this gnarled avenger.

As the game progresses further in the third quarter, the hysteria increases and it's hard to follow the play sequences or the score, and little details intrude on my mind:

- Little Cecil Turner, the swift black return specialist, running back a kickoff after the Packers score a touchdown, is finding daylight. As he works his way upfield, a black Packer screams to his teammates on the field, "Kill that dude!"
- O'Bradovich, coming off the field after hurling Peay around some more, sits down with his sleeves rolled up in a spot where he can avoid the heat from the side-line blowers—on a day when it's so cold that a man standing next to me is warming his hands over the open flame of his cigarette lighter.
- Willie Holman, Bear defensive tackle, barrels into Patrick as he tries to pass. The ball has no speed and is intercepted. Holman's shot actually rings in the ears for a moment. That night on the TV returns, you can't even tell that Holman caused the interception, because there is no sound, no sense of the brutality of the play.
- Butkus is dumped on his ass by Gale Gillingham as he tries to blitz Patrick. Gillingham is one of the very good offensive guards around

and it's an incredible shot. The only time I've seen Butkus go backward all year.

- Jim Ringo, the nine-year all-pro center who now coaches the Bear offensive line, winces with pain each time a Bear defensive lineman wipes out one of Green Bay's offensive linemen. It's obvious that Ringo simply hates all defensive players, even his own.

Late in the fourth quarter, with the game safely out of reach, 35–10, Butkus comes out and is replaced by John Neidert. Gibron and the defense are now very much interested in the game again. The Packers get a little drive going and are at the Bear 13. Neidert is getting a lot of information from the Bear bench, especially from Gibron. To show some respect for the rule that prohibits coaching from the side line while the clock is running, Gibron wants to call his signals discreetly. He is trying to whisper "Double-zone ax" across a distance of some 25 yards.

Double zone means that the cornerbacks will play the wide receivers tight, one on one. Ax means that the middle linebacker will take the tight end alone on the short drop. On the next play, Patrick completes a pass to the tight end for the score. As Neidert comes off the field, he is heartbroken and Gibron is screaming, "Neidert, whatsomatta witchoo? If you don't know it, say so. Did you have the ax in?" Neidert, who looks too confused to think, only nods and kneels down, looking as if he is close to tears. It's possible that at the end of this already decided football game, on a meaningless score, his football career might be over. It's the one upsetting thought in an otherwise brilliant day for the Bears.

Two months after the Packer game, after a trip to Los Angeles to play in the Pro Bowl, Butkus goes into the hospital to have his knee operated on. He leaves the hospital afterward but suffers great pain for days and finally returns to see if anything can be done about it. Butkus thinks a muscle was strained when the cast was put on; the doctor doesn't agree and can't understand why he is having so much pain. I went to visit Butkus at Illinois Masonic Hospital, a typically ugly yellow-walled institution. When I get to his room, he is playing gin rummy with a friend and is in a very scowly mood.

He doesn't look like a typical patient. He isn't wearing a hospital gown, just a pair of shorts, and his upper body is almost wider than the bed. The impression is that any moment he may get out of bed, pick it up as if it were an attaché case and walk out. He offers me a beer from a large container filled with ice and cans.

He gets bored with the rummy game very quickly and his guest departs.

"How do you feel?"

"Horseshit."

Butkus describes the pain he's been having in the side of his knee and tells me the doctor just keeps saying that Gale Sayers was up and around the day after his knee was operated on. He isn't happy with the doctor. His wife, who is nine months pregnant, enters. We all discuss the pain for a minute and she makes it clear that she thinks it may be partly psychosomatic.

Butkus talks about a condominium he's bought on Marco Island in Florida and a big Kawasaki bike that he hasn't been able to ride because of the operation. He is very uncomfortable and we get into some more beers.

I ask if he was trying to hurt Starr in the Green Bay game. "Nah," he says. "I just went in there with everybody else. That's what you gotta do. But you should see the mail from Wisconsin. I got a letter that said, 'You shouldn't hit old people.' Another one said, 'I hope you get yours.'"

Butkus continually reaches down to massage his leg, which is wrapped from hip to toe in a bandage. A nurse comes in with a paper cup containing an assortment of brightly colored capsules. He asks which one is the painkiller, but the nurse refuses to tell him. She explains that he has been taking a number of sedatives since his arrival in the hospital and Butkus is disturbed that he's been swallowing a lot of stuff that hasn't done any good. "We didn't want to give you anything too strong," she tells him archly. "We thought you were taking care of yourself with the beer." It is apparent that a lot of people are enjoying the fact that the big mean Butkus is acting like a six-year-old. He looks at the nurse with puzzlement and annoyance. He doesn't think that any of this is the least bit funny and goes back to rubbing his knee.

"Do you think the operation is going to make you cautious?"

"No. But nobody's going to hit this knee again. No way."

During the next few weeks, the knee continued to trouble him. He had an unusual reaction to the catgut that had been used to rebuild the joint and his body was trying to reject it. He was often in pain and became adept at squeezing pus and sometimes chunks of catgut from the suppurating incision. At the end of March, the doctor opened the knee again and cleaned it out.

This time, the doctor and Butkus were satisfied and a second operation, planned to rebuild the other side of the knee, was canceled because the joint seemed sound again.

Early in April, Butkus went to Florida to relax. He returned to Chicago after a brief stay and fell into an off-season pattern. Fool with the Kawasaki, have beers with O'Bradovich, spend Sundays with his family. In late May, he started to tune his body on the Universal Gym.

On a hot, rainy morning last June, I arrived at Butkus' house to find him sitting in the kitchen jouncing Matthew Butkus, who had been born in late February (8 pounds, 13 ounces) on his knee. The father was cooing and the son was grinning, as well he should, considering that he was spending much of his first few months surrounded by the protective comfort of those huge hands.

Butkus was still unsure of the knee. "I think I'll really be able to go on it around December first," he said. That would mean missing three months of the season. I didn't know if he was serious, and it occurred to me that he didn't either. He was to see the doctor that afternoon. I had an appointment to visit his parents, who live nearby, and as I left, his wife said, "If that knee isn't OK, I'm moving South. He'll be impossible to live with."

Butkus' parents are Lithuanian. They have seven children (Dick is the youngest and smallest of five boys) and 22 grandchildren; the family is loyal and gathers frequently.

When I got to the house, Mr. Butkus, 80 years old, a bushy-browed, weathered man of medium height, was working with a spade on the grounds. The rain had stopped and the day had turned sunny and hot. He was calmly digging out weeds in a small thicket bordering an expansive lawn that fronted the house. A white-plaster statue sat in the middle of the lawn. Mr. Butkus is a friendly man of few words who has little to say about his youngest son's success. It's simply not something that he relates to easily. The senior Mrs. Butkus is quite another story. She's a big woman who clearly supplied her sons' breadth of shoulder and chest. She is a bit immobilized now from a recent fall and thoroughly fills the armchair she is seated in. Butkus bought the house for his parents a few years ago. The living room is filled with the furniture and remnants of other places and times, and the harsh early-afternoon light seems to be cooled by its journey around the knickknacks to the corner of the room, where she is sitting. His mother says of Dick: "He didn't make any special trouble. He liked practical jokes a lot but never got into any real trouble. He was full of mischief and energy—like any other boy." There is something hard in her attitude, something that comes from raising a lot of children. Life is not wonderful, nor too simple, but it's not too bad, either. It's to be endured—and sometimes bullied. As she stares out the window, thinking about Dick, she says, "When he was a kid, his brothers would take him to the College All-Star game. He'd sit there and say, 'I'm going to play here. This is where I'm going.'" She pauses, and then continues: "You know, his brother Ronnie played for a while with the old Chicago Cardinals. He had to stop because of a knee injury." Then she turns to me and says, "I hope Dick gets well. It's his life."

Losing: An American Tradition

CHARLES M. YOUNG

Using Prairie View A&M's historic eighty-game college football losing streak along with recollections from his own dubious football career, Charles Young dissects the American obsession with winners and losers.

Young's realization of how few "winners" exist in a literal sense points out to all of us "losers" that we have plenty of company. And he's not afraid to take a shot at the revered leaders we so commonly accept to be winners. Unless our goal is to be a nation of people who pollute groundwater and screw fellow citizens out of their hard-earned money, maybe it's time for a re-evaluation of our very American status system. And if falling short of becoming Bill Gates means I'm a loser, well . . .

Maybe it's time to re-evaluate Prairie View's eighty-game losing streak. They only lost to Southern by nine touchdowns. I'm sure there's a winning lesson to be found somewhere in that. And really, eighty losing games in a row isn't *that* bad.

OK, maybe it is. I guess we're not ready to anoint them "winners" just yet, but it is important to note that very few teams win the last game, the one for all the marbles. And very few of us turn out to be Bill Gates, but our mothers manage to love us anyway.

J ust north of the north end zone of Blackshear Stadium at Prairie Vie A&M University in Texas is an unmarked grave.

"We buried last season," said Greg Johnson, the Prairie View Panthers' coach, during a break in football practice. "In March, just before the start of spring practice, we had them write down everything they didn't like about the past—being 0–9 last season, the record losing streak. We used the example of Superman, this guy that nobody could stop unless you got him near some green kryptonite. We asked them, 'Well, what's your green kryptonite? What is it that keeps you from doing what you need to do in the classroom and on the football field? Is it a female? Is it your friends? Is it a drug? Is it alcohol? Lack of dedication? Not enough time in the weight room? You got a nagging injury that you didn't rehab?' Whatever they wanted to bury, they wrote it down on a piece of paper. And the last thing we did, we looked at the HBO tape. The segment that Bryant Gumbel did on us for *Real Sports,* where they laughed at us and ridiculed us as the worst team in the country—'How does it feel to be 0–75 since 1989?' or whatever it was at that point. I said, 'That's the last we'll ever see of that tape,' and I put it in a big plastic trash bag with the paper. We took it to a hole I had dug near the gate, and we threw it in. All the players and all the coaches walked by. Some of them kicked dirt on it, some of them spit on it. Some of them probably thought I was crazy. I said, 'This is the last time we're going to talk about last year. This is the last time we're going to talk about the losing streak. The past is dead, and anything that's dead ought to be buried. It's history. It's gone.'"

That took place in September 1998, when Prairie View's NCAA-record losing streak stood at 0–77. Now skip ahead to the postgame interviews of the January 9, 1999, AFC playoff game, in which the Denver Broncos beat the Miami Dolphins 38–3. Shannon Sharpe, the Broncos' tight end, called Miami's Dan Marino a "loser." Universally, this was viewed as a mortal insult, far beyond the bounds of acceptable trash talk.

"I cringed when I read that," said Mike Shanahan, the Broncos' coach. "I was really disappointed. Dan Marino's no loser."

So Sharpe, much humbled (and probably at Shanahan's insistence), groveled after the next Denver practice: "In no way, shape, or form is Dan Marino a loser. Dan, if I offended you or your family, your wife, your kids, your mother or father, your brothers or sisters, I apologize. I stand before you and sincerely apologize. I would never disrespect you as a person."

Which is odd. Football, along with every other major sport, is constructed to create losers. On any given game day, half the teams win, and half the teams lose. By the end of the playoffs, exactly one team can be called a winner, while thirty other teams are, literally, losers. So given that 96.7 percent of the players in the NFL can't help but be losers, why should calling somebody a loser be considered such an egregious violation of propriety that the guy who won must debase himself in public for pointing out that the guy who lost, lost?

Consider *Patton,* winner of the 1971 Academy Award for Best Picture and a favorite of coaches, team owners, and politicians ever since. It opens with George C. Scott standing in front of a screen-size American flag in the role of General George S. Patton, giving a pep talk to his troops. Using sports imagery to describe war (mirroring the sportswriters who use war imagery to describe sports), Patton delivers a succinct sociology lesson: "Americans love a winner, and will not tolerate a loser. Americans play to win all the time. I wouldn't give a hoot in hell for a man who lost and laughed. That's why Americans have never lost, and will never lose a war—because the very thought of losing is hateful to Americans."

Which is a view of most Americans that's shared by most Americans. Certain women of my acquaintance refer to men who score low on the Multiphasic Boyfriend Potentiality Scale as losers. *Cosmopolitan* has run articles on how to identify and dump losers before they have a chance to inseminate the unwary.

In *Jerry Maguire,* Tom Cruise suffers his worst humiliation when he spots his former girlfriend dating a rival agent at a *Monday Night Football* game. She makes an L with her fingers and mouths, "Loser."

In *American Beauty,* Kevin Spacey announces during his midlife crisis: "Both my wife and daughter think I'm this gigantic loser."

In *Gods and Monsters,* Lolita Davidovich, playing a bartender, dismisses the possibility of sex with her sometime lover, played by Brendan Fraser: "From now on, you're just another loser on the other side of the bar."

In *200 Cigarettes,* set in the ostensibly alternative subculture of Manhattan's Lower East Side, Martha Plimpton works herself into a state of despair considering the idea that no one will come to her New Year's Eve party. Then, considering an even worse possibility, she weeps: "All the losers will be here!"

At the real-life sentencing last February of Austin Offen for bashing a man over the head with a metal bar outside a Long Island night club, Assistant District Attorney Stephen O'Brien said that Offen was "vicious and brutal. He's a coward and a loser." Offen, displaying no shame over having crippled a man for life, screamed back: "I am not a loser!"

In his book *Turbo Capitalism: Winners and Losers in the Global Economy,* Edward Luttwak equates losing with poverty and observes that Americans believe that "failure is the result not of misfortune or injustice, but of divine disfavor."

I could list a hundred more examples, but you get the point.

Shannon Sharpe, in using the word *loser,* implied that Dan Marino was: unworthy of sex or love or friendship or progeny, socially clueless, stupid, parasitical, pathetic, poverty-stricken, cowardly, violent, felonious, bereft of all forms of status, beneath all consideration, hated by himself, hated by all good Americans, hated by God. And Dan Marino is one of the best quarterbacks ever to play football.

I was standing on the sideline during a Prairie View Panthers practice one scorching afternoon when a large boy on his way to class stopped to watch for a moment. Someone pointed him out to Coach Johnson and suggested that the boy be recruited for the team. "No, he was out last year, and he quit," said Johnson. "He has female tendencies. He looks like Tarzan and plays like Jane."

Johnson didn't say that *to* the boy, but suddenly my unconscious was barfing up all kinds of post-traumatic stress disorder from my own athletic experience. The next day in his office, I asked Johnson about football as an initiation rite in which aspiring Tarzans get all the Jane beaten out of them.

"That's just an old coach saying," he said. "If I had my druthers, I'd cut a kid open and look at his heart. You never can tell just what tempo it's beating at until you put them in the heat of battle. Football is a test of manhood, a test of who has the biggest *cojones.* Win, lose, or draw, all my guys got great big *cojones,* 'cause they fight when they know the odds are against them."

Johnson's coaching record has ranged from 0–11 as an assistant at Tennessee Tech to winning a couple of championships as a head coach at Oklahoma's Langston University. Feeling the need to migrate out of his "comfort zone," he came to Prairie View for the '97 season, becoming the fourth coach during the losing streak.

Back on the sideline, Anthony Carr, a sophomore cornerback from Houston, told me: "All these people put the streak in your mind. We say that's the past, but when everybody reminds you, it's hard to forget."

One of the lamest clichés in football, I said, was that it's so hard to repeat as champion because the other teams get so fired up to play you. In my experience, they got a lot more fired up to pulverize someone they knew they could pulverize—the incentive being that if you lose to the last-place team, you're worse than the worst.

"Yeah, nobody wants to lose to us. The other team is going to catch it. We've been called the laughing stock of the nation. That hurts. And it will hurt somebody to lose to the laughing stock of the nation."

Josh Barnes, a 165-pound junior quarterback returning from knee surgery, said he had chosen Prairie View to "make history" by breaking the losing streak. "My freshman year was tough. Southern beat us 63–0, Jackson State beat us 76–20. It hurt me. I hate losing. The cynicism was terrible. We heard it from everybody: 'Yawl suck!' If you have any pride, it's hard to take."

"A lot of people say losing builds character. I got enough character for several lifetimes," said Michael Porter, a running back who graduated in 1997. At Jefferson Davis High School in Houston, he lost every game for three years, and at Prairie View, he lost every game for four years. He is now coaching football at his old high school. "It's hard to keep kids on the team when it's losing. It's hard to keep fans in the stands. But I just loved the game. I loved the spotlight. I didn't love losing. You never get used to that. Never. Ever."

So how did he keep going when he was getting crushed 60–0 in the fourth quarter?

"You got to have a nut check. Either I'm going to get whipped like a girl, or I'm going to come out like a man and get on with it. You may be winning on the scoreboard, but I'm going to whip your ass on the next play. It's war, man. That's what it is—and it's not for everybody. This is no girlie sport."

When I was losing football games in college, it seemed like the worst thing you could call somebody was a pussy.

"Oh yeah. You don't want to be called a pussy on the field. I remember the times they'd be calling us the Prairie View Pussy Cats, and maybe some names even worse than that. It was a bad situation, having your organization ridiculed all the time. And you really hated it when it happened on campus. But it's all about manhood. Football forces you to be mature, to be disciplined, everything a man should be."

Later, I asked Coach Johnson if there was anything to learn from losing.

"You learn what's wrong, and then you do the opposite. These kids will win even if they lose, because they're going to get their degree. Football helps keep them focused. Every kid wants discipline and structure and a chance to be special. When the world is telling them, 'You're not gonna be nothin',' football gives them a chance to prove themselves."

But maybe most people don't want to find out how good they are. If you give something a complete effort and fail, it would be logical to conclude that you are a loser. An incomplete effort offers the appeal of an excuse.

"Yeah, that's the real loser concept," said Johnson. "That's something you say on the porch with your wino buddies: 'Yeah, if I hadn't beat up that girl when I was sixteen, I'd still be playing football. If I hadn't taken that first drink or that first hit of marijuana, I'd be a star.' That's a penitentiary story."

The literal truth is, I may not be the worst college football player of all time. I've claimed that occasionally in the course of conversation, but I may be only the worst college football player of 1972. I was definitely the worst player on the Macalester College Scots of St. Paul, Minnesota, and we lost all of our games that season by an aggregate score of 312–46. The team went on to win one game in each of the following two seasons (after I graduated), then set the NCAA record with fifty straight losses. So, strictly speaking, the losing streak wasn't my fault. I do think I made a huge contribution to the atmosphere of despair and futility that led to the losing streak. I think that as Prairie View was to the '90s, Macalester was to the '70s. But in the final analysis, I think that over two decades at both schools, some athlete may have failed more than I did.

I may therefore merely be one of the worst, a weaker distinction that makes me even more pathetic than whoever it is who can make the case for sole possession of the superlative—if someone wants to make that case. No one, though, can question my credentials for at least a display in the Hall of Failure. In my junior year, on a team with barely enough players for one string, I was the only guy on third string. The coach wouldn't put me in the game even when the other team was winning by six touchdowns. In my senior year, we got a new head coach who had a terrifying policy: "If you practice, you play." And I did play in every game on the kickoff team, often getting a few additional minutes at strong safety after the game was hopelessly lost. The opposing third-string quarterback would throw a couple of touchdowns over my head just so I could feel as mortified as the rest of the team.

I got injured once. I came in too high to tackle a halfback and he drove his helmet into the left side of my chest. When I took off my shoulder pads in the locker room later, I was surprised to discover that I had a hemorrhaged pectoralis major muscle, which looked like a large, purple, female breast. To this day, when I am in the company of big American men and they compare their unstable knees, necrotic hips, herniated disks, cracked vertebrae, tilted atlas bones, arthritic shoulders, and twisted fingers, I can't make my wounded tit, as it was called back then, work even as a joke. No matter how I phrase it, they exchange "that guy's pathetic" looks. If your football injury made you look like Marilyn Manson, it definitely won't get you into the club of manly heterosexuals.

As many manly writers and equally manly psychologists have asserted, manhood is something you supposedly win. Females are simply born to womanhood. Males must wrest their manhood from some other male in a trial-by-fire ritual, the hottest of which in America is football.

I failed. I'm a loser.

Losing puts you in the center of a vast vacuum, where you are shunned by your own teammates, scorned by spectators, avoided by your friends. It's a lot like smelling bad. Nobody wants to talk about it in your presence.

Losing is hard to write about, too. Writing was why I went out for football, because the football players I knew had the best stories. I played two seasons. In my junior year, we won just one game, and the coach played me a total of sixty-three seconds over ten games. The losing wasn't quite mine, since I wasn't playing much, and the psychological distance made it possible to write a lot, mostly about stuff other than the actual games, because I didn't want to hurt the feelings of anyone on the team.

In my senior year, though, the shame became mine. Playing every game as a strong safety, I was supposed to line up about seven yards deep over the tight end. I could never figure out who the tight end was. The enemy huddle would break, and all I could see was this undifferentiated mass of enemy uniforms. "Strong left!" I would yell, which was part of my job. Our middle linebacker would turn around and hiss, "Strong right, you fucking idiot!"

In a chronic state of embarrassment, I wrote very little. The one long article I wrote was mostly about a Ping-Pong game I played with a sexually ambiguous linebacker named Wally. (If I won, I got to spend the night with his girlfriend; if he won, he got to spend the night with me.) I beat Wally, and suddenly the words began to flow in the brief absence of humiliating defeat, in the brief presence of a different sport, one in which we could make a farce out of the cult of achieved masculinity. Not that I could articulate that insight at the time, but that's what we were doing. Farce is the only refuge for losers.

A couple weeks after I left PVU, the Panthers won a football game, 14–12, against Langston University, ending the losing streak at eighty. The campus erupted in a victory celebration that was typical of the orgiastic outpourings that people all over the world feel entitled to after an important win. I was happy for them. I felt bad for Langston, having to carry the stigma of losing to the losers of all time.

There being virtually no literature of losing, I became obsessed with reading books about winning, some by coaches and some by self-help gurus. All of them advised me to forget about losing. If you want to join the winners, they said, don't dwell on your past humiliations. Then I thought of George Santayana's dictum: "Those who forget the past are condemned to repeat it." So if I remembered losing, I'd be a loser. And if I forgot losing, I'd be a loser. Finally, I remembered a dictum of my own: "Anybody who quotes George Santayana about repeating the past will soon be repeating even worse clichés."

That Christmas, my local Barnes & Noble installed a new section called "Lessons from the Winners." Publishers put out staggering numbers of books with "win" in the title (as they do with *Zen and Any Stupid Thing*), and they make money because there's a bottomless market of losers who want to be winners. Almost all of these books are incoherent lists of aphorisms and advice on how to behave like a CEO ("Memorize the keypad on your cell phone so you dial and drive without taking your eyes off the road"). Most of these books are written by men who have made vast fortunes polluting the groundwater and screwing people who work for a living, and these men want to air out their opinions, chiefly that they aren't admired enough for polluting the groundwater and screwing people who work for a living. I thought of the ultimate winner, Howard Hughes, who was once the richest man in the world, who had several presidents catering to his every whim, who stored his feces in jars. I got more and more depressed.

Maybe I was just hypnotized by my own history of failure, character defects, and left-wing politics. Maybe what I needed was a pep talk. Maybe what I needed was Ray Pelletier, a motivational speaker who has made a lot of money raising morale for large corporations and athletic teams. Pelletier, a member of the National Speakers Association Hall of Fame, wrote a book, *Permission to Win,* that Coach Johnson had recommended to me. Basically an exhortation to feel like a winner no matter how disastrous your circumstances happen to be, the book deals with losing as a problem of individual psychology. I asked Pelletier if he thought that the emphasis American culture places on competition was creating vast numbers of people who, on the basis of having lost, quite logically think of themselves as losers.

"I don't think you have to think of yourself as a loser," he said. "I think competition causes you to reach down inside and challenges you to be at your very best. The key is not to beat yourself. If you're better than I am and you're more prepared to play that day, you deserve to win. I have no problem with that. Every time I give a presentation, I want it to be better than the last one. I want to be sure I'm winning in everything that I do."

Yeah, but wasn't there a difference between excellence and winning?

"No, that's why I say that if I get beat by a team that's more talented, I don't have a problem with that."

When one guy won, was he not inflicting defeat on the other guy?

"No. I'll give you an example. The first time I worked with a female team before a big game, I was getting them all riled up and playing on their emotions, telling them how they deserved this win and how they worked really hard. A rah-rah, goose-pimple kind of speech. Just before we went on the court, the point guard said, 'Can I ask a question? Haven't the girls in the other locker room worked really hard, too? Don't they deserve to win, too?'"

Pelletier then veered off into a discussion of how the game teaches you about life, of how his talks are really for fifteen years down the line when your wife leaves you, or the IRS calls for an audit, or you can't pay your mortgage. I asked him how he replied to the point guard in the locker room.

"I said, 'Absolutely the other team deserves to win, too. What we have to do is find out if we can play together tonight as a team.' See, that's the biggest challenge facing corporate America today. We talk about teamwork but we don't understand the concept of team. Most of us have never been coached in anything. We've been taught, but not coached. There's a big difference. Great coaches challenge you to play at your best. The key is, you're in the game, trying to better yourself."

But Bill Parcells, the former coach of the Jets, is famous for saying that you are what the standings say you are . . .

"Winning is playing at your best. Do you know the number-one reason why an athlete plays his sport? Recognition. Once you understand that, everything else becomes easy. Lou Holtz says that win means 'What's Important Now.'"

That's just standard practice in books about winning, I told him. They redefine the word to include all human behavior with a good connotation. In *The Psychology of Winning,* Dr. Denis Waitley writes that winning is "unconditional love." Winning could hardly be a more conditional form of love. You are loved if you win, and scorned if you lose.

"I don't believe that."

If athletes play for recognition, don't they want to be recognized as winners? And if you've lost, won't you be recognized as a loser?

"I don't think they're labeled that way."

By the press? By the fans?

"To me, unconditional love is an aspect of winning. The problem is that you and I have not been trained to think positively. In one of my corporate seminars, I ask people to write down all the advantages there are to being negative. I want them to think about it seriously. It's an exercise that can taken fifteen or twenty minutes, and then they have the 'Aha!' There is no advantage to negative thinking. None. And yet the biggest problem we face in America is low self-esteem."

Low self-esteem has its uses, though. Whenever you see a couple of male animals on a PBS nature special duking it out for the privilege of having sex with some female of the species, one of the males is going to dominate and the other male is going to die or get low self-esteem and crawl off making obsequious gestures to the winner. The evolutionary value is obvious: Fight to the death and your genes die with you; admit you're a loser and you may recover to fight again or find another strategy for passing on your genes through some less selective female. Species in which one alpha male gets to have sex with most of the females—elephant seals are a good example—need a lot of low self-esteem among the beta males for social stability.

With 1 percent of the population possessing more wealth than the bottom 95 percent, the American economy operates a lot like a bunch of elephant seals on a rock in the ocean. And it simply must mass-produce low self-esteem in order to maintain social stability amidst such colossal unfairness.

According to the World Health Organization, mood disorders are the number-one cause worldwide of people's normal activities being impaired. In the United States alone, the WHO estimates, depression costs $53 billion a year in worker absenteeism and lost productivity. While that's a hell of a market for Ray Pelletier and the National Speakers Association, which has more than three thousand people giving pep talks to demoralized companies and sports teams, doled-out enthusiasm is a palliative, not a curative. In fact, demoralization is a familiar management tool; the trick is creating just enough. Too much and you have work paralysis, mass depression, and suicide. Too little and you have a revolution. Ever hear a boss brag that he doesn't *have* ulcers, he *gives* them? He's making sure his employees are demoralized enough to stay in their place.

Consider the book *Shame and Pride,* by Dr. Donald L. Nathanson, a psychiatrist and the executive director of the Silvan S. Tomkins Institute in

Philadelphia. Starting in the mid-1940s, Dr. Tomkins watched babies for thousands of hours and made a convincing case that humans are born pre-programmed with nine "affects"—potential states of emotion that can be triggered by a stimulus or memory. These affects are: interest-excitement, enjoyment-joy, surprise-startle, fear-terror, distress-anguish, anger-rage, dis-smell (*dissmell* is similar to *distaste*, but related to the sense of smell), disgust, and shame-humiliation. These affects "amplify" an outside stimulus or memory to give you an increase in brain activity that eventually becomes full-blown emotion.

Until recent years, shame was the "ignored emotion" in psychology. But a few people, Nathanson most prominently, built on Tomkins and discovered the key to . . . well, not quite everything, but an awful lot. According to Tomkins and Nathanson, shame erupts whenever "desire outruns fulfillment." An impediment arises to the two positive affects (interest-excitement and en-joyment-joy), and suddenly your eyes drop, your head and body slump, your face turns red, and your brain is confused to the point of paralysis. This is ob-servable in babies and in adults. This is also observable in the NFL, exquisitely so after the regular season, when the coaches of the teams that don't make the playoffs are ritually humiliated at press conferences. A variation on the theme, often seen in losing coaches who manage to keep their jobs for another sea-son, is the compensatory jutting chin and the disdainful stare, both directed at the press and usually accompanied by promises to examine every aspect of the organization and by pronouncements about "recommitment to winning." Players in this state of shame often attack journalists verbally, and sometimes physically. Sportswriters, who in general demand that losing competitors ex-hibit lots of shame for dramatic purposes and who reinforce the savage lie that losers aren't man enough to win, keep the system in place even as they com-plain about it.

So I called up Nathanson and asked if he had any thoughts about why athletes get so upset when they are called pussies.

"One of the major tasks of childhood is the formation of gender iden-tity, the shift from saying, 'I'm a kid,' to saying, 'I'm a boy,' or 'I'm a girl,' " he replied. "I don't think anyone gets over the shame we have of not being ade-quately identified by the right gender. We see a lot of that worry in adults, in the drive for perfection of the body through plastic surgery and steroids. Peo-ple don't just wish to be someone else anymore, they buy it. Men also face the problem of 'Am I masculine enough?' In Blake Edwards's remarkable movie *Victor/Victoria,* Alex Karras says something to the effect that a lot of men go into football because they want to undo any worry that they're not adequately masculine. Men are concerned that they'll be called not just female, but female genitalia. I don't think any of this is trivial, because of the risk of violence when someone is shamed in public. Sports are an analog of what goes on in everyday life, and it's amazing what people get away with on the so-called field of honor."

Sports events are often described as a morality play, I said, but there's nothing moral about it. Sports decide who will participate in power and who will be humiliated.

"That's understandable when you recognize that our sense of place in society is maintained by shame. Keeping people in their place is maintaining them at certain levels of shaming interaction at which they can be controlled. This issue of winning and losing, it throws us. It defines our identity, doesn't it?"

Calling someone a loser is probably the worst insult in the United States today.

"If you're calling someone that, the person must live in a perpetual state of shame. The only way he can live with himself is to have massive denial, disavowal of his real identity. He has to make his way in the world somehow, and he can't walk around constantly thinking of himself as a loser. Yet if someone in our eyes is a loser and he refuses to admit it, this is narcissism. He has an identity that can't be sustained by consensual validation."

Is there some value in competition, in creating all these losers?

"When you're young and you're learning and it's just a bunch of guys playing a game, that's not shame. That's just figuring out that Billy is faster than Johnny. When parents and schools and bureaucracies start getting involved and demanding wins, then it gets pathological."

Playing for the Chicago Bears, the Philadelphia Eagles, and the Dallas Cowboys from 1961 to 1972, Mike Ditka was All-Pro five times as a tight end, won an NFL championship with the Bears in 1963, won Super Bowl VI with the Cowboys, and was elected to the Hall of Fame. As the coach of the Bears from 1982 to 1992, he won Super Bowl XX with an 18–1 team generally acknowledged as one of the greatest ever and was named Coach of the Year twice. As the coach of the New Orleans Saints for the past three seasons, he had a 15–33 record and is now most vividly remembered for flipping off the fans and grabbing his crotch during and after an especially inept defeat. (He was fined $20,000.) I asked him if he thinks that football fans are inherently interested in the game, or in the hallucination of power they get when their team wins?

"They relate to the winning. Well, you can't say they aren't interested in the game. They watch the game. But the excitement comes from winning."

When football players snap at journalists in the locker room after a loss . . .

"That's only human nature. They probably snap at their wives when they get home, too. Are you saying, Does losing bother people? Sure it does. It's no different from a guy at IBM who loses a sale to a competitor. You just don't like to lose. Most people want to be associated with winning. When you work your butt off and don't get the results you want, you might be a little short-tempered as a coach. That's only life. But that's no different than any other segment of life. Football parallels society, period."

I've noticed that the worst thing you can call somebody in the United States is a loser.

"No. The word *quitter* is the worst thing you can call somebody. Lemme ask you something: If two teams play all year, and they reach the Super Bowl, the one that loses is a loser? Come on.

"I don't like the term. . . . It's not fair. I think as long as you compete and you do your best, if the other team is better, I don't think you really lose. I think you lose when you quit trying."

The problem with declaring a quitter to be a lower form of dirt than a loser is that you're still stigmatizing almost everybody. Studies indicate that up to 90 percent of children drop out of organized competitive sports by the age of fifteen. Extrapolating from my own experience, I would guess that they don't enjoy feeling like losers so that the jocks can feel like winners. Since they associate intense physical activity with feeling rotten, they grow up having problems with obesity and depression, both of which have become epidemic in the United States.

As Mike Ditka would say, it's not fair. But I think there's a way out. And I think that Alfie Kohn has seen it. Kohn, an educational philosopher, has helped inspire the opposition to standardized tests, an especially pernicious form of competition. His first book, *No Contest: The Case Against Competition,* cites study after study demonstrating that competition hinders work, play, learning, and creativity in people of all ages. (In fact, there is almost no evidence to the contrary in the social sciences.) The book is wonderfully validating for anyone who ever had doubts about the ostensible fun of gym class and spelling bees. I told Kohn that in my experience, people get unhinged when you question the value of making other people fail.

"Absolutely. It calls into question America's state religion, which is practiced not only on the playing field but in the classroom and the workplace, and even in the family. The considerable body of evidence demonstrating that this is self-defeating makes very little impression on people who are psychologically invested in a desperate way in the idea of winning. The real alternative to being number one is not being number two, but being able to dispense with these pathological ratings altogether. If people accepted the research on the destructiveness of competition, you wouldn't see all these books teaching how to compete more effectively. I hear from a lot of teachers and parents whose kids fall apart after losing in spelling bees and awards assemblies, and they feel dreadful about it. The adults start to think, *Hmm, maybe competition isn't such a good thing, at least for those kids.* It took me years to see that the same harms were being visited upon the winners. The kids who win are being taught that they are good only to the extent that they continue to beat other people. They're being taught that other people are obstacles to their own success, which destroys a sense of community as effectively as when we teach losers that lesson. And finally, the winners are being taught that the point of what they are doing is to win, which leads to diminished achievement and interest in what they are doing. What's true for kids is also true for adults. It's not a problem peculiar to those who lose. We're all losers in the race to win."

I'm very blessed that way. I didn't have the perspective to spell it out like Alfie Kohn, but I've known I was a total loser since my first college football practice. I've admitted it here publicly, and I am free. You, you're probably holding on to some putrefying little shred of self-esteem, denying that you're a loser in a country inhabited by Bill Gates and 260 million losers. You're still hoping to beat your friend at racquetball and make him feel as bad as you do when you lose, still looking to flatten some rival with just the right factoid in an argument, still craving the sports car in the commercial that accurately announces, "There's no such thing as a gracious winner." Give up, I say. Join me. Losers of the world, unite! You have nothing to lose but your shame.

The Biggest Play of His Life

RICK REILLY

Rick Reilly's *Sports Illustrated* column is alternately satirical, sarcastic, and serious. For years, subscribers have been starting with the magazine's back page first to get his take on modern sports topics in "The Life of Reilly."

For me, the most moving examples of Reilly's work come not from his assessment of sport's biggest stars, but from the human stories he finds in sport's more anonymous ranks. His telling of a gay high school football player's courage coming out to his team is one example of such work.

One of the captains of the high school football team had something big he wanted to tell the other players. "I was so anxious," remembers middle linebacker Corey Johnson, a senior at Masconomet High in Topsfield, Massachusetts, "I thought I was going to vomit."

He took a hard gulp. "I want to let all of you guys know something about me." He tried not to let his voice quake. "I'm coming out as an openly gay student here."

His teammates' eyes and mouths went wide as soup plates. "I hope this won't change anything," Corey quickly went on. "I didn't come on to you last year in the locker room, and I won't this year. I didn't touch you last year in the locker room, and I won't this year."

Awkward silence.

"Besides, who says you guys are good enough anyway?"

And you know what happened? They laughed! But that's not the best part. The best part is what happened next. Nothing.

Corey's teammates had no problem with his sexual orientation. His coach had no problem with it. His mom and dad and his sister had no problem with it. His teachers, his counselor—nobody—had a problem with it.

O.K., somebody scrawled FOOTBALL FAG on a door at school. True, one cementhead parent asked coach Jim Pugh to have the team take a new vote on the captaincy, but Pugh told him to stuff it. And, yeah, one week the opposing team's captain kept hollering "Get the fag!" but his coach finally benched him (and Masconomet fricasseed that team 25–0).

No opponent refused to play against Corey. No opposing coach said, "Boys, the Lord wants you to go out and crush that heathen!" Nobody held up a sign at a Masconomet game that read WHICH SIDE ARE YOU ON, COREY? Nope. Corey Johnson, guard–linebacker, wrestler, lacrosse player, just went out and played his senior football season, same as ever. Masconomet did well (7–4 for the season, 25–8 with Corey, a two-way starter for three years). Now Corey is getting on with his life, hopeful as ever. He'll graduate with his class next month, think about playing small-college football, and become a gay activist, a journey that began on Sunday at the Millennium March on Washington for Equality.

Can't wait for Corey to be on a gay parade float when some beer-bellied yahoo hollers, "Hey, girls! Shoe sale next corner!" The football captain might turn the poor schmo into a smudge mark.

Corey can take the hits now, but hiding the truth about himself was so depressing in his sophomore and junior years that he let his grades drop, skipped practice, and even skipped school. When an adult friend started ripping homosexuals at a Super Bowl party in January 1998, Corey couldn't decide whether to punch him or cry. He knew he had to do something.

First, he told a guidance counselor he was gay and then a few teachers. They all supported him. A year later he told his parents. Fine. Then his best friend, Sean. Uh-oh. Big problem. Sean started crying. Corey asked him what was wrong. "I'm sorry you couldn't share this with me before," Sean said. They're still best friends.

Since coming out, Corey says, he has heard from "hundreds" on the Internet, including athletes who wish they had the guts to come out, too. "But," says Corey, "they always say, 'At my school? No way. It'd be impossible.' "

At Masconomet, a public school with an enrollment of thirteen hundred, Corey is the football captain who had even more moral courage than physical. He's admired by his teammates. In fact, nothing much changed between them, except on bus rides home after wins, when the whole team sang *YMCA* together. Well, it isn't *Hunker Down, You Hairy Bulldogs,* but it works.

Maybe we're actually getting somewhere in the U.S. A young man who leads young men comes out as gay, and it makes such a ruckus you can still hear the crickets chirp. In fact, last month the Boston Gay, Lesbian, and Straight Education Network handed its Visionary Award not just to Corey, but also to his teammates. Can you imagine that? A high school football team getting an award for *tolerance?*

When I was growing up, my best friend was a hilarious kid I'll call Danny. Along about high school, he stopped coming around. Then, in college, he showed up in the Gay Club photo in the yearbook. After that, Danny didn't take my calls.

It's a lousy feeling. I guess I'm not the kind of person he could've shared that with.

The Minority Quarterback

IRA BERKOW

At a time when a young, black, ridiculously talented athlete, Michael Vick, is quarterbacking a team from the south and fast becoming the National Football League's most exciting and marketable player, it appears that many of the negative stereotypes that have hounded black quarterbacks are disappearing from football culture. Long-toiling Vick predecessors like Doug Williams and Randall Cunningham exploded the myth that blacks were not capable of leading professional football teams. And more recent successes such as Steve McNair, Donovan McNabb and Vick have cemented the transition to a more enlightened view.

But quarterback remains the most visible position in all of sports. And as long as there are quarterbacks suiting up on Friday nights and Saturday and Sunday afternoons, there will be scrutiny for those talented enough to play the game's most pivotal position.

As part of a Pulitzer-Prize winning *New York Times* series examining race in America, Ira Berkow found the dyslexic version of race stigma as it applies to football: the white quarterback as a minority. In "The Minority Quarterback," Berkow takes a look at Marcus Jacoby's indoctrination as the first white quarterback in the 76-year history of the black Southwestern Athletic conference.

Quarterback is the singular position in sports that can define a team. That Jacoby faced many of the hurdles traditionally encountered by blacks in a majority white society was as much a product of his position on the football field as any sociological aspect of his experience at a black college.

A late summer morning and the sun was already harsh on the dusty high school football field in Baton Rouge, Louisiana. The shirtless blond nineteen-year-old in shorts stained with sweat kept dropping back to pass, his hands at times so wet it was hard to grip the ball. He was throwing to a friend, working "up the ladder," as it is called, starting with short passes and ending long.

But his mind wasn't totally on his receiver. He could feel the eyes of the man in the dark glasses who sat in a car on the other side of a chain-link fence, a hundred yards away. The boy knew the man was watching. It had been subtly arranged. The National Collegiate Athletic Association does not allow tryouts, but if a college coach happens by a field where kids regularly throw the ball around, well, a coach may argue, where's the harm?

At that time, in July of 1996, Southern University, a football power-house among black colleges, desperately needed a quarterback, and the boy, Marcus Jacoby, badly needed a place to play quarterback. After half an hour, the man in dark glasses, Mark Orlando, Southern's offensive coordinator, had seen enough and drove off.

It had gone well. The boy was invited to the coach's apartment, where after a short visit he was offered a full football scholarship. The coach explained that the boy had a shot at the starting job, that the intended starter's poor grades had lost him his place on the team, and that the two backups did not have the coaches' confidence.

"Sounds good," Jacoby, who had been a star at Catholic High, one of Baton Rouge's schoolboy powers, recalled saying. "But I have to think about it—talk with my parents."

"Practice starts in four days," the coach responded. "We're going to need an answer soon."

Marcus Jacoby was unaware that if he accepted the scholarship, he would be the first white to play quarterback for Southern University. And he would be the first white to start at quarterback in the seventy-six-year history of the black Southwestern Athletic Conference. Jacoby had grown up in Baton Rouge, and yet he knew practically nothing about Southern, had never even been to the other side of town to see the campus. Until that July day he had spent his life surrounded by whites.

Southern's head coach, Pete Richardson, worked out of a modest wood-paneled office lined with trophies. In his three years there he had turned a laughingstock into a national force. Southern won eleven of twelve games his first year, 1993, and two years later it was the number one black college foot-ball team in the nation.

It is not easy for a black man to become a head coach. Despite his record, Richardson, fifty-four, has never had an offer from one of the 114 Division I-A colleges; only three of them have black head football coaches.

In college he played at the University of Dayton, hardly a major football school, and though he had limited natural talent, he reached the professional level, playing three years for the Buffalo Bills. He coached high school ball for a few years, then took the head coach job at Winston-Salem State in North Carolina. Finally, in 1993, he got his big break at Southern, which with its combined campuses is the largest historically black college in the nation.

"I can't get caught up with the thought that, 'Hey, why shouldn't I be at Notre Dame?'" he said in an interview. "I can't get sidetracked or go around with a chip on my shoulder." He is a stoical man and expected stoicism from his players.

That day in his office, the Jacobys said, they were impressed by his quiet intellect, the way he measured his words, his determination. Indeed, the president of Southern, Dr. Dorothy Spikes, often said that she had hired Richardson over better-known candidates not just because his teams had been winners but because of his reputation for integrity, for running a clean program.

Coach Richardson and the Jacobys discussed everything from Southern's rich athletic tradition to the engineering courses that interested Marcus, but for a long while they didn't mention the thing that worried the parents most. The quarterback is team leader. Would a black team accept a white leader? Would the black campus? The night before, at the Jacobys' home in the upper-middle-class white Tara section of Baton Rouge, talk had become heated. "What if they don't like Marcus?" Marian Jacoby had said, tears in her eyes. "What if there's some kind of . . . action?" Marcus had not been able to sleep he was so upset.

Now his father, Glen, an environmental engineer, asked the coach, "How are you going to protect my son?"

The room went silent, Glen Jacoby said later. "I realize that you're concerned," Richardson began, "but I just don't think it will be that big a deal. Sure, there will be some adjustments from all sides. But Marcus will have the backing of the administration as well as the coaching staff." Coach Richardson pointed out that there were other minorities on campus. He meant that of the 10,500 students, 5 percent were not black, but Mrs. Jacoby kept thinking about how it would feel to be in a stadium with her husband amid 30,000 black fans.

The coach didn't say it to the Jacobys, but no one knew better than he about the strain Marcus would feel being in the minority. As a successful black

man, Richardson was used to the stares of surprise. "Walking into a place with
a suit and tie on, you're always going to get that second look because you're
not supposed to be there." When he coached at Winston-Salem, he drove a
state government car. "Whites look at you and ask you what you're doing driving the state's car," he said. "You pull over to get some gas and people will address you the wrong way or policemen will look at you funny."

There was something else Richardson didn't say that morning. He was
well aware how hostile Southern's fans could be to any newcomer, regardless
of creed or color. Many had not wanted him hired. They felt he had come
from too small a college; they had wanted a big name in black college football.
They had even used race on him. Shortly after he arrived, a rumor started that
Richardson's wife, who is light-skinned, was white, and that his white offensive
coordinator was his wife's brother. None of it true, but Richardson didn't let it
get to him. He knew the best answer was to win, and since he had done so, he
was—as Southern's registrar, Marvin Allen, liked to point out—a campus god.

The coach thought he could make this Jacoby thing work. He wasn't
sitting there fretting about whether Marcus could learn to be part of the minority. The first game was only six weeks away. As he would say later, he didn't
have "ample time to find another black quarterback." Marcus would have to do
what all good players did, what the coach himself had done: suck it up.

To reassure the Jacobys, the coach told them about his staff. Of six assistants he had hired when he started in 1993, two were white, one Asian. He
was told Southern fans would never stand for that. But after his 11–1 debut
season—the year earlier they had been 6–5—a popular T-shirt on campus featured a photo of the integrated staff, with the phrase "In Living Color."

The parents wanted to think about it overnight, but Marcus did not.
He climbed into his Jeep, he said later, and went riding. He was getting his shot,
finally. There was nothing he loved like football. As a boy, when he couldn't
find a friend, he tossed footballs into lined-up garbage cans in his yard. His parents held him back in ninth grade so he would have time to grow and a better
chance to play high school ball. After starring at Catholic, he went to Louisiana
Tech, but there, prospects for playing were dim.

Now he envisioned a game night at Southern with a crowd cheering
as he threw yet another touchdown pass. When he stopped at a red light, he
lifted his head and at the top of his lungs screamed, "Praise God!"

From the Jacobys' home, Southern was a twenty-minute car trip, literally to the other side of the tracks. On the ride to the first practice, as he drove
over the Hump—the small hill that is one of the barriers between Southern

and white Baton Rouge—the momentousness of what he had done began sinking in. As he looked around, he began imagining himself playing a game, he recalled. "Would I see a white face?"

Southern's decision to sign a white quarterback made headlines, first locally, then nationally, and the reaction of some whites he knew startled him. When Jacoby called his girlfriend to talk about it, her mother answered. "The niggers over there will kill you," he recalled her saying. "There are bullets flying all over the place. It's a war zone." When his girlfriend got on the phone, she said, "Marcus, I don't want you to call me again." To many on the white side of town, who had never visited this campus bustling with middle-class black students on the bluffs of the Mississippi, it was as if Jacoby had voluntarily moved to the ghetto.

Like many white Americans, he knew there was still prejudice—though, he says, not at home. He had been raised to believe that, after generations of injustice, the country was now a fair place when it came to race—a level playing field, so to speak—and he had made a few black friends while playing high school ball.

The Jacobys were considered a little eccentric for Baton Rouge, having moved here from California when Marcus was three. His paternal grandfather was Jewish. His mother had attended Berkeley in the 1960s and still had some of the flower child in her. She was a fitness buff and had even tried putting her family on a vegetarian diet, stocking the refrigerator with so many oat products that Marcus's buddies asked whether they owned a horse. Marcus and his sister at first attended a private school, but their mother felt too many children there were spoiled by wealth. So she taught them at home for five years, until Marcus was a sophomore.

Friends and teachers at Catholic High remember him as hard-working, smart, and moralistic, with a strong Christian bent. "We'd make fun of his being so innocent," said John Eric Sullivan, one of his best friends. "By that I mean, he didn't do anything that most normal high school kids are doing. he'd be, 'Watch out, watch yourself,' when guys would be drinking. We'd say, like, 'Marc, relax, man.' " He told them he was waiting until he was twenty-one to drink.

The Southern coaches were impressed with his arm and had never seen a quarterback learn Coach Richardson's complex offense so fast. Jacoby stayed after practice to do extra throwing and often studied game films well past midnight. Southern at times uses a no-huddle offense, meaning the quarterback has to call plays rapidly right at the line, and Coach Richardson felt that of the three candidates, only Marcus Jacoby knew the system well enough to do that. Within days of arriving, he was first string.

That sparked anger among many of his new black teammates. For over a year they had been friendly with the two quarterbacks now relegated to backup, and they resented the newcomer, complaining that he had not earned his stripes. "He was *given* his stripes," said Virgil Smothers, a lineman. "There was a lingering bitterness."

Several felt the decision was racial. "It just became the fact that we were going to have this white quarterback," said Sam George, a quarterback prospect who was academically ineligible that year. "It wasn't about ability no more." Teammates picked at Jacoby's weaknesses—he didn't have "fast feet" and rarely scrambled—and joked that he was the typical bland white athlete, which angered Coach Richardson. "A lot of minorities, they want the flash," the coach said. "We felt we needed a system in order to be successful and a quarterback to operate within the confines of that system."

Except for the coaches, he was isolated. In the locker room, Jacoby recalled, "I would walk around the corner and people would just stop talking." Even in the huddles there was dissension. Scott Cloman, a Southern receiver, recalled: "The minute Marcus was like, 'Everybody calm down, just shut up,' they were like: 'Who are you talking to? You're not talking to me.' You know, stuff like that. If it was a black person it wouldn't be a problem. They all felt that 'I'm not going to let a white person talk to me like that.' "

His entire time at Southern, Jacoby kept his feelings about all this inside, "sucking it up," repeatedly telling the inquiring reporters what a great experience it was being exposed to a new culture. "As soon as I signed and walked onto the campus," he told one interviewer, "I felt like part of the family. I definitely feel at home here."

On September 7, 1996, Southern opened at Northwestern State, with Marcus Jacoby at quarterback. Of the 25,000 spectators, half had made the three-hour trip from Southern, not unusual for this football-crazy place. "Fans plan their lives around games," Coach Richardson said. "They fight to get schedules, to see where we're going to play so they can take holidays and go to games."

Southern University families like the Morgans will take more than twenty people to an away game, filling several hotel rooms. Mo Morgan, a supervisor at the local Exxon plant who attended Southern in the 1960s, went so far as to buy a motor home just for Southern football, which made him the object of good-natured ribbing. Friends insisted that "black people don't drive Winnebagos." His wife, Wanda, and about twenty-five of their relatives are

Southern graduates, and his youngest son, Jabari, a freshman drummer and cymbals player, was on the field for that same opening game.

For the youngest Morgan, the band was only partly about music. More famous than Southern's football team—having performed at five Super Bowls and three presidential inaugurations—it had real power and importance on campus. The 180-piece Southern band thrived on intimidating lesser rivals on the black college circuit. With its hard-brass sound and its assertive style, the group had a militant edge that old-timers on campus attributed to the influence of the civil rights era, when the band's show was honed.

Robert Gray, who played cymbals with Morgan, said: "When people think about Southern band, they think about a bunch of big, tough-looking, tight-looking dudes with psychotic looks on their faces, ready to go to war. I just think—Southern band—black, all male, just rowdy, loud."

Families like the Morgans were fiercely proud of their school and its role in helping generations of blacks into the middle and professional classes—even if the state had long treated it as second-rate. In the early 1900s, legislators planning to create a new campus for Southern considered several locations around Louisiana. But in city after city, white residents rose in protest, and finally the state settled on a site that no one else then coveted. In the 1950s, blacks like Audrey Nabor-Jackson, Wanda Morgan's aunt, were prohibited from attending the big white public campus across town, Louisiana State University. Southern was their only alternative.

Even as late as the 1970s, Louisiana's public higher education system was capable of inflicting deep racial wounds. Wanda Morgan was required to take several courses at LSU as part of a master's program at Southern. In one class she was one of four blacks, and for every exam, she said, the four were removed by the professor and put in an empty classroom across the hall, one in each corner, while the white students took the exam in their regular seats. The message was missed by no one: black students would cheat.

By the mid-1990s, change was brewing. The year before Jacoby arrived, Southern and LSU settled a twenty-year-old federal desegregation lawsuit. Both institutions pledged sharp minority increases on their campuses, with 10 percent of enrollment set aside for other races—more whites to Southern, more blacks to LSU. Alumni like the Morgans were worried. Would Southern soon become just another satellite campus of LSU? Was the white quarterback the beginning of the end?

Mo Morgan and Audrey Nabor-Jackson agreed with an editorial in Southern's student paper saying that a white quarterback did not belong. "There are plenty of young black athletes," it said, "who could benefit from

Jacoby's scholarship." Mo Morgan said, "I didn't like the fact that he was there."
About the only Morgan not upset was Jabari. Mo Morgan worried that his
eighteen-year-old son was not race-conscious enough. "I came through the
movement, I was confronted with things," said the father. "That's one of the things
that concerns me—that he hasn't." But it didn't concern Jabari Morgan—he
was consumed with the band. Long before starting college, he had begun as-
sembling on his bedroom wall what he called his shrine, a montage about the
Southern band that included a picture of the first white band member, in the
early 1990s.

Now, in his freshman year, his long-nurtured fantasy was coming true.
Standing there that day with cymbals weighing nine pounds each, ready to
march into Northwestern State's stadium, he was at the front of the band. The
director, Dr. Isaac Greggs, always positioned his tallest and most imposing players—his "towers of terror"—at the front, and Jabari Morgan, at six foot one,
was one of them. Football, he said, was about the last thing on his mind.

"It was like winning the lottery." He wouldn't have cared if Marcus Jacoby were purple, as long as Southern won and people stayed in their seats for
the halftime show.

Southern lost its first two games. The team was young—ten of eleven
offensive starters were new—but what people remembered was the 11–1 record the year before. For fans, the quarterback, more than any other player, is
the team—hero or goat. During the second loss, Jacoby recalled, "I heard the
entire stadium booing me."

Jean Harrison, the mother of the quarterback prospect Sam George,
remembered, "One lady had a megaphone and she was screaming, 'Get that
white honky out of there!' It made you sick."

Chris Williams, an offensive lineman, believed that the other team hit
Jacoby harder because he was white: "Teams took cheap shots at him. I really
believe that. I mean they hit him sometimes blatantly late after the whistle."
Scott Cloman recalled that after one Southern loss, opposing players said,
"That's what you all get for bringing white boys on the field."

Jacoby was hit so hard and so often during the first game that he was
hospitalized with a concussion. Glen Jacoby, Marcus's father, was sure the
blockers were sandbagging their white quarterback, but in interviews at the
time, the young man denied it. He still says he believes that it was just the mistakes of an inexperienced line.

After Southern's second loss, an angry fan threatened Jacoby. A coach
had to jump between them. For the rest of his career, Jacoby would have a po-

lice escort at games. There was a disturbance outside the stadium at another game. Gunshots were fired. Jacoby recalls thinking the shots were aimed at him. They were not.

The Tuesday after the second loss, Jacoby rose at 5 A.M., worked out in the weight room, then walked to the cafeteria for the team breakfast. No one was there. He checked his watch. Shortly after he sat down, Coach Orlando came in, took him by the arm, and led him through a nearby door. As Jacoby remembered it, the entire team and coaching staff sat squeezed into a small room. All chairs were taken, so he stood alone against a wall. No one looked at him. Coach Richardson stood. "I think Marcus should know what's going on," he said, adding, "Who wants to say something?"

Virgil Smothers, the senior defensive end, rose. The night before, he had talked about staging a strike. Now he mentioned some minor gripes, then added: "We're losing and we feel changes ought to be made. Some guys aren't getting a fair chance."

Someone else said, "Guys are playing who shouldn't."

Coach Orlando walked to the front. As offensive coordinator he naturally worked closely with the quarterback. But several players felt he favored Jacoby because they were both white. "Let's get this in the open," Orlando said, adding, "This is mostly about Jacoby, isn't it?" Insisting that the quarterback had been chosen fairly, he said: "You have to accept Marcus, he's one of us. We're 0 and 2, but we have to put this behind us."

Lionel Hayes, who had lost the quarterback job to Jacoby, interrupted Coach Orlando. "You're just saying that," Mr. Hayes said, "because you're Jacoby's Dad." It got a laugh, though his tone was angry. Jacoby said later: "There was a lot of hate in that room. I felt like I was falling into a hole, and I couldn't grab the sides."

Coach Richardson spoke again: "We win as a team, we lose as a team. Jacoby's doing what he's supposed to be doing, and he'll get better. We all will." He said practice would be at three. "If anyone doesn't want to be on the team with Jacoby as the starting quarterback, don't come."

Richardson remembered: "What I saw was a frustration by some players—mostly seniors—who weren't playing. They weren't playing because they didn't deserve to. And so they needed a scapegoat."

Jacoby remembers feeling like the invisible man. "It was almost as though I weren't there, and they were talking about me," he said. "I wasn't sure where to turn. I felt they didn't want me there—not me personally, but any white quarterback—that I was just another problem."

Three or four players didn't show up for practice, and Coach Richardson cut them. Not long afterward, Virgil Smothers and one of the coaches argued, and Smothers was told, "Clear out your locker."

When the players gathered the next day at practice, before the coaches arrived, Jacoby said, he stood to talk. A few tried to shout him down, but John Williams, a star senior cornerback and devout Christian who would go on to play for the Baltimore Ravens, rose and said, "Man, let the man talk."

"I don't care if you like me or hate me," Jacoby recalled saying. "All I ask is that we can go out and play football together. This is not a popularity contest. I'm trying to win. I'm just trying to be your quarterback."

Things improved dramatically. Southern won six of its next seven games, beating the two top-ranked black colleges, and was invited to the Heritage Bowl in Atlanta, the black college championship. "I wasn't getting booed nearly as much," Jacoby said. Some teammates began warming to him. More than anything, they were impressed by his work ethic. During a practice break, players drank from a garden hose. "Sorry, Marcus," one teased, "this is the black water fountain." They called him "Tyrone," and "Rasheed."

"I appreciated it," he recalled. "Things had changed to the extent that some of the players were calling me 'the man.'"

Before games, he and John Williams prayed together. One Sunday the two went to the black church where Williams was a minister. Occasionally strangers would wish Jacoby well. One day the band's legendary director, Dr. Greggs, greeted him warmly and urged him to persevere.

He felt he was developing real friendships with teammates and Southern students. When Scott Cloman needed a place to stay for a month, Jacoby had him to his parents' home and the two grew close. "Marcus was the first white person I ever really got to know," Cloman said. "I always felt a lot of tension around whites. I'd go into a store and I could just feel the tension. Sometimes you just feel like, 'I can't stand white people.' I didn't understand them. I really didn't want to be near them."

"His parents treated me like a son," added Cloman. Some players now joked when they saw him, "Where's your brother?"

"And some," he said, "called me 'white lover.' Didn't bother me. I had come to understand the Jacobys. A lot of times people fear what they can't understand. Because of being around the Jacobys, my attitude toward whites in general changed."

At the Heritage Bowl that first year, on national television, Southern took a 24–10 halftime lead against Howard University, then fell behind, 27–24. In the closing minute, Southern drove to Howard's fifteen-yard line. On third down, with forty-two seconds left, Marcus Jacoby dropped back and, under pressure, threw off the wrong foot, floating a pass into the end zone.

"I heard the crowd gasp," he said. "I couldn't believe this was happening." He'd been intercepted. "Their fans must have cheered, but I remember everything being silent." A camera captured Coach Richardson on his knees, hands over his head.

"I dragged myself off the field and sat on a bench and buried my head in my arms," Jacoby said. "A few people, like John Williams, came by and patted me on the back, to be encouraging. But I heard, 'You screwed up real bad this time, Whitey,' and, 'You're as dumb as they come.' It was the lowest point of my life."

After the game, Coach Orlando received an anonymous call: "If Jacoby ever plays for Southern again, we'll kill him—and you." The coach said he averaged a threat a week that season. Later, as Coach Orlando and Jacoby headed to their cars, the coach pointed to several trees. In the light of the street lamps, Jacoby could see a yellow rope hung from each tree. The ropes were tied in nooses.

On campus, Jacoby struggled with all the daily irritations that go with being in the minority. As a white who grew up among whites, he was used to being inconspicuous. Here he always felt on display. "I hated that," he said, "because it was like I had become just a novelty act."

He found that things he had done unconsciously all his life were suddenly brought to his attention and analyzed. One was the way he dressed. He liked to wear a T-shirt, shorts, and flip-flops to class; most students at Southern dressed up for class in slacks. Another was that the way he spoke, his slang, was different from the black majority's. "Many times I would say something at Southern and they would repeat it and I wouldn't get my point across," he said. "It would get lost in the mocking of how I said it instead of what I said. I might walk into a room and I'd say, 'Hey, how y'all doin'?'" Instead of answering, someone would do an imitation of a white person talking, enunciating slowly. "They'd say 'Hi, guy, how are you doing?' So I just learned to say, 'Hey.' " He believed the classmates were only needling him, but being constantly reminded was exhausting.

"People's eyes were on him," said Chris Williams, a teammate. "He just didn't blend in. I mean, like me, I just blended in wherever I went."

A white with a different personality might have fared better. There was one other white on the seventy-man squad, Matt Bushart. And though as a punter he was at the periphery of the team and little noticed by fans, Bushart had the personality and experience possibly to cope better as a minority. While

Marcus had seemed protected and naive even to the middle-class white students at Catholic High, Matt's years at a local public high school where most of his football teammates were black had taught him how to live comfortably among them. While Marcus was more introspective, a little too sensitive for some of his coaches' tastes, Matt was noisy, funny, sometimes crude—so outgoing, his girlfriend said, that he could talk to a wall.

When Bushart's teammates made fun of the country music he liked, he gave it right back to them about their rap, and kept listening to his music. "I get kidded about it," he said, "but there's been a song that's been playing and one of the black guys will come by and say, 'Play that again, that's actually not too bad.'"

Jacoby loved music too; playing guitar was an important outlet for relieving the pressure, but he would not play on campus. As he put it: "At times the rap just blared from the dorms; I longed for something that was my own. I couldn't play it on campus because for most of the time I was apologizing for who I was. I didn't want to cause any more turmoil than there was. I didn't want to make myself look like I was any more separate than I was."

Interracial dating is complicated at Southern. Ryan Lewis, Jacoby's roommate, says most black men would not openly date a white woman on campus. "They would keep it low so nobody knew about it but them," Lewis said. "I've never seen it."

As quarterback, Jacoby often had female students flirting with him. He felt uneasy, caught between the white and black sides of town. Among whites, he said, "everybody just assumed the worst, that I was dating a black girl now because I was at Southern." But even though there were some "gorgeous light-skinned black girls over there," he said, and a couple of women from his classes became good friends, he wasn't attracted. He thinks it was "a cultural thing."

Though college students are confronted with new ideas—sometimes only partially understood—and encouraged to speak out about them, Jacoby felt that when he did, he was criticized. At first, in his African-American literature class, when they discussed slavery, he said he tried to be conciliatory in an oral report. "I would say something like, 'I can't imagine how terrible it must have been, that people could do those kinds of things to other people.' And others in the class made some kind of jokes, but it was like bitter jokes: 'What are you talking about, Marcus? You're one of those whites.' It was like they were saying to me, 'Quit Uncle Tomming.'"

Then he worried he wasn't being true to his white roots. "I felt that I had lost my pride and the respect of friends that I had grown up with," he said.

For his next oral report, he decided to speak his mind and said that it was unhealthy for blacks to dwell too much on past racial violence. "There have been tragedies like slavery throughout time," he said. "I don't think one is more important than any other." When he finished, he recalled, "there was an eerie silence and I saw at least three or four people glaring at me."

Increasingly, being in the minority alienated him, made him feel alone. "I learned early on that I was a pioneer in all this and no one else had gone through it, and often the best advice I could get was from myself. Because I was the only one who knew the whole situation."

It didn't help that his preoccupied parents were going through a divorce. At one point when he was upset about not fitting in, his mother gave him a copy of *Black Like Me,* the story of a white man in the 1960s who dyes his skin and travels the South to experience being black during segregation. At the time, Jacoby said, "I resented my mother giving me the book. She was just trying to help me understand the other side, but I felt she was almost taking the other side."

Blacks, of course, are much better at being in the minority, since they have far more practice and, usually, no choice. When Jabari Morgan was considering colleges, his father told him he was free to pick Southern or a "white" college, but if he picked white, he had better be prepared. Then he gave him the talk about being in the minority that so many black American men give their sons. "You are going to face being called a nigger," Mo Morgan told Jabari. "Now, are you ready to deal with it? If you're not ready to deal with it, don't go."

The Morgans have a family council of elders that meets regularly to guide their young, and one message emphasized is this: "A black person in America has to be smarter and sharper and work harder to achieve the same things as a white person of the same abilities." Mo Morgan says, as a minority, he understands that "the majority is white, and you have control and you want to keep control."

But Jabari Morgan did not think like his father. He had always dreamed of attending Southern, but for him its great appeal was not as a racial sanctuary. He considered race simply part of the rough and tumble of life, the cost of doing business in a mostly white world. Southern was the place where he might be able to play in the best marching band in America, as his father had before him. He determined very early that the best high school marching bands, like the best college bands, were black, and so he fudged his address in order to attend a nearly all-black Baton Rouge school where the band rocked. He figured that that would give him an edge when he tried out at Southern.

As a marketing major who graduated in May, Morgan fully expects that he will one day work for a big white-controlled corporation. But as a marching band member at Southern for four years, he was in many ways the ultimate insider in the self-contained black-majority culture of the Yard, as Southern's campus is known. All the things that Marcus Jacoby found so foreign, and sometimes irritating, were second nature to Jabari Morgan—the music, the dress, the vernacular of put-downs and nicknames that is the campus currency. He loved African-American literature class because the poetry and stories reinforced what his family had taught him about black history.

Like all new band members, Morgan went through hazing. But as part of the majority, he never worried that it was about race. Jacoby, on the other hand, felt so unsettled as part of the minority that he often had trouble sleeping.

Morgan eventually joined a fraternity—a support in its own way as strong as the band's. And, where Marcus Jacoby the minority had no steady girlfriend during his years at Southern, Jabari Morgan the majority began, in his second semester, dating Monique Molizone, an economics major from New Orleans. She had also come to Southern partly for the band—to join the Dancing Dolls, who perform at the band's side.

As much as anything, what got Jacoby through his second year at Southern was a determination to avenge that Heritage Bowl interception, to show everyone—including himself—he could be a champion. He moved through the 1997 season with a passion, working so hard in the weight room that he could now bench-press 350 pounds; running endless drills to improve his foot speed; and doing so much extra throwing that by day's end it took an hour to ice and treat his arm.

Again he was first string, but he had competition. Sam George had returned from academic probation. George was a popular figure on campus, known not only for his hard-partying ways but for his small-man grit on the playing field. Though he was only five foot seven, he had a strong arm and terrific speed. His teammates, responding to his take-charge style in huddles, nicknamed him the Little General. "And," Scott Cloman said, "he was black."

Although Jacoby started, Coach Richardson liked bringing in George when the team seemed flat. Both quarterbacks saw race as the true reason behind the coach's substitutions. Jacoby was convinced that Richardson was giving the black quarterback playing time to pander to the black fans; George was convinced that Coach Richardson—influenced by Coach Orlando—was starting the white quarterback because of favoritism.

George wound up playing in five of twelve games. By Southern's third game, against Arkansas–Pine Bluff, both quarterbacks were bitter. After winning its first two games, Southern was losing to Pine Bluff 7–6 at the half. Coach Richardson decided to replace the white quarterback with the black. Jacoby was devastated; he felt he had proved effective and should not be yanked for one bad half.

Given his chance, George threw a last-ditch thirty-seven-yard pass that tied the game, and threw another touchdown in triple overtime for a 36–33 Southern win. And yet, come Monday practice, Jacoby was the starter again. Now George was frustrated.

Southern had a 9–1 record going into its two final games. A victory in the next game—the Bayou Classic, against Grambling, its archrival—would assure a return to the Heritage Bowl and a chance for Jacoby to redeem himself. His parents and teammates had never seen him so obsessed. He had trouble sleeping and little appetite. His father called Coach Orlando, worried that Marcus's weight was down.

In a journal account of that period, Marcus Jacoby wrote: "I sat down and wrote out a detailed plan of how I was going to get through these last two games, including my political and motivational moves. My survival as a person depended on these last two games. Nobody, including Coach Orlando, knew the amount of outside forces that were pressing on these last two games. I was at a point where I felt that I was crawling on my knees."

He added, "I dreamed of a team when I could just say that I had accomplished something, instead of fighting for respect, fighting in a classroom full of people who disagreed with everything I stood for, and could have a day of true rest."

Before the big game against Grambling, he pleaded with Coach Orlando. "If you don't pull me," Jacoby said, "I guarantee we'll win our next two games."

"You can't guarantee that," the coach said.

"I just did," Jacoby said. Coach Orlando suggested that if Marcus Jacoby played a little more like Sam George, sometimes scrambling out of the pocket, he might be more productive. Jacoby felt that he was being told to become something he was not, but he was so desperate, so nervous about being yanked, that he followed the advice. He scrambled, and it worked. In a 30–7 win against Grambling, Jacoby threw three touchdown passes and played the entire game. He was named the Bayou Classic's most valuable player.

A month later he achieved his redemption, throwing the winning pass in a 34–28 Heritage Bowl victory over South Carolina State, capping an 11–1 season that earned Southern the black national championship. "I was happier than I had ever been at Southern," he recalled. On the bus trip back from that game he slept soundly for the first time in months.

The more you achieve, the more is expected. After that 11–1 season, the talk on campus was that Southern would go undefeated in 1998. But in the opener, with the team trailing 7–0 at the half, Jacoby was pulled for George. Southern lost anyway, 28–7.

In practice on Tuesday, Jacoby overthrew a pass to one of his ends, John Forman, who yelled at him in front of everybody. Forman would say later that it was just the frustration of having lost the opener, but to Jacoby it was so much more—the final straw. He was sure that Forman was trying to subvert his control of the team to help George, his roommate. "If you have a choice, you choose black first," Jacoby would later say. "I felt that I was all alone again, on an island by myself. It was like I was right back where I had started two years before, with a lot of the same attitudes against me."

He quit football and Southern.

Coach Richardson was surprised and asked Jacoby to stay. But more recently he said he understood the decision. Because of "the type person he is," the coach said, "it was the best thing for Marcus because it would have killed him." The coach meant that Marcus Jacoby was not emotionally equipped to continue being the solitary white.

When Branch Rickey of the Brooklyn Dodgers wanted to break major league baseball's color line in 1947, he chose Jackie Robinson, not simply because he was a great black ballplayer—there were greater black stars—but because he had experience inside white institutions. Jackie Robinson was twenty-eight that first year in the majors, a mature man who had attended UCLA and served in the army. He knew what it was like to be in the minority.

When Coach Richardson went after Jacoby, he was just looking for a quarterback.

Reporters hounded Jacoby to find why he had left, but he never spoke openly about it. He never mentioned race. In brief interviews he told them he was burned out, and in a sense this was true. He had burned out on being in the minority. And as a white, he didn't have to be. In those last months at Southern, he often thought about returning to a white life. "You kind of look over your shoulder and see your old life and you say, 'I could go back.'"

There had been such anguish over the Jacoby-George quarterback battle, and all its racial nuances, but at least on the field, in the end, it didn't seem to make much difference. That year Southern, with Sam George at the helm, finished 9–3, once again winning the Heritage Bowl.

A white quarterback at Southern did make people think. Mo Morgan had been against it, but not after watching Jacoby at practices. "I looked at the three quarterbacks that were there, and he was the best at the time. I'm just telling you straight out. It wasn't his ability, and I'm not saying he was brighter than the other kids. He just put in the work."

Morgan's son Jabari said he, too, was sorry to see Jacoby go; he liked the idea of a white guy being open to attending a black college. This past year, as a senior, Jabari Morgan reached out to a white freshman tuba player, Grant Milliken, who tried out for the band. He helped him through the hazing. One of Morgan's friends said he had done it because Milliken was white, but Morgan said no, he had done it because Milliken was really good on tuba.

Morgan even helped Milliken create a dance solo full of shakes and shivers and fancy steps, which was performed at halftimes to wild applause. What the crowd loved, said Morgan, was not just that a white guy could dance. "The whole point of letting the white guy dance is that we were saying to the world, 'Hey, you can learn our culture just like we can learn yours.'"

Morgan's father continues to be both fearful of his son's more relaxed attitude about race and a little in awe of it. "He doesn't think it's something he can't overcome," said Mo Morgan, "and you know, I think he's right. You can get caught up in this, and it will screw up your thinking."

One weekend last fall, at the request of a reporter, Jacoby went to a Southern game for the first time since quitting. This was Homecoming Day, and from his seat in the stands he watched Southern seniors and their families being introduced to the crowd at midfield. It could have been his moment. Ryan Lewis, his old roommate, was there, and so was Matt Bushart, the white punter. Bushart's name was called, to applause. Jacoby had read in the newspaper Bushart's saying how much he had enjoyed Southern.

The team had won seven straight games at that point, and so Jacoby was surprised during the first quarter when Southern's starting quarterback was replaced after throwing an interception. Jacoby had always been so sure he'd been replaced with Sam George to pander to fans; now Coach Richardson was using the same strategy with two black quarterbacks. In the paper the next day, Richardson said he had just been trying to light a spark under the offense.

After the game, outside the stadium, a large black man spotted Jacoby and, extending his hand, said, "Hi, Marcus, how ya doin'?"

"Okay, Virgil," Jacoby said. "How you doin'?" The two chatted for a moment outside the stadium—the man said he had left school and was working as an account executive for a drug company—then they went their separate ways.

"That was Virgil Smothers," Jacoby said afterward. It was Smothers who had led the aborted strike against Jacoby. "I guess he figures it's all in the past."

It was not all in the past for Jacoby. Though he had moved on—he was now majoring in finance at LSU—his Southern experience still unsettled him. "Just last night I had a dream about it," he said. "Weird dreams. Like some of these people are coming back to haunt me in some way. By these people I mean some of those who I considered friends and who I felt kind of turned on me."

At times he talks about being lucky to have experienced another culture; at others he describes it as "a personal hell." His sister Dana says, "There are some scares that haven't gone away, from the bad things."

After leaving Southern, Jacoby took a while to realize how much pressure he had felt. "I remember one time a few months after I quit—and this was part of the healing process—I said something about country music, that I liked it. And I remember standing around with four white people and thinking, 'Oh, my God, I can't believe I just said that.' And then I caught myself right before I got through that whole thing in my mind and I looked at the people's faces and they were agreeing with me. I went 'Whoa,' I didn't have to apologize for that anymore."

These days he appreciates walking around anonymously on the mostly white LSU campus. "I got burned out as far as being somebody," he said. "At LSU I've just enjoyed being a part of the crowd."

A Name on the Wall

WILLIAM NACK

One of the cardinal sins of the American sports fan was exposed in an early '90s advertising campaign when Charles Barkley proudly reminded the country that he was not a role model. It is the easiest of life's traps to place athletes with superior physical gifts into a revered class of human being and endow them with supersized character traits that would be difficult for anyone to embody. Athletes on the field or court show a blend of competitive fire, determination, and God-given talent not on public display in other walks of life. For them, filling out a box score in the biggest game of the year and looking good doing it can translate into consideration for sainthood.

But in modern athletics, in the age of 24-hour cable sports, nearly constant examples of vanity run amuck amid pampered athletes have made it clear that our role models must be found elsewhere. Overpaid, over-exposed athletes show a spoiled sense of entitlement that prevents sports fans from identifying with today's superstars. Run-ins with the law, rumors of steroid use, corked bats, or generally surly demeanors incessantly replayed on pervasive cable sports networks have turned the modern athlete into more punch line than role model.

The poignancy of William Nack's Sports Illustrated story, *A Name on the Wall*, comes from understanding that Lt. Bob Kalsu was truly the embodiment of what America hopes for out of its athletes. Devotion to family, a work ethic that allowed him to overachieve athletically, and a willingness to forego the life of a professional athlete to serve in Vietnam are testament to a life dedicated to excellence, both on and off the football field.

Mr. Barkley, it is certainly debatable whether or not you are a good role model, but Bob Kalsu certainly is.

The feeling had gone out of everything. It was like we were zombies. You didn't care anymore. July was terrible. The [North Vietnamese] whacked Ripcord, that hill we were on, with mortars and rocket fire. Day after day, night after night. I was getting shell-shocked. I didn't care if I got out. At night you could hear the [enemy] yelling from the jungles all around, "GI die tonight! GI die tonight!" This was our deathbed. We thought we were going to be overrun.

—Spc. 4th Class Daniel Thompson
Wireman at Firebase Ripcord, Vietnam, July 1970

There were always lulls between the salvos of incoming mortars, moments of perishable relief. The last salvo had just ended, and the dust was still settling over Firebase Ripcord. In one command bunker, down where the reek of combat hung like whorehouse curtains, Lt. Bob Kalsu and Pfc. Nick Fotias sat basting in the jungle heat. In that last salvo the North Vietnamese Army (NVA), as usual, had thrown in a round of tear gas, and the stinging gas and the smoke of burning cordite had curled into the bunkers, making them all but unbearable to breathe in. It was so sweltering inside that many soldiers suffered the gas rather than gasp in their hot, stinking rubber masks. So, seeking relief, Kalsu and Fotias swam for the light, heading out the door of the bunker, the threat of mortars be damned. "Call us foolish or brave, we'd come out to get a breath of fresh air," Fotias recalls.

It was Tuesday afternoon, July 21, 1970, a day Kalsu had been eagerly awaiting. Back home in Oklahoma City, his wife, Jan, was due to have their second child that very day. (They already had a twenty-month-old daughter, Jill Anne.) The Oklahoma City gentry viewed the Kalsus as perfectly matched links on the cuff of the town. Jan was the pretty brunette with the quick laugh, the daughter of a successful surgeon. Bob was the handsome, gregarious athletic hero with the piano-keys grin, the grandson of Czech immigrants for whom America had been the promised land and Bob the promise fulfilled. As a college senior, in the fall of 1967, the six-foot-three, 220-pound Kalsu had been an All-America tackle for Oklahoma, a team of overachievers that went 10–1, beating Tennessee in the Orange Bowl. The next season, after bulking up to 250 pounds, Kalsu had worked his way into the starting offensive line of the Buffalo Bills, and at season's end he had been named the Bills' rookie of the year.

While in Vietnam, Kalsu rarely talked about his gridiron adventures. Word had gotten around the firebase that he had played for the Bills, but he would shrug off any mention of it. "Yeah, I play football," he would say. What he talked about—incessantly—was his young family back home. Jan knew her husband was somewhere "on a mountaintop" in Vietnam, but she had no idea what he had been through. In his letters he let on very little. On July 19, the day after a U.S. Army Chinook helicopter, crippled by antiaircraft fire, crashed on top of the ammunition dump for Ripcord's battery of 105-mm howitzers, setting off a series of explosions that literally sheared off one tier of the hill, the bunkered-down lieutenant wrote his wife. He began by using his pet name for her.

> Dearest Janny Belle—
>
> How're things with my beautiful, sexy, lovable wife. I love & miss you so very much and can't wait till I'm back home in your arms and we're back in our own apartment living a normal life. The time can't pass fast enough for me until I'm back home with all my loved ones and especially you and Jan and Jilly and Baby K. I love you and need you so very much.
>
> The wind has quit blowing so hard up here. It calmed down so much it's hard to believe it. Enemy activity remains active in our area. Hopefully it will cease in the near future.
>
> I'm just fine as can be. Feeling real good just waiting to hear the word again that I'm a papa. It shouldn't be much longer until I get word of our arrival. . . .
>
> I love you, xxx–ooo.
>
> Bob

Kalsu was, in fact, involved in the gnarliest battle going on at the time in Vietnam: an increasingly desperate drama being played out on the top of a steep, balding shank of rock and dirt that rose 3,041 feet above sea level and 656 above the jungle floor. From the crest of this two-tiered oblong promontory, on a space no bigger than two football fields, two artillery batteries—the doomed 105s and the six 155-mm howitzers of Battery A, Kalsu's battery—had been giving fire support to infantrymen of the 101st Airborne Division, two battalions of which were scouring the jungles for North Vietnamese while pounding the ganglia of paths and supply routes that branched from the Ho Chi Minh Trail in Laos, twelve miles to the west, spiderwebbing south and east around Ripcord through Thuathien Province and toward the coastal lowlands around Hue.

Atop that rock, Kalsu was caught in a maelstrom that grew stronger as July slouched toward August. On July 17, four days before his baby was due, Kalsu was made the acting commander of Battery A after the captain in charge was choppered out to have a piece of shrapnel removed from a bone in his neck. Kalsu and his men continued their firing missions as the NVA attacks intensified. With a range of thirteen miles, Battery A's 155s were putting heavy metal on enemy supply lines as far off as the A Shau Valley, a key NVA logistical base ten miles to the southwest, helping create such havoc that the enemy grew determined to drive the three hundred or so Americans off Ripcord. As many as five thousand NVA soldiers, ten to twelve battalions, had massed in the jungles surrounding Ripcord, and by July 21 they were lobbing more than six hundred rounds a day on the firebase, sending the deadliest salvos whenever U.S. helicopters whirled in with ammo and soldiers raced for the helipad to carry the shells on their shoulders up the hill.

Kalsu humped those ninety-seven-pound explosive rounds along with his men, an officer exposing himself to fire when he could have stayed in the bunker. "A fearless guy, smart, brave, and respected by his troops," recalls retired colonel Philip Michaud, who at the time was a captain commanding the ill-fated battery of 105s. "Rounds were coming in, and he was out there. I told him a few times, 'It's good to run around and show what leadership is about, but when rounds are blowing up in your area, you ought to hunker down behind a gun wheel. Or a bunker.' The guy thought he was invincible."

The grunts loved him for it, and they would have followed him anywhere. David Johnson always did. Kalsu and Johnson, by most superficial measures, could not have been more different. Kalsu was white and the only child of middle-class parents—city-bred, college-educated, married, a father, devoutly Catholic. Johnson was black and the seventh of eleven children raised on a poor farm outside of Humnoke, Arkansas. He was single and childless, a supplicant at the Church of God and Christ. What the two men shared was a gentleness and childlike humanity that reached far beyond race. So James Robert Kalsu, twenty-five, and Spc. 4th Class David Earl Johnson, twenty-four, became inseparable. "They just clicked," recalls former sergeant Alfred Martin. "You saw one, you saw the other."

That lull in incoming fire on July 21 nearly brought the two friends together again. Johnson was standing outside Kalsu's bunker on the pock-marked hill. Cpl. Mike Renner, a gunner, was standing by his 155 with a sergeant who was dressing him down because the jack on the gun had broken, leaving the crew unable to raise it to a different azimuth. At that moment Kalsu and Fotias rose out of the bunker. They stood at the door for a moment, Fotias with his back to it, and Kalsu started reading to him from a piece of paper in his hand. "[It was] a letter he had received from his wife," Fotias says. "I remember the joy on his face as he read the letter to me. He said, 'My wife's having our baby today.' "

Some rounds you heard falling, some you didn't. Fotias did not hear this one. Jim Harris, the battalion surgeon, was across the firebase when he heard the splitting crack and turned his head toward it. The 82-mm mortar landed five feet from the bunker door. "I can still feel the heat of the blast coming past me and the concussion knocking me over," says Renner. "It flipped me backward, my helmet flew off, and the back of my head hit the ground."

Johnson fell sprawling on the ground. Fotias, at the mouth of the bunker, saw the sun go out. "I remember this tremendous noise," he says, "and darkness. And being blown off my feet and flying through the door of the bunker and landing at the bottom of the steps, six feet down, and this tremendous weight crushing me. I couldn't see. I couldn't hear. I had dirt in my eyes, and my eyes were tearing. I rubbed them, and then I could see again. I pushed off this weight that was on top of me, and I realized it was Bob."

Kalsu was really a boy trapped inside a large man's body—a player of pranks whose high-pitched cackle would fill a room. He laughed so heartily that he drooled, the spittle coursing from the corners of his mouth down around his dimpled chin and on down his chiseled neck. Once, on hearing the punch line of an off-color joke, he slammed a fist so hard on an adjoining barstool that the stool broke into pieces. He had the appetite of a Komodo dragon, but he loved kids even more than food. Some valve must have been missing in his psyche: his ego, unlike that of most jocks, was not inflatable. He always favored the underdog (he arranged the selection of one girl as high school homecoming queen because no one paid her much mind), and he turned down a high school sports award on grounds that he'd already received too many. "It'll mean more to somebody else," he told his mother, Leah.

Kalsu was born in Oklahoma City on April 13, 1945, and he came of age in the suburb of Del City at a time when coach Bud Wilkinson was leading Oklahoma through its gilded age. From 1953 into '57 the Sooners won forty-seven consecutive games, still a record for a Division I school, and finished three straight seasons ('54 to '56) undefeated. Twice during that run, in '55 and '56, they were national champions. Like every other eighteen-year-old gridiron star in the state, Kalsu aspired to play in Norman. Even as Wilkinson's program faltered in the early 1960s—the Sooners were 16–14–1 in the first three years of the decade—the coach's aura was so strong that there was only one place for a local kid to go. When Wilkinson recruited Kalsu out of Del City High in '63, Kalsu signed on.

He was not the first in his family to make the big time in Oklahoma college sports. Bob's uncle, Charles Kalsu, played basketball at Oklahoma State for Henry Iba, whose legend in college hoops was writ as large as Wilkinson's was in football. The six-foot-six Charles was a second-team All-America in 1939 and played pro ball with the old Philips 66 Oilers. Charles's brother Frank Kalsu, three inches shorter and two years younger, yearned to follow him to Oklahoma State. "Frank and Charles were extremely competitive," recalls their younger brother, Milt. "Frank went to Stillwater thinking he could play. He lasted half a semester and came home." Frank married Leah Aguillard, of French Canadian ancestry, became a sheet-metal worker at Tinker Air Force Base in Midwest City, Oklahoma, and settled in Del City.

Frank saw in his son, Bob, an open-field run at fulfilling the dreams that he had left behind in Stillwater. "That's what made him drive his son to be a college athlete," Milt says. "He'd wanted to play basketball for Iba." Frank put the teenage Bob on a rigorous conditioning program long before such regimens were common. Milt still remembers Bob chuffing through four-mile cross-country runs among the tumbleweed and jackrabbits while Frank trailed behind him in the family car.

Early on, the boy began to live for the playing of games, for competition, and he approached everything as if it were a last stand. "He played every kind of ball imaginable," says Leah. "He was even on a bowling team. He loved to play cards—canasta, hearts. We'd play Chinese checkers head-to-head. We played jacks when he was seven or eight. He played jacks until he was in high school. He'd never quit when he lost. He'd say, 'Mom, let's play another.' "

Bob liked football well enough—the butting of heads, the grinding contact, the fierceness of play in the trenches—but the game he loved most was golf. He was a four or five handicap. On Sundays, Bob would go to 7:00 A.M. Mass at St. Paul's Church so he and Uncle Milt could make an 8:30 tee time. They sometimes got in fifty-four holes in a day, and they spent hours behind Bob's house hitting balls, always competing. "We'd see who could get [the ball] closest to a telephone pole," Milt recalls.

Kalsu never played a down for Wilkinson, who resigned after his freshman season. However, over the next four years, including a redshirt season in 1964, Kalsu matured into one of the best offensive linemen ever to play for the Sooners. He also developed his talent for leading men, which was as natural as the stomping, pounding gait that would earn for him the nickname Buffalo Bob. Steve Campbell, three years behind him at Del City High, remembers summers when Kalsu, preparing for the next Oklahoma season, would call evening practices for high school players and run them as if he were a boot-camp sergeant. He simply put out the word that he would be working out at the high school and that all Del City players should be there.

Kalsu would appear in a jersey cut off at the sleeves, in shorts and baggy socks and cleats, and begin sending the young men through agility and running drills, racing up and down the field with the players and finally dividing them up for a game of touch football. "We were ready and willing followers," Campbell says. "He had a very commanding air about him."

Fact is, in his comportment on and off the field, Kalsu rarely put a cleat down wrong. "He did everything the way you're supposed to," says former Sooners defensive end Joe Riley, who was recruited with Kalsu. "He didn't cut classes. He never gave anybody a minute's trouble. He became the player he was because he believed everything the coaches told him. He didn't complain. We'd all be complaining through two-a-days, and he'd just walk around with a little smirk on his face. He was a little goody-goody for some of us, but we respected him. And once you got to know him, you liked him."

By his third year of eligibility, 1966, Kalsu was starting on a squad that was showing signs of a pulse. The year before, in Gomer Jones's second season as coach, the Sooners had gone 3–7, and Gomer was a goner. In '66, under new coach Jim Mackenzie, Oklahoma went 6–4. When Mackenzie died of a heart attack in the spring of '67, Chuck Fairbanks took over, and his rise to the practice-field tower presaged the sudden ascension of the team, which would have one of the wildest years in Sooners history.

Like their 2000 counterparts, the '67 Sooners had not been expected to win their conference, much less make a run at the national title. For guards Eddie Lancaster and Byron Bigby, the tone of the season was set on the first play of the first game, against Washington State in Norman on September 23, when they double-teamed a defensive lineman and rolled him seven yards down the field, springing tailback Steve Owens for a twelve-yard gain. Next thing Lancaster knew, Kalsu was standing over him and Bigby and yelling, "Good god, awright! Look at this! Look at what you did!"

Bigby turned to Lancaster and said, in some amazement, "You know, we can do this." The Sooners won 21–0. They kept on winning, too, and nearly pulled off the whole shebang, losing only to Texas, 9–7. Kalsu was smack in the middle of it all. Elected team captain, he took the job to be more than that of a figurehead. He took it to mean that he should lead, which he did in the best way, by example.

Steve Zabel, an Oklahoma tight end at the time, recalls the day Buck Nystrom, the offensive line coach, got peeved at the taxi-squad players who were going against his linemen in the "board drill," in which two players lined up at opposite ends of an eight-foot-long plank and ran into each other like mountain goats, the winner being the one left standing on the board. Disgusted by what he saw as a lack of intensity, the 215-pound Nystrom—"the meanest coach I was ever around," says Zabel—got on the board and turned his cap backward. Without pads or a helmet, he took on all his linemen, one by one. Finally Kalsu got on the board.

Kalsu, at 220 pounds, had become the biggest hammer on the Sooners' offensive line. He took off down the board. "He hit Buck so hard that he lifted him off the board and planted him on the ground with his helmet on Buck's chest," says Zabel. "Everybody was running around yelling, 'Kalsu killed him! Kalsu killed Buck!'"

That night Zabel and center Ken Mendenhall were walking into a Baskin-Robbins when Nystrom came out, holding an ice cream cone in one hand and his two-year-old son, Kyle, in the other. He was wearing the same T-shirt he'd worn at practice, and his arms were discolored. "Zabel! Mendenhall!" Nystrom blurted. "Wasn't that the greatest practice you ever saw?" He handed his cone to Zabel, the boy to Mendenhall, and raised the front of his shirt, revealing the black-and-blue imprint of a helmet. "Look at this!" he said gleefully. "Boy, ol' Bob Kalsu liked to kill me!"

On the field that year Kalsu was everywhere, urging the troops on, picking them up off piles. Every time Owens, the tailback, looked up from the ground, there was Kalsu. Owens would win the Heisman Trophy in 1969, but in '67 he was an unbridled galloper who often ran up the backs of Kalsu's legs. One day the exasperated captain took Owens aside. "Listen, Steve, I'm on your side," he said. "Find the hole!"

Owens was in ROTC, and he remembers Kalsu, a cadet colonel, marching his battalion around the parade grounds like so many toy soldiers. "He was all over us all the time," says Owens. "He took that job seriously, too."

Before Kansas State played Oklahoma, Wildcats coach Vince Gibson, who had been studying film of the Sooners, approached Fairbanks on the field. "Kalsu is the best blocking lineman I've ever seen," Gibson said. In fact, after the Sooners' coaches studied all their game film of 1967, Fairbanks said that "our average gain on all plays going over Kalsu, including short yardage and goal line plays, is 6.2 net yards rushing. . . . That is what we coaches grade as . . . near perfection."

Kalsu "wasn't better than other players because of his ability," Fairbanks recalls. "He was better because he was smarter and technically better. He was a little more mature in his evaluation of what was happening on the field. There were no problems coaching him. You didn't have to try to motivate him. He came to practice every day with a smile on his face."

At season's end Kalsu appeared to have it all. An appearance in the Orange Bowl. All-America honors. A solid chance at a pro football career. And his marriage, after the Orange Bowl, to Jan Darrow. She and Bob had had their first date on October 15, 1966, and she knew that very night she'd found her mate. "A really cute guy who made me laugh," she says. "I came home, threw myself on my sister Michelle's bed, and said, 'I just met the man I'm going to marry.'"

Jan was the third of nine kids—five girls and four boys—and by the summer of 1967 Kalsu had been embraced as the tenth sibling in the Darrows' seven-bedroom house on Country Club Drive. "I always wanted brothers and sisters, and now I got 'em," he told Ione Darrow, the mother of the brood. Kalsu may have been a fearsome lineman, but what the Darrows discovered was a large, lovable kid who liked to scare trick-or-treaters by jumping from behind trees and who failed grandly in his experiments as a pastry chef. Diane Darrow, four years older than Jan, walked into the kitchen one day and saw Bob with his huge hands in a mixing bowl, squashing the batter. She asked him what on earth he was doing. He said he was making an angel food cake for Ione's birthday. Diane wondered why he wasn't using a wooden spoon. "The box says mix by hand," he said.

Around the Darrows' dinner table, everyone would stop to watch the spectacle of Kalsu's eating. Whole salads disappeared at two or three stabs of a fork. Glasses of orange juice vanished in a single swallow. Kalsu could devour a drumstick with a few spins of the bone, stripping it clean. He also played games endlessly with his new siblings, cheerfully cheating at all of them.

Bob and Jan were married on January 27, 1968, and when they returned from their honeymoon in Galveston, Texas, during spring break, the Darrow family sang the news: "Buffalo Bob, won't you come out tonight?" He had been drafted in the eighth round by the Bills of the American Football League. The NFL's Dallas Cowboys and the AFL's Denver Broncos had also shown interest, but both had backed away, leery of Kalsu's military commitment. Having completed ROTC, he would be commissioned a second lieutenant after graduation in May. He was not immediately called to active duty, however. By the time he reported to the Bills that summer, Jan was six months pregnant.

Within a few weeks with the Bills, Kalsu had worked his way into the lineup, taking the place of the injured Joe O'Donnell at right guard and starting nine games that season. No one watched Kalsu more closely than Billy Shaw, Buffalo's left guard and a future Hall of Famer. Shaw was twenty-nine in '68, nearing the end of his career, and he saw Kalsu as a threat to his job.

"Bob had a lot of talent," says Shaw. "He had real good feet, and he was strong, good on sweeps. In those days we had only one backup, and he was Joe's and my backup. Our forte was foot speed, and Bob was right there with us. He really fit in with how we played, with a lot of running, a lot of sweeps, a lot of traps."

Shaw and O'Donnell were mirror images of each other—both six-foot-two and about 252 pounds—and when Kalsu joined them, the three looked like triplets. At the Bills' urging, the six-foot-three Kalsu had gained weight by lifting weights and devouring potatoes and chicken ("His neck got so big that even his ties didn't fit him anymore," says Jan), and he was listed at 250 pounds on the Bills' roster. "The thing I noticed is that he was so mature for a young player," says Shaw. "He wasn't your normal rookie. He wasn't in awe."

Bob Lustig, the Bills' general manager at the time, says Kalsu "had a good future in pro football." Lustig recalls something else. "He not only had the talent, but he also had the smarts. He didn't make the same mistake twice."

Kalsu also brought to Buffalo the same love of horseplay and mischief that had marked his days in Oklahoma. He and one of his rookie roommates, John Frantz, a center from Cal, filled a trash can with water and carried it into the head at training camp. They thought their other roommate, rookie tackle Mike McBath, was sitting on the toilet in one of the stalls. They lifted the can and dumped the water into the stall. They heard a thunderous bellow that sounded nothing like McBath. It was six-year veteran Jim Dunaway, Buffalo's six-foot-four, 281-pound defensive tackle, who rose from the dumper like Godzilla and screamed, "Whoever did that is dead!"

Kalsu and Frantz bolted in a panic and hid in the closet of their room until Hurricane Dunaway had blown over, and they laughed every time they saw the big tackle after that. "Bob was always stirring the pot," says Frantz. "As good an athlete as he was, he was an even better person."

Frantz and McBath used to hit the night spots, chasing girls, but no amount of coaxing could get Kalsu to go along. "Some of the married guys chased around, but Bob, never," says Frantz. "He loved his wife and his kid. He was totally at ease with himself, confident in who he was. We'd go out, and he'd laugh at us: 'You guys can do what you want. I've got what I want.'"

Only seven active pro athletes would serve in Vietnam: six football players and a bowler. Most other draftable pro athletes elected to serve in the reserves. Kalsu's family and friends urged him to go that route. "I'm no better than anybody else," he told them all. It was early 1969. The Vietnam War was still raging a year after the Tet Offensive, and there was no hope of its ending soon. Frantz pleaded with Kalsu to seek the Bills' help in finding a slot in the reserves. "John, I gave 'em my word," Kalsu said, referring to his promise, on joining ROTC, to serve on active duty. "I'm gonna do it."

"Bob, it's hell over there," Frantz said. "You've got a wife, a child."

Kalsu shook his head. "I'm committed," he said.

That September, after nearly eight months at Fort Sill in Lawton, Oklahoma, Kalsu went home one day looking shaken. His uniform was soaked with sweat. "I have orders to go to Vietnam," he told Jan.

They spent his last weeks in the country at her parents' house, with Jan in growing turmoil over the prospect of losing him. They were in the laundry room washing clothes when she spoke her worst fear. "What if you die over there?" she asked. "What am I do to?"

"I want you to go on with your life," he said. "I want you to marry again."

She broke down. "I don't want to marry again," she said. "I couldn't."

"Jan, I promise you, it'll be all right."

They had been married in the St. James Catholic Church in Oklahoma City, and a few weeks before he left, they went there together. Jan knelt before the altar. "If you need him more than I do," she prayed silently, "please give me a son to carry on his name."

Bob was gone before Thanksgiving. In one of her first letters to him, Jan gave Bob the good news: she was pregnant again.

If his letters didn't reveal what he was facing in Vietnam, Jan got a sense of it in May 1970 when, seven months pregnant and with Jill in tow, she met him in Hawaii for a week of R and R. Bob slept much of the time, and he was napping one day in their room when fireworks were set off by the pool. "He tore out of that bed frantic, looking for cover," Jan says, "terror and fear on his face. I got a glimpse of what he was living through."

At the end of the week they said goodbye at the airport. "Bob, please be careful," she said.

"You be careful," he said. "You're carrying our baby."

Jan returned to Oklahoma, Bob to Vietnam—and soon to Firebase Ripcord. For the last three weeks he was on that rock, it was under increasing siege, and his men saw him as one of them, a grunt with a silver bar working the trenches of Ripcord and never complaining. "He had a presence about him," says former corporal Renner. "He could have holed up in his bunker, giving orders on the radio. He was out there in the open with everybody else.

He was always checking the men out, finding out how we were, seeing if we were doing what needed to be done. I got wounded on Ripcord, and he came down into the bunker. My hands were bandaged, and he asked me, 'You want to catch a chopper out of here?' " Renner saw that Kalsu had been hit in the shoulder. "I saw the bandage on him and saw he was staying. I said, 'No, I'm gonna stay.' "

The men of Battery A, trapped on that mountaintop, bonded like cave dwellers in some prehistoric war of the worlds. "Our language and behavior were pitiful," says Renner. "We behaved like junkyard dogs. If you wanted to fight or tear somebody else up, that's what you did. It was the tension. But I never heard Lieutenant Kalsu cuss. Not once. He was such a nice guy."

As was the other gentle soul of the outfit, David Earl Johnson. "A kind, lovable person," recalls his sister, Audrey Wrightsell. Growing up in their little Arkansas community, David played most sports. His junior high coach Leo Collins says that David was good at just about everything and best at basketball and track. "One of the best athletes you could ever wish for in a small school," says Collins. "He was so easy to manage, a coach's dream."

Like Kalsu, Johnson did not take the easy way out of the war. He was paying his way through Philander Smith College in Little Rock, majoring in business administration, when he decided not to apply for another student deferment. "I'm tired of this," he told Audrey. "I'm gonna serve my time."

So it was that Johnson landed on Ripcord with Kalsu, in the middle of the most unpopular war in U.S. history. In May 1970, during a protest against the war at Kent State in Ohio, National Guardsmen had fired on student protesters, killing four. Criticism of the war had become so strong that as the NVA massed to attack Ripcord, the U.S. command in Vietnam decided not to meet force with more force, which would have put even more body bags on the evening news. So Ripcord was left twisting in the boonies.

The men made the most of their fate. Kalsu tried to make a game of the darkest moments. He and Big John, as Johnson was known, "were always laughing and joking," says former sergeant Martin. "For [them], everything was a challenge." When the sling-loads of ammunition would arrive by chopper, Kalsu would call out, "Let's get that ammo off the pads!" He and Johnson would take three of those 97-pound shells apiece and hump them up the hill together. The contest was to see who could carry the most. "Johnson was the biggest man we'd seen until Kalsu came along," says Martin.

They died together at five o'clock that summer afternoon. Fotias rolled Kalsu off him and saw the flowing wound behind the lieutenant's left ear. Kalsu was pulled out of the bunker, not far from where Johnson lay dead, and Doc Harris came running over. He looked down at Kalsu and knew that he was gone.

Renner, dazed from the concussion, saw that Kalsu was dead and picked up Beals, wounded in the blast, and started to carry him to the aid station. "Lieutenant Kalsu has been killed," Renner said. "I don't know what the hell we're gonna do now."

In a hospital where he had been flown after taking shrapnel, Martin got word that Kalsu and Big John were dead. "I sat there and cried," he says.

That evening, the battalion commander on Ripcord, Lt. Col. Andre Lucas, learned of Kalsu's death. Lucas would die two days later, as the firebase was being evacuated, and for his part in defending it, he would win the Congressional Medal of Honor. As battle-hardened as he was, he seemed stunned by the news about Kalsu. "The tone went out of the muscles on his face, and his jaw dropped," Harris says.

On July 21, 1970, James Robert Kalsu thus became the only American professional athlete to die in combat in Vietnam.

At 12:45 A.M. on July 23, at St. Anthony Hospital in Oklahoma City, Jan Kalsu gave birth to an eight-pound, 15½-ounce boy, Robert Todd Kalsu. When Leah Kalsu visited her that morning, Jan fairly shouted, "Bob is going to jump off that mountain when he finds he has a boy!"

That afternoon, as the clan gathered in the Darrow house to head for a celebration at the hospital, there was a knock at the front door. Sandy Szilagyi, one of Jan's sisters, opened it, thinking the visitor might be a florist. She saw a uniformed Army lieutenant. "Is Mrs. James Robert Kalsu home?" he asked.

Sandy knew right then. "She's at St. Anthony Hospital," she said. "She's just given birth to a baby."

The young lieutenant went pale. Turning, he walked away. Sandy called Phillip Maguire, the doctor who had delivered the baby, and told him who was coming. At the hospital, the lieutenant stepped into Maguire's office and sat down. He was shaking. "Do you think she'll be able to handle this?" he asked. "I don't know what to do. I'm not sure I can do this."

Maguire led the officer to Jan's room, slipped into a chair and put his arm around her. "Jan, there's a man from the Army here to see you," he said.

"Bob's been killed, hasn't he?" she said.

The officer came in and stood at the foot of the bed. He could barely speak. "It is my duty . . ." he began. When he finished, he turned and left in tears.

Jan asked to leave the hospital immediately with her baby. She did one thing before she left. She asked for a new birth certificate. She renamed the boy James Robert Kalsu, Jr.

The funeral, a week later at Czech National Cemetery, brought people from all around the country, and the gravesite service was more anguished than anything Byron Bigby, Kalsu's old Sooners teammate, had ever seen. "I looked around," he says, "and there was not a dry eye. We walked out of there biting our lips."

Barry Switzer, who had been a young assistant under Fairbanks during the '67 season, was walking to his car when he turned and looked back. What he saw haunts him still. "Bob's daddy got his wife and Jan back to the car," Switzer says. "After everyone was gone from the gravesite, he went back and lay down on the casket."

Three decades have passed since Kalsu died. Jan has sought ways to deal with the void, but times were often difficult. She struggled financially, frequently living from one government check to another, determined to remain at home while raising her kids.

She did not have a serious relationship with a man until the mid-eighties, when she began seeing Bob McLauchlin, an Oklahoma businessman. In 1986 they visited the Vietnam Veterans Memorial in Washington, D.C. They found Kalsu's name on the wall, and McLauchlin shared Jan's bereavement. They married in 1988. Last fall McLauchlin took Jill and Bob Jr. to a reunion of Ripcord survivors in Shreveport, Louisiana. Her children persuaded Jan not to go. They didn't want to see her cry as she had for so many years.

Jill and Bob Jr. have suffered a keen ambivalence for years. From all they have heard about their father from Jan and the Darrow clan, they have grown to love and admire him without having known him. They are proud of all he accomplished and the honorable way he conducted his life, but they are angry at him, too. They grew up fatherless, after all, having to comfort a lonely, grieving mother whose pain and struggles continually touched them.

The children turned out well. Jill, outgoing and warm, is a housewife in Oklahoma City, the mother of three with a fourth on the way. Bob, soft-spoken and reflective, is an aviation lawyer in Oklahoma City and the father of two. Asked what he would say to his father, Bob says, "I would embrace him and tell him I love him. It would not be derogatory, and it would not be mean, but I would ask him, 'Did you fully contemplate the consequences of your decision? I feel like I lost out, and I wish you had not made the decision to go.'" Bob Jr. considers what he's said for a moment, then goes on: "I'm equally proud he made the decision. That's the kind of man I want to be, to have the integrity that he had." That, of course, is the rub. Bob Kalsu made that decision precisely because he was the kind of man he was.

All who knew him remember him in different ways. The clan, as a family man. The football players, as a tough jock. Then there are those who knew Kalsu on that terrible hill. They have the most painful and poignant memories of him. Fotias has trouble talking about Kalsu, his voice soft and filled with sorrow. So does Renner. He walked over to Kalsu's body lying outside the bunker and peered into his motionless face. He would see that face for years. Now, however, "I can't see the face anymore," Renner says. "I can see his silhouette. I can't see a lot of their faces, only their silhouettes."

Renner is having trouble getting out the words. They come in a whisper. "I've thought of him every Memorial Day," he says. "In my heart, I pay homage to him. And Johnson. They are all very important." He closes his eyes and bows his head and quietly weeps.

Permissions Acknowledgments